环球雅思学校雅思（IELTS）考

雅思写作 官方题库范文大全

全球10位著名雅思考官 联合推荐

杨凡 ◎编著

吉林出版集团有限责任公司

图书在版编目(CIP)数据

雅思写作官方题库范文大全 / 杨凡编著. -- 长春 : 吉林出版集团有限责任公司, 2011.7
ISBN 978-7-5463-5702-7

Ⅰ.①雅… Ⅱ.①杨… Ⅲ.①IELTS - 写作 - 自学参考资料 Ⅳ.①H315

中国版本图书馆CIP数据核字(2011)第118897号

雅思写作官方题库范文大全

编　　著:杨　凡
责任编辑:于　鑫　朱　玲
特约策划:王慧玉　宋美丽
封面设计:淡晓库
开　　本:787mm × 1092mm　1/16
字　　数:425千字
印　　张:26
版　　次:2011年8月第2版
印　　次:2012年8月第3次印刷

出　　版:吉林出版集团有限责任公司
发　　行:吉林出版集团外语教育有限公司
地　　址:长春市泰来街1825号
邮　　编:130011
电　　话:总编办:0431-86012683
发行部:0431-86012675　0431-86012826(Fax)
网　　址:www.360hours.com
印　　刷:北京市大兴区兴达印刷厂

ISBN 978-7-5463-5702-7　　**定价**:59.80元

版权所有　侵权必究　举报电话:0431-86012683

环球雅思图书编委会核心小组

总 策 划 张永琪 张晓东

执行策划 刘海华 王慧玉

图书编辑 李晟月 宋美丽 吕颜辉

主　　编 杨 凡

委　　员 李铁戎 李 钧 赵伯兰 杨维勤 林桂珍
郑兰宾 李桂芝 李铁成 郑芝梅 杨 林
张瑞娟 陈广平 郑芝真 冯光辉 张宝娟
郑珊珊 朱海霞 杨开宇 王 格 王 效
汪海静 杨文达 刘 虎 邓菲菲 刘孟媛
胡 珺 牟恒瀚 闫 曦 李帅亚 张忱欣
许 韧 赵 佳 赤云杰 赵姗姗 万汶林
胡文燕 曹玉倩 王 伟 唐艺绮 高莉钧
周 喆 朱海澎 杨恬甜 白小禾 郭 洋
董洪峰 葛 栗 张洁琳 董祥翔 莎日娜
赖奕萌 曹志强 崔建东 赵子佳 谢坤子
黄晓月 王 谦 尹 航 皮雪媛 姜 杰
赵骏杰 高 昂 张 蕾 彭 怡 郭琳琳
王 妍

推荐序

我与杨凡老师在环球雅思学校共事多年，其独特的语言教学法和对英语理论、应试英语的理解，在全国堪称独树一帜。将他的教学理论和授课实践的精华撰写成书以帮助更多的“烤鸭”，一直是我们和他所教授学生的夙愿。

谈《雅思写作官方题库范文大全》我想先介绍杨凡其人，许多见过杨凡老师的人都会觉得他有点“文弱书生”的感觉，其实“初见谈吐静如水，三句过后起波澜”是他教学中最鲜明的特点。杨凡老师的才思敏捷和风趣幽默曾吸引过许多学生，他喜爱博览群书，这个特点体现在他教学内容的精炼通俗上。多年相处，我觉得无论教学风格还是行事风格，用“以柔克刚”一词形容杨凡其人最为贴切。

今天，这本《雅思写作官方题库范文大全》是继《剑桥雅思词汇大全》之后的又一力作。《剑桥雅思词汇大全》自出版以来单月销量破万册，深受广大考生青睐。为此，杨凡老师根据最新的雅思写作考试动向，精心编写了《雅思写作官方题库范文大全》，旨在帮助考生在短期内突破雅思写作。此书可谓杨凡老师精心锤炼的产物，是他十几年来教学实践和经验的结晶。书中无不尽显杨凡老师关于写作的神机妙法。我真心代表环球雅思学校的全体师生员工向杨老师表示感谢。

书中所列举的题目囊括了目前最新雅思写作官方题库的所有题目，堪称史上最全的雅思写作官方题库。题目分类精细，译文精准流畅，范文典型地道。所收录的274篇范文均由雅思考官审定，是最权威的雅思写作官方题库范文大全。这本书对于将要备考雅思写作的广大考生而言，是一本难得的背诵宝典。杨凡在书中关于范文的点评和加分语句的提炼，可谓是“让优者更优，令弱者变强”(Reinforce the strong & Enpower the weak)，相信对考生写作考试成绩的提高和英语水平的巩固都会有绝佳帮助。

杨凡老师作为“全国环球雅思教学委员会GTRC”的主要发起人之一，一直积极推动将优秀教学成果转化为学术教材并向全国推广的活动。他致力于促进学生及教师的相互学术交流，及时沟通考试动态，随时总结发展应试英语学习法，不断超越自我，提升雅思教学水平，让全国广大考生得到优秀教师的精髓和真传。这些都确立了他在语言教学行业中的至高地位。愿杨凡老师和他的这本书能够成为广大考生的良师益友，并借助这本书能够早日实现出国之梦。

借此感谢广大师生多年来对环球雅思学校的信赖，使我们荣幸成为数十万学子人生脚下的前进大道。祝愿环球卓尔文化公司再创历史新辉煌！

环球雅思学校总校长

环球天下教育科技集团总裁

张永琪

2011年4月

如何使用本书备考雅思写作(自序)

雅思考生普遍感觉写作很难。考试中心的统计数据也表明,写作的平均成绩是四项中最低的。那么如何备考雅思写作呢?

根据多年的雅思写作教学经验,笔者建议大家,要提高写作水平和写作成绩,应该把如下两个方面结合起来。

▶一、仔细研读,背诵和模仿真题范文

本书包括了目前雅思写作官方题库的全部题目(包括Task 2和Task 1),每个题目都给出了高分范文。雅思写作考试,就是从该题库里出题。所以,这些题目,在大家实际考试时,都有可能遇到。同学们熟悉这些题目和范文,是保证雅思写作获得好成绩的关键。

本书包含274篇高分范文,考生们可以根据自己的情况选择一些题目和范文来学习。

对于范文,只读是不够的,还要背诵。背诵也不需要整篇背诵,而是背诵其中对自己有帮助的句子。常言说得好,"熟读唐诗三百首,不会作诗也会吟",读范文和背句子对于写作是非常重要的。写作是"输出"的,但没有"输入",就没有"输出"。读范文和背句子就是在"输入"。

为此,本书针对一些加分的句子也用蓝色粗体标出,请读者注意积累这些句子。

▶二、写几篇文章,并仔细修改

在阅读和背诵一定数量范文的基础上,考生还应该选择几个题目,自己写一写。一般Task 2写5篇,Task 1写5篇即可。写完之后,要找英语老师帮助仔细修改。

在本书写作过程中,得到了尹龙龙老师帮助。可以说,本书的体例很多来自于尹龙龙老师的想法。同时也得到了我的亲人,同事,朋友和学生李铁戎、李钧、赵伯兰、杨维勤、林桂珍、郑兰宾、李桂芝、李铁成、郑芝梅、杨林 、张瑞娟、陈广平、郑芝真、冯光辉、张宝娟、郑珊珊、朱海霞、杨开宇、王格、王效、汪海静、杨文达、刘虎、邓菲菲、刘孟媛、胡珺、牟恒瀚、闫曦、李帅亚、张忱欣、许韧、赵佳、赤云杰、赵姗姗、万汶林、胡文燕、曹玉倩、王伟、唐艺绮、高莉钧、周喆、朱海澎、杨恬甜、白小禾、郭洋、董洪峰、葛栗、张洁琳、董祥翔、莎日娜、赖奕萌、曹志强、崔建东、赵子佳、谢坤子、黄晓月、王谦、尹航、皮雪媛、姜杰、赵骏杰、高昂、张蕾、彭怡、郭琳琳、王妍的帮助,在此也深表谢意。

在本书编写过程中,参考了一些关于英文写作的书籍,在此对相关作者表示感谢。

个人博客:http://blog.sina.com.cn/yangyasi
个人微博:http://weibo.com/ieltsyang
电子邮件:yangyasi2@sina.com

杨凡
2011年4月于北京

目录

第一章 Task 2议论文题库全部题目和范文

▶第一大类:学生生活类话题

▶第四大类:媒体类话题

▶第五大类:动物类题目

▶第六大类:环境资源交通类题目

▶第七大类:传统与发展变化类题目

▶第八大类：政府类话题

▶第九大类：平等类话题

▶第十大类:社会问题类话题

第二章 图表作文题库全部题目和范文

第三章 书信题库全部题目和范文

附录

剑 8 写作真题解析

A 类

G 类

第一章

Task 2议论文题库全部题目和范文

第一大类：学生生活类话题

1. 大学生交学费

Topic:

Some people say university students should pay for their tuition fees. Some others say the government should pay for the tuition fees. What is your opinion?

Sample Answer

Owing to high qualities and considerable expertise they have, college graduates stand a better chance of securing an ideal job, thus being paid much more than those without a decent schooling. If that is the case, college students, according to some people, should pay all the full cost, such as tuition fees, by themselves rather than government do. Truly, if government is not obliged to shoulder the duty of paying for college students, a large sum of money can be saved to invest in other fields, but the subsequent detriments are more than alarming.

Initially, tremendous economic pressure will hinder students' learning efficiency. If students have to pay tuition fees alone, perhaps they will take up part-time jobs in their spare time, which ought to be spent on relaxation or review of the lessons learned. Consequently, physical exhaustion and mental stress deprive them of the possibility of studying efficiently. Furthermore, students usually lack social experience, so it is more likely that they are confronted with the dangers of being cheated or even life threatened. Such reports as female students as home tutors are raped or killed are not uncommon recently.

Moreover, if college students are required to pay all the full cost, some talents born in poor families can never enter higher education and it is a great loss for the country. Some students from destitute areas are really promising, and if they can further study in one particular field, they are sure to become outstanding enough and make a great contribution to society. However, lack of sufficient money to support their future learning, they have to drop out of school, and it is absolutely a shame for government, whose function is to serve the people.

All in all, the main duty of students is to acquire more knowledge, so it is never reasonable to impose economic pressure on them. It is government that should be responsible for students' expenses.

▶考官评分:8

题目:

一些人认为大学生应该支付他们的学费，另外一些人认为政府应该支付学费，你的观点是什么?

译文:

由于大学毕业生素质高且具备专业的知识，他们更有机会获得一份理想的工作，因此他们应该比那些没有受过良好教育的人获得更多的报酬。基于上述事实，有些人认为大学生理应自己支付所有的学习成本，例如学杂费，而不是由政府来支付。的确，如果政府不必承担大学生的花费，那么可以节省下一大笔钱并投资于其他领域，但随之而来的损害会超过人们的想象。

首先，巨大的经济压力会降低学生的学习效率。如果学生要独自支付学杂费，那么也许他们将在课余时间从事兼职工作，而这本应该是学习之外的放松和复习的时间。因此，身体的疲劳和精神压力使他们不可能高效率地学习。此外，学生们通常缺乏社会经验，所以他们很可能被欺骗，甚至受到生命威胁。女学生在做家教时被强奸或被杀害的报道最近就经常见诸报端。

此外，如果大学生必须支付全部的学习费用，在一些贫困家庭出生的人才，可能再也没有机会接受高等教育了，这将是国家的巨大损失。一些出身于贫困地区的学生非常有潜力，如果他们能在一个特定的领域深入学习，他们一定会变得非常优秀，并且为社会做出巨大贡献。然而，由于他们缺乏足够的资金继续学习不得不辍学，这对主要职能是为人民服务的政府来说绝对是一种耻辱。

总而言之，学生的主要职责是掌握更多的知识，所以对他们施加经济压力是极不合理的。学生的学习费用是应该由政府来支付的。

范文点评:

辩论型题目。范文使用一边倒结构，写了四段。开头段提出自己的观点：大学生不应该支付他们的高等教育费用。中间写了两个理由段。最后一段，重申自己的观点。全篇文章语言很好，好词好句比比皆是。

2. 考试对学生的影响

Topic:

Some people think that examinations have some bad effects on students. Some people say they have some good effects on education. Discuss both sides and give your opinion.

Sample Answer

In the long history of human education, great changes have taken place in every field of study. However, testing a person by examinations is still regarded as the only reliable and feasible method to measure one's knowledge and ability. From elementary schools to universities, students have to take many examinations. They even regard examinations as an indispensable part of their life.

Some people hold that examinations have negative impacts on students. First of all, examinations are unable to evaluate one's true ability. They can only test memory or the skill of working rapidly under pressure. Secondly, examinations encourage bad study habits. Students tend to lay emphasis on what will be tested. They are encouraged to memorize rather than to think. Finally, examinations lower the standards of teaching. Teachers have to train students in exam techniques instead of teaching their subjects.

Many other people, however, believe examinations have some advantages. In the first place, they serve as a driving force to stimulate students to work hard. Laziness is part of human nature. Without examinations, students tend to ignore their studies. Moreover, the results of examinations are just like mirrors for both students and teachers. Students can assess themselves and teachers can adjust their teaching method according to the information they obtain from examination. Finally, till now no better methods have been discovered to replace examinations. Other forms of assessment are too time-consuming and therefore are infeasible.

In my opinion, examinations have positive effects on teaching. They make students hard working. They also provide a clear objective standard by which the students can assess themselves and teachers can know what they should do next. Furthermore, at present no better methods are available. Therefore, I am sure examinations will continue to play an essential role in education.

▶考官评分:8

题目:

一些人认为考试对学生有负面的影响，一些人认为考试对教育有正面的作用，讨论双方观点并且给出你的观点。

译文:

在漫长的人类教育历史中，有关学习的各个领域都发生了很大变化。尽管如此，用考试来测试一个人的知识和能力仍旧被认为是惟一可靠和可行的办法。从小学到大学，学生要参加很多考试，考试甚至被视为他们生活中不可缺少的一部分。

有些人认为考试给学生带来了负面影响。首先，考试并不能衡量一个人的真正能力。他们只能测试记忆力或在压力面前迅速完成工作的技巧。其次，考试鼓励了不良的学习习惯。学生们容易偏重于那些将要被考到的内容。他们被鼓励去记忆而不是思考。最后，考试降低了教学质量。老师们不得不用训练学生们的应试技巧来代替他们所教的科目。

然而，其他很多人认为考试是有一些好处的。首先，考试是激励学生努力学习的一种动力。懒惰是人类的天性。没有考试，学生们容易忽视他们的学业。此外，考试的结果对老师和学生来说就像镜子一样。通过他们从考试中所获得的信息，学生们可以自我评估而老师们可以调整他们的教学方法。最后，至今还没有发现更好的方法来替代考试。其他形式的评估过于费时，因此是不可行的。

在我看来，考试对教学有积极的影响。它们使学生努力学习。同时它们也提供了一个清晰、客观的标准来让学生们自我评估，也让老师明白下一步该怎么做。另外，现在并没有更好的办法。因此，我确信考试将继续在教育领域扮演一个重要的角色。

范文点评：

辩论型题目。题目中包含“both sides”，所以，必须使用对称式结构。范文使用对称式结构，写了四段。开头段使用四句话介绍背景，是本篇文章的一个加分点。中间两段，双方观点各占一段。第二段，介绍考试的弊端，介绍了三个理由，每个理由写两句话左右。第三段，介绍考试的优点，介绍了三个理由，每个理由写两句话左右。最后一段，先介绍自己的观点：考试对教学有积极的影响。然后各用一句话改写第三段中的每个理由。整篇文章结构合理，理由充分。

3. 出国留学的利弊

Topic:

In recent years, many young people decide to further their study abroad. Do you think the advantages of study abroad outweigh its disadvantages?

Sample Answer

Over the last several years, along with the rapid development of economy, an increasing number of parents have been sending their children to study abroad. A majority of people hold the view that study abroad brings students many benefits, while others are of the opinion that students should finish university education in their motherland. It is quite natural that people from different backgrounds may have divergent attitudes towards it.

People, who advocate that study abroad has a lot of disadvantages, have their sound reasons. First of all, living far away from home, students will suffer from loneliness and homesickness. Overseas students often feel disoriented and depressed for lack of adequate knowledge and understanding of the local customs and lifestyle. Secondly, many students do not want to return to their native country after graduation because most of them want to seek a more comfortable life and a brighter future overseas. This may result in a serious brain-drain and our country will inevitably incur a huge loss of talents.

To this issue, some other people hold a different attitude, arguing that students should go abroad to study. To begin with, it can broaden the students' vision. They get a chance to experience a totally different culture. The knowledge of social customs acquired in the other countries helps them to become more open-minded. Next, there are academic advantages. Students can learn advanced science and technology. They receive a different education. The book resources are more up-to-date. The professors are aware of all the latest development in their fields. Therefore the standard of teaching is much higher. Moreover, when they finish their study abroad, they will have more choices for their future career. All the above merits are conducive to their self-betterment and self-realization.

For my part, I stand on the latter opinion that while overseas study has its drawbacks, the advantages are more obvious. It can broaden one's horizon. Students have easy access to the first-rate facilities and the latest development in science and technology. In addition, when they finish their study, they have more job opportunities. Therefore, as long as it is financially feasible, an overseas education may do a person more good than harm.

▶考官评分:7

题目:

近几年来许多年轻人选择出国留学深造，你认为出国留学的利大于弊吗?

译文:

近年来，随着经济的发展，越来越多的父母送他们的孩子出国留学。很多人认为出国留学会给学生带来很多好处，也有人认为学生应该在本国完成大学学业。背景环境不同，对出国留学的看法自然也不同。

认为出国留学有很多弊端的人理由充分。首先，离家在外，孩子要承受孤单寂寞和想家的痛苦。只身国外，人地生疏，留学生常会感到迷茫和沮丧。另外，很多学生毕业后不想回国，因为他们中的大多数人想在国外追求更加舒适的生活和更加光明的未来，这就会导致严重的人才流失，使我们的国家不可避免地遭受巨大的人才损失。

对于这个问题，其他的人有不同的看法，他们认为学生应该出国留学。首先，它可以拓宽学生的眼界。留学使他们有机会体验完全不同的文化。在国外学习的有关社会风俗的知识使他们的思想更开明。第二，学术上的优势。学生可以学到尖端的科学和技术。他们接受到完全不同的教育，拥有更新的书籍资源，接触到深谙领域前沿科技的导师。因此，教学水平会更高。第三，一旦他们在国外完成了学业，他们未来在事业上也会有更多的选择。上述所有的优势都有助于他们的自我完善和自我实现。

依我看来，我赞成后一观点：虽然去国外学习有些弊端，但是优势是更明显的。它会拓宽我们的眼界。学生可以接触到一流的设备和最新的科学技术知识。当他们完成了学业，会有更多的工作机会。因此，只要在经济上允许，出国留学还是利大于弊的。

范文点评：

辩论型题目。必须使用对称式结构。范文使用对称式结构，写了四段。开头段第一句介绍背景,然后介绍双方观点，最后一句引起下文。中间两段，双方观点各占一段。第二段，介绍出国的弊端，介绍了两个理由，每个理由写两句话左右。第三段，介绍出国的优点，介绍了三个理由，每个理由写两句话左右。最后一段，先说出自己的观点：出国的积极影响。然后各用一句话改写第三段中的每个理由。

4. 大学生就业困难的原因

Topic:

Nowadays it is difficult for university graduates to find a job. Analyze the individual and social reasons and offer some solutions.

Sample Answer

The job market for college graduates is getting tighter and tighter. According to a survey, in 2005 only 60 percent of college graduates found jobs. Why do college graduates find it increasingly difficult to get jobs? There are some personal and social reasons.

Graduates themselves are responsible for the situation. Nowadays university students cannot concentrate on their studies. High technology brings them many interesting things which can easily attract their attention such as watching TV, surfing the Internet and playing games. They are addicted to these activities, totally neglecting their studies. In addition, some graduates set too high salary standard and they are reluctant to seek a job in the less developed areas, where there are many opportunities for success and career development. Furthermore, there is no denying the fact that the students better equipped with practical knowledge are more competitive in job hunting, while those majoring in history, geography and the like have few job opportunities.

Should students assume all the responsibility? There are some social reasons, one of which is the boom of college graduates. For example, in China, only half of high school graduates were admitted to colleges and universities in 1997, but in 2001 two-thirds of them entered colleges. Obviously we will experience a sharp increase in the number of college graduates. Moreover, the world economy is in depression, which makes the situation of job market worse than ever. Another reason is that there exist some unreasonable employment policies such as sexual discrimination and residence permit restriction.

In order to solve the problem, college graduates should spend more time on their learning to improve their academic performance. They also need to have a moderate salary requirement. Meanwhile, the government should encourage the development of the economy to create more job opportunities to young people. All the unreasonable policies should be abolished.

▶考官评分:8

题目:

目前大学毕业生难就业，分析个人和社会的原因，并提出解决办法。

译文:

大学毕业生的工作市场越来越紧张了。根据调查，2005年仅有百分之六十的大学毕业生找到了工作。为什么大学毕业生找工作日益艰难？这里有社会和个人双方面的原因。

大学毕业生自己应对此负责。现在的大学生不能集中精力在学习上。高科技给他们带来了很多有趣的东西，很容易吸引他们的注意力，例如，看电视，上网及玩游戏。他们沉溺于这些，完全忽视他们的学习。第二，一些学生设置太高的薪水标准而且他们不愿意去一些欠发达的地区工作，而那些地区有很多成功或事业发展的机会。而且，不可否认，有实践知识的学生在找工作中更有竞争力，而以历史、地理等为专业的学生工作机会很少。

是不是学生应该承担全部的责任呢？还有一些社会原因，其中之一就是大学毕业生的数量在增加。例如，在中国，1997年仅有一半的高中毕业生可以进入大学，但是在2001年三分之二的高中毕业生都可以进入大学。很明显在大学毕业生的数量上有了急剧的增加。而且，全球经济陷入经济萧条，就业形势也因此比以前更艰难了。另一个原因是存在一些不合理的就业政策，例如性别歧视和户口的限制。

为了解决这个问题，大学毕业生应该花更多的时间在学习上以提高学习成绩，并且有一个适度的薪金要求。同时，政府应鼓励经济发展以提供给年轻人更多的工作机会。所有不合理的政策应该被废除。

范文点评:

解释型题目。注意题目要求说明个人原因和社会原因，不要遗漏。范文采用“一边倒结构”写法。开头段先介绍背景，然后引起下文。中间两个为原因段，一段介绍个人原因，一段介绍社会原因。最后一段介绍解决办法。

5. 上大学的原因

Topic:

People attend college or university for many different reasons (for example, new experiences, career preparation, increased knowledge). Why do you think people attend college or university?

Sample Answer

College is a place where students can gain more new knowledge and experience. Of course, different people have different reasons for attending college: some may want to further their study in college; some hope to find a good job while some others wish to exchange their present situation through studying in the college. In my opinion, college study can be best defined as a preparation for one's future life.

Firstly, students can gain new knowledge and experience from studying in college. Teachers and professors in college who possess not only abundant professional knowledge but also plentiful teaching experience will supply students with new knowledge and direct them to solve problems in reality. With their help, students can be equipped with knowledge in a specific area, which will pave the road for their future career.

Secondly, students can learn how to arrange time efficiently. Before studying in college, their life may often be arranged by their parents, and their study by teachers. It is very different for them to live and study in college, because they will have to arrange their life and study by themselves. They have to decide things such as when to get up, when to play, and when to finish their assignment etc. This experience is of great importance for their work and life in the future.

Thirdly, studying in college gives students an opportunity to live with others and learn to cooperate with others. Usually, people feel uncomfortable about living with strangers because of different habits and values. But in the long run, it will turn out good for them because in the process of forcing themselves to cooperate with others and solve problems together, they will learn to care for and understand other people. It is a preparation for students to cooperate with others in society.

All in all, students can not only gain lots of new knowledge but also accumulate much more experience, such as how to arrange time and how to cooperate with other people. Therefore, college study serves as an important preparation for their future work and life.

▶考官评分:8

题目:

不同的人上大学有不同的原因：学习更多的知识，想找一个好工作，还有一些人想有新的体验。你认为为什么要上大学?

译文:

大学是一个让学生获得更多新知识与新经验的地方。当然，不同的人上大学有不同的原因：有些人想到大学进一步学习，有些人想找一个好工作，而还有一些人希望通过大学学习改变他们目前的状况。在我看来，对大学学习最好的定义就是一个人对未来生活做的准备。

首先，学生能够通过在大学学习获得新知识与新经验。大学里的老师和教授不仅拥有丰富的专业知识，而且还有大量的教学经验，他们可以为学生传授新知识并且指导他们解决现实中的问题。在他们的帮助下，学生能够在一个特定的领域用知识武装自己，这些知识将成为他们未来职业生涯的铺路石。

其次，学生能够学习怎样有效地安排时间。在上大学之前，他们的生活也许经常是被父母安排的，学习是被老师安排的。对于他们来说大学的生活和学习是非常不同的，因为他们将不得不自己安排他们的生活和学习。他们不得不决定一些事，例如什么时候起床，什么时候玩，什么时候完成作业等等。这些经验对于他们未来工作和生活是非常重要的。

再者，大学学习给学生一个与别人生活和学习及与别人合作的机会。通常，因为不同的习惯和价值观，人们觉得与陌生人生活不舒服。但是从长远看，这个机会对他们是有利的，因为在迫使自己与别人合作共同解决问题的过程中，他们将学会关心和理解别人。这会是学生为将来在社会上与他人合作所做的准备。

总而言之，学生不仅能够获得许多新知识，而且能够积累更多的经验，例如如何安排时间和如何与别人合作。因此，大学学习可当作是对他们未来工作和生活的准备。

6. 大学教育的目标

Topic:

Should the goal of college education be to ensure that the students find a good job or should it aim at cultivating the students' overall abilities?

Sample Answer

What should be the purpose of college education? No doubt, different people, or even different universities, may see it quite differently. As to me, I tend to support the view that it should aim at cultivating the students' overall abilities.

First of all, social progress needs overall-developed college graduates in the long run. When we ask ourselves the question: "What kind of college graduates does the society need?" The answer is just too obvious: ones with a good command of the knowledge in their own fields of study, ones with a healthy body, ones with a healthy mentality, ones with good communication skills, ones with teamwork spirit, ones with creative, innovative ability or the ability for implementation. What are all these things? Again, the answer is just simple: overall abilities.

Second, an overall developed graduate would find a job more easily. You can ask around an employer of a certain enterprise: What type of employees do you wish to employ? If this question is a little unclear, we can make it more specific by letting him make a choice: A. an overall developed college graduate; B. a none-overall developed college graduate. Supposing every other things remain equal, we have sound reasons to believe that he will definitely select A.

Admittedly, it is praiseworthy of universities to be concerned about their graduates' job-hunting issues, for anyone should first solve the problem of making a living before talking about later on development. Besides, it is also the shared aspiration of all college graduates to have a well-paid job that they like and that points to a good prospect in the future. However, no one would ever deny the fact that to cultivate the overall abilities of the students is always closely related to and in no way conflicts or contradicts good job opportunities.

From the foregoing discussion, we can come to the conclusion that the purpose of college education should always target at cultivating the overall abilities of the students.

▶考官评分:8

题目:

大学教育应以给学生找份好工作为目的还是以培养学生的综合能力为目标?

译文:

大学教育的目的究竟应该是什么呢?毫无疑问,人们肯定会有不同的看法,甚至各个大学之间也会观点相左。我个人倾向于培养学生的综合能力。

首先,从长远角度讲只有全面发展的学生才是社会发展所真正需要的人才。我们可以问问自己:社会发展需要什么样的大学毕业生呢?很明显答案是:有良好的专业知识、有健康的体魄、有健康的心态、有较好的沟通能力、有团队精神、有创新力或执行力。这一切的一切归纳起来是什么呢?答案很明了:综合能力。

其次,全面发展的学生必然更容易找到好工作。随便问一个企业的雇主:你希望雇用什么样的员工?如果这个问题有些不明确,那就把问题具体化。请您选择:A:一个全面发展的大学毕业生;B:一个不是全面发展的大学毕业生。在其他条件都相同的情况下,我们有充足的理由深信这位雇主肯定会选择A。

诚然,大学关心自己毕业生的工作问题是值得称颂的,因为任何人都首先需要谋生,然后才能谈进一步的发展。有一份自己喜欢的、收入好、工作前景好的工作也是大学毕业生们所期盼的。但是,谁也不能否认,培养全面发展的学生与好工作机会之间永远都是密切相关的,绝对不是相冲突、相矛盾的。

基于以上论证,我们可以清楚地认识到:大学教育应该永远以培养学生较强的综合能力为目标。

7. 上大学和参加工作的利弊

Topic:

Some people think that studying in a college or university is the best way for students to prepare for future career. But others think they should leave school as soon as possible to develop their career through work experience. Discuss both views and give your own opinion.

Sample Answer

While some people think that the best way to get prepared for future career is studying in a college or university, there are others who hold that one should leave school as early as possible and develop his career through work experience. In this essay, I will discuss the two views from the following aspects.

Firstly, going to college is very useful. One needs to learn and acquire a lot of fundamental and theoretical knowledge that will prove to be of practical significance in his future career development. In this respect, a college education can well serve as a means to the end. It is not hard to reckon that the theoretical and fundamental knowledge one acquires at college will at least help broaden his vision and horizon and thus give him the edge over those who have not done so.

Secondly, one's success, especially financial success, is not determined by whether or not he has been educated in college. It seems that work experience and opportunity play a more important role. I have quite a few friends who merely managed to finish primary or junior high school and went into business right away. Some of them struck rich in a few years and are now managing very large companies which employ over 1,000 workers, most of their employees being college graduates.

However, our society is undergoing fast development and changes, thus raising higher and higher requirements for knowledge. In this context, people's education levels gradually reveal their corresponding advantages and disadvantages. So far as employment is concerned, those who have received a college education naturally have more chances than those who have not. And in terms of the new models of achieving success, tremendous fortune is increasingly related to the trend of scientific and technological development, fully demonstrating the value of going to college.

So, even though there are quite some success stories of people without a college education, we can assert from the development trend of the world that this will become rarer and rarer. Therefore, if one has the chance, it is more advisable for him to go to college.

▶考官评分:8

题目:

有人认为读大学是为将来的职业发展做准备的最佳方式，也有人认为他们应该尽早离开学校并通过积累工作经验来发展事业。讨论双方观点并给出你的观点。

译文:

有人认为读大学是为将来的职业发展做准备的最佳方式，也有人认为人们应该尽早离开学校并通过积累工作经验来发展事业。在本文中，我将从以下几个方面对这两种观点进行探讨。

首先，上大学很有用。一个人需要通过学习获得大量基础的理论知识，这些知识将在他日后的职业发展中发挥实际作用。在这一方面，大学教育完全可以作为达到此目的的一种手段。不难推断：一个人在大学里所获得的理论和基础知识至少会有助于他开阔视野，从而使他比那些未读过大学的人更有优势。

第二，一个人的成功，尤其是金钱上的成功确实不是由是否读过大学而决定的。在这一方面，经验和机遇似乎发挥了更重要的作用。我有不少朋友，勉强小学或初中毕业，然后便马上开始经商了。几年后，他们中有些人发财了，现在经营着超过千人的大公司，而且员工中大学毕业生占据多数。

然而，社会在快速发展、变化，对知识的要求越来越高。在这一背景下，教育程度的高低便逐渐显现出相应的优势和劣势来了。从就业角度讲，读过大学的就是要比没有读过大学的有更多机会。从新的成功模式看，巨大的财富都是越来越与科学技术发展的趋势相联系的。这也充分体现了上大学的价值。

由此可见，现实生活中虽然不乏没读大学而取得成功的例子，但是，我们可以从世界发展的趋势断言：这种情况将越来越少见了，因此如果有条件，还是读大学为好。

8. 直接上大学的利弊

Topic:

Some people believe that students who want to go to university after graduation from high school should have about one year's time to get a job to obtain work experience or have a travel to enlarge their vision. Do you agree or disagree? What's your opinion?

Sample Answer

In most countries, most high school graduates go directly to university. Some people oppose this practice. They claim that students should get a job or have a travel for one year before starting their university education. They argue that, by this way, students can obtain work experience and their sights can be enlarged. However, I doubt whether the arguments could hold much water.

First, it is a waste of time. Since students are in their formative years, the main task of students is to study hard and learn what is needed for the development of our nation. The knowledge and skills which they have gained in high school are surely inadequate. Compared with studying, working and traveling, to some extent, are more relaxing and less painstaking, so after one-year exciting experience outside campus, some young people tend to give up their learning. At least, they cannot concentrate on their studies. It is a great loss to themselves as well as a great misfortune for our country.

Second, young students may be hurt psychologically. The job or the trip may expose them to social ills at an age when they cannot differentiate good from bad. Their early contact with the complicated society makes them more easily contaminated by unwholesome influence. For example, they maybe become money-oriented.

Finally, studying in university can also enrich their social experience and widen their vision. The university is a small society so university students have to communicate with teachers, peers and other people and they have to deal with some problems. During holidays, they can find part-time jobs and go out to travel.

In conclusion, students should continue their studying after graduation from high school. Social experience can be gained after finishing their studies.

▶考官评分:7

题目:

在大多数国家，大多数高中毕业生直接进入大学学习，但有些人反对这种做法。他们认为，学生应先工作或旅行一年，再开始上大学。他们认为，通过这种方式，学生可以获取工作经验并且可以扩大他们的视野。你的观点是什么?

译文:

在大多数国家，大多数高中毕业生直接进入大学学习，但有些人反对这种做法。他们声称，学生应先工作或旅行一年后，再开始他们的大学教育。他们认为，通过这种方式，学生可以获取工作经验并且可以扩大他们的视野。然而，我反对这种观点，我认为这种观点站不住脚。

第一，它会浪费大量的时间。学生的主要任务就是努力学习，用知识来促进我们国家的发展。他们在高中学的知识和技能当然是不够的。与学习相比，工作和旅游更放松，也不累，所以在校园外工作一年，往往会使一些青年人放弃自己的学业。至少，他们不能专注于学业。对于他们自己这是一个很大的损失，对于我们的国家也是一个极大的不幸。

第二，可能会使年轻的学生受到心理上的伤害。在工作或旅行中他们可能会面对许多的社会弊病但又分辨不清其好与坏，过早接触社会的复杂状况将会使他们更容易受到不良影响。例如，他们可能成为拜金主义者。

最后，在大学学习也可以丰富他们的社会经验并开阔他们的视野。大学也算是一个小社会，学生要学会与老师，同龄人和其他人的交往，而且要学会处理一些问题。在节假日里，他们也能够做兼职工作并且可以外出旅行。

总而言之，高中毕业的学生应当继续他们的学业，等到完成学业后再去获取更多的社会经验也不迟。

9. 全民高等教育

Topic:

Some people believe that a college or university education should be available to all students. Others believe that higher education should be available only to good students. Which view do you agree with?

Sample Answer

There is no denying that a college or university education is very beneficial. Those who receive higher education have more opportunities. They often hold better jobs, earn a higher income and enjoy a more comfortable and secure lifestyle. Unfortunately, places in university are often limited and reserved for "good" students. It is my belief that this practice is not only detrimental to those "bad" students, but to the society as a whole. Therefore, higher education should be available to all students.

One reason that higher education should not be limited to good students is that not all secondary students study in equal circumstances. The facilities and teaching at some high schools are superior to those at others, and the students who study there enjoy a great advantage. In addition, a student's performance can be affected by his or her home environment or family financial pressure. It is often more difficult for a student from a disadvantaged environment and school district to perform well. However, this does not mean that the students would not appreciate and benefit from higher education if given the opportunity.

Another reason for making higher education available to all is to encourage less capable students to improve. If marginal students believe that they have no hope of entering university, they may feel that there is no point in studying diligently. However, if they see a more direct relationship between their academic performance and their future opportunities, they will be more motivated. In this way, a poor student may turn out to be a good one.

Finally, a better educated population contributes to the growth and prosperity of a society as a whole. For this reason, it is advantageous to educate as many young people as possible. Furthermore, by denying higher education to students who do not make their mark in their secondary education, the country may be ignoring a future Einstein. When every person in the society is given the opportunity to reach his or her full potential, the society will benefit.

For all of these reasons, I believe that higher education should be available to all students, not only to those with good academic performance in high school. Of course, it is desirable to encourage good performance in students. This can be done by offering financial support in the form of scholarships to those who work hard. In this way, we can ensure that students have the ability to take advantage of the opportunities available to them.

▶考官评分:8

题目:

一些人认为高等教育应该全民化，一些人认为高等教育应该只是针对好学生，你是如何看待这一观点的？

译文：

大学教育非常有益，这是不可否认的。受过高等教育的人会拥有更多的机会，通常也会有比较好的工作，赚比较多的钱，并享有比较舒适的生活和安全的生活方式。可惜的是，大学的入学资格通常是有限制的，而且都是保留给“好”学生的。我相信，这样的做法不但对那些“坏”学生是有害的，整体来说对社会也不利。因此，高等教育应向所有学生开放。

高等教育不应该只限于给好学生。原因之一是，并非所有的中学生都在平等的环境中学习。有些中学的设施和教学比其他的学校好很多，这使得他们的学生占了很大的优势。此外，学生的表现也可能受到家庭环境和家中经济压力的影响。对来自贫困和落后地区的学生来说，要学好需要克服更多困难。然而，这并不表示，如果这些学生有机会接受高等教育，他们不会心存感激并且会从高等教育中获益。

另一个应将高等教育全民化的原因是它可以鼓励那些能力较差的学生进步。如果边缘学生认为自己没有进大学的希望，那么他们也许会觉得用功读书是没有用的。然而，如果他们知道现在的学业表现和未来的发展机会有很直接的关联，他们便会更有动力学习。如此一来，原本学习很差的学生也可能会变成学习优秀学生。

最后，就整体而言，受良好教育的国民会促进社会的发展与繁荣。因此，让尽可能多的年轻人受教育是有好处的。此外，国家如果不让高中成绩未达标准的学生受高等教育，可能会因此埋没了一个未来的爱因斯坦。当社会中的每个人都有机会充分发挥潜力时，整个社会都将获益。

基于这些理由，我认为所有学生都应该接受高等教育，而不是只限于那些在高中时期学习好的学生。当然，鼓励学生有好的表现是可取的。我们可以通过提供奖学金的方式对认真学习的学生进行经济资助。如此一来，我们就可以确保学生有能力充分把握他们可获得的机会。

10. 学校和父母谁应该对孩子的教育负责

Topic:

Who should be more responsible for children's education, the school or the parents?

Sample Answer

Recently, parents tend to attach greater importance to their children's education. Some parents hold the opinion that the school has the main duty to educate their children. However, some teachers take the view that parents should also assume the responsibility. Views on this issue vary from person to person.

People who hold the opinion that the school should shoulder the major responsibility to educate children have some sound reasons. In the first place, most of the children's waking time is spent in schools, and their purpose to attend school is to receive education. Secondly, the parents of the children pay for the education of their children, so they have the rights to receive correspondent services. As an institution of education, the school has the sole responsibility to educate the younger generation. Moreover, there are well-equipped facilities and well-trained teachers in schools.

However, the other side of the coin voices its strong opposition, saying that the parents should assume the main duty of children's education. First of all, the parents know their children more than the school, and they know what to teach and in what way it can be accepted. In the second place, it is beneficial to teach children in accordance with their specific features. Furthermore, in school, each child gets inadequate individual attention, and sometimes his or her particular needs are passed over.

Admittedly, there are merits to both arguments. From my own perspective, I would like to take a more balanced position. Schools and parents are both essential to children's all-around development and they should take the responsibility together.

▶考官评分:7

题目:

是学校还是父母应该对孩子教育承担主要责任?

译文:

最近，父母们更重视孩子的教育。有些父母认为学校有教育他们孩子的主要责任。有些教师认为父母也应该承担这个主要责任。人们的观点各不相同。

认为学校应该承担主要教育责任的人有这些理由：第一，孩子的绝大多数时间是在学校度过的，他们去学校的目的是接受教育。第二，家长为他们孩子的教育付钱，所以孩子有权利接受相应的服务。作为一个教育机构，学校有责任教育年轻一代。而且，学校有良好的教学设施和训练有素的教师。

然而，另一方强烈反对，提出父母应该承担主要责任。首先，家长比学校老师更了解他们的孩子，而且更清楚应该教孩子什么和以何种方式教孩子能更加容易让孩子接受。第二，因材施教对孩子是有益的。而且，在学校，孩子无法得到特别的关照，以致他们的特殊需求被忽视。

必须承认，双方都有道理。我愿意持有一个更平衡的立场。学校和父母对孩子的全面发展都很重要，他们应该一起承担责任。

11. 寄宿学校和走读学校

Topic:

Some people think young children can have better education in a boarding school far from home, while others claim that a day school is a better one. What's your opinion? Give your reasons.

Sample Answer

When asked what kind of school, a boarding or day school or home, is better for young children's education, some people think a boarding school is more desirable while some prefer a day school or home.

Those for a boarding school are justified, I think, in holding that children can learn to be independent earlier when they are far away from home at an early age. Being away from home, young children are less likely to be spoiled by their parents or grandparents. They have to care for themselves, like washing clothes, buying necessities of life etc. They also think that living in a boarding school, together with people of the same age, is greatly beneficial to the building-up of children's personality. Young children can learn what cannot be learned at home, such as getting on well with others, the idea of cooperation, collectivism, and caring for others.

However, those for a day school think quite the opposite. They argue that family education is also very important in addition to school education because family care and love amount to much in the development of children's personality, particularly in their childhood. There will be some psychological defects in a person, like being indifferent, unsociable, and cruel, if he does not enjoy enough family care and parental love during the formation of his character. The second reason is that young children need parents' supervision and guidance because they are still not mature enough to restrain themselves. Although teachers play a part, they can not spare enough attention for each student.

As far as I am concerned, I think there is truth in the arguments of these two parties. I would like to have a balanced view—a day school and home living are good for children in their childhood. When they are old enough to go to high school, it will be more desirable for them to go to a boarding school.

▶考官评分:8

题目:

有些人认为寄宿学校有助于青少年的教育，而有些人认为走读学校更有助于青少年的教育，讨论双方并且给出你的观点。

译文:

当被问及是寄宿学校还是走读学校更有助于青少年的教育时，有些人认为寄宿学校更可取，然而有些人更喜欢走读学校。

支持寄宿学校的人持有的观点是寄宿可以使那些在幼年就离开家的孩子更早学会独立。离开家，可以尽量避免孩子被他们的父母或者祖父母宠坏。他们不得不自己照顾自己，像洗衣服，购买生活必需品等。他们还认为生活在一所寄宿学校，与他们同龄人在一起，这更有利于培养孩子们的个性。孩子们可以学到在家中学不到的知识，例如如何与其他人相处，合作的意识，集体观念和如何照顾别人。

然而，那些喜欢走读学校的人却并不这么认为。他们认为除了学校教育之外家庭教育同样重要，因为家庭的关心和爱护对正在成长的孩子很重要，尤其是在他们童年。如果他在性格形成期间没有享受到足够的家庭关怀和父母的关爱，他们将有一定的心理缺陷，例如：冷淡，不爱交际，残忍。第二个原因就是孩子们需要父母的监督和指导，因为他们还没成熟到能够克制自己。尽管老师也起到一定的作用，但是他们不可能足够重视每一位学生。

对我来说，我认为这两个观点都是正确的。我有一个折衷的观点——在孩子们的童年时期走读学校对他们更有利。当他们长大要上高中的时候，选择寄宿学校对他们来说更可取。

12. 公立学校和私立学校

Topic:

Nowadays there are two kinds of school: public and private. Discuss the merits of each.

Sample Answer

These days, there is a growing tendency for students to enter private schools. A large number of people hold the opinion that private schools play a more important role in education than public schools. Other people, however, hold the opinion that public schools offer their children more advantages. For my part, I think both public schools and private schools are indispensable to our society.

On one hand, it is increasingly acknowledged that private schools, with their unique characteristics can provide their students with more practical skills, which makes them more competitive in the job market. Generally speaking, a private school is renowned for certain fields of study, such as law or medicine in which many eminent authorities serve as tutors. In general, private schools, financed mainly through contributions and high tuition fees, have plenty of funds to invest in advanced teaching facilities, which can make the students' lives and studies more convenient and comfortable. But, at the same time, high tuition fees are an obstacle for gifted but poor students.

On the other hand, the great contributions of public schools cannot be ignored. Poor students have easier access to the public schools that are supported by the government. Schools, ideally, should provide profound, systematic learning of various subjects. The public school that provides wide-ranging subjects for the students is ideal for such training. Furthermore, since education is being more and more emphasized nowadays, the government will, undoubtedly, invest more money in public schools.

From what has been discussed above, we may safely draw the conclusion that both public schools and private schools are necessary to train young people for our country ' s development and construction.

▶考官评分:8

题目:

目前社会上私立学校与公立学校并存，讨论双方的优点。

译文:

最近，进入私立学校的学生数量呈现上升趋势。很多人认为与公立学校相比，私立学校在教育中起着更重要的作用。而其他人则认为公立学校为他们的孩子提供了更多有利条件。从我的角度来看，我认为公立和私立学校都是我们社会中不可或缺的。

一方面，人们逐渐认识到，私立学校通过其独一无二的特征，可以为学生提供更多能使他们在未来职场上更具竞争力的实用技能。总的来说，私立学校以某一特定领域的学习见长，例如法律或药学，都有许多杰出的学术权威作导师。总体而言，私立学校的资金主要来源于捐赠和高昂的学费，有充足的资金购买先进的教学设备，可使学生的生活和学习更加便利和舒适。但与此同时，高昂的学费对于那些有天赋却家境贫穷的学生而言是一个障碍。

另一方面，公立学校的巨大贡献不容忽视。家境贫穷的学生更容易进入政府扶持的公立学校。理想中的学校应为学生提供深入、系统学习各种学科的机会。而公立学校就可达到这种效果。除此之外，如今教育越来越受到重视，政府毫无疑问将会在公立学校投入更多的资金。

从以上的讨论中我们可以顺理成章地得出这样的结论——在为我们国家的发展和建设培养年轻人的过程中，公立和私立学校都是必不可少的。

13. 大学宿舍与校外公寓

Topic:

Students at universities often have a choice of places to live. They may choose to live in university dormitories, or they may choose to live in apartments in the community. Compare the advantages of living in university housing with the advantages of living in an apartment in the community. Where would you prefer to live?

Sample Answer

At most universities there is a variety of housing options for students to choose from. Two of the most common ones are university dormitories and off-campus apartments. Each of these options has its advantages, so students should make their decision carefully.

When moving into a university dormitory, students will find the following advantages. First, it is usually located on the campus and so it is very convenient for students to get to their classes, the library, and other university facilities. They will save the time that they would have otherwise spent commuting to campus. Second, living in a campus dormitory offers students a convenient life. They do not have to worry about cooking meals or paying utility bills on time because all these services are included. They will be able to devote more time to their studies and extracurricular activities. Finally, living in a dormitory makes it easy for students to meet others and develop friendships. In addition to sharing living and recreation space, students can meet others through activities organized by the university or the dormitory itself. This is especially helpful to new students.

As for off-campus apartments, there are also several advantages. First of all, living away from the university allows students to develop more independence. Having more responsibility for their daily needs when they are students, they may find it easier to adjust to life on their own after graduation. In addition, the more independent lifestyle offers more freedom. Without university restrictions, the students can keep their own hours and set their own limits. Finally, students who live off-campus have more personal space. They do not have to share their bedrooms or bathrooms with many other people. This may allow them to better relax when they are not in class.

In conclusion, both university dormitories and off-campus apartments offer certain advantages to students. Which one to choose depends on what is important to the student. As for me, I would choose to live in a university dormitory for the first year. This would allow me to make friends and get accustomed to school life without the distraction of having to worry about my daily needs. Later, I would move into an off-campus apartment in order to develop my independence and enjoy a freer lifestyle.

▶考官评分:8

题目:

大部分大学都有很多居住方式供学生选择,其中最常见的两种就是大学宿舍与校外公寓,讨论双方观点并且给出你的观点。

译文:

大部分大学都有很多居住方式供学生选择，其中最常见的两种就是大学宿舍与校外公寓。这两种方式各有优点，因此学生应该谨慎地选择。

当搬进大学宿舍时，学生可以发现以下一些优点。首先，因为宿舍通常都在校园内，因此对学生来说，无论要去上课、去图书馆，还是要去使用其他校内设施都很方便，可以省下住在其他地方所需的交通时间。其次，住校内宿舍使学生生活很方便。他们不必担心要煮饭或按时缴水电费的问题，因为所有的这些公共设施都由宿舍包办，他们可以花更多的时间在学业方面或参加课外活动。最后，住宿舍让学生更容易认识其他人并培养友谊。除了能与别人共享生活与休闲空间外，学生还能通过校方或宿舍所发起的活动认识新朋友，这对新生而言特别有帮助。

住在校外公寓也有一些优点。首先，住在校外可以让学生更独立。如此便可以使他们在学生时代就能对自己的日常生活所需负责，毕业之后也许更能适应自力更生的生活。此外，较独立的生活方式可以给学生更多的自由。由于没有学校的束缚，学生就能安排自己的时间，并且自我约束。最后，住在校外的学生能拥有较多的私人空间，不需要和很多人共用寝室或浴室，这会让他们在课余时间更能放松。

总之，住在校内宿舍或校外公寓对学生而言都有一些好处。应该怎么选择，要看哪些好处对自己比较重要。对我来说，大一时我会选择住在校内宿舍，这会让我有交友的机会，并且熟悉校园生活，不用因为一些日常所需而分心。之后，我就会搬到校外公寓，这样才能培养自己独立生活的能力并享受更自由的生活。

14. 住家和住校

Topic:

Is it better for students to live at home with their parents or in school accommodations? Give your own opinion on the issue. Use your own experience or an example to support your idea.

Sample Answer

Many parents would like to spend more money sending their children to boarding schools so that they can receive a better education. However, there are many others who prefer to let their kids stay at home. In my point of view, it is better for students to live in school accommodations.

In the first place, living in school accommodations can cultivate students' ability to live independently. Students have to deal with many problems when they live on campus, such as learning how to adapt to a new environment and how to get along with other people. For instance, I began to live in boarding school since high school. Though at first I found it difficult to live alone, I gradually became open-minded and understood how to solve different problems on my own. These benefited me a lot in my later career life. I acquired many interpersonal communication skills and knowledge through living in school.

Furthermore, living on campus can broaden our vision and horizon. Living in school accommodations, we are closer to many other students coming from various parts of the country and with diversified cultural backgrounds. Communicating with them enables us to learn from one another and make progress together. Unavoidably, we will be faced with some different opinions. Nevertheless, it is these counterviews that make us learn more.

Of course, everything has two sides. Likewise, living in school also has its drawbacks. For example, students will have to be confronted with many psychological problems, for they often feel lonely and helpless in a new environment. However, these experiences may be something beneficial to their future development.

Therefore, living in school has more advantages than living at home with parents.

▶考官评分:8

题目:

住在家里好还是住在学校里好？结合你自身经历和所见所闻谈谈你的观点是什么？

译文:

为了让孩子接受更好的教育，许多家长愿意多花钱送孩子去寄宿学校。然而，仍然有许多家长比较喜欢让孩子住在家里。在我看来，让学生住校更好。

首先，住校可以培养学生的独立能力。当他们住在学校时，学生不得不独自处理许多问题。他们不得不学习怎样适应一个新环境以及怎样与他人相处。举例来说，我高中就开始住校，虽然刚开始时我觉得很困难，但我逐渐变得开朗起来，并且从独立生活中学到了很多怎样解决问题的经验，这使我在以后的职业生涯中受益匪浅，我从住校的经历中提高了人际交往的能力，并获得许多相关知识。

除此之外，住校可以开阔学生的视野。在学校，我们会遇见许多有不同文化背景和来自不同地方的学生。通过交流，我们互相学习，共同进步。我们会遇到一些不同意见也不可避免，然而，正是这些不同意见才使我们学到了更多。

当然，任何事情都有两面性，住校同样也有缺点。例如，学生会面临许多心理上的问题，因为在一个新的环境里，他们经常感到孤独和无助。然而，这种经历对于将来的发展也可能是件好事情。

由此可见，学生住校要比在家与父母同住的好处更多。

15. 大班和小班

Topic:

It is much easier to learn in a small class than in a large one. Do you agree or disagree with this statement? Use specific examples and reasons to support your answer.

Sample Answer

People's views on the size of a class vary. While some people hold that a small class is better for learning, there are others who argue that a big one is better. On a personal note, I am convinced that a small class is better for learning.

In the first place, with a small number of students in one class, the classroom atmosphere would be relatively quiet and, therefore, it would be possible for students to concentrate on their learning. This can be easily understood, for, after all, the noise made by 10 or 20 people is much lower than that made by 100 or even 200 people!

Also, with fewer students, the teacher would find it much easier to manipulate the class, that is, to have the whole class under complete control. If there are too many students, the teacher would be at a loss as to what to do because controlling the situation itself would be challenging enough.

Besides, in a small class, the students could have more interactive activities with the teacher and the teacher can give each student whatever instructions or help that he or she needs. When the number of students in a class is much too big, one-to-one or one-to-several tutoring is simply impossible.

From the above discussion, we can safely come to the conclusion that the size of a class does have much influence on the students' learning effect. A small class is better for learning.

▶考官评分:7

题目:

小班学习比大班学习效果更好。你赞同这种观点吗？举例说明并给出你的原因。

译文:

在大班学习效果好还是在小班学习效果好的问题上人们会有不同的看法：有人认为小班好，也有人认为大班好，依我看来小班更有利于学习。

首先，由于小班中的学生人数少，教室里会相对安静些，学生可以安心学习，这一点毋庸置疑，毕竟10人、20人所制造出的声音会远远低于100人、200人所制造出的声音。

其次，学生人数少，任课教师容易掌控课堂。人太多时，教师会感到无所适从，因为要掌控整个局面本身就不是一件简单的事儿。

另外，学生人数少，可以与教师形成互动，教师也就可以对学生实行针对性的指导。如果学生多，一对一的指导或者说一对几的指导根本是不可能的事情。

基于以上论证，我们可以说班级规模的大小会对学生的学习产生很大的影响，小班更有利于学习。

16. 新生入学遇到的困难

Topic:

Many young people find their first days at high school or college difficult, because they feel very lonely. What do you think are the other difficulties they face on their first days? What can schools and colleges do to make them feel more comfortable?

Sample Answer

For many teenagers, dealing with their first days at a new school not only means encountering many exciting new things, but also means overcoming difficulties. They may be delighted to start pursuing more advanced study, another step towards their future success. But on the other hand, unpleasant sentiments, including loneliness, might hit them, when they have to work under the huge psychological pressure of adjusting to a new life of study.

Part of the difficulties they face over this period is due to a changed academic environment. When proceeding to a university or a new school overseas, a student may face a different set of academic norms and expectations. The differences are significant enough to require adjustments in their learning style and attitudes to knowledge, when difficulties arise. Challenges also come from their peers. To ensure that their study performance is equal to or better than their fellow students, they need to work very hard, under great psychological pressure.

However, there are more problems when they commence their new school life. For many students, this may be their first foray beyond the borders of the family home, perhaps living in another city or country. It may take them time to acclimatize and adapt, and local food might not suit their tastes. Sharing accommodation, they may not be able to get along well with other fellow students and suffer from the strain related to interpersonal relationships with relative strangers. To make matters worse, these new students are likely to find it hard to get used to and blend into the local culture, especially in the case of overseas students. In short, lack of familiarity adds to their homesickness, making them even more uncomfortable.

School authorities may play an important role in helping students to settle in. First of all, the orientation programs could last long enough to enable students to feel at home. Furthermore, such programs should be on a more individual basis so that new students can get a clearer picture of school rules and facilities, in addition to accommodating special needs of particular students. Moreover, it would be a good idea for schools to organize some excursions and outings during the first days. Such activities would give students a better understanding of the local culture, as well as promoting better mutual understanding between peers.

▶考官评分:8

题目:

许多高中或大学新生会有孤独感，他们在入学初还要面对哪些困难？学校可以怎么帮他们？

译文:

学生入新校不但会接触许多新鲜的事物，而且还要克服许多困难。他们也许因开始新的学习而高兴（这是迈向成功的一步），另一方面，当面临巨大的心理压力时，他们也会不愉快，比如感觉孤独。

新生面临困难一部分是由于改变了学习环境。进入大学或海外一所学校，学生会面临不同的学业要求。在出现困难时，这种差异非常重要，有时学生不得不改变他们的学习方法和对知识的态度。对于他们来说，同伴也是竞争者。为了确保自己在学习上的表现与同伴一样或者比同伴更好，他们就得在巨大的心理压力下努力学习。

然而，在他们开始新的学习时会发现很多问题。很多学生都是第一次离开家乡住在另一个城市或国家，他们要花时间适应那里的生活，包括饮食。他们或许与同屋的人相处很好，与那些陌生人打交道也会有压力。更糟的是，他们会发现他们很难习惯和融入当地的文化。总之，各种不适应会让新生们更想家，也会让他们觉得更不舒服。

校方在帮助学生适应新生活方面起着重要的作用。首先，介绍会要长一点，直到使学生有宾至如归的感觉。另外，这样的安排应该更个性化以满足个别学生的特殊要求，使他们更清楚地了解学校的规定和设施。这样的活动也会让学生更好地理解当地的文化，促进他们与同龄人的相互理解。

17. 学术课程和实用技能

Topic:

It is often said that the subjects in schools are too academic and that it would be more useful for children to learn about practical matters such as home management, work and interpersonal skills. Do you agree or disagree?

Sample Answer

A criticism often heard these days is that the subjects taught in schools tend to be too academic, and contribute little to preparing a young person for the real-life tasks he or she will have to perform after graduation. They say that academic subjects are rooted in the past, and are not useful for solving modern problems. I disagree with this point of view for three reasons.

My first reason is that it is the duty of parents, not teachers, to prepare their children to deal with the practical affairs of life. The home, not the classroom, is the ideal place to learn about home management and interpersonal skills. As for work abilities and attitudes, they are best learned on the job and under the supervision of an experienced older worker.

My second reason is that academic subjects have withstood the test of time. They represent the accumulated wisdom of our ancestors down through the ages, and, far from being impractical, they equip us with the knowledge and confidence to make sound judgments about any problems which may crop up. In addition, academic subjects are good for training us in mental discipline, while practical subjects are weak in this regard.

My third reason is based on the saying "Man does not live by bread alone." Schooldays devoted solely to instruction in down-to-earth practical matters would be dull indeed. Lessons in the best literature of the world and the epoch-making scientific and geographical discoveries of the past enrich our lives and make us feel that we are part of the great family of mankind.

All in all, the teaching of academic subjects in schools is entirely appropriate. It is my firmly held view that practical subjects have no place in the classroom. On the contrary, the curriculum should be more academic.

▶考官评分:8

题目:

人们常说,学校学科的定位过于学术化,而孩子们如果能学习到有关家政管理、工作以及人际关系技巧等方面的实际知识会对他们更有用,你是否同意此观点?

译文:

最近经常能听到这样一种批评言论——学校教授的课程过于学术,且对一个年轻人来说对他或她在毕业后不得不面对的实际生活中的考验用处不大,他们说学科的设置根植于过去,而对于解决当代问题并非那么有用。我不同意这种观点,理由有三。

我的第一个理由是教孩子们处理生活中实际问题应是父母的责任,而非老师。家庭是学习家政管理和人际关系技巧的理想地方而非教室。至于工作能力和态度,则最好在一名经验丰富的老工人监督下学习工作。

我的第二个理由是学术科目已经经受住了时间的考验,它们代表了我们祖先在各时代积累下的智慧,而且,它们并非不切实际,它们给予了我们面对突发事件时能够作出公正判断的知识和自信。此外,学术课程很有利于锻炼我们的心理素质,而实践课程则在这方面比较薄弱。

我的第三个理由是基于"人不能单靠面包活着"的言论之上,教学时一味地夯实解决实际问题的能力确实会非常枯燥,世界上最好的文学课程和过去那些具有划时代意义的科学和地质上的大发现丰富了我们的生活,使我们有人类大家庭的认同感。

总而言之,在学校教授学术知识是完全妥当的,我坚持认为实践课程并不应在教室中教授。不但如此,课程应当更学术。

18. 理论课程和实用课程

Topic:

College students should give priority to practical courses over traditional ones?

Sample Answer

I frown when I hear people suggest that job-oriented programs should get a bigger share than traditional ones in curriculums of tertiary educational institutions in the hope that graduates can get easy access to employment. In my opinion, their view is short-sighted and flawed. Indeed, equal attention should be paid to both academic excellence and preparation for a working life.

Every subject performs a unique and important role in a student's personal and mental development. It is true that practical courses like computer science and business courses are very useful and students who are adept at them will have a unique advantage in seeking a job. However, if they know nothing beyond these job-oriented skills, they will become robots rather than human beings. As a result, nations, in the long run, will lose their cultural identities.

In fact, knowledge of history and geography is an integral part of human beings' overall qualities. This knowledge, which may seem less practical, is fundamental and necessary to shape students as useful members of society. For example, history teaches people about the development of their country, thus establishing a sense of national identity and pride. People with a knowledge of geography are generally more environmentally conscious, which, in the long run, is essential to achieving sustainable economic development and ensuring the survival of human beings.

In fact, without the benefit of knowledge of history and geography, students cannot do well in learning practical courses either. Students pursuing business courses will be involved in cross-cultural communication. When promoting their products in foreign markets, knowing the local culture, history and geography is a key for them to work out a successful marketing strategy.

A graduate with a wide range of knowledge besides his specialized and practical skills will get on better in society, and such a society will better off as a result. For these reasons, traditional courses deserve at least equal attention as practical ones.

▶考官评分:8

题目:

是不是实用课程比传统理论课程更重要?

译文:

每当我听到人们建议与求职相关的课程应该在高等教育中占主导地位，从而使学生能够很容易找到工作时，我都不是很赞成。我认为这种观点是缺乏远见而且是不完美的。事实上我们应该既要重视学术成绩也要为工作生活做准备。

每一门科目对学生个人和智力的发展有与众不同而且重要的作用。的确，像计算机科学和商务这种实用课程对学生非常有用，那些熟练掌握这些课程的学生在寻找工作的过程中具有得天独厚的优势。然而，如果除了这些求职技能之外一无所知，他们就会成为机器人而不是真正的人。其结果是民族可能会失去她的文化特性。

事实上，历史和地理知识是人类综合素质不可分割的部分。这些知识，看上去好像不是很实用，但是，它们是让学生成为社会有用之才的基本和必备知识。比如说，历史帮助人们了解国家的发展，从而树立民族认同感和自豪感。了解地理知识的人们通常对环境很敏感，这对维持经济发展和确保人类生存是必不可少的。

事实上，缺乏历史和地理知识，学生也很难学好实用的课程。学习商务课程，也要了解跨文化交流的知识。要想在异国促销产品，就要了解当地文化、历史和地理背景，这也是成功打开营销市场的一把钥匙。

一个既懂得专业技术和实际技能又学识渊博的毕业生能够很快地适应社会，拥有这样人才的社会也会越来越好。综上所述，传统的课程应该得到与实际课程同样的重视。

19. 理论知识和实践培训

Topic:

Some people think that the university should not provide theoretical knowledge, but to give practical training. Do you agree or disagree? Use your own experience and knowledge to support your idea.

Sample Answer

Whether theory and practice are contradictory to each other has long since been a controversial issue and is still unresolved. Some people claim that university should not provide theoretical knowledge but to give practical training, which sounds unreasonable and even ridiculous to me. What my viewpoint towards this issue is that university should function as a comprehensive academic institution which can provide both theoretical knowledge and practical training.

At first, I would like to point out that university is an intermediate stage where the graduates from high school prepare themselves for their future in society. As we all know, high schools focus relatively more emphasis on elementary education, which means the teaching in high schools is based on theoretical knowledge instead of practical training. Provided the university only attaches importance to the practical training, how can the college students adjust themselves to society and make contributions later without learning about applying theory into practice?

Secondly, theoretical knowledge has settled foundation for practical training which serves as essentially as a cornerstone. The latter will not even be able to exist without the former one's guiding and directing. Take my own experience for example. When I was a freshman in university, I was offered a part-time job as a proofreader in a press. I accepted it without any hesitation considering it to be an extremely rare and valuable opportunity for practical training. Less than two weeks later I was dismissed by the chief editor who was mainly in charge of proofreading. The reason is simply that I was not qualified for the job due to lack of some correspondent theoretical knowledge.

Thirdly, theoretical knowledge itself derives from practice via a demanding and sophisticated course of refining and abstracting. To provide proper amount of theoretical knowledge can consequently save money as well as time which are supposed to be devoted to practical training.

In general, I stand my position that university ought not to replace theoretical knowledge teaching with practical training. Instead, we should attach the same importance to both aspects.

▶考官评分:8

题目:

理论和实践在大学学习中是否矛盾？结合你的亲身经历谈谈你的观点是什么。

译文:

理论和实践是否矛盾一直是一个有争议的问题，这一问题尚未解决。一些人认为，大学不应该教理论知识而是让学生多去实践。我认为这种说法是不切实际的，甚至是荒谬的。对于这个问题，我的看法是，大学应该是一个既能够教授理论知识又能教授实践技能的机构。

首先我想提出的是：大学是为高中毕业生步入社会做打算的中间过渡阶段。众所周知，高中比较着重于基础教育而不是实践，假如大学生只重视实践，没有学会用理论知识去实践，大学生怎样能把自己融入社会呢？更谈不上为社会做贡献了。

第二，理论知识从本质上讲可作为基石为实践提供稳固的基础，没有前者的向导和指示，后者甚至不会存在。就拿我自己的经历作为例子来讲吧，在我上大一的时候，去了一家出版社做兼职，当一名校对员。我毫不犹豫地接受了这项工作，因为考虑到这是一个非常难得而又有价值的社会实践。但不到两周，我被校对的主管解雇了，原因就是我没有通信方面的理论知识，也就没有资格去做这项工作。

第三，理论知识本来就源自于不断的实践，是经过复杂、严格的提炼和总结获得的，教授适量的理论知识可以为学生节省金钱和时间投入到实践中。

总之，我的观点是大学不应该用理论知识来替代实践，而要同等重视这两方面。

20. 学生选课

Topic:

Some people think the students should take the subjects which are decided by the government in the university. Others think that students can apply for the subjects they prefer. Discuss the two situations and give your opinion.

Sample Answer

Some people hold that college students are supposed to study imperative courses assigned by the government while others argue that they should be endowed with the right to select whatever subjects appealing to their own interest. As far as I'm concerned, I side with the latter viewpoint and will demonstrate it in the following aspects.

First and foremost, it is the basic human right to make personal choices, including what to study on campus, as schools are mere places for receiving education rather than military camps forcing people to accept everything imposed on them. Students, despite the fact that they just step into adulthood and may thus be inexperienced, actually don't need the government to confine them to a tiny little framework of knowledge. As an independent university student, one is both supposed to and able to apply for any subject he's keen on and shoulders all responsibilities for the decision.

In the second place, each individual is distinctive, meaning that one doubtlessly has his own aptitudes as well as weaknesses. As is known to all, one man's meat could be another's poison. Therefore, the government should be sensible enough to entitle every single student to design or at least decide on his own curriculum according to his specific learning styles and preferences. It would have been a total catastrophe to have forced Beethoven to major in math and Einstein to work on opera.

Every coin has two sides. Admittedly, there are still a few merits for students to take subjects determined by the government. For instance, students can better comprehend and pursue the latest trend of the country's cultural orientations, if they want to. What's more, they can lead a relatively easier academic life simply by following what is already prepared for them by the government. However, as we can clearly notify that these incentives are just for the sake of convenience.

To sum up, to select subjects at one's own will contributes more to students' all-round development and it conforms more closely to human nature as well.

▶考官评分:8

题目:

部分人认为大学生应该学习政府为他们设计的课程,而另一部分人坚持学生应该有权选择自己感兴趣的课程。你的观点是什么?

译文:

部分人认为大学生应该学习政府为他们设定的课程，而另一部分人认为学生应该有权选择自己感兴趣的课程。就我而言，我支持后者的观点，并将会从以下几个方面来论证。

首先，可以自己做决定是最基本的人权，其中就包括有权决定自己在校期间的学习内容，因为学校只是吸收知识的地方，而非强迫大家接受其灌输一切的军事基地。虽然大学生刚步入成年期，也可能涉世未深，但他们依旧无需政府来为他们设定应学的课程。作为独立的大学生，他们有权也有能力选择自己想学的课程，且为自己的选择负责。

其次，每个个体都有其独特性，也就是说，每个人都会有其擅长和薄弱的方面。众所周知，彼之甘露，我之毒药。明智的政府理应让每个学生根据自身特有的学习风格和偏好去设计或至少去决定自己的课程表。可以想象，如果逼着贝多芬学数学，爱因斯坦学歌剧，将是多大的灾难啊!

诚然，事物都有两面性。按照政府要求来选课也非一无是处。比如，如果学生愿意听从政府安排听课的话，可以更好地理解和学习国家最新的文化发展方向。另外，学生也可以生活更轻松，因为他们只要紧跟政府做出的安排就可以了。然而，不难发现的是，这样做的动机无非是贪图轻松。

综上所述，根据个人意愿来选课更有利于学生的发展，也更切合人性。

21. 书本知识与社会经验

Topic:

It has been said , "Not everything that is learned is contained in books ." Compare and contrast knowledge gained from experience with knowledge gained from books. In your opinion, which source is more important?

Sample Answer

People always are learning and practicing through their whole lives. From reading words in textbook such as toy, car etc. , people develop concepts and ideas. They further understand the actual meaning of these words by playing toys and riding cars etc. Education(books) and experience are the two main channels for people to gain their knowledge. Each plays a different role for people. In my opinion, knowledge from experience is more important than that from books.

Experience firstly can prove whether the knowledge from books is true or false. Textbooks are very wonderful in teaching people essential principles. However, people can only understand the real meaning of those from books and justify them if they are right through practices. A few hundred years ago, people learnt from textbooks that the earth was flat. However navigators found that was wrong through observations and voyage.

Knowledge from experience can improve and advance the world and our society. As books have limitations, they only teach us about what people found in the past. The knowledge from the books is constrained to the certain conditions and environment. For example, the university course only taught me very simple cases. Most knowledge I possess is obtained from various difficult and complicated cases in my career. There are a lot of new inventions and new products, which could not be found yet in textbooks. Our society and world are developed through continuous practices. Some knowledge, never found in books, such as internet, e-business etc. are all developed through new practices.

"The truth comes from practices and experience", so goes an old saying. People are continually discovering new things and assessing the credibility of knowledge written in books. The knowledge from experience helps us much more than that from books.

▶考官评分:8

题目:

读书不能学习到所有知识。比较从书本获取的知识和实践中获取的知识，谈谈你认为哪种更重要。

译文:

人们一生都在学习和实践。当从书上读到诸如玩具、汽车等词语时，人们才有这样的概念和想法，而他们更深入地理解这些词语的意思是在玩玩具和驾驶汽车的时候。书本和实践是人们获得知识的两个主要途径，在获得知识的过程中它们扮演了不同的角色。依我看来，通过实践获得知识比通过书本获得知识更重要。

实践首先可以检验那些从书本获得的知识是否正确。教科书在教授人们基础知识时很有用。但是人们只有经过实践才能明白那些概念的真正意义和判断它们的对错。几百年前，人们从教科书上学到地球是平的，但是航海家通过观测和航海旅行发现那是错误的。

从实践得到的知识可以改善和发展世界和社会。书本有它的局限，它只能教授我们过去的发现，书本上的知识受限于某时的条件和环境。比如，大学的课程仅仅教授我非常简单的东西，我的大部分知识是从处理工作中各种各样困难和复杂的事件中获得的。有很多新的发明和产品并不是在书中能够找到的。我们的世界和社会是在持续的实践中发展的，一些事物，比如因特网，电子商务等，当时从没在书中出现，它们是在新的实践中发展起来的。

古谚说"实践出真知"。人们在不断地发现新的事物和验证书本上知识的可信度。从实践中获得的知识要比书本上获得的重要得多。

22. 学习与实践

Topic:

Some people believe that the best way of learning about life is by listening to the advice of family and friends. Other people believe that the best way of learning about life is through personal experience. Compare the advantages of these two different ways of learning about life. Which do you think is preferable?

Sample Answer

As we grow, we learn many things about life. Some of these lessons are easy and some are difficult. What is the best way to learn them? Some believe that they can learn best by listening to the advice of others, while some people believe that it is better to learn through personal experience. Both methods have their advantages.

In the first case, learning by listening to others, we have the benefit of learning from others' mistakes and are thus being able to avoid them ourselves. We can take advantage of the experience and wisdom of our friends and family. This will help us to make better decisions and avoid costly errors. Furthermore, the people who know us well can advise us effectively because they understand our strengths and weaknesses. At the same time, they are sometimes able to see situations more objectively than we are.

In the second case, learning through doing, we have the advantage of gaining meaningful experience. We will no doubt better remember the lessons we learn when we enjoy the rewards or suffer the consequences ourselves. Moreover, we can often develop other skills through personal experience and can learn from our mistakes. Finally, no two people are exactly alike. Therefore, what family and friends think may be suitable for them, but not appropriate for us.

Given a choice between these two ways of learning about life, I would still choose the former, learning through the advice of others. This is because I believe I should take advantage of all the resources available, and the experiences of my family and friends are a valuable resource. For example, if I were preparing to take my first trip abroad on my own, the advice of others who have already experienced such a trip could only help me. Just as we can learn from history, we can learn from the past actions of those close to us.

▶考官评分:8

题目:

有些人认为,他们可以通过听取家人和朋友的建议而获得最好的学习效果,而有些人却认为最好是通过亲身体验来学习。讨论双方论点并且给出你的想法。

译文:

在成长过程中,我们会学到生活中的许多事情。其中有些教训很简单,而有些却很困难。什么是获取教训最好的方法?有些人认为,他们可以通过听取别人的建议而获得最好的学习效果,而有些人却认为最好是通过亲身体验来学习。这两种方法各有优点。

第一种方法是听取别人的建议而学习,因为我们可以从别人所犯过的错误中学习,避免再犯相同的错误。我们还可以利用家人和朋友的经验或智慧来帮助我们做出更好的决定,避免犯下代价高昂的错误。此外,因为他们了解我们,知道我们的优缺点,所以能提出有用的建议。同时,他们可以比我们更客观地看待事物。

第二种方法是从行动中学习,这样我们可以从宝贵的经验中获益。毫无疑问,当我们因为自己所做的事情而享受成果或承担后果时,我们会对这些教训记忆得更加深刻。此外,通过亲身体验,可以培养其他技巧,而且也能从错误中学习。最后,没有两个人是完全相同的,因此,家人或朋友的想法也许只适合他们自己,不见得适合我们。

若要我从这两种学习人生的方法中选一个,我仍然会选择前者,也就是从别人的建议中学习。因为我认为,应该利用所有可获得的资源学习,而家人与朋友的经验就是宝贵的资源。例如,如果我初次要准备自己出国旅行,那么有类似出国旅行经验的人所提供的建议对我就很有帮助。正如我们能从历史中学习一样,我们也能从周围的人的经验中学习。

23. 书本知识和个人实践

Topic:

Which is more important for you in your life: knowledge from books you read, or personal experiences in reality? Please use details to explain your answer.

Sample Answer

Books and experience are the main two channels for people to gain their knowledge. Each plays different roles for people. In my opinion, knowledge from experience is more important than that from books.

To begin with, experience can prove if the knowledge from books is true or false. Textbooks are very wonderful in teaching people essential principles. How does the world look like? What is the basic law of change of people and things? We can learn a lot through primary school, secondary school until university. However, people can only understand the really meaning of those from books and justify them if they are right through practices. A few hundred years ago, people learnt from textbooks that the earth was flat. However, navigators found that was wrong through observations and voyage.

Next, the knowledge from experience can improve and advance the world and our society. As books have limitation, they only teach us what people found in the past. The knowledge from the books is constrained to the certain conditions and environment. For example, mould and tools design for plastics industry, the university course only taught me very simple cases, most knowledge are obtained from various and complicated cases in my career.

Furthermore, there are a lot of new inventions and new products which could not be found from textbooks. Our society and world are developed through continuous practices, those knowledge, never found in books, such as Internet, e-business etc. are all developed through new practices.

Just as the saying is "The truth comes from practices and experience", people are continually discovering new things and assessing the creditability of the knowledge written in books. The knowledge from experience helps us much more than those from books.

▶考官评分:8

题目:

书和个人实践哪个是人们获取知识的主要途径，请简单阐述你的观点。

译文:

书和实践是人们获取知识的主要途径。对人们来说，每一种途径都起着不同的作用。我认为，从实践中学到的知识比从书本中学到的知识更重要。

首先，实践可以证明我们从书本中学到的知识是对还是错，教科书对于教授人们知识有着不可替代的作用。这个世界看起来是什么样的？什么是人与物的变化的基本规律？我们从小学，中学到大学的过程中能学到很多东西。然而，人们只有通过实践才能真正懂得从书本里学到的知识的意义。几百年前，人们从教科书上学到地球是平的。但是，航海家们通过观察和实际航行证明了这是错的。

其次，从实践中学到的知识能够帮助世界和社会进步。书本的知识是有限的，它们只能教给我们人们在过去发现的东西。从书本中学到的知识多会受到特定条件和环境的限制。例如，工具支持塑料生产，但是在大学中只教过我非常简单的案例，大多数知识是在我工作之后从很多复杂的事情中学到的。

除此之外，这里还有很多教科书中找不到的新发明和新产品。我们的社会和世界在不断的实践中不断发展，这些知识，在书本中永远找不到，就像互联网，电子商务和其他很多东西一样，都在练习中不断发展。

就像"真理来源于实践和经验"这句话说的，人们不断地发现书本中没有记录的新事物。从实践中学到的知识远比从书本中学到的知识有用。

24. 学生必须上课

Topic:

Some people believe that university students should be required to attend classes. Others believe that going to classes should be optional for students. Which point of view do you agree with?

Sample Answer

Some people may believe that going to classes should be optional, but I disagree. I don't understand how university students can expect to learn anything if they don't attend classes. Personal experience can help people learn about themselves and the world outside the classroom, but when it comes to learning about academic subjects, students need to be in class.

In class they receive the benefit of the teacher's knowledge. The best teachers can do more than just go over the material in the textbook. They draw their students into discussion on the material. They present opposing points of view. They schedule guest speakers to come, give the students additional information, or show documentary films on the subject.

Also classes on any subject provide more than just facts. The students are taught how to learn, how to get information and then apply what they've learned in other situations. Their teacher is the best one to help them with these skills. They can't learn them just by reading the textbook.

By going to class, the students can learn how to work with the other members of the class. Many times, students will be given group assignments. This is different from what they did in secondary school. Here they are with people from different backgrounds and experiences. In this situation, they learn how to cooperate with people different from themselves to achieve a common good.

In short, by going to class, students get more than just information from the teacher. They also learn how to learn, how to work with others, and how to work responsibly. These are not optional skills in life, so attending classes should not be optional.

▶考官评分:8

题目:

一些人认为应该要求大学生必须去上课，而另一些人则认为是否上课应由大学生自己选择，你的观点是什么?

译文：

一些人可能觉得去不去上课应该自由选择，但是我不同意这种观点。我不明白大学生如果不去课堂如何能学到所有知识。个人经历可以帮助人们在课外了解自我和世界，但是如果要学习专业知识，学生就需要到课堂中去。

在课堂上，学生们从老师的学问中受益。最好的老师可以做的不仅仅是传授教科书的内容。他们组织学生就书上的内容进行讨论，他们列出对立的观点，他们请人来给学生讲授更多的知识，或者放相关主题的资料片。

同时课堂教给学生的不仅仅是书本上的内容，还教授学生如何学习，如何获取信息并在其他的情况下将所学的内容加以应用。他们的老师是帮助他们获取这些技能的最佳人选。仅仅依靠读教科书，学生们不能学到这些。

在教室里，学生学到了如何与同学合作。许多时候，学生们会被分成若干个小组，然后会共同完成指定任务，这与他们在中学时的学习方式不同。在这里他们与有着不同背景和不同经历的人合作。在这种情况下，他们学习如何与不同的人合作来达到共同的目标。

一句话，在课堂中，学生们获得的不仅仅是老师传授的知识。他们同时学习了怎么去学，怎么同别人合作，怎么负责任地工作。这些是生命里必不可少的，所以学生必须要来上课。

25. 学生评价老师

Topic:

Some people think that, in order to improve the quality of education, students should be encouraged to evaluate and criticize their teachers. Others feel that this will result in a loss of respect and discipline in the classroom. What do you think?

Sample Answer

In many universities, students are asked to evaluate their teachers after each course. Some people believe the system has many advantages to the students and the teachers. Others argue that it would lead to poor discipline in the classroom. Indeed, evaluation of their teachers by students has both pros and cons.

There are many drawbacks in student assessment. First of all, students are very young and, compared with their teachers, are less knowledgeable both in theory and practice on a subject. Therefore, they are unable to evaluate their teachers' performance in a sound way. Secondly, student assessment would lead to poor discipline in the classroom. If each of the students is allowed to decide on what, how and when to learn, classroom management would become impossible. Thirdly, in order to gain a better evaluation, teachers would seek to please each of the students by lowering the study requirements. This would do harm to students' academic performance in the long run.

However advocates of student assessment have their reasons. Firstly, this kind of feedback can be used to improve teachers' performance. Teaching methods can only be successful if they are student-centered. Therefore, listening to the students' constructive suggestions, teachers will have a better idea of what students' needs are and can then adjust their teaching to meet them. Secondly, the process of writing evaluations will help the students think in their own way independently. Students should be encouraged to learn by even challenging their teachers' thinking. Thirdly, the matter could be considered in a commercial way. Teachers are those who provide paid educational services while students, paying for their education, are customers. In this way, it can be fully justified that students have the right to evaluate the services they receive.

In my own opinion, student evaluations of teachers would be beneficial to both teachers and students. Teachers can adjust their teaching according to the information they obtain from the evaluation. Students' ability of independent thinking and learning can be greatly improved. Moreover, the practice is the outcome of market economy. Students have rights to evaluate their teachers.

▶考官评分:8

题目:

一些人认为,为了提高教学质量,应该鼓励学生对老师进行评价和批评。其他人则认为这将导致课堂上对老师的尊重和良好纪律的缺失。你认为呢?

译文:

许多大学要求学生在课后对该课程的教师做出评价。一些人认为这种做法对于学生和教师都有很多益处。另外一些人则认为这样做可能导致不良课堂纪律。事实上,学生对教师的评估有利有弊。

学生的评估有很多缺点。首先,学生都非常年轻,并且与他们的老师相比,他们在某一学科的理论和实践方面都缺乏知识。因此,他们无法对教师的表现做出恰当的评估。第二,学生评定有可能导致不良课堂纪律。如果每个学生都可以决定学什么、如何学和什么时候学,课堂管理将变成不可能的事情。第三,为了获得更好的评估结果,教师可能通过降低学习要求的方法来取悦学生。从长远角度来讲这样会对学生的学习效果产生不良影响。

然而,提倡学生评估的人也有他们的道理。第一,这种反馈可以用于提高教师的教学水平。只有以学生为中心的教学方式才是成功的。因此,听取学生的建设性的建议,可以使教师更加了解学生的需求,并且帮助他们调整自己的教学以满足学生需求。第二,写评估的过程可以帮助学生以他们自己的方式独立思考。应该鼓励学生学习,即使是以挑战他们老师的观点的方式。第三,可以站在商业的角度考虑这个问题。教师们提供的是有偿的教育服务,而学生为教育付费,学生是消费者。如此说来,学生有权评价他们得到的服务,这是完全合理的。

我个人认为,学生对教师的评估对教师和学生都是有益的。教师可以通过从评估中获得的信息来调整他们的教学。学生独立思考和学习的能力可以得到极大的提高。而且,这是市场经济的结果。学生有权利评估他们的老师。

26. "师"从电脑还是师从老师

Topic:

Nowadays, we can learn from computers and we can also learn from human teachers. What do you think are the advantages and disadvantages of these two kinds of "teachers"?

Sample Answer

People's view on the advantages and disadvantages of learning from computers and from human teachers vary from person to person. While some people believe that learning from computers is more convenient and more economical than learning from human teacher, there are others who hold that learning with the help of human teachers can ensure better learning effect. On a personal note, I argue that these two approaches both have positive and negative aspects and thereby a combination of these two approaches of learning is the best policy.

First, nowadays with the development of computer science, we use computers almost in every aspect of our life, especially in education. Some people predict that one day computer will take the place of human teacher. Is that true? It is true that it is both convenient and economical to learn this way. For example, we can listen to online lectures without leaving our homes and can stop at any time we want. We can also take free courses on the Internet.

But we also have to admit that if we have doubts and problems while we are listening to the on-line lecture, which is sure to happen from time to time, no one can help us out right away. To solve this problem, what we need to do is perhaps to send e-mails and then wait for the reply for days or even for weeks. However, we don't have to face such problems if we learn from human teachers as they can help us out at once. Also, they can adjust their teaching process according to how well we can follow them, that is, they can adapt their teaching methods to suit our actual levels.

While learning from human teachers does possess many an advantage, it is also a fact that we will have to go to school every day and in so doing, we will have to spend a lot of time traveling to and from schools, thus suffering from traffic jams and all the kinds of inconveniences.

As a whole, both computer teachers and human teachers have their advantages and disadvantages in their own special and unique way. Therefore, I'm sure they will exist side by side in the future. This means that it is most advisable for us to combine these two ways of learning.

▶考官评分:8

题目:

当今,我们既能从电脑中获取知识,也能从老师那学到知识,你认为这两种"老师"各自都有哪些优缺点?

译文:

对于"师"从电脑和师从教师学习的优势与劣势问题,人们各有不同的看法。有的人认为"师"从电脑要比师从老师更为方便和经济,也有人认为只有师从老师才能有更佳的学习效果。从个人角度而言,我认为这两种方式都有着积极的和消极的方面,因此,将两者结合起来才是上策。

首先,如今伴随着电脑科学的发展,我们几乎在生活中的每一个方面都在使用电脑,特别是在教育方面。有人预计,有朝一日,电脑将取代老师。真的会如此吗?当然,有一点倒是真的,即:以这种方式学习既方便又经济。举例说吧,我们无需离开家便可上线听课,而且可以随时叫停。我们还可以在因特网上听取免费的课程。

但是,我们还必须承认:如果我们线上听课过程中有疑问和问题了(这一点是肯定会不时发生的),没有人能够马上帮助我们。要解决这个问题,我们所要做的也许就是发邮件,然后等待数日甚至数周才能等来答复。然而,如果我们师从教师,那就不会出现此类问题,因为他们可以马上帮我们释疑解惑。另外,教师还可以根据我们的听课情况来调整教学进度,也就是说,他们可以调整自己的教学方法来适应我们的实际水平。

师从老师的确具有很多的优势,但另外一个事实是:我们不得不天天去学校上学,如此一来我们就要花费很多的时间在学校和家之间奔波,从而遭受交通拥堵之苦和所有各种各样的不便。

总体而言,电脑教师和真人教师自有其特殊和独特的优势与劣势,因此,我相信他们将在未来并存。这就等于是说我们最可取的做法就是将两种学习方式结合起来。

27. 自学和跟老师学

Topic:

Some people think that they can learn better by themselves than with a teacher. Others think that it is always better to have a teacher. Which do you prefer?

Sample Answer

I would argue in this essay that learning from teachers is more advisable in that with the help of teachers, we can learn faster and learn in a more enjoyable manner.

First of all, learning from teachers can make sure that we learn more quickly. As we all know, teachers have received professional trainings which means that they are supposed to know much more than we do on a certain subject. Besides, they have rich experience which can help ensure that we learn more effectively and that we can quickly understand what we should understand. This will be hard to achieve if we learn by ourselves, for, after all, both our knowledge and ability to solve problems are limited; otherwise, we would not need teachers at all.

Second, it is more fun to learn from teachers. As we know, learning is a long process which requires a lot of patience and endurance to be carried on. This naturally poses a great challenge to us all: how can we make it? The answer is simple: to develop interest. As the saying goes, "Interest is the best teacher." With interest, we would feel that learning, which used to be so boring, suddenly becomes so much fun and thus we are happy and self-motivated to learn. To do this is nothing easy because the entire process of learning is full of hardships and despairs. However, our teachers are capable of making their class teaching lively and interesting which in turn, can greatly arouse our passion and enthusiasm for learning and finally enable us to find fun in it, thus carrying it on and on.

Based on the above discussion, we see that learning under the guidance of teachers can make the learning process itself easier and more enjoyable.

▶考官评分:8

题目:

一些人认为没有老师他们凭自己学得更好,其他人认为有老师的指导总是有利的。你同意哪个观点?

译文:

我认为跟着老师学习会更好，因为有了老师的帮助，我们可以学得更快、更有趣。

首先，跟着老师学会比自己学要快得多。我们都知道，老师是受过专业训练的，在某一门特定的科目上肯定比我们知道的多得多，而且，老师有丰富的教学经验可以让我们不走弯路，让我们很快明白我们应该明白的一切，这一点是我们自学所做不到的，毕竟我们的知识有限，解决问题的能力有限，否则，我们就根本不需要老师了。

其次，跟着老师学会更有趣。学习是一个漫长的过程，没有耐心和毅力是难以坚持到底的。这就对我们提出了挑战：如何才能够坚持到底呢？答案很简单：要培养兴趣。俗话说：兴趣是最好的老师。有了兴趣，我们就会感到原本枯燥乏味的学习突然间变得有趣了，我们愿意学习了。而做到这一点绝非易事，因为学习的过程可能充满了艰辛和苦恼。但是，老师有办法使自己的课堂生动有趣，这就在很大程度上激发了我们的学习热情，从而使我们能够从学习中发现乐趣并坚持到底。

综上所述，在老师的指导下学习可以使学习本身成为一件轻松快乐的事情。

28. 教师的职责

Topic:

Some people think that teachers should be responsible for teaching students how to judge right and wrong and how to behave well. Some say that teachers should only teach students about academic subjects. Discuss both views and give your opinion.

Sample Answer

There is no denying that a teacher's role in the overall development of a student is multifaceted. As a teacher, one's primary obligation is to teach students academic knowledge. Yet, it is equally important for him to make sure that the students make progress in other aspects.

First of all, whether one can effectively pass academic knowledge to the students makes the first and most important criterion for judging him as a qualified or unqualified teacher. The main task for the students to perform at school is to lay a solid foundation for their study at a higher level, thus the task for a teacher is to assist them to achieve this goal.

Second, a teacher's obligation is not just confined to passing on academic knowledge to the students. The students are also supposed to develop their ability to judge right from wrong, thus becoming good citizens when they step out of school. To do this, a teacher will have more roles to play than just teaching academic subjects. He will have to set a good example of morality himself and share or discuss with his students his viewpoints towards different phenomena in society. In a sense, apart from the role as a pure academic teacher, he also serves the roles of students' parents at school.

Admittedly, a teacher can relatively be more sure about the academic progress of the students, but not that sure about their moral development for the simple reason that society is a big dyeing pool in which one's being dyed into a certain colour is the result of many factors of which family and many other things also have a role to play. Therefore, seen from this perspective, the influence of a teacher is, after all, limited.

From the above discussion, we can come to the conclusion that apart from teaching students academic subjects, a teacher should also try his best to mould their personality and moral image. Meanwhile, the society as a whole is also supposed to work together to ensure the students' overall development.

▶考官评分:8

题目：

一些人认为老师应该教导学生如何辨别是非，如何行为规范。一些人则认为老师仅仅教授学生学术知识就可以了。讨论这两种观点并提出自己的观点。

译文：

毋庸置疑，老师在学生全面发展的道路上所发挥的作用是多方面的。作为教师，首要任务就是向学生传授学术知识，然而，确保学生在其他方面取得进步亦是同样重要的。

首先，能否有效地向学生传授学术知识是评判一名教师合格与否的首要的、同时也是最为重要的标准。学生在校期间的主要任务就是为更高层次的学习奠定扎实基础，因此，教师的任务就是帮助他们达到预期的目标。

第二，老师的职责并非仅仅局限于向学生传授学术知识。学生还应该不断提升自己辨别是非的能力，从而可以在走出校门时成为好公民。要做到这一点，老师要扮演的角色就不只是教授文化课这么单一了。他需要为学生树立道德典范并针对社会上诸多现象与学生分享或交流的观点和看法。从某种意义上讲，除了扮演了纯粹的学业教师外，他还扮演了学生们在学校里的父母的角色。

诚然，老师可以相对保证学生学习方面的进步，而在道德规范方面就不见得这么有把握了。这主要是因为社会是个大染缸，最终被染成什么颜色是多方面共同作用的结果，这其中就有家庭和所有其他方面的影响，所以，从这个方面来讲，老师的作用毕竟还是有限的。

由此，我们可以得出这样的结论：老师除了教授学生学术知识外，还应该竭力塑造他们的个性与道德形象，同时，全社会应该协力确保学生们的全面发展。

29. 学生是否应该穿校服

Topic:

Should students wear school uniforms? What is your opinion?

Sample Answer

It is a common practice for schools to require their students to wear school uniforms. It is very understandable that school authorities carry out such a policy, because it obviously benefits not only schools but also their students.

Schools are the places where students receive formal education. A sound study environment can contribute to students' satisfactory study performance. To require students to be in school uniforms is part of a school's efforts to create a good learning environment.

Wearing school uniforms is also seen to offer other benefits to students. An obvious one is to ease the financial burden for students. Being in school uniform from Monday to Friday means that there is almost no need for students to buy many other clothes to wear. Another potential advantage is the effect it may have on the students' personal development. School uniforms give children a sense of student identity and belonging to a particular school. Realizing this, students tend to work harder on their courses.

One might argue that the requirement to wear uniforms may discourage individuality and creativity. As a matter of fact, such an argument is flawed. School uniforms of the same colour and design instill the notion that an organization has greater importance on value than an individual's creativity. In fact, in today's highly organized society, it is this view which should prevail.

In conclusion, school uniforms play a significant role in encouraging the students to be hardworking and disciplined.

▶考官评分:8

题目:

学生应该穿校服吗?请谈谈你的看法。

译文:

很多学校都要求学生穿校服。校方制订出这样的政策是可以理解的。穿校服不仅仅对学校有益而且也对学生有益。

学校是学生接受正规教育的地方。良好的学习环境有助于学生达到满意的学习效果。要求学生穿校服是校方为了营造良好的学习环境所做出的努力之一。

穿校服对于学生来说也是有好处的。最显而易见的优点就是能减轻学生的经济负担。从周一到周五都穿着校服意味着学生不需要再花钱去买别的衣服。穿校服的另外一个潜在的好处就是对学生的性格培养有益。校服显示出学生的身份以及属于哪个学校。考虑到这一点,学生会努力学习。

可能有人会说要求学生穿校服会妨碍他们的个性和创造力的培养。而事实上,这种观点是不正确的。校服的颜色和款式向学生灌输了一种观念——集体的价值高于个人的创造性。实际上,在当今高度组织化的社会里,这种观点非常流行。

总之,校服对于鼓励学生努力学习并遵守纪律起着非常重要的作用。

30. 上大学之前先工作或者旅行一年的利弊

Topic:

In some countries young people are encouraged to work or travel for a year between finishing high school and starting university studies. Discuss the advantages and disadvantages for young people to do this.

Sample Answer

It is quite common these days for young people in many countries to have a break from studying after graduating from high school. The trend is not restricted to rich students who have the money to travel, but is also evident among poorer students who choose to work and become economically independent for a period of time.

The reason for this trend may involve the recognition that a young adult who passes directly from school to university is rather restricted in terms of general knowledge and experience of the world. By contrast, those who have spent some time earning a living or travelling to other places have a broader view of life and better personal resources to draw on. They tend to be more independent, which is a very important factor in academic study and research, as well as giving them an advantage in terms of coping with the challenges of student life.

However, there are certainly dangers in taking time off at that important age. Young adults may end up never returning to their studies or finding it difficult to readapt to an academic environment. They may think that it is better to continue in a particular job, or to do something completely different from a university course. But overall, I think this is less likely today, when academic qualifications are essential for getting a reasonable career.

My view is that young people should be encouraged to broaden their horizons. That is the best way for them to get a clear perspective of what they are hoping to do with their lives and why. Students with such a perspective are usually the most effective and motivated ones and taking a year off may be the best way to gain this.

▶考官评分:8

题目:

在一些国家，年轻人被鼓励在上大学之前先工作或者旅行一年。讨论这么做的优缺点。

译文:

近年来，有种情况很普遍，很多国家的年轻人都在高中毕业后间隔一段时间再去上学。这种趋势不仅限于有钱去旅行的富学生，在穷一点的学生中也很明显，他们选择去工作并且取得一段时间的经济独立。

出现这种趋势的原因可能是人们认识到了直接从中学上大学的年轻学生在知识和经历上都比较有限，然而相比较而言，如果他们先花了一定的时间去赚钱谋生或到其他地方旅行，他们对生活就会有更宽广的视野，也有可以使用的更好的个人资源。此外，他们会更加独立，这不仅在他们的学术学习和研究当中是一个非常重要的因素，还会让他们在处理学生生活的各种挑战时获得一种优势。

但是，在如此重要的时期离开学校当然会存在一定的风险。有些年轻学生可能就不回来学习了，或者发现很难再重新适应学习环境了。他们或许认为继续做某个工作会更好，或者去做一些跟大学课程完全不同的事情。但是总体来说，我觉得这在今天的情境下不太可能，因为学术资格证书对于找到一份不错的工作是十分必要的。

我的观点是，我们应该鼓励年轻人去开阔他们的眼界。这是让他们清晰地知道将来他们希望做什么以及为什么的最好的方式。有这种认识的学生往往是学习最有效和最有动力的人，间隔一年后再去上大学是最好的方式。

31. 兼职工作的利弊

Topic:

In many countries, students participate in some kind of paid work in their spare time. Some people think this is wrong, but others believe that such work will extend students' knowledge and increase their sense of responsibility. What is your opinion?

Sample Answer

When it comes to whether children should be allowed to work outside school hours, some educators are strongly against it, claiming that part-time work may have a negative influence on their study. Obviously, if students spend too much time on employment, it may contribute to poor academic performance. However, if they do a part-time job over reasonable hours, it may be extremely valuable for them.

One of the clear advantages is that they could finance part of their education from their own earnings, easing the financial burden on their parents. The extra money earned may enable them to get better access to various educational resources, such as books, stationery, special courses, and special-interest clubs. Using money of their own, they tend to value such opportunities more. In return, this will undoubtedly benefit them a great deal in their study.

What matters even more is that when they do part-time jobs, they may learn something practical that they could never be taught at school. A student working part-time in a software company could keep himself well-informed about the latest software not even installed in his school's computer lab.

Students in part-time employment would also stand a chance of being exposed to different types of people, thus helping them to become mature when dealing with interpersonal relationships. Let's take the example of a student working in sales. To sell products, the young person is constantly obliged to assess and satisfy the needs of his customers. By and by, he learns to be considerate in associating with other people. This must be very beneficial for his future success.

In a word, students should be encouraged to take up part-time employment outside school hours.

▶考官评分:8

题目:

许多国家的学生会在课余时间做许多不同的兼职工作。一些人认为这是错误的,但是其他人相信这样的工作能够拓展学生的知识并且增加他们的责任感。你的观点是什么?

译文:

当谈到孩子是否可以在学习之余打工时，一些教育工作者表示强烈反对，认为兼职工作会给孩子们的学习带来负面影响。显然，如果学生花费过多的时间在工作上，势必会影响他们的学习。然而，适量的兼职工作，对孩子们会非常有益。

其中一个很明显的益处就是他们可以自己负担一部分教育费用，减轻家里的经济负担。额外的钱也可以帮助他们获得更多的学习资源，如书、文具、特殊的课程和加入感兴趣的俱乐部。花自己的钱会让他们更加珍惜这样的机会，毫无疑问，这也会使他们在学习中受益颇多。

更重要的是他们可以在兼职工作中获得书本上学不到的东西。比如业余时间在软件公司打工的学生可以接触到最新的软件，而这些软件在学校的计算机房里可能根本都没有。

兼职学生可以有机会接触不同类型的人，让他们在今后处理人际关系时更成熟。我们以做销售的学生为例。为了卖出产品，年轻人就要尽量满足客户的要求。逐渐地他懂得和别人交流时要替别人考虑。这对他今后的成功非常有益。

总之，应该鼓励学生在课余时间做一些兼职的工作。

32. 兼职工作的利弊

Topic:

Some say part-time jobs are useful for full-time students, because they not only earn money but also gain career experience. Do you agree or disagree?

Sample Answer

There is a growing tendency these days for students to take part-time jobs, even though they are following full-time higher-education courses. Many people criticize this on the grounds that working even part-time interferes with their studies and gives them little or no useful experience. Besides, they say, the little extra money they earn does not compensate for the fatigue incurred by working and studying at the same time.

But it seems to me that working at a part-time job is useful for helping a student to learn how to arrange his or her time properly. We all must learn to plan our time so that we do not become absorbed in one single task, no matter how important it is. In later life, the student will have to be able to balance the demands of a career with the demands of his or her family, and at the same time handle various unexpected crises.

As for the money earned from part-time jobs, I firmly believe that it is not only useful but also necessary nowadays for students to earn extra money, no matter how little. Tuition fees and the prices of books, not to mention the cost of living, are soaring by the day. As a result, sometimes even a small sum of extra money can make all the difference between passing or failing a course.

To sum up, I agree that full-time students should take part-time jobs. Working while studying teaches the student good time-management habits. Most students need extra money, and if the jobs are chosen properly they can benefit not only the students' pockets, but also their health and studies as well.

▶考官评分:8

题目:

有人认为对于全天上课的学生来说,临时工作不仅能挣钱而且可以获得工作经验,你赞成这种观点吗?

译文:

如今有越来越多的学生在做兼职工作，即使他们上全日制的高等教育课程。很多人以兼职工作妨碍了他们的学习，并且几乎无法给予他们有用的经验为理由，批判这一现象。此外这些人还认为，由工作所挣来的微薄收入并不能补偿他们由于同时工作和学习所导致的疲劳。

但依我看来，兼职工作在帮助学生学习怎样合理地安排时间这方面是非常有用的。我们所有人都必须要学习怎样去安排我们的时间，不能将全部的精力只全神贯注地投入到一件事情上，无论这件事情有多么重要。在以后的生活中，学生将要去平衡事业和家庭的需求，与此同时，他们还要处理各种意想不到的危机。

至于那些他们从兼职工作中赚到的钱，我确信这不仅仅是有用的，而且如今赚钱对学生来说是非常必要的，无论那些钱有多少。如今学费和参考书的价钱都飞涨，更不用说生活费了。所以，有时即使是一笔额外的小的收入，都可能会造成能否通过一个科目的不同。

总而言之，我同意全日制的学生去做兼职工作。在学习的同时工作可以教会学生合理安排时间。多数学生都需要额外赚钱，如果他们选择的工作合适，那么不仅可以满足自己的钱包，对他们的健康和学习也有好处。

33. 出国工作的利弊

Topic:

What do you imagine are the advantages and disadvantages of working abroad, as far as individuals and countries are concerned?

Sample Answer

In an era of economic globalization, working abroad is emerging as an inevitable trend. A recent study has revealed that the number of people who are employed overseas across the world still keeps rising. What does this tendency imply for individuals and nations?

Advantages can be expected from such an experience. Being exposed to different cultures, individuals can get a clear picture of the way other people live. Work experience overseas can also broaden one's horizons about the world and lead one to a more objective attitude toward it. This results from being able to view things in different ways and from different cultural angles. Ultimately, one could also become more tolerant. When this is the case for a great number of individuals, the collective impact may even produce less conflict and promote peace between countries. As far as nations suffering from overpopulation and high unemployment are concerned, another benefit from the trend of working abroad can be perceived, as it may ease employment pressure there. For countries that receive employees, the influx might satisfy the demand for labour.

However, in some cases, overseas employment may bring some undesirable consequences for individuals as well as nations involved. There is a likelihood of encountering language barriers and culture shock, when one finds oneself try to adapt to local customs and culture. Living overseas also means being away from one's family and, as a consequence, this weakens family ties. A good case in point is that a couple who live apart often ends up divorcing. In addition, because talented people prefer developed areas as their destinations, these places are more liable to become overcrowded with high-calibre experts. At the same time, the underdeveloped countries are in urgent need of such people.

On the whole, I would say that the advantages of working overseas far outweigh its disadvantages.

▶考官评分:8

题目:

请从国家和个人的角度分析出国工作的利与弊。

译文:

在经济全球化的时代，出国工作成为一股不可阻挡的潮流。最近的一项研究表明全球海外工作人员的数量还在上升。这种趋势对于国家和个人来说有什么影响呢?

这种经历有好的一面。深入到不同的文化氛围，人们可以清楚地了解其他民族的生活。海外工作经历可以开阔一个人的视野。从多种渠道和不同的文化角度来观察事物，有助于让人持有更为客观的态度并最终变得更加宽容。海外工作者数量的增多，相互影响，有助于减少冲突并促进和平的集体效应。对于一些国家人口过剩，失业率居高不下，出国工作还有另外一个好处。这种潮流能够减少就业压力。需要劳动力的国家可以接纳这种劳动力。

然而在某些情况下，无论对个人还是国家海外工作还可能带来一些意想不到的后果。当海外工作者面对当地的文化和风俗时，将会出现语言障碍或者文化冲突。在海外生活会远离家人，使家庭纽带松懈。夫妻长期两地分居就会造成离婚就是这方面的例子。此外，有才干的人往往喜欢去发达地区，因此在这些地方汇集了很多的专家，而不发达国家恰恰又急缺专家。

总之，我认为海外工作利大于弊。

34. 出国留学的利弊

Topic:

The idea of going overseas for university study is an exciting prospect for many people. But while it may offer some advantages, it is probably better to stay at home because of the difficulties a student inevitably encounters living and studying in a different culture. To what extent do you agree or disagree with this statement?

Sample Answer

There is no doubt that going to study in a foreign country, with its different language and culture, can be a frustrating and sometimes painful experience. But while overseas study has its drawbacks, the difficulties are far outweighed by the advantages. Indeed, people who go abroad for study open themselves up to experiences that those who stay at home will never have.

The most obvious advantage of overseas university study is real-life use of a different language. While a person can study a foreign language in his or her own country, it cannot compare with constant use of the language in academic and everyday life. There is no better opportunity to improve second-language skills than living in the country in which it is spoken. Moreover, having used the language during one's studies offers a distinct advantage when one is applying for jobs back home that require the language.

On a campus, the foreign student is not alone in having come from far away. He or she will likely encounter many others from overseas and it is possible to make friends with people from all around the world. This is not only exciting on a social level, but could lead to important overseas contacts in later professional life.

Finally, living and studying abroad offers one a new and different perspective of the world and, perhaps most importantly, of one's own country. Once beyond the initial shock of being in a new culture, the student slowly begins to get a meaningful understanding of the host society. On returning home, one inevitably sees one's own country in a new, often more appreciative angle.

In conclusion, while any anxiety about going overseas for study is certainly understandable, it is important to remember that the benefits offered by the experience make it well worthwhile.

▶考官评分:8

题目:

出国留学似乎是每个人的希望。不过它也是有利有弊,有的时候还是留在本土学习比较好,因为在外学习会遇到很多如生活环境和不同文化背景的冲突。你是否同意这个观点?

译文:

毫无疑问，去一个语言及文化背景不同的国家进行学习是一段令人感到受挫且痛苦的经历。尽管留学有这些不足之处，但它的优点还是远远超过了其困难之处。确实，去国外留学的人将放开自己，去体验那些留在国内的人未曾拥有过的经历。

留学最显而易见的优势就是实实在在地使用一门外语。一个人在自己的国家学习外语同在学业与日常生活中经常使用外语的情况是不能相提并论的。提高一门外语最好的机会就是在使用该语言的国家生活。此外，当一个人回国申请有外语要求的工作时，以此语言完成学业的经历便成为一个显著的优势了。

在大学校园里，外国学生不会因为远道而来而觉得孤零零。他/她可能会遇到许多其他留学生并且很容易交到来自世界各地的朋友。这不但在社交层面上令人兴奋，而且还能为日后职业生涯建立宝贵的海外人际网。

最后，在国外学习和生活给予一个人对于世界，也许最为重要的是，对于自己的祖国一个全新的、不同的视角。一旦度过最初的文化冲突后，学生就会慢慢地了解东道国文化的意义。回国后，他必然会用一种全新的、更有欣赏力的视角看待自己的祖国。

总而言之，虽然对于出国留学的任何担心都可以理解，但重要的是要记住这段经历所带来的好处使其非常有价值，不虚此行。

35. 学外语是否必须出国学

Topic:

Studying English in an English-speaking country is the best but not the only way to learn the language. Do you agree?

Sample Answer

Studying a language in a country where it is widely spoken has many advantages. It is, therefore, a good idea to study English in a country such as Australia. However, I believe it is not the only way to learn the language.

In the first place, most students in non-English speaking countries learn English at middle school, and some even at university nowadays. Although their spoken English is not usually of a very high standard, their knowledge of grammar is often quite advanced. This is certainly useful when students come to an English-speaking country to perfect the language.

Secondly, studying the basics of English at secondary school is less stressful than learning the language while overseas. This is because students living at home do not have to worry about problems such as finding accommodation, paying for their study and living costs, and trying to survive in a foreign country where day-to-day living causes much stress.

However, there are obvious advantages of learning English in Australia. Every day there are opportunities to practice listening to and speaking with Australians. Also, students can experience the culture first-hand, which is a great help when trying to understand the language. This is especially true if they choose to live with Australians, as part of a homestay family, for example. Furthermore, if students attend a language school full-time, the teachers will be native speakers. In this case, not only will students improve speaking and listening skills, but attention can be paid to developing reading and writing skills as well.

In general, even though it is preferable to study English in an English-speaking country, a reasonable level of English can be achieved in one's own country, if a student is gifted and dedicated to study.

▶考官评分:8

题目:

在讲英语的国家学习英语是最好的但并非惟一的学习语言的方式。你同意这种观点吗?

译文:

在一个广泛使用这种语言的国家来学习这门语言具备诸多优势。因此，在这样一个国家比如澳大利亚学习英语就是一个很好的主意。然而我相信，这并不是惟一学习英语的方式。

首先，非英语国家的大多数学生从中学时代开始学习英语，而现今甚至有些学生从大学时代才开始。尽管他们的口语通常并不具备很高的水平，但是他们的语法知识却相当深厚。这对学生们到讲英语的国家去完善语言当然是非常有用的。

其次，学生们在中学学习基础英语的压力要比在国外学习这门语言小很多。这是因为学生们住在家里并不需要担心诸如找宿舍、承担他们学习和日常生活的开销等问题。而在国外生存日常生活方面会有很大的压力。

但是，在澳大利亚学习英语有明显的优势。每天都有机会和澳大利亚人练习听力和口语。此外，学生们能够亲身体验文化，这对试图了解一门语言有很大的帮助。如果他们能同澳大利亚人住在一起，例如，作为寄宿家庭的一部分，这一点尤为正确。再者，如果学生能参加全日制语言学校，教师将会是以英语为母语的人。在这种情况下，不仅学生们听说技能可以得到提高，而且也能注意提高阅读和写作技巧。

一般来说，尽管在说英语的国家学习英语更为可取，但如果一个学生有天赋并且努力学习，那么他在自己国家依旧可以使英语达到尚好的水平。

36. 学习一门外语是否必须学习该国文化

Topic:

In order to learn a language well, we should also learn about the country as well as the cultures and lifestyles of the people who speak it. To what extent do you agree or disagree?

Sample Answer

I fully support the assertion that to learn a language well, we should also be familiar with the country as well as the cultures and lifestyles of the people who speak it.

Let's first see how we normally define "learning a language really well". To my understanding, learning a language well means being able to speak the language in a proper way. Here, with speaking it properly, we need to know that due to cultural differences, many things are just so different from culture to culture. For example, the Chinese often greet each other by asking "Have you taken your meal?" which, to the Western ears, would make an invitation to lunch or dinner. Therefore, the lack of a knowledge of the cultures of different countries will give rise to wrong interpretations of the message issued or received and as a result, lead to misunderstandings. In this way, we can not say that we are speaking the language properly and further, we can not say that we speak it well.

Second, the ultimate purpose for us to learn a language is to use it in our communication with other people who speak it, mainly the native speakers. Suppose we know nothing about the US or Britain, including its government, its people, its tradition, and its other aspects. Do you think you can speak English properly, thus achieving effective communication with the American or British people? I'll say at least I can't.

Third, the lifestyles of the people whose language we are learning are also something we need to know in order that we can speak their language properly. For instance, the Chinese eat pork, but this is not the case with Muslims. Also, Muslims are very religious people and perform rituals many times a day. If we don't know these things, how can we expect to communicate with them without incurring troubles? In this logic, if we cannot make sure that we are speaking their language properly, how can we say that we have learned their language well?

From the above discussion, we finally draw the conclusion that to learn a language really well, we also need to be familiar with the country as well as the cultures and lifestyles of the people who speak it.

▶考官评分:8

题目:

为了学好一门语言，我们还有必要了解这个国家及其文化和生活方式，你赞同这个观点吗?

译文:

我完全赞成这种观点，即：要学好一门语言，我们还应该了解讲这门语言的国家、文化和人们的生活方式。

首先来看看我们一般情况下是如何定义“真正学好一门语言”的。按照我的理解，学好一门语言意味着能够恰到好处地去应用。这里，对于恰当地应用这门语言，我们需要知道：由于文化上的差异，很多东西会大相径庭。比如，中国人常通过问“吃了吗?”来表达问候，而这对于西方人来讲便认为是午饭或晚饭的邀请。因此，缺乏了对不同国家文化方面的知识，就会引起对所发送或接收到的信息的错误理解，结果便会导致误解。这样一来，我们就不能说我们讲得妥当，再进一步，我们就不能说我们讲得好。

第二，我们学习一门语言的最终目的是用它与讲这门语言的人进行交流，主要是母语为这门语言的人。设想我们对美国或英国什么也不了解，包括其政府、人民、传统以及其他方面，你想你能恰当地讲英语，从而与美国人或英国人达到有效的交流吗?我会说：至少我做不到。

第三，我们还需要知道我们所学语言国家的人们的生活方式才能恰到好处地使用这门语言。举个例子：中国人吃猪肉，但穆斯林人不吃。还有，穆斯林宗教气氛浓郁，每天举行多次仪式。如果我们不知道这些事情的话又怎能指望与他们顺利交流而不招惹麻烦呢?按照这一逻辑，如果我们不能保证恰当地讲好他们的语言，我们又怎么说他们的语言我们学得很好呢?

由此，我们可以最终得出结论：要真正学好一门语言，我们还必须了解这个国家及其文化与人们的生活方式。

37. 性格迥异的朋友和兴趣相投的朋友

Topic:

Some people like different friends. Others like similar friends. Which kind of friend do you prefer? Explain why.

Sample Answer

Which kind of friends is more desirable, different friends or similar friends? Since people's criterion for friendship differs, they may never agree on the above issue. Personally, I have made friends with people from all walks of life, and these different friendships are such a precious treasure for me.

In the first place, a mixture of friends can bring us many practical benefits. As the saying goes, a friend in need is a friend indeed. Since we all need to move on in life, we need new friends to lead us to new adventures, new career opportunities and new life. In fact, most of us have to make new friends when we leave school and find employment. Besides, different friends can help us with the different difficulties that we encounter in life. And the friend in a foreign country might be able to arrange cheap accommodation for a holiday.

In the second place, the contact with different friends gives us a broad outlook to life. As the Chinese sage Confucius put it, "When three persons walk together, one of them can surely be my teacher." Since we all have our own weaknesses, the strengths of different friends can always complement each other. For example, from a friend who majors in computer, I have learned how to design my own web page; by exchanging e-mails with an American pen-friend, I have greatly improved my English writing. In addition, different friends can help me to enjoy a variety of interests, and we can always attract each other with our different hobbies, different ideas and different experiences. I feel that I can always find new things to learn from my various different friends.

All in all, although "birds of a feather flock together," I would like to fly with "birds" of different feathers, which would certainly make my life more colourful.

▶考官评分:8

题目:

有些人喜欢与自己性格迥异的人交朋友,有些人喜欢和自己兴趣相投的人交朋友,你喜欢和哪种类型的人交朋友呢?请说明理由。

译文:

哪种朋友值得交,性格迥异的还是兴趣相投的?不同的人对友谊的判断标准也不相同,他们对上述问题也许不会达成一致。就我个人而言,我和各行各业的人交朋友,这些性格迥异的朋友对我而言就是宝贵的财富。

首先,各种各样的朋友可以带来一些切实的好处。常言说得好,患难见真情。因为我们都需要在生活中不断前进,所以我们需要新朋友带给我们新的挑战、新的工作机会和新的生活。实际上,我们中大多数人需要在毕业和找到工作后结交新的朋友。此外,不同的朋友可以帮助我们解决生活上遭遇到的各种困难。如果我们有一个身处国外的朋友,在度假的时候他可以帮我们找到便宜的居所。

其次,与不同的朋友接触,会让我们对生活有更多的见解。正如中国古代哲学家孔子所说,"三人行,必有我师。"我们都有我们自身的弱点,性格迥异的朋友可以优势互补。例如,从一个计算机专业的朋友那里,我学到了如何设计我自己的网页;通过电子邮件与一个美国的笔友交流,我的英语写作有了很大的提高。另外,不同的朋友可以让我享受到多种兴趣爱好的乐趣,我们往往会被对方不同的爱好、想法以及经历所吸引。我感到我总是能够从很多不同朋友的身上学到东西。

总之,虽然说"物以类聚,人以群分",但我更喜欢结交不同的朋友,这将一定会使我的生活多姿多彩。

38. 年轻人谈恋爱

Topic:

Most young people without a partner would prefer to have a boyfriend or girlfriend. Yet being in a relationship when you are young is not always a good idea. Do you agree or disagree?

Sample Answer

When you are young, there is often a great deal of peer pressure put upon you to be in a relationship. Although most young people spend a lot of time dreaming about finding the right boyfriend or girlfriend, I believe that early relationships can lead to many problems which young girls and boys might not be able to solve easily.

Firstly, having a special friend is a large responsibility. It takes a lot of time to look after the needs and interests of another person. It could be better to spend the time studying or playing sport. After all, there will be plenty of opportunities for young people to share their lives later, when they are grown-up.

Next, there is the financial situation to consider. Some activities are cheaper to do together, but most are not. Often one partner has more money than the other and has to pay for both when, for instance, they go to the movies or to a restaurant. Also, young people love to buy each other gifts, and may try to impress by spending more than necessary.

Some people argue that today's youth are better informed than their parents were, and, therefore, might be more capable of making a relationship succeed. This may be true, but young people today still have many emotional problems to face; especially in a relationship it is more difficult. For instance, it is hard to have complete trust in someone without a strong commitment. Jealousy can be very destructive, especially at an early age.

In general, while it is true that, for young people, being together and in love is wonderful, there are often many difficult issues to cope with in a full-time relationship.

▶考官评分:8

题目:

很多没有伴侣的年轻人都愿意找一个男朋友或者女朋友,但是在年轻时就谈恋爱不太好,你同意这个观点吗?

译文:

当你年轻的时候，往往很大程度上来自同辈间的压力将你们弄在一个恋爱关系里。虽然很多年轻人花了很多时间来梦想着找个合适的男朋友或者女朋友，我还是认为早恋仍然给年轻人带来了很多困惑，并且是很不容易解决的困惑。

首先，有一个特别的朋友是意味着承担很大的责任。需要花很多时间照顾对方的需求和兴趣，如果这些时间用来学习或者运动岂不是更好，毕竟，当年轻人长大成人后，他们有很多机会去和别人一起分享他们的生活。

其次，从财政状况考虑，一些活动大家一起做就能便宜些，但大部分并非如此。往往是伴侣中比较有钱的一个花钱更多或全部买单，比如看电影或下饭店。此外，年轻人喜欢互相买礼物，并为了摆阔气花更多不必要的钱。

有些人争辩说，今天的青年比他们的父母年轻时更见多识广，因此，可能会更有能力维持社会关系。这可能是正确的，但今天的年轻人仍然要面对许多情感问题，尤其是在这种相互关系中更加困难。举例来说，没有一个强有力的承诺很难完全做到彼此信任。嫉妒会极具破坏性，尤其是在年纪还小的时候。

总而言之，诚然，对于年轻人而言，在一起并相爱是美好的，但在一起交往的过程中往往要面对很多困难，一定要妥善处理。

39. 一小群朋友和一大群朋友

Topic:

Some people prefer to spend time with one or two close friends. Others choose to spend time with a large number of friends. Compare the advantages of each choice. Which of these two ways of spending time do you prefer?

Sample Answer

Friends play a very important part in everyone's life. And each of our friends is special and unique. Some friends may be good advisors or confidants while others challenge our opinions or push us to try something new. Therefore, we may like to pursue different activities with different friends, and we may like to be with a large group of friends or spend time with just one or two. Each has its advantages.

One advantage of spending time with one or two close friends is that these friends usually know us well. We can communicate with them easily and are unembarrassed to share our feelings. We know that these good friends won't judge us. In addition, we are likely to share many of the same interests and will, therefore, find it easy to talk about many things. Finally, it is much simpler to arrange activities when only two or three people are involved.

Spending time with large groups of friends also has its advantages. First, being with a wider variety of people exposes us to many more new ideas. We may be introduced to new things and develop new interests as a result. Also, we will be more likely to find someone to do things with when we associate with many friends. Last but not least, being with a large group of people can be fun and happy. There will always be enough people to play any game or make up a team.

As for me, although it can be fun to spend time with a large group of friends, I prefer to stay with one or two close friends. It is easier for us to match our schedules and arrange a time to meet. Also, we have a deeper relationship, so I find the time that I spend with them to be very valuable. No matter how we like to spend time with friends, there is no denying that friends are very important to us.

▶考官评分:8

题目:

有些人喜欢只与几个亲密的知己在一起,有些人喜欢和一大群朋友在一起,比较两种方式各自的好处,并说出自己的选择。

译文:

朋友在每个人的生活中都扮演着很重要的角色。我们每一个朋友都是独一无二的。有的朋友可能是很好的顾问或是心腹知己，而有的朋友则会质疑我们的看法或驱使我们去尝试新事物。因此，我们可能会喜欢和不同的朋友从事不同的活动，可能会喜欢和一大群朋友在一起，或和一两个知己在一起消磨时间。每一种方式都各具优点。

和一两个知己消磨时间的好处之一就是知己通常很了解我们，我们可以轻易地和他们沟通，分享自己的感受时也不会不好意思。因为我们知道，知己是不会去评判我们的好坏的。此外，我们也可能因为分享许多共同的兴趣而找到更多共同话题。最后一点也是非常重要的一点，要安排只有两三个人的活动真是简单多了。

和一大群朋友消磨时间也有它的好处。首先，和一大群各种各样的人在一起能让我们接触到更多新的想法。我们可能因此接触到新的事物，或培养出新的兴趣。此外，和很多朋友来往，也让我们更容易找到可以一起做事的伙伴。最后一个要点是，和一大群人在一起本身就是一件既有趣又快乐的事情。因为永远都有足够的人来玩游戏或组个团队。

至于我呢，虽然和一大群朋友消磨时间很有趣，但我还是比较喜欢和一两个知己在一起。因为这样一来，规划行程或安排时间见面都比较容易。此外，因为我们的关系较密切，所以我会觉得和他们共度的时光格外珍贵。不论我们想要以哪种方式和朋友在一起相处，朋友对我们的重要性是不可否认的。

40. 学生的态度

Topic:

Many problems in schools are aroused by the attitudes of students. How do these problems form? What should we do to change the situation?

Sample Answer

School violence becomes very protrusive in many countries, most of which are caused by the attitudes of students. Some governments and the authorities show great concerns about the problems. From my point of view, these problems are aroused by three factors, the development of society, the influence of family and media and the weakness of school education.

The rapid development of the society offers young students more opportunities to contact the outside world. Due to the lack of social experience, some youngsters are not capable of distinguishing right from wrong. Curiosity drives them into imitating what they have seen on TV or from the people around them. Therefore, it is easy for them to be addicted to alcohol, smoking and drugs. Some students even smoke or take drugs at school.

Family violence is another major factor causing problems in schools. Family violence hurts children both physically and psychologically. Physically, family violence will hurt their tender body because children are still in the stage of development. Psychologically, physical punishment will hurt children's self-confidence and make them have a tendency of violence. Recently, school gunshots hit the headlines frequently, which should be partly attributed to family violence.

Finally, the weakness of school education is an important factor causing school problems. Some schools only stress students' achievements in their study, while neglecting their moral education. Therefore, even some top students are apt to stride on the criminal road.

To solve these problems, I think we should take the following measures. Firstly, schools should strengthen students' moral education, giving them correct directions and cultivating their ability to tell right from wrong. Secondly, parents should spare some time to communicate with their children, resolving difficulties and troubles for them timely. If the school and family can join hands in solving these problems, I think the students will develop healthily and the environment in schools will become much clearer.

▶考官评分：8

题目：

很多的校园问题都是由学生态度引起的，这些问题是怎样形成的呢？如何改变这种情况呢？

译文：

校园暴力已成为许多国家日渐突出的问题，其中大部分是由学生的态度所引起。一些政府和专家都对此极为关注。以我个人而言，这些问题是由三方面因素导致的：社会的发展、家庭和媒体的影响及学校教育的缺陷。

快速发展的社会为年轻学生提供了更多接触外面世界的机会。由于缺少社会经验，一些年轻人没有明辨是非的能力。好奇心驱使他们去模仿电视节目中的内容及周围人们的所作所为。结果，他们很容易就会对酗酒、吸烟和吸毒成瘾。有些学生甚至在学校里吸烟，吸毒。

家庭暴力也是引起学校暴力的另一主要因素。家庭暴力造成了孩子们生理和心理上的伤害。生理方面，因为孩子们正处在成长阶段，家庭暴力将会伤害他们脆弱的身体。心理方面，体罚会伤害孩子们的自信心并使他们产生暴力倾向。最近，校园枪击事件频繁出现在报纸的头版头条，而部分原因应该归咎于家庭暴力。

最后，学校教育的缺陷也是诱发这些校园问题的重要因素。一些学校只重视学生的学习成绩，而忽视了对他们的道德教育。结果，即使是成绩优异的学生也有走向犯罪道路的倾向。

为了解决这些问题，我认为我们应采取以下措施：首先，学校应加强学生的道德教育，给予他们正确地指导并培养他们辨别是非的能力。第二，家长应该花些时间与孩子沟通交流，及时帮助他们解决困难，摆脱困境。如果学校和家庭能够携起手来解决这些问题，那么学生将会健康成长而校园的环境也将得到更大程度的净化。

41. 开卷有益

Topic:

As reading is important for a good education, we should encourage our children to read whatever appeals to them. Do you agree or disagree?

Sample Answer

The famous English philosopher Francis Bacon said, "Reading makes a full man". Reading books can strongly shape you inclination, mature your thoughts, widen you horizon and enrich your personality. Life is limited, but knowledge is boundless. The more books we read, the more knowledge we get. Hence, we should encourage our children to read more books.

However, books can also be harmful, particularly the pornographic books. Bad books always contain evil thoughts. In them, there might be much description about violence, superstition, and sex. Let's suppose that you are in the position of a parent. Would you allow your children to read whatever appeals to them? If your answer to the question is "yes", you are either extremely permissive or just plain irresponsible. If children read bad books, the evil thoughts would poison their mind gradually. They will be dispirited and perhaps commit a crime.

Good books, on the other hand, teach and help children to do good things. Good books are children's real companions, and they are both instructive and inspiring. Children know past events from history books, study communication by language book, learn space and numbers through mathematics books. In a word, different kinds of good books can give them a large amount of ideas and knowledge.

Consequently, those who read good books can be inspired to grow healthily, while those who read bad ones will lead a wicked life and meet with miserable failure. So before we encourage our children to read books, we should teach and help them to identify good and bad books.

▶考官评分:8

题目:

读书对成功的教育来说不可或缺，我们应该鼓励孩子看任何书籍，你是否同意这个观点?

译文:

英国著名哲学家培根曾说过，“阅读使人完善。”读书能强有力地塑造你的爱好，磨砺你的思想，拓宽你的眼界，丰富你的个性。生命有限，但知识无限。我们读的书越多，获得的知识就越多。因此，我们应该鼓励我们的孩子多读书。

然而，书也能带来危害，特别是色情书籍。坏书往往涵盖着邪恶的思想。其中可能充斥着许多对暴力、迷信和性的描述。让我们想象一下假如你身处父母的立场。你是否能允许你的孩子读任何吸引他们的书籍？如果你的回答是肯定的，那么你不是极端放任主义就是明显的不负责任。如果孩子接触了坏书，邪恶的思想将逐渐毒害他们的头脑。他们将会沮丧或者可能犯下罪行。

从另一方面来说，好书可以教育和帮助孩子去做有益的事情。好书是孩子们真正的朋友，它们都是富有教育性和鼓励性的。孩子们从历史书中了解过去，从语言书中懂得交流，从数学书中学习空间和数字。总之，不同种类的好书能教给他们很多想法和知识。

因此，那些阅读好书的孩子将在鼓舞下健康成长，而阅读坏书将导致他们生活败坏并遭受痛苦的失败。所以当我们鼓励我们的孩子读书时，我们应该教会和帮助他们去鉴别书的良莠。

42. 言传身教

Topic:

Children learn best by observing the behaviour of adults and copying it. Do you agree or disagree?

Sample Answer

The process of growing up is very complex for children. Among countless factors that influence children's growth, the behaviour of adults plays a significant role in shaping children's inclination and character. After the baby is born, the first and the nearest adults are his/her parents. The little babies have started to learn from their parents by observing and copying the adults' talk. This learning environment is important for the babies.

There is a special case reported by the press. A baby was abandoned when she was born. A sow fed her as a piglet. When she was about eight years old, some villagers found her,

her intelligence was just similar to the two-year old baby and all of her behaviours were looked like a pig. From this case, we know child is a “mirror” which will reflect the behaviour of the closest adults.

Along with the children’s growth, adults will influence them much more, such as logical thinking, making a decision, cooperation with others, etc. The behaviour of adults can give children both good and bad influence. Most of the behaviours represent adults’ inclination. For instance, if media report chiefly on the seamy side of the society, children will easily incline to violence and excessive sex. Therefore, they will be infected with bad mental state.

Behaviour is a direct and convincing method to teach children. Things are easier said than done. Parents always tell children those principles repeatedly, but most children can not accept it through these boring method. Adults’ behaviour is the most effective education method to let them observe the whole process of how to deal with the problems. The children will learn from the adults naturally.

Children are like young trees, they need to be carefully irrigated, fertilized and trimmed. Adults’ behaviour will be greatly helpful to shape them into useful talents.

▶考官评分:8

题目:

孩子通过观察和模仿大人能够很好地学习，你同意这种观点吗?

译文:

孩子长大成人的过程是非常复杂的。在无数影响孩子成长的因素中，成人的行为在塑造孩子的爱好和个性方面扮演着重要的角色。在宝宝出生后，首先面对的也是最亲近的成年人就是他们的父母。宝宝们已经开始通过留心和模仿大人的谈话从父母那学习。这种学习氛围对宝宝们来说很重要。

这里有一篇特殊报道。一个孩子出生时就被遗弃了。一头母猪把她当小猪一样喂养了她。当她大约八岁时，一些村民找到了她，她的智力跟两岁的婴孩差不多，而且所有举止行为都跟猪相似。通过这个案例，我们知道孩子像一面可以反映出最亲近的大人的行为的镜子。

在孩子的成长过程中，成人将在更多方面影响着他们，比如逻辑思维、制定决策，和他人合作等。大人的举止会从好、坏两方面影响着孩子。孩子的大多数行为反映了成人的举止倾向。比如，如果媒体主要报道社会阴暗面，孩子们将容易倾向于暴力和纵欲。因此，他们将被感染上不良的心理状态。

言传身教是直接而有力的教育方法。说起来容易做起来却很难。父母总是再三地给孩子们讲道理，但是大部分孩子不能通过这种枯燥的方式来接受。最有效的教育方式是大人行为的潜移默化，让他们观察如何解决问题的整个过程。孩子们自然会向其学习。

孩子们就像小树苗，需要精心的灌溉、施肥和修葺。大人们的行为可以极大地帮助他们成为有用的人才。

43. 孩子的空闲时间是否应该用在学业上

Topic:

Some people believe that children should engage in educational pursuits in their spare time, otherwise they are wasting their time. Do you agree or disagree?

Sample Answer

Today, education has become a priority for many parents seeking to secure a good future for their children in this rapidly changing world. They believe that if their children apply themselves and work hard at school, then they will increase their opportunities to go for a higher education and eventually get a good job. Of course they are right, and as access to the best education and best job is becoming more competitive, then it is true that children have to make the best of their study time when they are young.

However, the parents who do not allow their children sufficient free time for leisure activities outside school hours are misguided. Such activities are far from being a waste of time for the children simply because they are not academic. It is important to remember that children need to develop skills other than intellectual ones, and the best way to achieve this is through activities such as sports, games and playing with other kids. If they cannot play make-believe games, how can they develop their imagination? How can they learn physical co-ordination or learn important social lessons about the winning and losing if they do not practise any sports? Many children develop strong personal relationships with their friends they play with, and without the opportunity to this, they could grow up emotionally immature or unformed.

Finally, I think it is also important to remember that children need to relax as well as work. If everything they do must have some educational or academic relevance, then they will soon get tired of studying altogether, which is the last thing parents would want.

▶考官评分:8

题目:

有些人认为孩子们的课余活动必须是有教育意义的，否则完全是浪费时间。你是否同意这种说法?

译文:

现如今，在这个飞速变化的世界，为了使孩子有更好的未来很多家长都重视教育。他们相信如果他们的孩子能充分发挥自己的实力并且在学校里努力学习，然后他们就会获得更多的机会去接受更高的教育，并且最终获得不错的工作。当然他们是对的，因为获得最好的教育或者最好的工作竞争非常激烈。当孩子还小的时候，他们就应该充分利用他们的学习时间。

然而，那些不允许孩子们在课余时间有充分的时间去做课余活动的家长，是被误导了。这些活动对孩子来说远非浪费时间而已，只是因为这些活动不是学术性的。而重要的是要记住孩子需要发展知识以外的技能，并且最好的方式就是通过这些活动来培养，例如体育、游戏以及和同龄人一起玩耍。如果他们连游戏都不能玩，又怎么能培养他们的想象力呢？又怎么能学习身体协调呢？或者如果他们不参加任何体育活动，又怎么能学会得与失的社会经验呢？许多孩子和一起玩耍的朋友们建立友好的关系。没有这种机会，孩子们可能长大后，情感发展会不成熟。

最后，我认为要记住：孩子们不仅需要学习，而且也需要放松。如果他们做的每一件事情都必须是有教育意义或者学术意义的，他们很快就会厌倦一切学习，这恐怕也是家长最不想看到的。

44. 高中生选择专业

Topic:

High school students should remain in general schools until 17 years old. Only then can they know themselves enough to choose the specialty for their future career. Do you agree or disagree with the statement?

Sample Answer

Some people think high school students should remain in general schools till 17 years old so that they are mature enough to know what speciality is suitable for their future careers. My opinion is identical with theirs.

In the first place, the policy tallies with the psychological traits of an average teenager. An average person won't become mature enough until they reach the age of 17 or 18. Students at the age of 17 will have a better understanding about themselves. They learn to be responsible for what they decide.

In the second place, staying in high schools for longer years helps student to enlarge their common knowledge before they choose their speciality, which enables them to discover their real interests and strong points. With longer years in high school, students may have more experience which helps to understand life and the society so that they may choose their speciality according to the demand of the society. As a result, they may avoid detours.

Of course, I am not denying the merits of leaving high school earlier, before 17. Some people mature earlier not only psychological but intellectually. They may find quite inappropriate for them to remain in high school until 17. Those who leave high school earlier to receive higher education or pursue their careers will certainly possess an apparent advantage over others who don't. Therefore, we shall allow people to decide for themselves according to their specific condition.

Frankly speaking, both views are well-grounded. However, if I have to choose one of these two, I am in favour of the first opinion that students should stay in general schools till 17, which can ensure a sound and solid foundation for all the students to further their study at the tertiary level or pursue their career.

▶考官评分:8

题目:

高中生在17岁之前应该在普通学校接受教育，只有那时他们才能充分地了解自己并选择自己将来的职业方向。你是否赞同此观点?

译文:

一些人认为高中生在17岁以前还是应该留在普通学校接受教育，直到他们足够成熟知道选择哪个专业对他们将来的事业最合适。我同意他们的观点。

首先，这项政策符合青少年心理特征的平均水平。按平均算人们只有到了17或18岁的时候才足够成熟。学生到了17岁的时候将对自己有一个更全面的了解。他们学会对自己所做的决定负责。

其次，中学阶段可以帮助学生扩大知识面，然后选择他们自己的专业，这能够使他们发现自己真正的兴趣和优势。在较长的高中生活中，学生可以丰富自身的经验，这有助于他们理解社会生活，使他们可以根据社会的需要选择自己的专业。因此，他们可能会避免走弯路。

当然，我不否认在17岁之前较早地离开高中也有一些优点。有些人不仅在心理上成熟较早，在智力上也同样如此。他们可能会觉得留在高中一直到17岁对他们来说是非常不合时宜的。那些较早离开高中而选择接受高等教育或者追求事业的人，无疑比那些继续高中学习的人拥有明显的优势。因此，我们应该让人们根据自身的条件做出决定。

坦率地讲，这两种观点都很有道理。然而，如果我不得不从两者中选其一，我更加赞成第一种观点，那就是学生应该留在普通学校接受教育直到17岁，这可以确保所有学生拥有健全和坚实的基础，从而进一步接受高等教育或者追求他们的事业。

第二大类:家庭生活类话题

45. 照看老年人

Topic:

Some people think that old people should be taken care at home, while others think they should be placed in old people's house. What is your opinion?

Sample Answer

Thanks to the development of medical science, there are an increasing number of elderly people in the world. Some people believe that the seniors should be looked after at home. Indeed, it is the children's responsibility and obligation to take care of their parents when they are old. However, as for me, a better way to ensure them to live a happy life is to send them to the nursing home.

First of all, in such retirement homes, aging people can receive intensive medical care from professional doctors. Besides, they can receive a proper diet prepared by dieticians to meet their individual requirements. This is especially good for those old people in poor health. Moreover, they could have regular medical check-ups so that any disease could be diagnosed in its early stage. What is the most beneficial is that if any disease strikes them, medical services are immediately available.

Living in nursing homes, they have more opportunities to communicate with their peers. They do not feel lonely and can do a great deal of things together, such as doing morning exercise, playing games, and exchanging memories and stories from their past. On the contrary, if they live at home, they are often left alone when their children and grandchildren are away working or studying.

Some people may say that children have duties to take care of their old parents. However, nowadays people are confronted with fierce competition and suffer from great pressure. They are too occupied to spare time for their old parents. There are benefits for children's work and study when nursing homes take over the task of caring for the elderly. Children, free from care, can devote themselves to work or study and achieve more success.

Since nursing homes benefit seniors and other family members so much, I believe that old people should be sent to nursing homes.

▶考官评分:8

题目:

有人认为老年人应该被赡养在家中，而也有人认为他们应该被送到养老院，你的观点是什么?

译文:

由于医学的进步，这个世界上老年人越来越多。有些人认为老年人应该赡养在家中。确实，当父母老的时候，照看他们是子女的责任和义务。但是我认为一个确保能让父母快乐健康的更好方法是把他们送到养老院去。

首先，在养老院里，老人可以得到专业医生精心的医疗护理。此外，他们还可以接受营养师准备的合理膳食来满足他们各自的需要。这对健康状况不好的的老人是十分有益。而且，他们会接受定期的身体检查，这样可以使任何疾病在发展初期就能被发现。最有益处的是当有任何疾病侵害他们的时候，可以立刻进行医疗救护。

在养老院里生活，他们有更多的机会与同龄人进行交流，互相交往，他们不会感到孤独而且还可以一起做很多事情，比如晨练、玩游戏、一起交流过去的记忆和故事。相反，如果他们在家里生活，那么当孩子或者孙子在外工作或者学习的时候，他们就会感到很孤单。

有人可能会说孩子们有责任照看他们年迈的父母。然而，现在人们面临激烈的竞争，承受巨大的压力。他们太忙了，不能分出时间给他们的父母。确实，养老院接管了看护老人的工作对孩子的工作和学习也是有好处的，从看护中解放出来的孩子可以对工作或者学习投入更多，从而获得更大的成功。

既然养老院对老人和其他家庭成员都有益处，那么我认为老人应该被送到养老院去。

46. 孩子缺少父母关注

Topic:

Some people think that children do not get as much attention from their parents as children did in the past. To what extent do you agree or disagree with the opinion?

Sample Answer

In recent years, many parents have little time for their children. Some people are of the opinion that children do not get as much attention from their parents as children did in the past. On the other hand, towards the same issue, other people have a different attitude. Before giving my opinion, I think it is important to look at the argument on both sides.

There are several reasons which suggest that children do not get as much attention from their parents as children did in the past. On one hand, people face fierce competition and suffer from great pressure. They have to devote more time and energy to their careers and therefore have no time with their children. On the other hand, high technology brings them more interesting things which can easily attract their attention such as watching TV, surfing the Internet and playing games. They are addicted to these activities, totally ignoring their children. More importantly, the record of divorce rate has been constantly renewed. Obviously, children from broken family get less care and attention from their parents.

However, there are a large number of people who hold a different view concerning this case. They believe that children gain more attention from their parents than children did in the past. For one thing, with the development of technology, more and more machines replace men's labour. Therefore, people enjoy more and more free time at home with their children. For another, with the development of economy, people earn more money. Some parents even give up their decent job and devote all their energy to their children. Last but not least, there is a sharp decrease in the number of children a family has. Consequently, each child gets more attention and care from their parents.

Both opinions make sense, and consequently it is hard to decide which one is more reasonable. From my own perspective, children get more attention from their parents than children did in the past. Parents spend more time with their children. They have more money to ensure their children's needs. In addition, the number of children decreases dramatically.

▶考官评分:7

题目:

有些人认为现在的孩子不像以前的孩子那样能得到父母很多的关注。你是否同意这种观点?

译文:

近年来，很多父母几乎没有时间照顾他们的孩子。一些人认为现在的孩子不像以前的孩子那样能得到父母很多的关注。另一方面，对于同样的问题，还有一些人持有不同的看法。在给出我的意见之前，我认为应该看看双方的观点。

有很多原因支持现在的孩子不像过去的孩子那样能够获得父母很多的关注的观点。一方面，人们面临激烈的竞争，承受巨大的压力。他们不得不在事业上投入更多的时间和精力。因此，没有时间和他们的孩子在一起。另一方面，高科技带给他们更多有趣的事情，它们可以很容易地吸引人们的注意力，例如看电视、网上冲浪或者打游戏。人们沉溺于这些活动中，完全忽视了他们的孩子。更重要的是，离婚率屡创新高。很显然，来自破碎家庭的孩子得到父母的关心和关注更少。

然而，有很多人对于这个问题持有不同的观点。他们认为现在的孩子得到父母的关注要比以前的孩子多。首先，随着科技的发展，越来越多的机械化操作取代了人工劳动。因此，人们享有越来越多的空闲时间在家中和孩子在一起。其次，随着经济的发展，人们挣更多的钱。有些父母甚至舍弃自己体面的工作全身心地照顾孩子。最后，每个家庭孩子的数量急剧下降。因此，每个孩子从父母那里得到的关注和关心更多。

双方都有道理，因此很难决定哪一方更有道理。在我看来，现在的孩子得到父母的关注要比以前的孩子多。父母会花更多的时间和孩子在一起。他们有更多的钱满足孩子的需要。而且，每个家庭孩子的数量急剧下降。

47. 家庭成员关系不亲密

Topic:

It is generally acknowledged that the relationship among family members is not as close as it used to be. Give possible reasons and your recommendations.

Sample Answer

Nowadays, couples quarrel more often than they used to do. Brothers and sisters talk less and take less care of each other. Children turn less to their parents for advice. These scenes are just part of the whole picture of today's family alienation. As far as I am concerned, there are several reasons for the above phenomena.

The first reason is that people spend more time on their studies and work. Nowadays, people face fierce competition and suffer from great pressure. As a result, they have to devote more time and energy to their careers. Some people are too busy to spare time for their family. What is more, many jobs require people to work in other cities and many children have to leave their parents at an early age to study or work elsewhere. As time passes, these people become emotionally estranged from their families.

The alienation among families is also attributed to the increasing number of entertainments available. High technology brings modern people more interesting things which can easily attract their attention, such as watching TV, surfing the Internet or playing video games. Consequently, people are addicted to these activities, totally neglecting the feelings of their family members.

Last but not least, people are now more independent than before. Apart from their family, they can easily get help from their friends and it is much easier to make more friends as a result of the rapid improvement in telecommunication. Therefore they are not as dependent on their families as before.

To bring families closer, people put forward various suggestions. First, we should spare more time with our family members, no matter how occupied we are. Second, teach children the sense of family when they are still young. Last but not least, the government should organize activities to promote public awareness of the importance of a harmonious family relationship.

▶考官评分:8

题目:

人们现在普遍承认家庭成员的关系不像过去那样亲密了，请给出可能的原因并提出你的建议。

译文:

现在夫妻吵架的现象比过去多了，兄弟姐妹之间相互交流少了，彼此关心也少了。同过去相比，孩子们向父母征求建议的情况也少了。这些变化只是现代家庭关系疏远的部分情况。在我看来，发生上述现象主要有以下几点原因：

第一个原因是人们将更多的时间投入到学习和工作中。现在，人们面临激烈的竞争，承受巨大的压力。因此，他们不得不在他们的事业上投入更多的时间和精力。一些人太忙了以至于很少有空余的时间留给他们的家人。而且，一些工作需要人去其他的城市，一些孩子不得不在他们很小的时候离开他们的父母，在其他的地方学习或者工作。随着时间的流逝，一些人就会在感情上疏远他们的家人。

家人的疏远还由于娱乐形式的不断增加。现在高科技带给现代人更多有趣的事情，它们可以很容易地吸引人们注意，例如看电视、网上冲浪或者打游戏。因此，人们沉溺于这些活动中，完全忽视了家人的感受。

最后，人们比过去更加独立。除了他们的家人，他们很容易从朋友那里得到帮助。而且，随着通讯的快速发展，人们更容易交到更多的朋友。因此，他们不再像从前一样依赖家庭。

为了使家庭更亲密，人们提出了很多建议。首先，无论我们有多忙都要抽出时间陪自己的家人。其次，我们应该在我们的孩子还小的时候教会他们家庭观念。最后，政府应该组织活动来提升公众对和谐家庭关系重要性的认识。

48. 学校教育孩子如何做父母

Topic:

Some people think it would be a good idea for schools to teach every young person how to be a good parent. Do you agree or disagree with this opinion?

Sample Answer

Generation gap, which is inevitable between youngsters and elders, is not strange to modern people. As for the solution to that problem, various methods have been adopted including introducing relevant courses in schools to educate students how to be a good parent. I am in total favour of that idea.

If students can be provided with sufficient knowledge of what constitutes a qualified parent, they can better understand their parents. As we know, some generation conflicts derive not from intrinsic contradiction, but lack of mutual understanding, so if it is possible that children can have access to how to be good parents, they will recognize how much enormous sacrifice their parents have made to bring children up. Accordingly, a harmonious relationship between parents and children can be definitely established.

Additionally, through schooling about qualifications of parents, children are more prepared for their future adult life. It is generally agreed that the ultimate purpose of most education is to furnish students with essential skills to cope with problems confronted when stepping into society. One day, youngsters will not be naive, and they form their own families and become parents themselves. Thus some early information about desirable attributes of parents is that invaluable and indispensable to blessed families. After all, the early bird catches the worm.

However, there should be some limitations on that practice. As children, nowadays, have been already overburdened with study, education of being good parents need not take up too much time. Secondly, taking children's premature cognitive power into account, teachers had better select such materials as can be easily understood for those still young children. Only in this way, can the desirable effect be achieved.

Overall, I welcome the reform that when children are at their early age, they know how to be a good parent. Perhaps, the term "generation gap" will be soon rendered out-of-date since parents and children begin to behave more like friends than strangers without too much in common.

▶考官评分:7

题目:

一些人认为在学校教授每个年轻人如何成为一个好家长将会是一个不错的想法。你同意这个观点吗?

译文:

在年轻人和年长者之间不可避免地存在代沟,对于现代人来说并不陌生。关于解决这个问题,采取了许多方法,包括在学校介绍这方面的相关课程,去教育学生们如何成为好的家长。我完全支持这种观点。

如果孩子们学一些关于什么才是合格的家长的知识,他们会更能理解他们的父母。我们知道,一些代沟矛盾的产生并不是来源于固有的矛盾,而是彼此缺乏理解,因此如果孩子们可能学到如何成为好家长的知识,他们会意识到他们的家长为了抚养他们长大成人付出了多么巨大的牺牲。相应地,家长和孩子之间一定会建立一个和谐的关系。

此外,通过学习如何成为合格的家长,孩子们可以为以后的成人生活提前做准备。现在人们普遍地认为教育的最终目的是当孩子们步入社会时给他们提供必要的面对问题和解决问题的能力。总有一天，年轻人将会成熟，他们会组建自己的家庭并成为父母。因此关于理想父母的特征的早期信息对于幸福家庭而言是最宝贵且必不可少的。毕竟，早起的鸟儿有虫吃。

然而，那种做法也会有一些局限。作为孩子，现在，已经不堪学习的重负，成为好家长的教育不能占用太长的时间。其次，考虑孩子们过早的认知能力，老师们最好选择那些孩子们容易理解的材料。只有通过这种方法，才能达到理想的效果。

总之，我欢迎在孩子们小的时候让他们知道如何成为好父母的改革。只要家长和孩子相处时更像朋友而不是没有共同点的陌生人，“代沟”这个词将会在不久的将来可能被淘汰。

49. 父母和老师

Topic:

Parents are the best teachers. Do you agree or disagree?

Sample Answer

Obviously, the earliest teachers we have in our lives in most cases are our parents, and they are generally the most involved in the development and education of their children. Yet neither are all parents good teachers nor are those good parents, in most cases, the best teachers.

First of all, not all parents are good teachers. As normal individuals, some parents more or less have bad habits. Even though parents almost instinctively devote themselves to cultivating their offspring, the outcome might turn out to be disappointing, for all children tend to unconsciously or subconsciously copy everything from their parents. Another deficiency of parents as teachers is the fact that most parents lack the common senses of education. All too often we observe that some parents tend to pursue their own cherished but failed dreams by forcing their children to develop in a prearranged direction.

Moreover, some parents are qualified as good teachers, but not all of them are the best ones. When children are in the preliminary school, it is not surprising that parents are capable of teaching their children almost every subject. But the situation will not last long. We live in a world where knowledge is accumulated by multiplying and at the same time becomes more and more specialized. Therefore, to be a professional in a certain field today takes a much long time than ever before. No parent is able to be professional in all fields, though they might be experts in one or more fields.

Most parts of children's education is virtually beyond teachers' reaches. In a word, it is rather superficial to simply say that parents are the best teachers.

▶考官评分:8

题目:

家长是最好的老师，你是否认同此观点?

译文:

显然，大多数情况下，我们的启蒙老师就是我们的父母，他们一般对孩子的教育和发展起着至关重要的作用。但是，不是所有的父母都是好老师。而且，在大多数情况下，那些好父母也未必是最好的老师。

首先，不是所有的父母都是好老师。作为一个普通人，有些父母或多或少有一些坏习惯。即使父母几乎本能地投入于培养他们的孩子，但是结果可能令人失望。因为所有的孩子都趋向于下意识地或者刻意地模仿他们父母的行为。父母作为老师的另一个缺点是大多数父母缺乏教育孩子的常识。我们常常看到这种情况，父母通过强迫他们的孩子按照制定好的计划发展方向来实现他们自己向往但是却没有实现的梦想。

其次，虽然一些父母能成为好老师，但都不是最棒的那一个。当孩子还在初级学校时，父母有能力在几乎所有科目上指导孩子。但是，这种情况并不会持续太久。我们生活在一个知识飞速积聚并且专业化越来越突出的时代，因此，在今天成为某个领域的专家比以前困难得多。尽管一些父母可能是一个或者多个领域的专家，但是没有人可以精通所有领域。

孩子们大部分的教育实质上在父母的能力范围之外。概括来讲，简单的说父母是最好的老师是很不全面的。

50. 童年最重要

Topic:

A person's childhood years (the time from the birth to the age of twelve years) are the most important years of a person's life. Do you agree or disagree?

Sample Answer

It is generally accepted that a person's childhood years are very important years of their life. But it is hardly appropriate to say those years are the most important.

We do not reject the importance of childhood years. Actually it is rather important for the later part of a person's life. Our lives are subject to surroundings. Our world views have been structured from our childhood. Therefore, every one actually sees his own world differently to others. Even though we all live in a single world, every one of us in fact lives in a distinctive world, which are determined by our distinctive perceptions from individual to individual. Hence, we should not suspect that a person's life is influenced by one's childhood.

Childhood, however, is merely one of several factors that shape one's later life. Among various factors is one's learning ability. Human beings are superior to any other animals simply because of their ability to learn. Psychology teaches us that training and self-training can alter our characteristics which may eventually alter our lives. Furthermore, learning is a life long process, which means every part of one's life could be an essential period and could play an indispensable role in one's life. For example, Einstein was taken for an idiot by his teacher when he was a child. The awkward attitude of his stupid teacher made Einstein's childhood an awful one. Nevertheless, Einstein did lead a wonderful life.

Most parents nowadays seem to believe that childhood is the most important phase of one's life, and therefore often force their children to learn those alleged essential skills. The fact is, such behaviour is rather presumptuous, because, there are still many other important factors that affect one's life.

▶考官评分:8

题目:

一个人的童年（从出生到12岁）是一生中最重要的阶段，你同意这种观点吗?

译文:

大家都公认的是，童年在人的一生中是非常重要的时光，但是很难说是最重要的。

我们不否认童年的重要性。的确，它对一个人日后的生活是相当重要的。我们的生活受环境的支配。我们的世界观在童年就已经形成。因此，每一个人对他或她所处的世界的看法与别人都是不同的。即使我们都生活在同一个世界里，事实上，我们中的每一个人都活在一个与众不同的世界中。这是因为每个人对世界都有着不同的感知。因此，我们不应该怀疑一个人的童年的确影响着人生。

然而，童年仅仅是一个人成长的几个因素之一。学习能力也是这众多的因素之一。人类优越于其他动物的原因只不过因为学习能力。心理学告诉我们训练和自我训练能够改变我们的性格从而最终改变我们的人生。此外，学习是一个长期的过程，这意味着人生的每一步都是至关重要的时期，并且学习也扮演着人生中不可分割的角色。正如，爱因斯坦小时候就被他的老师称之为白痴。这位愚蠢的老师的态度造成了爱因斯坦糟糕的童年。然而，爱因斯坦的一生是非常精彩的。

大多数的家长都认为童年是人生中最重要的阶段，因此常常强迫他们的子女去学习那些所谓的重要技能。但事实是，这种做法是相当专横的。因为还有很多其他影响人生的重要因素。

51. 孩子早送幼儿园

Topic:

Nowadays, nurseries and kindergartens take care of children from an early age, so women can return to their work and children can get used to the society early. Is this a good thing? What's your opinion?

Sample Answer

Child care is a big issue in all families, and there is a heated debate on the best method of handling it. Nowadays there is a growing tendency for parents to send their children earlier to nurseries and kindergartens. Some even go to nurseries and kindergartens at age 2 or 3 so that mothers can be freed from child care and pursue their own careers. People from different backgrounds, however, hold different attitudes toward the matter in question.

Some people claim that children should be sent to nurseries earlier. First of all, psychologically speaking, the child needs more opportunities to communicate with his peers. The main task of the child care establishments is to inculcate honesty, courage, discipline, cooperation, friendliness, and good manners. Second, it is beneficial for them to receive systematic and scientific care and rudimentary knowledge from well-trained professionals. Last but not least, sending children earlier to nursery schools enables mothers to devote more time and energy to their jobs. In this way, career success becomes more possible, which is very beneficial to the whole family.

However, people rarely reach an absolute consensus on such a controversial issue. The opponents argue that sending children earlier to nursery schools has its demerits. In the first place, it may lead to poorer parent-child relationship for lack of emotional communication. In addition, with mother staying at home, children will be better cared for and given more attention. On the other hand, in nurseries and kindergartens, there is the possibility of lacking adequate care and attention because there are so many children in a class. Moreover, although the family may lose some income, its expenditure will also be greatly reduced. It will no longer be necessary to pay for attending nurseries and kindergartens.

Undeniably, there are points in both sides of the argument. But after a careful consideration of the above reasons, I stand on the side of the opponents. To start nursery schools too early is harmful for children mentally. Children who are sent earlier to nursery schools lack the affection of parents. Furthermore, mothers are the first teacher of their own child and exert profound impact on the child's future growth.

▶考官评分:8

题目:

现如今孩子们很早就被送去托儿所或幼儿园，这样他们的母亲就可以回到工作岗位，而且孩子们也可以从小适应社会。这样是否有利？你的观点是什么？

译文:

照顾孩子对所有家庭来说都是一个大问题，对于解决这个问题的最好的方法存在着一个激烈的争辩。如今家长提早把孩子送去幼儿园或托儿所的趋势逐渐增大。有些孩子甚至在2、3岁时就被送去托儿所，以便他们的妈妈能从照顾孩子中解脱出来追求他们自己的事业。然而，不同背景的人们在这个问题上持有不同的观点。

有些人认为孩子们应该更早些被送去托儿所。首先，从心理学上讲，孩子们需要更多的机会来和他们的同龄人交流。托儿所的主要任务是教导他们做到诚实、勇敢、守纪、协作、友善和礼貌。其次，从训练有素的专业人员那里受到系统和科学的照顾并得到初步知识对孩子们是有益的。最后一点也很重要，早些送孩子去托儿所能让母亲们在她们的工作上投入更多时间和精力。这样，事业更有可能获得成功，这对整个家庭都是有益的。

然而，人们在这个有争议的问题上很少能达到绝对的共识。反对者提出过早地送孩子们去托儿所是有缺陷的。首先，由于缺少情感交流，这可能导致更糟糕的亲子关系。此外，当母亲留在家里时，孩子们能够得到更好的照顾和更多的关注。另一方面，在托儿所，由于一个班级里孩子众多，所以会存在缺乏足够的照顾和关注的可能性。另外，尽管家庭可能会损失一部分收入，但家庭支出也会大幅减少。支付入托费也不再是必须的了。

不可否认的是，争论的双方都有很多的道理。但是经过对以上原因的仔细考虑之后，我站在反对者一边。过早的开始托儿所生活对孩子们的心理是有害的。那些被过早送去托儿所的孩子们缺乏父母的关爱。此外，母亲是孩子的第一位老师，而且对孩子们未来的成长有着意义深远的影响。

52. 体罚孩子

Topic:

Corporal punishment has been practiced in families for quite a long time. In recent years, people's attitudes towards this practice have undergone drastic changes. Nowadays many people strongly oppose it. Should corporal punishment be abolished?

Sample Answer

Psychologists warn the parents to respect children's freedom and rights. A good old-fashioned corporal punishment is out of the question. On the other hand, cases of corporal punishment are reported to take place in families now and then. Indeed, the issue whether or not corporal punishment should be abolished has aroused a heated discussion among people.

Those who strongly advocate that corporal punishment should not be abolished have cogent reasons for it. First of all, as a proverb says, "spare the rod, spoil the child". Children should be taught to respect discipline, which is the basis of all achievements. Little children are like young trees. In order to grow well, they need to be carefully irrigated, fertilized and trimmed. Furthermore, it helps to reinforce the authority of teachers and parents. Children are hardy creatures. Sometimes they will test the patience of their parents and teacher; teachers and parents should not be too permissive; otherwise they will spoil the children.

But the people who hold the view that corporal punishment should be abolished also have sound reasons. In the first place, it seriously violates the legal rights and interests for children. Children are human beings too. They enjoy the same equal human rights as adults do. Their parents have no right to exercise corporal punishment on them. In addition, children may be hurt psychologically. Researches reveal that students who suffer from corporal punishment tend to resort to violence in their future life. Last but not least, it endangers children's physical development. It is a kind of brutality and cruelty which may lead to injury or even death of the children. Recently it is reported in the newspaper that one child lost his hearing due to his father's cruelty.

When we consider these two sides more carefully, we can see that corporal punishment does more harm than good to children. Their rights are violated by the uncivilized action. It is detrimental to children's physical and mental development. Therefore, corporal punishment should by all means be forbidden in families.

▶考官评分:8

题目:

很长时间以来，体罚孩子是家庭中的一个惯例。但是最近几年中，人们对这一惯例的观念发生了巨大的变化。现在有很多人强烈地反对这一观点。体罚应该被废除吗？

译文:

心理学家警告家长应尊重孩子们的自由和权力。那种传统的好办法：体罚是根本行不通的。另一方面，据报道这种肉体惩罚的案例却会偶尔出现在家庭之中。关于肉体惩罚是否应该被废止的问题确实在人群中引起了一场激烈的讨论。

那些强烈赞成体罚不应该被废除的人理由充分。首先，就像谚语说的一样，“不打不成材”。我们应该教育孩子们去尊重纪律，这是取得一切成就的基础。小孩子就像小树苗一样。为了茁壮成长，他们需要被仔细灌溉，施肥和修剪。此外，这种惩罚有助于老师和家长巩固他们的威信。孩子们是很倔强的。有时他们会考验他们父母和老师的耐心，而父母和老师们不应该太过娇惯他们。否则就会宠坏孩子。

而那些认为体罚应该被废除的人也是义正言辞。首先，它严重违反了孩子们的合法权力和利益。孩子也是人。他们和成年人享有同等的权力。家长们没有权力去对孩子们实行肉体惩罚。另外，孩子们可能会遭到心理上的伤害。研究表明遭受过肉体惩罚的孩子在以后的生活中更易于使用暴力。最后，这会危及孩子们的身体发育。这是一种野蛮而且残忍的行为，很可能会导致孩子的受伤甚至死亡。最近报纸上的报道说一个孩子因为他父亲的残忍行为而失聪。

当我们仔细考虑这两方面意见时，我们会发现肉体惩罚对孩子是弊大于利的。他们的权力被这种很不文明的举动侵犯了。这对孩子心理和生理的发育成长都是有害的。因此，应该尽一切办法禁止家庭中的肉体惩罚。

53. 惩罚孩子

Topic:

Different people hold different views as to whether parents should adopt an instruction or punishment as the principal method for raising their children. If punishment is chosen as the main method, in what ways would you recommend that parents carry it out?

Sample Answer

Some people believe that parents should resort to instruction and edification as the main ways to raise their children, while many others maintain that the predominant measure parents ought to take is to discipline them, to make sure that they don't fall into the same pits in the future. Personally I agree with the latter opinion. Moreover, I believe that the best results can be obtained in the following ways.

In the first place, parents should try to create a family milieu in which the character development of their children is not suppressed and the young feel free to air their own points of view on various matters. The result will be that the young people will grow up to be men and women of honesty, sincerity, professional commitment and expertise.

In the second place, parents should show due respect for their children's personal interests and inclinations as regards their future careers. Some parents try to blueprint the entire future development paths of their children when they are convinced that their authority allows no challenge and their discipline will do the young no harm. However, parents should be on guard against any overuse of preaching and discipline lest it provokes nothing but resentment and rebellion.

All in all, disciplining the young can indeed impress upon their minds the conduct they are expected to adopt in society. Yet, the aim of punishment should not be to make the children regard their parents as dictators and fear them. Parents should do all they can to leave plenty of latitude for the development of their children's characters, and not over-use the lever of discipline.

▶考官评分:8

题目:

对于家长应该主要采取教导还是惩罚的方式来教育孩子长大的问题，不同人持有不同的观点。如果选择后者，对于该怎样将其付诸实际你有什么提议？

译文:

有些人认为应该将指导和启迪作为培养孩子的主要方式，但是其他人却觉得约束孩子是父母抚养孩子首先应该要做的事，以确保孩子将来不会再犯以前犯的错误。我个人同意后一种看法。而且，我认为通过以下几种方法来培养孩子能够获得最佳效果。

第一，父母应该尝试这样一个家庭氛围，孩子性格可以自然形成，不被压抑，且他们在家中对任何事都有言论自由。这样，孩子们长大后就能成为一个诚实、有敬畏心并有专业技术和素养的人。

第二，父母应该尊重孩子们的兴趣爱好和他们对未来职业生涯的规划。有些父母会为他们的孩子设计好未来的发展蓝图，他们确信他们的权威不受任何挑战而且他们的约束对孩子有益无害。然而，父母要注意不应该说教约束过度，这样不仅没有任何好处，而且还会引起孩子们的愤恨和反抗。

总之，约束孩子们能让孩子确信他们能够被社会所接纳。还有，惩罚的目标不应该是让孩子们觉得他们的父母是独裁者并对他们感到恐惧。父母应该尽一切可能为孩子们的性格成长留下足够的空间，而不是将约束这个杠杆用过度了。

54. 孩子犯罪父母是否应受罚

Topic:

If a five-year old child commits a crime, should his/her parents have the responsibility and be punished? What is the age of a child when parents no longer bear the responsibility for children's behaviour? What is your opinion?

Sample Answer

It is not uncommon that numerous youngsters are involved in heinous crimes and some kids are only five or six years old, which is really alarming to adults. Who should take the responsibility for this social deterioration, parents or other relevant people? Undoubtedly, as legal guardian and early mentor, parents cannot evade the responsibility and are the main culprits.

Of course, we have to admit the fact that social immoral atmosphere, such as the flooding of on-line games, contributes to increasing juvenile delinquency, for violence and pornography contained in the content exert a negative impact on children's vulnerable minds. According to the latest survey, the majority of youth crimes take place in the net bar, where there are actually no effective measures to supervise the operation. Parents, however, are more to blame for compared with social factors.

In comparison, parents are far more influential to their children's development. Due to lack of economic independence, kids have to spend the majority of their time living with their parents, so inevitably, what parents have done and said will affect underage children to a large extent. If parents commit a crime, then their children will take it for granted and follow suit.

In modern society, that divorce rate rockets aggravates the youth crimes. As youngsters undergoing growth both physically and psychologically, a healthy family provides invaluable love and guidance for vulnerable children, who often fall victim to abuse and injury. If that is true, it is not difficult to perceive desperate feeling suffocating poor kids when parents choose to depart from each other and at that time perhaps their children resort to crimes to revenge themselves on their parents.

Numerous tragedies have revealed the truth that parents are the immediate contribution to the increase in youth crimes. Perhaps when kids grow to 18 or above, there is no need for parents to be criticized, for by comparison society is a more direct reason.

▶考官评分:8

题目:

如果一个5岁的孩子犯罪，他/她的父母是否负有责任并且接受惩罚？孩子12岁时父母不再对他们的行为负责了呢？请谈谈你的观点？

译文:

经常可以听到很多年轻人卷入残忍的犯罪中，而且一些孩子只有五六岁。对于成年人来说，这真是触目惊心。谁难逃其咎？是孩子的父母还是相关的人？毫无疑问，作为合法的监护人和早期的指导者，父母是主要的罪魁祸首，无法逃避责任。

当然，我们承认不道德的社会氛围，例如充斥各个角落的网络游戏，加剧了青少年犯罪，因为网络游戏中的暴力与色情毒害孩子们脆弱的心灵。根据最新调查，大部分的青少年犯罪发生地都集中在网吧，那里几乎没有有效的监控手段。然而，与社会因素相比，父母有更大的责任。

相比而言，父母对孩子的影响力更大。由于缺乏经济独立，孩子们不得不长时间与父母住在一起。不可避免地，父母的一言一行很大程度上影响着未成年的孩子们。如果父母犯罪，孩子就会想当然做出同样的事情。

当今社会持续激增的离婚率加剧了青少年犯罪。随着孩子身心的发展，他们会常常面临虐待与伤害，此时，健康的家庭会给那些脆弱的孩子们提供非常宝贵的关爱与指导。不难想象，当父母决定离婚时，可怜的孩子处于多么绝望的境地中。或许犯罪是他们向父母复仇的手段。

无数的悲剧都证明了这个事实：父母是导致青少年犯罪增加的直接导火索。也许孩子18岁以后如果再犯罪，就没有必要批评父母了，因为那时社会就是更直接的原因了。

55. 父母是否应该花更多的时间陪孩子

Topic:

Some people think that parents should spend more time with their children. Do you agree or disagree?

Sample Answer

In China, the parents both have their jobs. With the development of economy, people tend to pursue high quality living conditions. **Most of the parents try their best to offer their children comfortable circumstances, but they seldom have time to stay with their children.** In my point of view, no matter how busy they are, they should make the best use of their time to stay with their children.

First, the relationship between children and adults will be enhanced with parents' spending more time on their children. Children could feel parents' affection through the genial conversation and sharing their pleasure with them. **Every time when parents take them to the amusement park, help them to prepare their birthday parties, applaud for them when they are competing in the sports meeting, the time they spend with children will become treasure in their memories.**

Second, children need the direction from their parents. There are some wrong behaviours in our society such as dishonesty, corruption, violence and eroticism and so on. Children have weak resistance in defending this detrimental influence. In this case, parents' instructions seem to be very important to children's growth. Parents should sit down and talk with them about what they should and shouldn't do. In addition, if parents often spend time in staying with their children, adults' good behaviours will greatly influence their children.

Here I do not deny that there are some disadvantages in spending too much time on children. Some parents restrict their children, and give them little freedom to develop their interests. Therefore, I emphasize that parents should educate and instruct their children appropriately in their spare time apart from their busy works.

▶考官评分:8

题目:

有些人认为父母应该多陪陪孩子，你同意这种观点吗？

译文:

在中国，父母都有他们自己的工作。随着经济的发展，人们趋向于追求高品质的生活环境。大多数的家长尽他们最大的努力给孩子提供舒适的环境，但是他们很少有时间与他们的孩子在一起。我认为，不管他们有多忙，他们都应该抽出足够的时间去陪陪他们的孩子。

首先，父母与孩子共处的时间越多，他们之间的关系就越亲密。孩子们可以通过友好的交谈感受家长的爱并且分享他们的快乐。跟父母一起去游乐园，和父母一起过生日以及父母为自己在赛场的表现呐喊助威，这段与孩子们一起度过的时光将会成为他们珍贵的记忆。

其次，孩子们需要家长的引导。目前我们的社会中有许多不良的行为，比如，不诚实、腐败、暴力和色情等等。孩子对这些不良影响的抵抗力很弱。因此，家长的指导看起来对孩子们的成长非常重要。家长应该坐下来并且与他们交流应该做什么和不应该做什么。另外，如果家长经常花时间与孩子呆在一起，他们成熟得体的举止将对他们的孩子影响颇深。

我不否认花过多的时间在孩子身上有一些缺点。有些家长约束他们的孩子，孩子甚至没有培养自己的兴趣的自由。因此，我强调家长应该在忙于工作的同时抽出适当的空闲时间来教育和指导他们的孩子。

56. 接种疫苗

Topic:

Should parents be obliged to immunize their children against common childhood disease? Or do individuals have the right to choose not to immunize their children?

Sample Answer

The issue of whether we should force parents to immunize their children against common diseases is, in my opinion, a social rather than a medical question. Since we are free to choose what we expose our bodies to in the way of food, drink, or religion for that matter, why should the question of medical "treatment" be any different?

Medical researchers and governments are primarily interested in overall statistics and trends and in money-saving schemes which fail to take the individual's concerns and rights into consideration. While immunization against diseases such as tetanus and whooping cough may be effective, little information is released about the harmful effects of vaccinations which can sometimes result in stunted growth or even death.

The body is designed to resist disease and to create its own natural immunity through contact with that disease. So when children are given artificial immunity, we create a vulnerable society which is entirely dependent on immunization. In the event that mass immunization programs were to cease, the society as a whole would be more at risk than ever before.

In addition there is the issue of the rights of the individual. As members of a society, why should we be obliged to subject our children to this potentially harmful practice? Some people may also be against immunization on religious grounds and their needs must also be considered.

For these reasons I feel strongly that immunization programs should not be obligatory and that the individual should have the right to choose whether or not to participate.

▶考官评分:8

题目：

家长是必须让他们的孩子接种疫苗以便抵抗儿童疾病还是家长有权利选择他们的孩子不接种疫苗呢？

译文：

我们是否应该强迫家长让他们的孩子接种疫苗以便于抵抗儿童疾病，在我看来，这是一个社会问题而不是医学问题。既然我们能自由地选择以多种方式来彰显个性，比如在食物、饮品以及宗教信仰方面，在这个医学治疗的问题上又有什么不同呢？

医学研究人员及政府主要对总体数据和趋势以及省钱的方案感兴趣，很少考虑到个人的忧虑和权益。尽管接种疫苗对预防某些疾病是有效的，例如，破伤风以及百日咳，然而政府几乎不发布关于接种疫苗会产生的副作用，即使接种疫苗有可能导致发育不良甚至是死亡。

人类的身体能够有计划地抵抗疾病并且能够通过接触那种疾病产生抗体。因此当孩子们接受了人工疫苗时，我们就创造了一个脆弱的完全依赖于疫苗的社会。在这种情况下，如果群众接受免疫的项目被叫停，那么整个社会将会面临前所未有的危险情况。

此外，这关系到个人权益的问题。作为社会成员，为什么必须让我们的孩子去做一个面临潜在危险的练习呢？还有一些人反对接种疫苗也是出于宗教信仰的考虑，他们的这种需求应该值得认真考虑。

根据以上这些原因，我强烈反对疫苗项目的义务化和责任化，个人应该享有接受或者不接受的权力。

第三大类：现代科技类话题

57. 飞机是最重要的发明

Topic:

Nowadays the jet plane is considered to be one of the most important and influential inventions in the world. To what extent do you agree or disagree with this opinion?

Sample Answer

Since jet plane appeared in the 1950s, it has had some revolutionary effects. Many people are of the opinion that it is one of the most important and influential inventions in the world. Some others, however, disagree with them. It seems quite clear to me that one of the most important and influential inventions in the world has been the development of jet plane. My arguments for this point are listed as follows.

One of the reasons is that jet travel brings us great convenience and efficiency. A hundred years ago, it took weeks to cross the Atlantic or Pacific oceans by ship. Today, those same trips can be completed in a matter of hours. One can attend a meeting in Paris and have dinner in New York at the same day. These amazing speeds have changed people's concepts of space. Today the world is much smaller than it was in the past.

Another reason why I advocate the attitude is that jet travel is relatively cheap. An international journey one hundred years ago was extremely expensive. Only wealthy people could afford to travel comfortably in first class. Poor people had to save for years to purchase a ticket, and the conditions in which they traveled were not very good. Today it is possible for more and more people in every country to travel in comfort. Thus it is possible for business people to do business all over the world, for students to attend universities in other countries, and for tourists to take vacations anywhere in the world.

For the reasons presented above, I strongly commit to the notion that jet plane is one of the most important and influential inventions in the world. The speed and low cost of jet travel have changed the world. Individual nations are not as isolated as they were in the past, and people now think of the whole planet as they once thought of their own hometowns.

▶考官评分:7

题目:

喷气式飞机被认为是当今世界上最具影响力也是最重要的发明之一，对此观点你是同意还是不同意呢?

译文:

自从喷气式飞机在20世纪50年代问世以来，它就产生了革命性的影响。很多人认为它是世界上最重要也是最具影响的发明之一。然而，还有一些人不同意这个观点。我认为，世界上最重要、最有影响的发明之一就是喷气式飞机的发展。论据如下:

原因之一是乘喷气式飞机旅行为我们带来方便的同时，也提高了我们的效率。100年前，乘船穿越大西洋或太平洋需要几周的时间。而今天，同样的旅行大约几个小时就可以完成。一个人在同一天可以在巴黎开会而在纽约享用晚餐。这些令人惊异的速度已经改变了人们对空间的概念。当今，世界比过去更小了。

我赞成这个观点的另一个原因是乘喷气式飞机旅行相对便宜些。100年前一次国际旅行的费用是相当昂贵的。只有有钱人才能够支付得起最舒适的旅行。穷人不得不用几年的积蓄来买一张票，而且他们旅途中的条件并不是很好。如今，各国越来越多的人能够舒适地旅行。因此，商人可以在世界范围内做生意、学生可以到其他国家的大学学习、旅游者可以在世界范围的任何一个角落度假，这些都有可能实现。

根据以上的原因，我坚定地认为：喷气式飞机是世界上最重要、最具影响的发明之一。乘喷气式飞机旅行的高速度和低成本已经改变了世界。国家之间也不像过去那样互相隔绝，并且人们把整个星球都当成了自己的家。

58. 互联网的利弊

Topic:

What are the advantages and disadvantages of the Internet?

Sample Answer

In recent years, the Internet has been gaining its popularity at an amazing rate. It seems that anyone who knows little about the Internet is out of date and lags far behind the times. The Internet plays such an important role that it undeniably becomes the biggest concern of the world.

Those who favour that the Internet has many advantages give their reasons as follows. In the first place, the Internet brings us great convenience and efficiency. For example, we can send e-mails to our friends in other countries in a few minutes while sending a traditional letter takes us at least a week and costs much. In the second place, we can make friends with people from all parts of the world. It overcomes the geographical barriers and makes the world smaller. Furthermore, the Internet accelerates the flow of information and spreads education to all corners of the globe. We can have easy and quick access to the latest information worldwide.

However, the other side of the coin voices its strong opposition, saying that the Internet has many weaknesses. For one thing, it can easily lead to psychological problems. An Internet-addicted person tends to be isolated, self-centered and unsociable. For another, there is a sharp rise in the number of cyber crimes. More and more financial crimes such as money laundering are committed via the Internet. In addition, it also has negative impacts on young people because there are a lot of obscene and violent contents on line. Researches reveal that people who watch too much violence tend to resort to brutal behaviour when arguments happen.

For my part, I completely agree with the latter view that the Internet has more disadvantages than advantages. It gives rise to people's mental problems. It results in various computer crimes. What is more, it is harmful to the growth of the young. Some measures should be taken as soon as possible to protect people from the negative effects of the Internet.

▶考官评分:8

题目:

互联网的利与弊各是什么?

译文:

最近几年中，互联网以惊人的速度越来越受人们欢迎。好像是不知道互联网的人就代表了过时与落后。互联网扮演着非常重要的角色，不可否认它成为全球关注的焦点。

那些认为互联网有很多好处的人给出了如下的原因。第一，互联网给我们带来很大便利的同时也提高了我们的效率。比如，我们给国外的朋友发电子邮件只需要几分钟时间，传统的邮件至少要花费我们一周的时间并且费用也很高。第二，我们可以与世界各地的人交朋友。它可以克服地域上的障碍，使世界变小。此外，互联网促进了信息的流通，使教育波及到世界的每一个角落。我们可以方便快捷地了解到全世界最新的信息。

然而，反对的人认为互联网有很多弊端。一方面，它很容易导致心理问题。一个沉迷于互联网的人会越来越孤立，以自我为中心，并且不善于交际。另一方面，它使网络犯罪的人数激增。通过互联网的经济犯罪越来越多。另外，它对年轻人也有负面的影响，因为在网上有很多淫秽和暴力的内容。经研究表明，看了太多暴力的人，当发生争执时，倾向于使用残忍的行为。

依我来看，我完全同意后者：互联网弊大于利。它引发人们精神上的问题。它导致各种各样的电脑犯罪。而且，对年轻人的成长是非常有害的。必须要采取措施，尽快尽可能地保护人们免受网络的负面影响。

59. 科技发展的利与弊

Topic:

The development of science and technology benefits our life. Do you think the benefits outweigh the drawbacks?

Sample Answer

The development of science and technology makes our life more comfortable and convenient. However, scientists have created many problems, which are not easy to be resolved, such as air pollution, the deterioration of environment and the scarcity of natural resources, to which we must find some solutions.

Modern science and technology render people many advantages. Modern telecommunication shortens the distance between people and makes communication much easier. Internet is widely used now not only for collection of abundant information but also for correspondence. E-mail, the most effective communication device now, is becoming very popular. Besides, telephone and mobile phone make contact more convenient than before.

Modern transportation, such as airplanes and high-speed trains make our journey smooth and fast. With the help of modern transportation, people can go everywhere they prefer to. The journey to outer space and other planets is not a dream any more. Rockets and space shuttles can help us realize the dream of space travel.

Modern medicine prolongs people's life and relieves patients of sufferings from many diseases. Cancer and AIDS are fatal to people's health. Thanks to the endeavors scientists have made, these diseases become treatable.

However, the process of scientific development also arouses many severe problems to our human beings. Internet, though widely used in modern communication, is easy to be destroyed by computer viruses. Outer space exploration has produced much waste in the space. A tiny metal, a screw, for example can destroy a flying man-made satellite. Industrialization is making natural resources become scarce.

Confronted with these problems, scientists are seeking prompt and feasible solutions. The development of science and technology brings about both positive and negative effects to us. We must eliminate the negative effects to the least extent.

▶考官评分:8

题目:

科学技术的发展给我们的生活带来了很多好处。你认为好处要胜过不利吗?

译文:

科学技术的发展让我们的生活更加舒适和方便。然而，科学家也带来了许多不容易解决的问题，例如大气污染、环境恶化以及自然资源匮乏，对于这些问题我们应该采取一些解决措施。

现代科学技术使人们获益颇多。现代通信缩短了人与人之间的距离，使得交流变得更加便捷。网络不仅被广泛地用于收集大量的信息，而且也频繁地用于通信。电子邮件作为当前有效的交流方式已经变得非常普遍。除此之外，电话和移动电话使得人与人之间的联系比以前更方便。

飞机和高速列车这样的现代交通工具使我们的旅程平安而快捷。因为有现代交通工具的帮助，人们可以去自己想去的任何地方。去外太空和星球旅行不再是一个梦。火箭和航天飞机能帮助我们实现太空旅行的梦想。

现代医学延长了人的寿命，并且减轻了患者的痛苦。癌症和艾滋是致命的疾病。由于科学家付出了大量的努力，使得这些致命的疾病也可以治疗。

然而，科学发展的过程中给人类带来了许多严重的问题。尽管网络被广泛地用于现代交际中，但它容易被电脑病毒摧毁。外太空探索已经产生了许多的太空垃圾。一个小小的金属螺丝钉就能毁坏一颗人造卫星。工业化使自然资源变得短缺。

面对这些问题，科学家们正在寻找及时可行的解决办法。科学技术的发展对我们有积极的作用也有消极的影响。我们应该将消极的影响降至最低。

60. 科技发展是否总是好的

Topic:

Do you agree or disagree that technological development is always good?

Sample Answer

Technology threatens and inflicts damage upon our quality of life. The technological developments of this century are creating widespread plagues that could soon destroy the entire world.

Let us take air for example. Due to massive air pollution, what we breathe is not relatively safe like it used to be. The fumes from the exhausted pipes of automobiles, trucks and factories blow waste material into the atmosphere. After a period of time, atmospheric changes occur. The fumes, that are collected in the atmosphere, are slowly eating away at the ozone layer. This layer of the atmosphere is what shields us from solar ultra-violet rays. Once this layer is gone, our natural protection against the sun would be gone, and if we were hit by one ray of the sun, we'd burst into flames and turn into a cinder.

Another plague of technology is nuclear power. The power that can energize entire cities with electricity could also be the power to destroy. After 1945, the research on nuclear power has increased significantly. Contrary to the belief that it is safe, nuclear power has a way of destroying the whole city. It is not like a fire that can be put out with water or CO_2, but special equipments have to be used. Afterwards that place would remain radioactive for quite a long time, devoid of life and sound.

So you see, if technology cannot be halted, our fate is unknown. Our end will not come about by natural means, but by our own technological achievements, and life on Earth would cease to exist.

▶考官评分:8

题目:

你是否同意科技进步总是有益的这种观点?

译文:

科技正威胁和影响着我们的日常生活质量。本世纪科技发展造成了广泛的、能摧毁整个世界的灾祸。

以空气为例。由于大量的空气污染，我们呼吸的空气不再像以前那样安全。从排气管中排出的汽车尾气，货车尾气和工厂废气在空气中传播。一段时期之后，大气开始发生改变。从空气中聚集的烟雾慢慢吞噬着臭氧层。大气中的臭氧层保护着我们免受紫外线的侵扰。一旦臭氧层消失，我们对太阳光线的自然保护就消失了，如果被其中一种光线照着我们就会突然着火化成灰烬。

另一种带来灾难的科技是核能。这种力量虽然能够为整个城市供电，但也能够摧毁整个城市。1945年后，世界对于核能的研究显著增加。与安全信念相反，核能可以摧毁整个城市。它不像火焰能被水或二氧化碳扑灭，它需要使用特殊的设备去消除。然后，这个地方会在很长一段时间里具有放射性，不会出现任何生命和声音。

因此你看，如果不能停止使用科技，我们的命运就会是未知的。我们的终结将不会以自然的方式进行，而是被我们自己的科技成就所终结，地球上的生命将会不复存在。

61. 20世纪的科技发展

Topic:

There have been many technological developments in the 20th century. Choose one of them, describe the changes it has brought about and discuss whether all the changes are positive.

Sample Answer

The last century featured many technological revolutions the world over. Among them, computer technology has been the most remarkable. Its rapid development and proliferation of use have changed everything from the way the work is done to cutting-edge scientific research.

First of all, computers free us from heavy workload. With the advent of word processors, mistakes in articles can be corrected and editing done without the need to rewrite or retype the entire paper. It is also possible to generate large, stylized type for headings and illustrations so that books can be prepared ready for print.

The computer has also brought about great changes in the financial and scientific world. A good case in point is the use of computers in banking. With its help, financial institutions are able to keep track of balances and transactions automatically and more efficiently than they did in the past. In the scientific community, one of its advantages is its "number-crunching" power. This has made accurate weather forecasting possible. Its power has also enabled scientists to get a clearer picture of the human genome.

However, not all the changes have had a positive impact on human beings and as a whole. There are quite serious health consequences of a sedentary life in front of a computer, the most obvious being eye strain. Furthermore, it is the social consequences that are more alarming. The computer and the Internet have made direct human contact less and less necessary, which had led to human relationships becoming less close and more confusing.

Although some undesirable consequences have arisen from using computer, on the whole, I feel we should embrace the technological advance. There is every reason to believe that computers represent even more efficiency and effectiveness in the future.

▶考官评分:8

题目:

二十世纪拥有许多科技发明，选择其一，描述该发明带给人们的变化并且讨论这些变化是否都具有进步意义。

译文:

上个世纪，在世界范围内发生过很多次重要的科技革命。其中最引人瞩目的就是计算机技术带来的变化。计算机科技的快速发展和广泛应用使整个社会产生了巨大的变化，这种变化是从工作方式延伸到边缘科学的研究。

首先，计算机把我们从繁重的工作中解脱出来。随着文字处理器的使用，人们不需要重写或是重新打印，就可以改正文章中的错误并且编辑整张报纸。计算机还能够为即将印制的书籍制作大的格式化的标题和插图。

在金融和科技领域里，计算机也带来了巨大的变化。计算机在银行中的使用就是一个很好的例证。在计算机的帮助下，金融机构比过去能够更加自动有效地了解余额和交易。在科学领域里，计算机的优势"数字捣弄"功能，能够使人们准确地预报天气。这个功能还能够帮助科学家绘制更清晰的人类基因组。

然而，并不是所有的变化都对人类产生积极的影响。在计算机前坐得过久会严重影响人们的身体健康，最明显的就是眼部疲劳。此外，它的社会影响也很令人担忧。计算机和互联网减少了人们的直接交往，使人与人之间的关系越来越疏远，越来越混乱。

尽管使用计算机带来一些令人不愉快的后果，但总的来说，我认为我们应该欢迎科技的进步。有充分的理由相信，计算机在未来会带来更高的效率。

62. 现代科技是否有助于学生学习

Topic:

With the help of technology, students nowadays can learn more information and learn it more quickly. Do you agree or disagree?

Sample Answer

It is undeniable that developing technologies have brought tremendous benefits, especially in learning area. Learning has become easier than before. For example, today, new devices, such as MP3 or MD players, are offered in market and relevant learning materials are easily and free to download on the Internet. However, it is a little bit hasty to assert that students can learn more information and more quickly, simply because technology helps.

Technologies always contribute both benefits and detriments. For example, computers help students a lot in various ways, but at the same time have many negative even harmful impacts on the students. Most students nowadays play computer games. Sitting before the table, staring at the screen, clicking mouse button; the outcomes are cerebrum fatigue, visual deprivation and time waste. Chatting on the Internet is another great way to kill precious time, and one of negative side-effects of key. Board dependence makes students spelling incorrectly. Worst of all, investigations have shown that more than half of time that students have spent online was exhausted on browsing porn movies, fictions or erotic photos etc.

Students certainly want to learn more information and to learn more quickly. But technology is not the solution. Learning is a skill and it only develops by practice. Computers and other devices can certainly help, but they won't make study any less painful. Technologies provide no solution to overcome indolence that everyone has. Learning has never been easy, and will not become easier merely because of technologies. It always requires tremendous effort and determination. Too much advocate of the fancy benefits of technologies will merely mislead, much more than virtually help.

▶考官评分:8

题目：

由于科技的发展，学生可以更快速地获取更多的信息，学到更多知识，就此观点，你是否同意呢？

译文：

不可否认科技的发展给我们带来了巨大的利益，特别是在学习方面。学习变得比以前容易多了。例如，现在很多新的设备，像MP3、MD播放器在市场中都能买到。有关的学习资料很容易从网上免费下载。然而，认为学生只凭借科技的帮助就能学到更多的信息而且学得更快，这有一些过于草率。

科技是一把双刃剑。例如，电脑在很多方面能够帮助学生，但同时对学生会造成很多消极的甚至有害的影响。现在大部分学生玩电脑游戏，他们坐在电脑桌前盯着屏幕，点着鼠标键盘，这会造成大脑疲乏、视力下降而且浪费时间。网上聊天是另一种消磨宝贵时间的方式，也是最关键的负面影响之一。依赖键盘使学生的拼写不正确。调查表明最糟糕的是学生在网络上花费一半以上的时间浏览黄色电影、小说和色情照片等。

学生肯定想要学到更多的信息，而且想快速地学到。但是，科技并不是解决办法。学习是一种技巧，它只有通过练习才能不断进步。电脑以及其他设备的确能有所帮助，但是它们不能使学习变得不那么痛苦。科技不能为每一个人都有的懒惰提供解决方案。学习从来都不是一件简单的事情，并且也将不会因为科技而变得容易。它通常需要付出巨大的努力和决心。大力提倡科技带来好处只能给人误导，而不是事实上的帮助。

63. 计算机对孩子的影响

Topic:

Computers do not help children to learn more effectively. In addition, their usage has negative effects on both the physical and mental development of young people. To what extent do you agree or disagree?

Sample Answer

Some people think that computers do not help children learn more effectively. The use of computers in schools has negative effects on children's physical and mental development. Personally, I am not in favour of the point. I think children can benefit a lot from using computers.

Now there appear good educational softwares that enable children to develop and practise some fundamental skills. They can help them learn, for example, about letters, numbers, shapes, and rhythm. Good softwares can also help children develop their procedural thinking and creative expression. Besides, computers help children to be in control of their experience, to set their own pace, and to select the level of challenge with which they feel comfortable. They learn more effectively with the aid of computers than only by means of traditional techniques.

It is also good for children's mental development to use computers in schools. By using computers children develop self-confidence and self-esteem as they master computer skills. And they will build positive attitudes toward technology. In addition, in the classroom setting children often prefer working with one or two partners over working alone, which leads to the development of social skills.

It is true that frequent and prolonged computer sessions may pose physical health risks for children, such as harmful effects of radiation, and posture and skeletal problems. In the case of normal usage and normal operating conditions, however, research has shown that computer monitors are safe and do not harm our eyes and that computer monitors emit little or no harmful radiation.

To sum up, computers are good tools for children in study and beneficial to children's mental and physical health.

▶考官评分:8

题目:

电脑并没有帮助孩子们更有效地学习。另外，电脑的使用对青少年的身体和心理健康都有着负面作用。你是否赞同此观点?

译文:

一些人认为电脑并不能帮助孩子们更有效地学习。在学校里使用电脑对孩子们的身心都有消极影响。就我个人而言，我并不同意这种观点。我认为孩子们能从使用电脑中获得很多益处。

现在出现了很多好的教育软件能帮助孩子们发展和练习一些基础技能。例如，这些软件可以帮助他们学习字母、数字、形状和节奏等知识。好的软件还可以帮助孩子们发展他们的程序化思维和创造性表达。此外，电脑帮助孩子们根据自己的经验，调整自己的进度和选择他们自己觉得舒服的挑战级别。由于电脑的帮助，他们的学习效率比只用传统方法学习的效率高很多。

在学校使用电脑对孩子们的心理发展也有好处。通过使用电脑，孩子们会因掌握了电脑技能而培养自尊和自信。他们会用积极的态度面对科技。另外，在教室中比起单独工作孩子们更喜欢和一两个伙伴一起工作，从而促进社会技能的发展。

的确，长时间使用电脑可能会对孩子的身体健康构成危害，如辐射、姿态和骨骼问题。然而，在正常使用的情况下，研究表明电脑显示器是安全的，并不会伤害我们的眼睛，也很少或根本不会发出有害辐射。

总而言之，电脑是孩子们学习的有利工具，而且对孩子的身心健康都非常有益。

64. 机器翻译替代外语学习

Topic:

Some people say that computers can translate all kinds of languages. Therefore, it is not necessary for children to learn foreign languages. To what extent do you agree or disagree?

Sample Answer

The fantastic development of computers has made it possible for people to live better than ever possible before. It seems that people can never do without them. One good illustration is that with computers updating, all kinds of languages can now be translated by computers. Some people even hold the opinion that with this, children do not need to learn foreign languages. The argument seems reasonable, but speaking for myself, I totally disagree with it.

The quality of computer translation cannot be ensured. It is clear that computers can only translate literally or word by word. Sometimes, we find ourselves confused by the head-scratching puzzlement about what they really want to tell. What makes matters worse is that machine translation is used in literature and science translation. The prime of some masterpieces can never be appreciated and some facts may be distorted.

Additionally, a foreign language is always closely related to a country's cultures and customs. To study a foreign language well, one is supposed to not only focus on language learning itself, but also attach importance to a country's cultures and customs from which the language stems. This practice can only be experienced by a learner himself. Computer translation, in this case, settles nothing and cannot replace people's own efforts.

The charm of a language also lies in the fact that it is a precious gift of human beings. When studying a foreign language, students can develop their intelligence, stimulate their imagination and creativity, form a good habit of industry and strengthen their confidence. The process of learning a foreign language is actually the way to cultivate students' all-around development. Computer translation, no matter how wonderful it is, can never play such a role in this process.

Eye-catching as computer translation may seem, it is by no means a cure-all solution. Maybe, with it, students can study a foreign language better. However, it cannot replace the role of students in learning a foreign language. After all, it is human beings who are the master of languages.

▶考官评分:8

题目：

有些人认为电脑可以翻译所有语言。因此，没有必要让孩子去学习外语。你同意还是不同意这个观点？

译文：

电脑不可思议的迅速发展，使人们的生活比以前更好了。这似乎在说，没有电脑人们什么也做不成。一个很好的实例是随着电脑的不断发展，所有的语言现在都能由电脑完成翻译。有些人甚至有这样的观点，孩子们不需要学习其他国家的语言。这样的观点似乎是合理的，但是就我而言，我完全不同意这个观点。

电脑翻译的质量不能保证。很明显，电脑只能从字面上或者逐词对应翻译。有时候，我们发现我们自己会因为不知道电脑到底想要说什么而抓耳挠腮，并感到困惑。更糟的是电脑被用于翻译文学作品和科学论文。一些重要的名著不再值得欣赏，一些基本的事实可能被扭曲。

此外，一种外语通常是和那个国家的文化和风俗习惯密切相关的。学好一门外语，不仅单纯地关注学习这门语言本身，而且要从这个国家的文化与风俗习惯中探寻这门语言的来源。学习者只能自己去获得这些实践经验。在这一方面，电脑翻译什么也不能解决，并且无法代替人们自己所付出的努力。

语言的魅力也在于这样的事实：它是人类珍贵的礼物。当我们学习一门外语时，学生们可以培养他们的智慧，激发他们的想象力和创造力，养成勤奋的好习惯并且增强他们的自信心。学习语言的过程事实上也是一种培养学生全面发展的方法。电脑翻译，不论它有多么神奇，也不能在这个过程中扮演这样的角色。

就像引人注目的电脑翻译，也不可能解决所有的问题。也许，有了它，学生们可以更好地学习外语。然而，它不能代替学生在学习外语中所扮演的角色。毕竟，人类才是语言的主人。

65. 计算机取代教师

Topic:

The computer is widely used in education and some people think teachers do not play an important role in the classroom. To what extent do you agree or disagree?

Sample Answer

As the pace of digital technology speeds up, computers are now widely applied in education and winning tremendous popularity. However, there is no yet absolute agreement on the question whether teachers are of no use with this trend. As I see it, although computers employed in education enjoy an array of benefits such as high speed, easy accessibility and great efficiency, teachers are still of significance.

On a substantive level, computers have reshaped the teaching as well as studying way. For teachers, computers make the teaching method more colourful, vivid and interesting. For students, computers help them finish their homework efficiently, obtain up-to-date information, expand their horizon and stimulate their interests in science.

In spite of this, that teachers' roles will be replaced is a plausible hypothesis rather than reality. It is always the case that teachers can play an indispensable and imperative part that computers cannot. Teachers not only teach us knowledge, but render us many other things such as the positive attitude to life, moral instructions, the courage to overcome difficulties, a host of practical skills, to name just a few. As for students, they are often more crucial than knowledge itself. It is hard to imagine that without teachers, computers can perform as well as teachers do.

Another point to note is that students are immature and are easily affected by adverse influence by computers. Nowadays, it is not rare to see that many students are addicted to computer games and live in a virtual world per day. As a result, they cannot concentrate on their study. What is even worse is that many youngsters are indulged in the Internet where violence, pornography and bloody contents are pervasive. Due to their inexperience and gullibility, they may go astray after watching too many these programs. From this angle, the existence of teachers is a must for the simple reason that they can supervise and educate students.

Above all, I am still inclined to support the opinion that computers can never replace teachers. After all, the computer is only a vital assistant in teaching and it is teachers who make a difference in education.

▶考官评分:8

题目:

计算机广泛应用于教育领域，有人认为教师在课堂上不再发挥重要作用。你是否同意这种观点?

译文:

随着数字技术的飞速发展，计算机被广泛应用于教育方面，并赢得了巨大的声望。然而，在这种趋势下，人们在教师是否有用的问题上并没有完全达成共识。在我看来，电脑虽然在教育行业中有着如高速、便捷和高效的好处，教师的存在仍然具有重大意义。

在本质上，计算机重塑了教育和学习的方式。对教师而言，电脑使教育方法更加丰富多彩、生动有趣。对学生而言，电脑帮助他们更快地完成作业，获得最新的信息，开阔眼界，激发他们对科学的兴趣。

尽管如此，教师的角色将被替代与其说是现实而不如说是一个合理的假设。教师总是可以扮演一个必不可少的、极其重要的角色，而计算机则不能。教师不仅教我们知识，而且在其他方面也给我们很多，例如积极的人生态度、道德培养、克服困难的勇气、许多实用技能，这里仅列举几个例子而已。对于学生而言，这些比知识本身更重要。很难想象如果没有教师，计算机能否完全代替教师的工作。

另一点值得注意的是，学生们尚未成熟，容易受到网络的不利影响。如今，学生每天沉溺于电脑游戏和生活在虚拟世界中的现象并不稀奇。因此，他们不能集中精神学习。更糟的是，许多年轻人沉溺于充斥着暴力、色情、血腥等内容的网络。由于他们缺乏经验和容易受骗，在看了太多这样的节目之后他们可能会误入歧途。从这个角度看来，教师有必要存在，原因很简单，他们可以监督和教育学生。

总之，我仍然倾向于支持电脑不能代替教师这一观点。毕竟，电脑只是一个重要的教学辅助工具，在教育中起重要作用的还是教师。

66. 计算机取代博物馆

Topic:

Some people claim that public museums and art galleries will not be needed because people can see historical objects and works of art by using a computer. Do you agree or disagree with this opinion?

Sample Answer

It is simply absurd to assert that with historical objects and works of art being able to be seen through a computer, public museums and art galleries will no longer be needed.

First of all, computers can never replace real public museums and art galleries. No matter how real and vivid computer images are, they are only images, not the historical objects and works of art that we see in real or even might be allowed to touch with our fingertips. For those who claim museums and galleries are no longer needed because they can see all they want to on a computer screen. I'd like to suggest that they marry a wife or husband in the computer rather than in real life!

In the second place, visiting real museums and art galleries is a rewarding experience in many respects. For one thing, it is a good exercise. While we are making the trip to a museum or art gallery and then strolling about on site, we take some exercise which does a lot of good to our health. For another thing, we can feast our eyes on all kinds of things there and experience the wonder, beauty and exquisite workmanship with our own eyes in an active way instead of in a passive manner by looking at what are being displayed to us by others on the screen. For yet another thing, we protect our eyesight by moving away from the computer screen and see the real objects on site.

It is true that computers have brought great conveniences to our life. At certain times, especially when it is temporarily impossible for us to visit museums and art galleries in person, we can get a rough picture of what are on display on site. However, what we see from a computer screen is, after all, not exactly the same as what we see and feel with our own eyes on site.

In conclusion, computers will never be able to replace real public museums and art galleries. Therefore, it is ridiculous to say that one does not need to go to museums and art galleries as historical objects and works of art can be appreciated on a computer screen.

▶考官评分:8

题目:

一些人认为由于人们可以通过电脑来看到历史文物和艺术作品，因此公共博物馆和艺术画廊都不再需要了，对此你是同意还是反对呢?

译文:

因为历史文物和艺术作品都可以从电脑上看到，因此公共博物馆和艺术画廊便不再需要了的观点简直就是荒唐。

首先，电脑永远替代不了真正的公共博物馆和艺术画廊。不管电脑影像何等真实、形象，它们依然仅仅是影像而已，不是我们真正看到的、或者还会被许可用指尖触摸一下的历史文物和艺术作品。对于那些认为可以从电脑屏幕上看到想看的一切，所以对于那些认为博物馆和艺术画廊没有继续存在必要的人们，我想建议他们就从电脑里娶个太太或者嫁个丈夫得了，而不用去娶嫁真实生活中的人!

其次，参观真实的博物馆和艺术画廊在很多方面有益。一方面可以锻炼身体：在我们赶往博物馆或者艺术画廊并漫步现场的过程中，我们得到了一些锻炼，这对我们的身体健康有诸多好处。另一方面我们可以大饱眼福，亲眼看到那里的所有物件并切身体会那种神奇、美妙和精湛的工艺。这个过程是主动地看我们想看的一切，不是被动地去看别人在电脑屏幕上展示给我们的。最后就是我们离开电脑去现场观看真实物件可以保护我们的视力。

电脑给我们的生活带来了很多方便，这是真的。有时候，特别是当我们暂时不能亲临博物馆和艺术画廊时，我们可以大概了解一下现场都展示了哪些东西。然而，我们从电脑屏幕上看到的与我们现场亲眼看到和感受到的毕竟不完全一样。

由此我们可以得出结论：电脑永远不可能替代真实的博物馆和艺术画廊。因此，不需要去博物馆和画廊因为历史文物和艺术作品都可以通过电脑屏幕来欣赏，这种说法是荒谬的。

67. 计算机对教育的作用

Topic:

Are computers an essential feature of modern education? Are there aspects of a good education that cannot be taught using computers?

Sample Answer

Computers are now essential in many areas of life—modern banking, retail and information exchange among others. However, this is not true for education. At a simple level, some subjects may be better taught using computers, but to explain important concepts a human teacher is still indispensable.

There are some subjects in which a computer can be used successfully to teach. Elementary mathematics, elementary language learning, any area which requires a student to memorise basic facts through repetition is well suited to computer learning. The computer can be programmed to provide an endless number of simple questions, and as the students answer these questions, the facts are learned and reinforced.

However, in the learning and practice of more complex ideas, the computer is not adequate. A computer can evaluate an answer as right or wrong, but it cannot determine why. It cannot find out why a student is making mistakes, and then re-present important concepts in a different way so the student will understand. It cannot determine at what stage in a mathematics problem the student has made an error, it can only indicate that the final answer is wrong. Tasks involving reasoning cannot be taught by computers, as there are too many variables for a computer to deal with successfully.

Thus, while computers may be useful as a tool for practising simple skills, they are not an essential feature of modern education, because they cannot monitor a student's grasp of concepts, nor evaluate a student's reasoning. Until further developments in computers are made, the human teacher will remain indispensable.

▶考官评分:8

题目:

电脑是现代教育的必需品吗？良好教育有哪些方面是电脑无法实现的？

译文:

现在计算机在我们生活的许多方面都是必不可少的——现代化银行业务、零售业和信息交流。然而，这个对于教育而言并不一定是正确的。一些学科在简单的层次上，也许用计算机教学会更好一些，但是当解释重要概念时，教师仍然是必不可少的。

有一些学科可以成功地用计算机进行教学。基础数学、基础语言学习、一些要求学生记住的基本事实并需要通过反复加强记忆的领域是适合用计算机进行教学的。计算机可以编程准备无休止的简单问题，然后当学生回答这些问题时，这些事实就被学习和强化。

然而，对于很多复杂问题的学习和实践，仅凭计算机是不足够的。计算机能评价一个答案的正确或者错误，但是不能解释为什么。它找不出来为什么学生犯这个错误，然后用一个能让学生理解的不同的概念描述。它不能解释这个数学问题在哪个阶段学生做错了，它只能指出最后的结果是错误的。一个涉及推理的任务不可以用计算机教学，因为当一个任务含有很多变数的时候，计算机也不能成功地处理。

因此，虽然计算机也许作为一种工具来从事简单的技能时非常有用，但是它们不是现代教育必不可少的特征。因为它们不能监督学生对概念的掌握，更不能评估一个学生的推理能力。教师将一直是不可缺少的，除非计算机更进一步的发展。

68. 电脑和教师的重要性

Topic:

The computer is widely used in education, and some people think teachers do not play important roles in the classroom and they will be replaced by computers. To what extent do you agree?

Sample Answer

The computer is playing an increasingly important role in our daily life and it is also widely used in education. Some people even propose a suggestion that we will never need teachers from now on. There have been two quite different views on this issue.

The use of computers in education seems to have important benefits for both students and teachers. First, the computer has the ability to accommodate to individual differences in learning speed, and so students can control the pace of lessons. Another advantage is that a computer can give immediate feedback. Most important of all, the computer offers numerous merits to teachers in preparing instructional materials, managing their classes and keeping students' records, thereby cutting down on time-consuming paperwork.

Compared with the computer, however, teachers are indispensable to students. First, the computer's capacity is limited, so attending lectures is very essential for students whose ability of independent study is not fully established. Second, it is the professionally trained teachers' duty to give students moral education. Apart from the knowledge and skills, children in school also learn how to behave themselves, how to abide by the rules and regulations of the society and how to adjust themselves to the society. But the computer can do little in this aspect. The self-control ability of children is not enough. Without teachers' supervision, they tend to ignore their study.

In my opinion, even if the computer can be of great help to teachers as well as to students, it will never replace teachers' work. We should never be so dependent on computers. If so, we humans would sooner or later become slaves of machines.

▶考官评分:8

题目:

随着电脑技术在教育行业的广泛应用，一些人认为教师不再是课堂的核心，他们的地位将被电脑取代。在什么程度上你同意或是反对此观点呢?

译文:

在我们的日常生活中电脑正发挥着越来越重要的作用，并广泛应用于教育。有些人甚至提出一个建议，从现在开始我们将不再需要教师。但对这个问题有两种截然不同的看法。

对学生和教师而言，在教育方面使用电脑似乎都有很大的好处。首先，电脑能够适应不同的学习进度，因此学生可以控制课程的节奏；另一个优点是，电脑可以立即反馈。最重要的是电脑给教师提供了诸如准备教学材料，管理班级和记录学生档案的种种好处，从而减少在文书工作上浪费的时间。

然而与电脑相比，教师是学生不可缺少的。首先，电脑的能力是有限的，对于那些还没有独立学习能力的学生而言上课是非常有必要的。第二，受过专业训练的教师有责任让学生受到道德教育。除了知识和技能，孩子在学校还需学习如何表现得体，如何遵守规则和条例以及如何调整自己去适应社会。但是，在这方面电脑一点也做不到。孩子们的自我控制力不强。没有教师的监督，他们将会忽视自己的学习。

在我看来，即使电脑可以有助于教师教学和学生学习，但它永远也不会取代教师的工作。我们永远不能太过于依赖电脑。如果这样，人类迟早会成为机器的奴隶。

69. 不会使用电脑的弊端

Topic:

What disadvantages will people meet if they cannot use computers? What should our government do?

Sample Answer

The computer plays a very important role in people's work and life. We can't imagine what our world would be like without computers. With the popularization of computer knowledge, more and more people can use computers. But there are still others who are not familiar with it. From my point of view, I think they will confront a lot of trouble and difficulties.

Firstly, most machines and equipment are controlled by computer nowadays, such as, automobile industry, manufacturing, power station and even airplanes, which can improve the efficiency of our work. If a person can not use computers, he will have difficulty in operating machines. It is hard to imagine that a pilot can fly an airplane without intimate knowledge of computer. Without knowing computer knowledge, people will not fit in with the rhythm of our society.

Secondly, people can acquire rich information on computer through Internet, which is abundant in valuable information. We can get a lot of information about world events, arts, movies and the latest development of science and technology. If a person can not use computers, he / she will be out of fashion and lag far behind the others.

Finally, the computer plays a very important role in education. For instance, students have to revise their thesis when they are fulfilling their thesis. Without a computer, the revision work will be very tedious. In addition, students can study some long-distance courses on computer through Internet, which can enlarge their knowledge.

Taking into account of the disadvantages people will meet, I think the government should do something to popularize computer knowledge. Firstly, the government and the authorities concerned should popularize computer knowledge in primary schools and secondary schools. Secondly, the society and the communities should organize some training courses to the people who cannot use computer.

To sum up, in the rapidly developing society, if people cannot use computer, they will meet many difficulties in their work and life.

▶考官评分:8

题目:

不会使用电脑的人会遇到哪些难题呢？政府应采取什么措施呢？

译文:

电脑在人们的工作和生活中扮演了一个非常重要的角色。我们不能想象没有电脑我们的世界会变成什么样子。随着电脑知识的普及，越来越多的人会使用电脑。但是仍然有些人不能熟练地使用它。我认为他们将要面临很多的问题和困难。

首先，当今多数的机器和设备由电脑控制，比如，汽车工业，机器制造业，发电厂，甚至飞机。它可以提高我们的工作效率。如果一个人不会使用电脑，他将很难去操作机器，很难想象一个飞行员没有很多的关于电脑的知识去驾驶飞机飞行。没有电脑知识，人们将无法适应社会节奏。

其次，人们可以在电脑上通过因特网获得丰富的信息，这些信息是大量的有价值的信息。我们可以得到很多关于世界性事件，艺术，电影和科技最新发展的信息。如果一个人不会使用电脑，他/她将脱离时代并且落后于别人。

最后，电脑在教育方面扮演了一个非常重要的角色。例如，当学生正在完成他们的论文而不得不去修改时，没有电脑，这个修改的工作将会变得非常冗长乏味。另外，学生们可以在电脑上通过因特网学习一些远程课程，这可以扩大他们的知识领域。

考虑到人们所遇到的困难，我认为政府应该做一些事来普及计算机知识。第一，政府和有关机关应该在小学和中学去普及电脑知识。第二，社会和社区应该为那些不会使用电脑的人安排一些教学课程。

总之，在这个飞速发展的社会，如果人们不会使用电脑，他们将会在生活中与工作中遇到很多困难。

70. 远程办公

Topic:

"Telecommuting" refers to workers doing their jobs from home for part of each week and communicating with their office using computer technology. Telecommuting is growing in many

countries and is expected to be common for most office workers in the coming decades. How do you think society will be affected by the growth of telecommuting?

Sample Answer

The spread of telecommuting is sure to have far-reaching effects on society. But itself, telecommuting refers to office workers spending much of their employers. The broader implications of telecommuting, however, may involve changes to corporate structure, workers' lifestyles and even urban planning.

The most obvious changes may be apparent in the "normal" offices of companies, governments and other organizations. If even half the working week is spent telecommuting from home, then we would initially expect many empty desks in the office. As offices grow smaller, workers coming in for the day would be expected to share desks with their absent colleagues. This, in turn, may affect the social atmosphere of an organization. However, less social contact with one's colleagues could harm morale and loyalty.

For the individual office worker, telecommuting would mean spending more time at home. For a parent with young children, this may be a blessing. Moreover, many telecommuters would be able to work the hours they wished: having a nap in the afternoon, for example, but working some hours in the evening. One substantial benefit for all telecommuting workers is that there will be no need to travel to work, allowing more free time.

The structure of urban life is also likely to be affected by telecommuting. We would expect to see fewer cars on the road during peak hours and, eventually, a smaller concentration of offices in cities' central business districts. In short, people will have fewer reasons to travel to city centres from outlying areas. As more people work and live in the same location, shops and cultural events will likely relocate themselves out of the city centre.

In sum, telecommuting will serve not only to change the way we work but also the way we live.

▶考官评分:8

题目:

远程办公指的是人们通过互联网，实现非本地办公，从而每周有一部分时间在家里办公。远程办公在许多国家都有发展并且在未来几十年将会成为办公的主要形式。对于远程办公的发展给社会带来的影响你是怎么看的呢?

译文:

远程办公的发展毫无疑问对于社会有着深远影响。但是远程办公本身涉及到员工会耗费老板很多钱。然而远程办公更广泛的意义应该包括公司结构、员工的生活方式甚至城市规划的改变。

最显而易见的改变应该出现在公司、政府部门和其他组织团体的“常规”办公室。如果一半的工作日都在家远程办公，我们首先会想到办公室里有很多空着的桌子。随着办公室的缩小，每天都上班的员工会分享未到公司上班同事的桌子。这样的结果就是，可能会影响这个团体的社交氛围。然而，社交联系的减少会对同事间的士气和忠诚造成伤害。

对于独自工作的员工来说，远程办公就意味着在家里度过更多的时间。对有孩子的家长来说，这是件大好事。此外，每个远程办公者都能在他愿意的时间里工作，例如下午小睡一会儿，但是在晚上工作几个小时。对于所有的远程办公者来说最可观的好处就是，不需要赶去上班了，有了更多空闲时间。

现代城市的生活模式可能也会被远程办公影响。我们会看到高峰时段路上的车辆少了，最终是城市中心商务区的办公集中区变小了。简而言之，人们从城市外围赶去市中心的原因减少了。随着人们在同一地点既工作又居住，商店和文化项目可能会从市中心迁走。

总而言之，远程办公改变的不仅是我们的工作方式，还有我们的生活方式。

71. 限制使用计算机

Topic:

Some people think that the use of computers should be restricted. Do you agree or disagree?

Sample Answer

In this IT age, computer literacy has become a skill-required of workers in practically every field. In some countries, computers have even been introduced into the classrooms of primary schools. However, some people advocate limiting the use of computers in such classes, arguing that they might retard children's ability to read, write and calculate. In my opinion, such restriction is totally unnecessary.

Two or three decades ago, when pocket calculators were popular, some people were concerned that their use by primary school children might hamper their ability to calculate. But this was not the case, and it was the children who learned to use pocket calculators at that time who grew up to design personal computers (PC). As a result, the PC-based Internet has increasingly become an integrated part of the world, and people can no longer afford to be computer-illiterate.

Therefore, it is clear that the more skillful you are at computer use, the more competent and efficient you will be. It is imperative to arm young people with computer knowledge as early as possible. To limit the use of computers by pupils in primary schools is to limit their access to a powerful tool. This will put these children in an unfavorable position in the future job market when they compete with others who had been given free access to computers earlier.

It is foolish to insist on using shields and spears when you have guns and tanks, due to the mere concern that soldiers will be physically less strong. You can still use your mind to think when you have a computer, and the use of computers and training in writing and calculating are not mutually exclusive.

We have always worried about the potential harmful impact on people, especially children, posed by the introduction of new technologies. But time after time, such worries have proved to be unfounded.

▶考官评分:8

题目:

一些人认为应该限制使用电脑。对此你是否同意呢?

译文:

在这个IT时代,电脑知识已经成为各领域里员工必备的一门技能。在有些国家里,电脑已被引入小学课堂。然而,有些人主张应该限制电脑在课程上的使用,因为他们认为电脑可能会阻碍儿童读写和计算能力。在我看来,这种限制是完全没必要的。

二、三十年前,袖珍计算器非常流行。有些人担心小学生使用袖珍计算器可能会妨碍他们的计算能力。但情况并非如此,这些学会了如何使用袖珍计算器的孩子们在他们长大的时候设计出了个人电脑(PC机)。因此,基于PC的互联网已日益成为整个世界的一部分,人们再也不能成为计算机文盲了。

因此,很明显可以看出你对电脑的使用越熟练,你的能力和效率就会越突出。当务之急是尽早武装青年人的电脑知识。在小学,被限制使用电脑的小学生也会被限制获得一个功能强大的工具。这会使他们在未来的职场竞争中,与其他在很小就能自由使用电脑的人相比,明显处于不利地位。

这看似是很愚蠢的事情,当你拥有枪和坦克的时候,你却坚持使用盾牌和长矛,因为你担心士兵会因此身体虚弱。当你有一台电脑,你仍然可以运用你的大脑去思考,电脑的使用和读写的训练是并不相互排斥的。

我们一直担心,新技术的引进会对人们有潜在的负面影响,特别是对那些儿童。但是,一次次的事实证明这种担心是毫无根据的。

范文点评:

这是典型的辩论型题目,范文一共写了5段,采用的是一边倒结构。开头段先写了限制使用电脑的一些理由,然后提出自己反对的看法引导下文。中间三个段落是理由段,第二段以计算器为例子类比了电脑,第三段从社会竞争力的角度来说明电脑的使用是不应被限制的,第四段以兵器为比喻引出观点。结尾段点题,重申自己的看法。全文的结构合理,论据丰富多样,语言上运用流畅自如,句式变换丰富,运用的模板句型很少,是一篇优秀的作文。

72. 飞机

Topic:

Now, air travel has become much cheaper than in the past. Some people say that is a positive development, while some people disagree with this. What do you think? Give your reason.

Sample Answer

Nowadays, people can choose to travel by bus, train, ship, and airplane. In the past, travelling by air was too expensive to be popular, but things are different now: air travel has become much cheaper. Therefore, I argue that this is definitely a positive development.

Firstly, airplane travels extremely fast, thus it saves us a lot of time. We know that in the past, travelling from Britain to America by ship would take at least a month, but now it only needs five to eight hours. One can start out from Britain in the morning and join friends in the States for dinner! In fact, thanks to the fast speed of airplane, many lives have been saved.

Secondly, traveling by air is safer than by any other means of transport. There are car crashes happening here and there on highways, taking away thousands of lives every day. People may think that train and ship are much safer than airplane, but statistics show that the rate of an airplane crash is far lower than these two means of transport. I have travelled by air dozens of times and am quite confident about the safety of air traveling.

Sure enough, apart from some worries about the safety of airplane, people are also worried that due to the cheaper prices of air tickets, there will be more and more people choosing to travel by air, thus resulting in huge consumption of fuel and severe air pollution. This is indeed a problem worth our deep consideration. However, I firmly believe that with the development of science and technology, new types of fuel will definitely be found and then, air travel will pose no threat at all to the environment.

From the foregoing discussion, we can see that air travel becoming cheaper and cheaper is absolutely not a bad thing.

▶考官评分:8

题目:

乘飞机旅行已经比过去便宜许多。一些人认为这是个积极的进步，但一些人持反对意见。你是怎么看的呢?

译文:

现在，人们可以自由选择乘公共汽车、火车、飞机或轮船等多种交通工具旅行。但在过去，飞机票价格不菲，没有几个人能够承受得起。现在情况不一样了，乘飞机已经便宜多了。所以，我认为：这绝对是个积极的进步。

首先，飞机速度极快，因此可以为我们节省很多时间。我们知道，过去乘船从英国去美国至少需要一个月的时间，但现在仅需5-8个小时。一个人早上从英国出发，耽误不了在美国与朋友共进晚餐！事实上，由于飞机速度快，挽救了很多人的生命。

其次，乘飞机比乘坐任何其他交通工具旅行都安全。公路上到处都有撞车事件发生，每天带走数千人的生命。人们可能认为火车和轮船要比飞机安全，但统计数据表明：飞机失事的几率远远低于这两种交通方式。我乘飞机旅行有几十次了，深信其安全性。

当然，有人除了担心飞机的安全性之外，还担心由于机票价格低廉，人们乘飞机旅行会越来越普遍，由此便会带来巨大的燃料消耗和严重的空气污染。这确实是值得我们深思的一个问题。然而，我深信：随着科技的发展，新型的燃料肯定会被发现，那样，乘飞机旅行就不会对环境构成任何威胁了。

基于以上论证，我们可以看出：飞机旅行越来越便宜绝对不是一件坏事情。

73. 空运水果和蔬菜

Topic:

Air transport is increasingly used to export types of fruits and vegetables to countries where they can not be grown or are out of season. Some people say it is a good thing, but other people think it can't be justified. Discuss both views and give your own opinion.

Sample Answer

Nowadays, we have more choices of fruits and vegetables in our lives. For example, people living in the south of China are able to eat fruits and vegetables from the north or even from abroad. This should be attributed to the convenience brought about by air transport.

First of all, airplanes have made possible the transport of fruits and vegetables over long distances. In the past when there were no airplanes, this was completely impossible as fresh fruit and vegetable get bad and rotted easily. With the appearance of air transport, what would have taken several days, a few weeks or even months in the past now only takes a couple of hours to be done. Therefore, fruits and vegetables from faraway places are able to get onto our tables as fresh as newly picked.

Second, air shipping fruits and vegetables has enhanced the economic development and the quality of life of the people of both the exporting and importing places. If the fruits and vegetables of a certain place can be transported within a short period of time to other places or countries, the local people and the government would benefit in the first place. This is easy to understand in that both the local people and the government would have cash in hand. In the second place, the people and governments of the places where fruits and vegetables are transported to are also benefited. The markets would have more varieties to offer and the governments would have more tax to collect.

Sure, air transporting fruits and vegetables consumes large amounts of fuel and human labour and these make the prime reasons for many people to say no to it. Besides, due to the high cost of shipment, these fruits and vegetables are usually very expensive when they finally appear on the markets. However, it is consumers who decide whether they will buy them or not, therefore, it is always a good thing that they at least have more choices.

From the foregoing discussion, we see that air transporting fruit and vegetables is fully justified.

▶考官评分:8

题目:

随着水果和蔬菜空运出口的发展，许多国家也可以吃到本国不生长或非本季的蔬果和水果。有些人认为这是件好事，但是其他人认为这样会导致不公平定价。讨论这两种观点并给出你的看法。

译文:

现在，人们可以选择的水果和蔬菜品种日益增多。比如，生活在南方的人可以品尝到来自北方甚至是国外的水果和蔬菜，这要归功于空运所带来的便捷了。

首先，飞机使得水果和蔬菜的长途运输成为可能。在过去还没有飞机的时代，这些事情都是完全不可能的，因为新鲜水果和蔬菜很容易变质、腐烂。有了空运，原来需要几天甚至几周、几个月才能做到的事情现在几个小时便可做到了。因此，来自远方的水果和蔬菜得以新鲜如期地被端上我们的餐桌。

第二，空运水果和蔬菜促进了输出地和输入地的经济繁荣与人民生活水平的提高。如果某地的水果和蔬菜能够在短时间内被运送到其他地区或国家，那首先受益的就是输出地的人民和政府，这一点很容易理解：因为当地人和政府都有钱了。其次，水果与蔬菜输入地的人民与政府也会受益：市场上会有更多的品种提供，政府则会有更多的税收来源。

当然，空运水果和蔬菜肯定要浪费大量的燃料和人力，这也是许多人表示反对的主要原因。除此之外，由于运费高，所以，最终出现在市场上的水果和蔬菜也就必然昂贵。然而，买与不买是消费者说了算，因此，人们有更多的选择永远都是一件好事情。

由此可见，空运水果与蔬菜是完全站得住脚的事情。

74. 太空研究

Topic:

Billions of money has been spent on the space research. Some people say that it should be spent in improving the living standard of the people on the earth. Do you agree or disagree?

Sample Answer

It has been almost forty years since Armstrong proudly uttered, "That's one small step for a man, one giant leap for mankind." Indeed, it is worthwhile to celebrate such a feat for human beings since space research of the moon-landing was totally unbelievable in the past. Some people, however, maintain that life is the same without any dramatic change. I strongly doubt the validity of this statement.

Without the exploration of unknown places, human beings can never solve the alarming energy crisis. Economic development around the world has accelerated the demand for energy substantially, which leads to resources crisis on the earth. If there is no petrol, coal or natural gas for humans, then the day of destruction will not be a fairy tale. Space research provides mankind with chances of locating new resources, something like water and minerals indispensable to humans.

Moreover, successful research in outer space encourages people to be more adventurous, and that valuable spirit is essential to historical advance. From barbarian states to modern civilizations, no progress can be achieved without exploring unknown places and the invention of airplanes is the best example. If humans, who have long yearned to fly in the sky like birds, fail to engage themselves in daunting experiments, it is not hard to imagine that long-distance travel can only be realized in people's wildest dreams.

Indeed, space research means tremendous investment from national purse, causing due alarm from people. It is not a secret that billions of money has to be spent making sure a successful launch of satellites or spacecrafts. The possibility of new resources and the boost of people's morale, however, justify such a considerable input.

Obviously, only through space research, can people live a truly decent life. Meanwhile, it is a must that this research should not serve a military purpose, and benefiting humans is the prerequisite.

▶考官评分:8

题目:

大量的钱花在太空研究上。一些人认为这些钱应该花在提高地球上人民的生活水平上。你是否同意?

译文:

自从阿姆斯特朗骄傲地宣布,"对我一小步,对人类一大步",已经将近四十多年了。的确,这是人类值得庆祝的盛事。因为在过去登月是完全无法想象的。然而,一些人坚持认为生活一如既往,没有太多显著的变化。对于这种说法,我完全怀疑其正确性。

没有探索未知领域的活动,人类就无法解决令人警惕的能源危机。全球经济发展加速了对能源的极大需求,这直接导致了地球上的能源危机。如果人类没有汽油,煤炭,或天然气,那么毁灭之日就不是童话。太空研究为人类提供了找到新资源的机会，像水、矿物质等对人类不可或缺的资源。

而且，成功的外太空研究激励人们更加具有冒险精神，这种精神对于历史的进步是不可或缺的。从蛮荒到文明，没有哪一次进步不是通过探索未知领域完成的，其中飞机的发明就可以很好地佐证这一点。长久以来，人类都渴望像鸟儿一样在天空飞翔。如果人们不投身到那些令人胆战心惊的试验中，不难想象，长途旅行是永远不可实现的。

太空研究的确意味着国库的巨大开支。这不可避免地引起人们的警惕。众所周知，一次卫星或飞船的成功发射意味着几十亿的投资。然而，有可能发现新的能源以及人们士气的提高使我们相信这笔投资是值得的。

很明显，只有通过太空研究，人们才能过上真正幸福的生活。同时必须确保研究用于造福人类，而不是为了军事的目的。

75. 国家是否应该进行太空探索

Topic:

Should countries undertake space research?

Sample Answer

In the past, there were just two nations which undertook serious space exploration, namely the United States and the former Soviet Union. In fact, the "space race" began in the late 1950s, with the Soviet Union launching the first manned rocket. It became a matter of national pride, as each country attempted to outdo the other in enhancing its international standing. When Americans landed the first man on the moon, it clearly represented a monumental national achievement.

Furthermore, space research has produced a variety of practical and beneficial discoveries and applications. For instance, Teflon, a non-stick surface used in cooking utensils, such as frying pans, was developed as a result of the space program. Moreover, we have a better understanding of climate patterns, together with a modern system of electronic communications, as a direct result of the hundreds of satellites which encircle our planet.

On the other hand, space research has considerable disadvantages. Obviously, space research is often carried out for military purposes. It undoubtedly adds to the arms race, endangering world peace. Think, for example, of American "Star Wars" project. How on earth does this benefit mankind?

Environmentally, there are significant reasons against launching rockets into space. The huge boosters used by vehicles escaping the earth's gravity produce considerable pollution, damaging the precious ozone layer. In addition, there are countless pieces of "space junk" floating around above our planet which one day could constitute a serious hazard.

▶考官评分:8

题目:

国家是否应该进行太空探索?

译文:

在过去，仅仅有两个国家认真地进行过宇宙空间探索，即美国和前苏联。事实上，空间竞赛始于上个世纪50年代，前苏联发射了第一颗载人火箭。这已经成为了民族的骄傲，因为每个国家都希望超过其他的国家，提高自己在国际社会中的地位。美国人首次登陆月球无疑代表了国家取得的巨大成就。

此外，空间研究还提供了各种各样的实用而有益的发明和应用。在空间研究项目中，研制出一种叫做Teflon不粘的表面材料，可以运用在烹饪器皿，如煎锅中。此外通过现代的电子通信系统和上百颗围绕着我们的星球卫星，我们还可以更好地了解气候模式。

从另一方面来看，空间研究也存在着相当大的弊端。显而易见，空间研究常常用于军事目的。毫无疑问这就促进了军备竞赛，威胁到世界和平。试想一下美国的"星球大站"计划，真的能够造福人类吗?

从环境方面看，也有很多充足的理由反对发射火箭升空。火箭运载工具使用的巨型助推器在摆脱地球引力时会造成严重的污染，从而破坏珍贵的臭氧层。还有大量的"宇宙垃圾"漂浮在我们生活星球的上空，总有一天会对我们造成严重的危害。

范文点评:

这是个辩论型题目，作者采用了并列式写法，一共写了四段，前两段是从正面来说空间探索带来的好处，举了很多例子。后面两段从空间研究的弊端来写该项目给人类带来的忧患。作者并没有明确表达自己的观点，而是从两面切入主题，写法巧妙，文章布局合理，理由充分，举例也比较多，语言上运用的模板句型很少，采用了许多不常用的独特句型，是一篇佳作。

76. 太空探索对人类的影响

Topic:

Space travel to the moon is cited as a big step for the mankind. Some people think it made little difference to our daily lives. To what extent do you agree or disagree?

Sample Answer

With the incredibly rapid advancement of science and technology, space exploration, which is considered to be a big step for human beings, has been carried out by many countries around the world. I disapprove of the claim that space travel to the moon made little difference to our daily lives, for it will benefit human race in many ways to a large scale.

In the first place, the investment of time and money in space exploration could, in future, be paid back to humanity many times over; especially the discovery of resources in outer space could be of great benefit to our planet. It is universally acknowledged that, the shortage of natural resources, nowadays, becomes one of the most severe problems throughout the world. There is possibility of finding some resources available on the moon, which may help us to solve the intractable problem.

Besides, the potential that other planets, taking the moon as an example, hold for colony could prove to be a salvation of the human race. Due to the population explosion on earth, humans begin to worry about the limited living space for their offspring. Therefore, it may be wise to exploit a completely new living space.

On the other hand, some political analysts claim that the Space Race has led to unnecessary competition between nations and a consequent failure to cooperate and collaborate on international issues. Moreover, many sociologists argue that colonies in space would create more social problems than they would solve. Nonetheless, I am still in favor of space travel, for its merits far outweigh its demerits.

In conclusion, in spite of some worries about space travel, it will, undisputedly, exert favorable effect on the human race, such as the discovery of new resources, the exploration of new colonies, and so on. Hence, it is of great necessity to conduct space travel to the moon.

▶考官评分:8

题目:

月球之旅被视为是人类的一大进步，有的人认为这对我们日常生活没有什么影响。你在多大程度上同意此观点?

译文:

由于科技的飞速发展，被誉为人类一大进步的太空探索在世界很多国家进行。我不同意月球旅行对我们日常生活没多大影响的说法，因为它将在很多方面并从很大程度上使人类受益。

首先，在太空探险上所花费的时间和金钱在未来会加倍地偿还给人类，尤其是外太空资源的开发对我们的星球极为有益。众所周知，自然资源的匮乏如今成为了全世界最严重的问题之一。可能在月球上寻找到可利用的资源，这或许能帮助我们解决这个棘手的问题。

另外，其他星球比如说月球有作为殖民地的潜力，这将拯救人类。由于地球上的人口爆炸，人们开始担心子孙后代极为有限的生存空间。因此，开发全新的生存空间是非常明智的做法。

另一方面，一些政治家分析指出，太空竞赛会导致国家之间不必要的竞赛，并随之导致他们在国际事务中合作的失败。另外，在外太空开发殖民地所造成的社会问题将大于解决的问题。尽管如此，我还是赞成太空探险，因为它的好处远远大于坏处。

总之，虽然人们对于太空探险很担忧，但毋庸置疑，它将对人类产生有利的影响，比如资源的发现和殖民地的开发等。因此，月球探索是极有必要的。

77. 我们是否应该投资于太空研究

Topic:

Should we invest money in space research?

Sample Answer

For over fifty years, a number of nations have been involved in the exploration of outer space. This research has been very costly. Has this money been well-spent or wasted?

Some people believe that the research should be eliminated because of its expense, not only in terms of money, but also in terms of the scientific and human resources. These people point out the fact that it cost billions of dollars to send astronauts to the moon, but they just brought back worthless rocks. These people say that the money and effort could be spent on more important projects right here on Earth, such as providing housing for homeless people, improving the education system, saving the environment, and finding cures for diseases.

However, other people believe that space research has provided many benefits. They point out that hundreds of useful products, from personal computers to heart pacemakers to freeze-dried foods, are the direct or indirect results of space research. They say that weather and communication satellites are also products of space programs. In addition, supporters of the space program point to the scientific knowledge that has been acquired about the Sun, the Moon, the planets, and even our own Earth as a result of space research.

I agree with those people who support space research. Space research, has already brought many benefits to humanity. Perhaps it will bring even more unimaginable benefits in the future. Moreover, just as individual people need challenges to make their lives more interesting, I believe the human race itself needs a challenge, and I think that the peaceful exploration of outer space provides just such a challenge.

►考官评分:8

题目:

我们应该投资在太空研究上吗?

译文:

在过去的五十年间，很多国家都致力于外太空的研究。这项研究耗资巨大。这是物有所值还是一种浪费呢?

一些人认为这项研究因为它的费用而应停止，不仅仅在金钱方面，还包括那些科学和人力资源。这些人指出花费了数十亿美金将宇航员送到月球，但是他们仅仅带回来无用的岩石。这些人说这些资金和努力在地球上能被用于更重要的项目上，例如为无家可居的人提供住房，改善教育系统，保护环境和为疾病找出治疗的方法。

然而，另一些人认为对空间的探索已经带来了巨大的利益。他们提到了许多有用的产品，从个人电脑到心脏起搏器，又到冷冻干燥食品，这些都是太空研究直接或者间接的结果。这些人还指出气象和通讯卫星也是太空研究的产物。此外，太空项目的支持者也指出那些已知的有关太阳，月亮，行星，甚至我们的地球的知识本身就是太空研究的产物。

我同意那些支持太空研究的人们的观点。太空研究，已经为人类带来了巨大的利益。以至未来它可能会带来更加不可思议的好处。此外，正如个人生活中需要挑战从而得到更多的乐趣，我坚信人类本身就需要挑战，而我想，和平的外太空探索就恰好为我们提供了这样一个挑战。

78. 太空研究是否浪费

Topic:

More than three decades ago, man for the first time set foot on the moon. Some people think that space research is a waste of energy and money. Discuss and give your opinion.

Sample Answer

It is an undeniable fact that it has been over thirty years since man's first landing on the moon, and his fascination with outer space has a much longer history than that. Some people believe that this type of study is a sheer waste of time and money. However, in my opinion, this issue has both pros and cons, and it should not be judged one-sidedly.

On one hand, it indeed requires a great deal of time and money to train people to carry out research work in this sphere, to put the research into actual practice, and to sustain countless test failures. In addition, doubtlessly the time and money spent on space research and exploration is hard to calculate, as it is carried out by several nations. From this perspective, the research in question can be considered a waste of time, money and resource.

One the other hand, however, once the research findings are transformed into productivity, we will see the situation in a different sight. For example, knowledge of other planets and stars may make possible the colonization of space. At that time, the expenditure that seems so wasteful now will serve to expand and extend the scope of human existence. Currently, the progress made by scientists who have dedicated much time and energy to this research has demonstrated this point clearly and forcefully.

In short, it truly takes a lot of time and money to carry out studies of outer space, for such research tests man's intelligence, patience and perseverance to the utmost, long before any concrete results are visible. Nevertheless, people of vision will indubitably recognize the abundant benefits to be reaped once the research is completed and its findings are put into production.

▶考官评分:8

题目:

三十多年前，人类第一次登上月球，一些人认为空间探索是能源和金钱的浪费。讨论你对此的看法。

译文:

不可否认，自从人类第一次登上月球已经三十多年了，而人类对外太空的痴迷历史比之更长。有些人觉得这种研究完全是浪费时间和金钱。然而，我却认为，这个问题有正反两方面的争论，不应该只从一方面来评判它。

一方面，为了培训相关人员在这个领域做好研究工作，将研究应用于现实并承受无数的实验失败，确实需要大量的时间和金钱。并且，由于它是由几个国家共同承担的，花在太空研究和探索上的时间和金钱是难以衡量的。从这种视角来看，太空研究无疑认为是对时间、金钱和资源的浪费。

然而，从另一方面来看，一旦研究结果能够投入生产，我们就会以一种不同的眼光来看待这个局面。举个例子来说，对其他星球和恒星的认知能够使太空移民成为可能。在那个时候，当时看起来是浪费的支出现在将会因为扩大了人类的生存范围而成为正当的花费。以现在看来，在这项研究上投入了大量时间和精力的科学家们取得的进展已经有力且清楚地证实了这一点。

总之，对外太空的研究的确花费了大量的时间和金钱，在这种能在极大程度上考验人类的智力、忍耐力和毅力的研究上，一切具体的结果在很早以前都是不可见的。然而，毋庸置疑，一旦这项研究完成并将其研究结果应用于生产，有远见的人都将认识到其带给他们的巨大利益。

79. 电话的利与弊

Topic:

Discuss the advantages and disadvantages of the telephone.

Sample Answer

During the last century, the telephone was undoubtedly seen as one of the most important inventions. Its rapid development and proliferation of use throughout the world have been remarkable. Being part of modern life, it has affected society in a variety of ways, both positively and negatively.

On the positive side, the telephone has been used as one of the most popular communication tools and favourably applied in many fields, such as doing business, communicating with people, providing more employment opportunities and dealing with emergencies. For example, the telephone has made doing business much easier and more efficient. Simply through a phone line, people can place or check on orders, saving the time when shopping for necessities.

The telephone has also made the world seem smaller, since it allows us to stay in touch at any time with anybody, both near and far. In addition, with the advent of the telephone, telecommunication companies have been established, creating many job opportunities. In handling emergencies, the telephone seems to play a most important role. If your life is in danger, all you need to do is to dial 120, and doctors can be sent for immediately.

On the negative side, the telephone can be a big time waster, both at work and at home. When at work, people are often distracted by one unwanted ring after another and, as a result, are kept away from finishing their daily tasks. At home, the telephone seems very inviting for some people who desire to communicate. Those in need of communication are often on the phone line just for casual talk for one hour or more. This, as a result, has made direct face-to-face human contact less and less necessary, which has led to human relationships becoming more confusing.

The advantages this powerful invention has brought to us are obvious, while its disadvantages should not be ignored. Despite some of its negative influences on our society, its benefits will assure its future use.

▶考官评分:8

题目:

请谈谈电话的利与弊。

译文:

毫无疑问电话已经被看成是上一世纪最重要的发明之一。它的发展速度之快和使用之频繁已经被全世界所关注。作为现代生活中不可分割的一部分，它已经在很多方面影响到社会，这种影响既有积极的也有消极的。

电话有其积极的一面。它已经成为最受欢迎的交流工具之一，并且成功地被应用在很多领域，比如做生意、聊天，招聘和处理紧急事件。例如，通过电话进行商业活动更方便快捷。仅仅通过一根电话线，人们就能够进行订货和核查订单，节约了购买生活必需品需要花费的时间。既然它能够使我们在任何时间，任何地点与任何人保持联系，电话也就使世界看起来更小。除此之外，随着电话的出现，电讯公司相继成立，创造了许多就业机会。在处理紧急事件上，电话看起来更是发挥着重要的作用。如果生活中你遇到危险，你所需要做的就是拨通120，医生就会迅速赶到。

电话也有其消极的一面。它有可能会在工作和生活方面浪费大量时间。在工作的时候，人们总是被一个又一个的意外电话所打扰，结果他们不能完成每天的任务。在家时，电话看起来是为那些渴望交流的人们预备的。有这种需要的人们占着电话线，仅仅只是一些日常聊天就能花费一个多小时。结果，这也导致人们面对面接触的机会越来越少，从而使人们之间的关系越来越淡漠。

这项伟大发明带给我们的益处是显而易见的，然而它的弊端也不容忽视。尽管它对我们的社会有不利的影响，它的益处也确保着它在未来的使用地位。

80. 小汽车

Topic:

The unlimited use of cars may cause many problems. What are those problems?

Sample Answer

The fast increase in the number of cars have brought along many related problems which are well worth our greatest attention.

First of all, urban traffic is getting from bad to worse. I'd like to cite my own experience as an example. Five years ago, it took me about 30 minutes to drive from home to office. One year later, I needed to spend about 40 minutes on the way. Then two years later, I had to start out from home at least 1 hour earlier in order to get to my office on good time for work. And then, since last year, it has just been too normal for me to spend about one and half hours to make it. The traffic just moves like a worm!

Second, with the ever growing number of cars, air quality in urban areas is deteriorating with each passing day. We used to see clear blue sky and breathe fresh air, but now this would be a real luxury. Car exhaust has seriously polluted the air and people's health is greatly endangered. It seems certain that we human beings have already made a fatal mistake that could only be remedied by bringing down the number of cars hugely.

Sure, we can not deny the fact that cars have brought up speed, comfort and greater mobility. However, these have already been history. We are suffering much more from cars than benefiting from them. Our health conditions are going down rapidly both due to the polluted air that we have to breathe every second and our lack of exercise as a result of the ever increasing amount of time we have to spend behind the wheel!

What can we do? From the forgoing discussion, I'm sure we have already found a solution: to discourage people to use cars! I know very well that science and technology are developing very fast and there might be better solutions coming up in the future, but, before that, let's first salvage ourselves in such a passive way!

▶考官评分:8

题目:

轿车数量的无限增长带来很多相关问题，请说明都有哪些问题。

译文:

轿车数量的快速增长带来很多相关问题，值得我们高度重视。

首先，城市交通每况愈下。这里我想拿自己的亲身经历作为例证。五年前，我从家里开车到办公室大约花30分钟。一年后，我路上大约花40分钟。两年后，为了准时到达工作岗位，我至少要提前1个小时从家里出发。之后，从去年开始，花1.5小时到达成为家常便饭。交通就像毛毛虫一样在蠕动！

第二点，随着轿车数量无休止的增长，城市中的空气质量正日趋恶化。我们过去还能看到蔚蓝的天空，呼吸到新鲜的空气，但现在这成了一种奢望。汽车废气已经严重污染了空气，人们的身体受到了严重威胁。似乎已经很明确：我们人类已经犯了一个致命的错误，惟一能够弥补的便是极大地减少轿车的数量。

是啊，我们不能否认，轿车给我们带来了速度、舒适和机动性。然而，这一切都已经成为过去。我们从轿车上所蒙受的灾难要远远大于我们所获得的益处。由于我们每一秒钟都要呼吸被污染了的空气，以及我们在汽车上必须要花费的时间日益拉长因而缺乏锻炼的双重原因，我们的身体状况正越来越糟。

我们该怎么办呢？从前面的论证中，我相信我们已经找到了解决方案：鼓励人们少开车！我很清楚科学技术也在快速发展，将来也许会有更好的解决方法，但是，在这一切成为现实之前，让我们先通过这种被动的方式来自救吧！

81. 私家车的利与弊

Topic:

Please state the advantages and disadvantages of the development of private cars.

Sample Answer

With the fantastic spur both in industry and in economy in China, the number of people who own private cars is on the rise. Some people have bought cars of their own, and others are planning to buy cars. But there have been two quite different views on this phenomenon.

Some claim that there are many advantages brought about by cars. First, the automobile industry provides jobs for countless workers and strong support for other industries. Second, if conditions permit, owning a car can make us work more efficiently. Finally, life will become more convenient. A car allows one to move freely and with a car there is no need to wait for the bus in the cold or under the burning sun.

However, others strongly object to the increase in developing private cars. They hold that automobiles will give rise to a series of problems. In the first place, as more and more cars are produced and run in the street, a large volume of poisonous gas will be given off, polluting the atmosphere and causing actual harm to the health of people. Next, private cars contribute to traffic congestion so greatly that the advantages gained in comfort and freedom are often cancelled out by the frustration caused by traffic jams. The last problem is the increasing number of car accidents which have killed and will kill a lot of people in a friction of a second.

In my opinion, although automobiles have been playing a vital part in the daily activities of our society, they also bring us numerous troubles such as more serious environmental pollution, more traffic accidents and more energy consumption. They drink up huge amounts of fuel and throw out huge amounts of pollutants. Traffic accidents kill thousands of people each year and cripple more. Jams waste our precious time. Therefore, I am against developing private cars.

▶考官评分:7

题目:

请说明发展私家车的利与弊。

译文:

中国随着工业和经济的飞速发展，拥有私家车的人数正在不断上升。有些人已经拥有自己的私家车，还有一些人正在计划着购买汽车。但是，对于这种现象有两个不同的观点。

有人认为，汽车会带来很多好处。首先，汽车行业为无数工人提供了就业机会，并且强有力地支持了其他行业的发展。其次，如果条件允许，拥有一辆汽车可以使我们更高效地工作。最后，使我们的生活会更加便利。汽车可以使出行更加自由，而且有了私家车就不用在寒冷的冬日或炎炎烈日下等待巴士了。

但是，其他一些人坚决反对增加私家车。他们认为，汽车将会产生一系列的问题。首先，随着汽车的大量生产，行驶在大街上的汽车也会越来越多，有毒气体将会大量排放，污染大气，实际上是损害人类的健康。其次，私家车带来的舒适和自由常被交通堵塞带来的沮丧所取代。最后一个问题是日益增多的交通事故所造成的死亡，将会继续倾刻间夺去许多人的生命。

在我看来，尽管汽车在我们的社会生活中充当着一个重要的角色，但是，它们也给我们带来了许多的麻烦，比如更加严重的环境污染，频繁的交通事故和大量的能源消耗。汽车消耗了大量的燃料，同时也制造了大量的污染物。每年的交通意外造成数千人的死亡和更多人的残疾。交通堵塞浪费了我们大量的宝贵时间。因此，我反对发展私家车。

82. 化肥和杀虫剂

Topic:

Modern technology, such as fertilizer, pesticide and modern machinery can feed the world better. However, it is negative to human health. To what extent do you agree or disagree with this opinion?

Sample Answer

With the rapid development of science, many modern agricultural technologies, such as fertilizer and modern machinery have been applied with the view to enhance the output of produces. Undoubtedly, this increases the volume of crops. But in the meanwhile, some people show their great concerns about the negative effects aroused by modern agriculture.

Firstly, the utilization of fertilizer causes great changes of the structure of soil. In the long run, this will make the soil infertile, which means that we can only have a good harvest with the help of fertilizer. Furthermore, the change of the structure of soil can cause serious environment problem.

Secondly, pesticide can kill most of the insects harmful to crops. But at the same time, it also kills many insects, which are friendly to the crops and human beings. The abuse of pesticide also seriously threatens the health of human beings. When people eat the vegetable and crops with pesticide sediment, their health will be in danger and their digest system and neural system will be damaged.

Finally, the use of modern machinery saves people a lot of time and energy. But this will cause serious environmental problems. In the ancient times, most of the field labor is undertaken manually or with the help of some tamed animals, such as cattle and horses. But now, modern machinery takes the place of human beings and animals and plays a major role in modern agriculture, which will cause serious environment pollution and the scarcity of natural resources.

To sum up, the employment of modern technology helps to improve people's living, but meanwhile, we should raise the awareness of protecting our environment and us and takes some measures to ensure people's health.

▶考官评分:8

题目:

现代技术，如化肥，农药和现代机械能更好地养活地球人。然而，它对人类健康有负面影响。在何种程度上你同意或不同意?

译文:

科学的迅速发展使得现代农业技术，如化肥和现代机械，迅速地提高了农作物的产量。毋庸置疑，农作物的产量是增加了，但是同时一些人也担心现代农业带来的负面影响。

首先，化肥的使用引起了土壤结构很大的变化。土地将因此不再肥沃了，化肥的使用仅仅能帮助我们取得一次大丰收，而且土地结构的改变引起了严重的环境问题。

第二，杀虫剂杀死了很多危害农作物的昆虫，但是同时它也杀死了对人类和农作物有益的昆虫。杀虫剂的滥用，严重地威胁了人类的健康。当人们吃了沾有杀虫剂的蔬菜和谷物时，他们的健康将处在危险之中，他们的消化和神经系统将受到损害。

最后，使用现代机械节省了人们的时间和精力，但是，这也会引起严重的环境问题。在古代，很多的田间工作都是人工或家畜协助完成的，如牛和马，然而目前现代机械取代了动物和人，在现代农业中起着重要作用，不仅带来了严重的环境污染，同时也牺牲了自然资源。

总而言之，现代技术的使用是提高了人们的生活，但是同时我们也应该时刻警醒保护环境和我们自己，确保人民身体健康。

83. 转基因植物

Topic:

Some people think that genetically modified plants may be harmful and should be banned. What do you think?

Sample Answer

Genetically-modified (GM) plants are part of the latest developments in our ever-changing world. Some people are against them because they are concerned that such plants may cause unpredictable problems. I believe this concern is totally unnecessary, as GM plants have the following three advantages.

First, research and development of GM plants will help us to produce better foodstuffs in terms of quantity and quality. For example, disease-resistant rice with high yields can help eradicate famines and food shortages that have been plaguing the people of many countries. With GM plant technology, we can develop fish without bones, apples that taste of meat and other delicious and exotic foods. The possibilities, to some extent, are only limited by man's imagination.

Second, GM technology opens a new dimension for scientific research. Scientists have been working hard to decipher the secrets hidden in all organisms. GM plant technology will help them to better understand how nature works. Some day, I believe, we will be able to decode all plants' genetic makeup, and bring the whole plant growth process—from blossoming to fruit bearing—under our control.

Third, GM plants may assist us to achieve a perfect ecological balance by producing species to cover the gaps in the biological chain due to wanton abuse of natural resources by human activities. We can develop organisms that can decompose and digest the garbage produced by mankind to make this world greener and cleaner.

Of course, GM plants, like other scientific developments, may cause some problems. But I believe that, with careful regulation and control, the advantages will far outweigh the disadvantages.

▶考官评分:8

题目：

有些人认为，转基因植物可能是有害的，应该禁止，你的观点是什么？

译文：

在我们瞬息万变的世界中转基因植物是一项最新科技进步。考虑到这些转基因植物有可能引发的种种难以预测的问题，有些人反对这项技术。而我认为这样的担忧是完全没有必要的，因为转基因植物有以下三个优势。

首先，转基因植物的研究和发展将会帮助我们生产数量更多、质量更高的食物。例如，高产量的抗疾病大米有助于解决困扰着许多国家人民饥荒和食物短缺的问题。有了转基因植物技术，我们可以养出没有骨头的鱼，有肉味的苹果或其他美味的国外食物。某种程度上说，可能性只取决于人类的想象力。

其次，转基因技术为科学研究开创了一片新天地。科学家们一直在努力破解所有有机体背后隐藏的秘密。转基因技术将帮助他们更好地理解大自然是如何运转的。我相信总有一天，我们将能够破解所有植物的基因结构，并使得植物从开花到结果的整个生长过程能为我们所控制。

再次，转基因植物可以让我们通过再生物种，来弥补由于人类滥用自然资源而给生物链造成的破坏，从而重新达到生态平衡。我们可以创造出有机体，这种有机体能分解消化人类产生的垃圾，让世界变得更绿色更清洁。

当然，与其他科学进步一样，转基因植物也会产生一些问题。但是我相信，只要认真规范和约束，它的优势就会远远超过劣势。

范文点评：

典型的辩论型题目。范文使用一边倒结构，写了五段。开头段使用“欲扬先抑式”，提出自己的观点：人们的担心是不必要的，转基因植物有它们的优势。中间写了三个理由段，从三个不同方面提出了自己的理由，论据充分，是本篇文章的一个加分点。最后一段，重申自己的观点。整篇文章结构合理，理由充分。在语言上，全篇文章使用了比较多的模板式句型，但也没超过100字。而且，其他非模板式句型写得也很好，所以，考官评分为8分。

第四大类：媒体类话题

84. 电视疏远家庭成员的关系

Topic:

Some people think that it is the television that makes the relationship of family members not as close as before. To what extent do you agree or disagree?

Sample Answer

As one of the most important inventions of the past century, TV is playing a more and more important role in modern life. However, some people are starting to worry about its negative effects on traditional families. I am convinced that the existence of TV has brought about alienation among family members.

First, watching TV occupies our time to communicate with our families. TV provides a ready means of relaxation for people who spend their days doing routine and busy jobs. As soon as TV enters our home, most of our free time is controlled by it. What is more, the one-eyed monster requires absolute silence and attention. If any member dares to open his mouth, the others order him to shut up immediately. Therefore we communicate less with our family members.

Furthermore, families often quarrel over what programs they should watch. Thanks to hard-working TV workers, we enjoy more TV channels and more colorful TV programs. But a question has arisen: it is difficult for families to choose a common channel because they have different interests. It is inevitable to give rise to quarrel among them.

In addition, poor-quality TV programs can have severe effects on people's mood and behavior. For instance, a person who watches too many idealized programs may become unrealistic. In addition, unhealthy programs which contain obscene and violent contents may cause people's curiosity. All these things will inevitably have negative influence on the family relationship.

In conclusion, I think that TV indeed has led to alienation among family members. We should be aware about the problem. Something should be done as soon as possible to protect the families from the negative effects of television. For example, we should reduce the time spent in front of the little screen and spend more time with our families together.

▶考官评分:8

题目:

有些人认为是电视使家庭成员间的关系不像以前那么亲密了，你是否同意此观点?

译文:

作为上个世纪最重要的发明之一，电视在现代生活中扮演着越来越重要的角色。然而，有些人开始担心起它对传统家庭的负面影响。我承认，电视的存在使得家庭成员之间的关系疏远了。

首先，看电视占用了我们同家人交流的时间。看电视是那些每天从事有规律而繁忙工作的人的休闲方式。电视一进入我们的生活，就控制了我们大部分的空闲时间。更甚者，电视要求绝对的安静和关注。如果哪一个家庭成员胆敢讲话，其他人会命令他马上住嘴。所以，我们与家人的交流减少了。

此外，家人经常因为看什么节目而争吵。多亏了不辞辛劳的电视工作者，我们才有越来越多喜爱的电视频道和有趣的电视节目。但是，有个问题产生了：家人很难选出共同的频道，因为他们有着不同的兴趣，这就不可避免地引起争吵。

另外，品质低劣的电视节目会严重影响人们的情绪和行为。例如，一个人看了太多理想化的节目，可能会变得不切实际。另外，包含淫秽和暴力内容的不健康的电视节目可能会引发人们的好奇心。这些将不可避免地对家庭成员的关系有负面的影响。

总之，我认为，电视的确导致了家庭成员之间的关系疏远。我们必须意识到这个问题。必须要做点什么，尽快尽可能地保护人们不受电视的负面影响。例如，我们应该减少花在电视屏幕前面的时间，而多花些时间陪陪家人。

85. 广告的利与弊

Topic:

Some people think that advertisements should be restricted. Do you agree or disagree?

Sample Answer

Everywhere, and almost at any time, we find ourselves surrounded by all kinds of advertisements. Some people suggest that the government should impose restrictions on advertisements. But on the other hand, there are also many people who strongly advocate that advertisements should not be restricted.

It is quite easy to find reasons for attacking advertising. First, it is extremely costly to put up an advertisement. TV advertising, for instance, costs more than 100,000 *yuan* RMB per minute during prime time and this cost must eventually be paid by the consumers. Second, Advertisements are misleading and cheating. It is because advertisements have powerful influence that the profiteer often tricks the public by them. In addition, surplus advertisements have interfered in people's normal life. Every ten minutes a television program will be interrupted by commercials for a couple of minutes, which ruins good movies and exciting television shows.

However, other people also argue in defense of advertising. In the first place, it has a valuable informative function, helping potential customers know about the characteristics and prices of products or where they can buy a particular product cheaply. In the second place, we would have to pay a great deal more if advertising did not create mass markets for products. It is precisely because of the heavy advertising that consumer goods are so cheap. Finally, advertisements also provide money for newspapers, magazines, radios and TV stations. Many kinds of media could not survive without advertisements.

In my opinion, advertisements should not be restricted. They provide us with much useful information. They reduce the price of commodity. What is more, they play a crucial role in the development of media.

▶考官评分:7

题目:

有人认为广告应该受到限制，你是否同意此观点?

译文:

在每个角落，我们随时都会发现我们是被各种各样的广告所包围的。一些人建议政府应当对广告有所限制。但在另一方面，也有许多人强烈提倡广告是不能受限制的。

找到攻击广告的理由是相当容易的。首先，做广告的成本是相当高的。例如电视广告，黄金时段每分钟要支付10万元人民币，而且这种成本最终是由消费者支付的。第二，广告有误导性和欺骗性。正是由于广告的强大影响力，奸商才利用广告来欺骗公众。另外，过多的广告干扰了人们的日常生活。每十分钟，电视节目就被广告中断几分钟，这样再好的电影和电视节目也索然无味了。

然而，另一些人支持广告。首先，它有提供大量有价值信息的功能，帮助潜在的消费者了解产品的特点和价格以及他们在哪里可以很便宜地买到某种特殊的商品。第二，如果没有广告打开产品市场，我们花的钱会更多。正是由于广告，商品才那么便宜。最后，广告为报纸、杂志、电台和电视台提供资金。没有广告，很多媒体不会生存下去。

在我看来，广告不应该被限制。它们不但为我们提供了很多有用的信息、降低了商品的价格，而且在媒体的发展中起到了重要的作用。

86. 广告促进销售但不反映真实的需求

Topic:

Today, the high sales of popular consumer goods reflect the power of advertising and not the real needs of the society in which they are sold. To what extent do you agree or disagree?

Sample Answer

Nowadays, there are lots of advertisements on television or on the streets. Some people think that the advertising boosts the sales of goods and it encourages people to buy things unnecessarily. This argument may be true. In my country, many advertising companies produce advertisements with famous and popular actors or singers. People, especially youngsters, buy goods that their favourite singer advertises, although they do not really need the products.

Also, on the television screen, a product may look gorgeous and of good quality. As a result of it, people often buy goods without enough consideration. Consumers may not actually need it, but they buy goods impulsively soon after they watch the advertising. Furthermore, as many customers buy a particular product due to its advertising campaign, the other people may be affected by the trend, even if the product is not the real needs of the society.

On the other hand, there are various aspects against these arguments. Moreover, it is people's choice to make a decision to buy goods. Advertising may be not a cause of customers' buying habits. Individuals have their own spending habits. If they have got enough disposable income, then the right to make a decision is given to them. No one actually can judge whether the goods sold are the real needs of the society or not. In addition, as there should be a limited amount of disposable income consumers are able to spend, people try to allocate their budgets. They cannot be simply swayed by those advertisements.

In conclusion, as customers have their own strong opinions and standard of good quality goods, it is better to leave them to make their own decision in buying goods. It is fairly difficult to say everyone is swayed by advertising and buy goods impulsively. However, in sensitive area of businesses such as toy industries, it may be necessary to ban advertising to those children as they have not got enough ability to control themselves or to know what they need.

▶考官评分:8

题目:

消费品的大量销售反映了广告的威力，而不是社会真正的需求。你是否同意此观点?

译文:

现今，电视上和大街上都有很多广告。有人认为广告促进了产品销售，并且促使人们买一些根本不需要的东西。这种想法可能有一定的道理。比如，在我们国家很多广告公司让一些著名演员或流行歌手来做产品的代言人。于是，人们，尤其是年轻人，就会买他们所喜爱的明星代言的产品，尽管他们可能实际上不需要这些商品。

同时，很多产品在电视屏幕上看起来质量会很好，很不错。因此，人们经常不经深思熟虑就掏钱去买。也就是说，消费者虽然实际上并不需要，但是一看完广告，他们就容易冲动消费。并且，当很多人由于广告的宣传买了某种商品，其他的人也可能会受此影响跟风，即使这种商品不是社会真正的需求。

但是，这种观点又有很多方面站不住脚。首先，买东西是人们自己做出的决定，广告并不是消费者购买习惯的成因。每个人都有自己的消费习惯。如果收入高，他们完全自己决定买还是不买。因此，我们无法判断产品销量是否反映社会的真实需求。另外，假设消费者可支配的收入有限，人们就会尽量安排好花费，他们不可能简单地被那些广告左右。

总之，鉴于消费者各有自己的看法，并对产品质量有自己的判断，买东西的时候还是他们自己做决定比较好。我们很难说每个人都会受到广告左右而冲动消费。而在一些比较敏感的商品上，比如玩具行业，可能需要明令禁止针对儿童的广告，因为他们自控能力不强，也不知道自己想要什么。

87. 广告对孩子的影响

Topic:

In some countries, advertisers persuade children to buy some goods, such as snacks, toys, and other goods. As for this phenomenon, parents object such practice on children. But some advertisers claim that there is useful information in these advertisements. Discuss both views and give your opinion.

Sample Answer

It is a common phenomenon that an overwhelming number of advertisements regard children as the target group, and persuade them, especially their parents to buy clothes, toys and even some luxuries. Urgently, this advertising means needing a thorough examination as for its justification.

There is no doubt that such advertisements exert a repercussion on children's family. Generally speaking, children can influence the family's purchasing orientation, which is best illustrated in Chinese families where the family planning is strictly pursued. Due to this national policy in China, and adults unwilling to have more kids, children are usually spoilt and every need, even seemingly unreasonable ones, will be satisfied by their parents. Under such circumstances, some manufacturers take advantage of children's inexperience and impulsion, designing fancy advertisements to draw their attention and even cheat kids, which will drag families under unbearable economic burden.

The side representing the interests of manufacturers and advertising agencies, of course, insists that there must be advertisement belonging to youngsters. According to their understanding, children can benefit from those specific advertisements just as adults do, and otherwise it is unfair in that they have no other channels to know any commodity information concerning their particular world. As for me, however, the main responsibility children assume at their age group is to acquire as much knowledge as possible, so in the future they can make a substantial contribution to society. If what they pay attention to is about fashion, then their learning efficiency is really doubted.

My view is that in view of children's vulnerable mentality and weighty responsibility, advertisements for children should be limited. Even if we allow some ones, they must be public service advertisements arousing concern for social vulnerable groups rather than encouraging buying.

▶考官评分:8

题目:

在一些国家，广告商说服孩子去买一些商品，例如零食，玩具，和其他商品。至于这种现象，父母反对广告商在孩子身上做文章。但是广告商认为，这些广告里有有用的信息。对双方观点进行讨论并给出你的观点。

译文:

现在有很多广告把孩子作为他们的目标群，并且说服他们，尤其是让他们的父母去买衣服，玩具还有一些奢侈品，这是一个普通的现象。迫切的是，至于广告商的正当理由，需要对这些广告的手段进行一个全面的检查。

无疑的是，这些广告对孩子的家庭有影响。总的来说，孩子可以影响这个家庭的购买倾向，最好的说明就是实施严格计划生育政策的中国家庭。由于中国的这种国家政策，并且家长不愿意多要孩子，孩子通常会被宠坏并且满足每个要求，甚至看来是不合理的要求家长也会满足孩子。在这样的循环下，一些制造商利用儿童的经验不足和冲动，设计奇特的广告去吸引他们的注意力，甚至是欺骗孩子，这样就会给家庭造成难以承受的经济负担。

当然，制造商和广告代理商坚持认为必须有些广告是年轻人看的。根据他们的理解，孩子可以像成年人一样，从这些特定的广告中受益，否则，这是不公平的，因为他们没有其他渠道知道世界任何其他特殊商品的信息。然而，对我来说，孩子在他们成长阶段最主要的责任就是尽可能学到更多的知识，这样他们才可以在未来对社会做更多的贡献。如果他们在时尚方面花太多精力，他们的学习效率也很值得怀疑。

我的观点是，鉴于孩子脆弱的心理和重大的责任，对儿童的广告应该被限制。即使我们允许插播一些广告，他们必须使发布的这些广告能够引起对社会弱势群体的关注，而不是鼓励消费。

88. 媒体影响人们的行为

Topic:

How does modern mass media such as movies or television influence people's behavior?

Sample Answer

The impact that modern mass media has had on our daily life, and society in general, is undeniable. Already, it can be seen that western movies are exerting influence on our youthful generations: they grow long hair regardless of their sex, commonly part of which is dyed gold; they wear jeans every season, usually the knees of which are deliberately tattered.

The major means that mass media influences the public is by creating topics of discussion in the society. Mass media offers people (the consumers) issues to talk and think about. Antiwar movies such as *Tears of the Sun* and *All Quiet On The Western Front* among numerous others have been raising many questions. Is any war really to uphold justice? Is it really worthwhile that an individual makes sacrifices to his country, and at the same time ignores his own family or his personal values?

Mass media also shapes our understanding of what is important, and what is not important. The "important" issues are to be found on the first pages of the newspaper or at the beginning of a television program. The "unimportant" stories are the ones that are not being told at all. The "not very important" stories are probably very short and hidden in the last pages. Even though there are critical thinking individuals in any society, they are a definite minority; the public in whole indeed lack the skills of critical thinking, and therefore they are often led by the media.

In brief, mass media, by offering topics and affecting the ways in which we discuss "the important issues", has a strong influence on our perception of the truth, of the world or of the structure of our society. We have to admit that it has a role in our lives as a source of information, experiences, entertainment.

▶考官评分:8

题目:

电影或电视等现代媒体如何影响大众的行为?

译文:

现代大众传媒对我们的日常生活和整个社会的影响是不可否认的。我们已经看到西方电影对年轻一代的影响：他们留长头发而不再在意是什么性别，而且部分头发被染成金黄色；他们无论什么季节都穿牛仔裤，通常膝盖处还故意弄破。

大众传媒影响人们的主要方式是创造社会中讨论的话题。媒体为人们提供问题去谈论和思考。反战电影如《太阳之泪》和《西线无战事》等曾带给人们很多思考：每场战争都是正义的吗？一个人真的值得为了国家利益而忽略自己的家庭和个人价值吗？

大众传媒也形成了我们对于“什么重要，什么不重要”的理解。“重要”的事件通常被放在报纸的头版或者新闻节目的开头，“不重要”的事件甚至不提，“不是很重要”的通常特别短并且藏在最后一页。即使社会上有个人评论家，但他们一定是少数。总体上讲大众缺乏评判能力，因此他们往往被媒体牵着走。

简而言之，大众媒体在提供话题和影响我们讨论“重要”话题的思路时，对人们关于真理世界或社会结构的感知有巨大的影响。我们必须承认传媒作为信息、经历、娱乐的来源，在我们生活中所起的作用。

范文点评：

范文使用了类似于一边倒结构的形式，写了四段。开头作者介绍背景，并举例阐述媒体对个人的影响，后面用了两段说明媒体的作用，每段都用了一个主题句+几个支持句的写法。条理清晰。最后总结全文并再次点题：“媒体在生活中扮演了重要角色。”整篇文章结构合理，理由充分。语言丰富，并且引用了生动的例子来说明问题。所以考官评分为8分。

89. 媒体的不良影响

Topic:

Some information in films, books and on the Internet has bad influence on young people and even on society. What are these bad influences and what should we do to prevent them?

Sample Answer

Nowadays with the development of globalization media has a more and more important status in spread and communication. However, some drugs of western culture are also spread into China, just like the flies in the fresh air, and they have great blights on the juvenile.

First of all, the x-rated films affect the juvenile a lot. The erotic pictures are contaminating the children's pure mind. This is a poison to their lovely lives. Secondly, the TV plays violent movies which lead the juvenile to go to the wrong way of their lives. In the recent years, if you open your TV set, many violent movies will meet your eyes everywhere. Since children's feeling is fragile, they cannot undergo such fierce impact. Thirdly, it seems that bad news dominates the headlines of all kinds of media. There is no doubt that the juvenile who read these magazines will have a wrong worldview.

To keep our juvenile away from such ill factors and let them grow in a good environment, the government should take the following measures. Firstly, examine the movies imported carefully and limit the degrees strictly. Then tell people which kind of movie the juvenile cannot see. In the meantime forbid the unhealthy magazines and books' issue. Secondly, produce more programs which are good to juvenile on TV. They need salubrious programs and they need their own programs. Thirdly, to improve the education of juvenile not only teaches them knowledge on science and technology, but also tells them how to face difficulties. Let them become an outstanding and moral talent.

In a word, there are still many disadvantages in the media and in our society, to which we must pay great attention. If we obviate them in proper ways, I believe, tomorrow will be better.

▶考官评分:8

题目:

电影，书籍和网络中的一些信息对年轻人乃至社会产生了不良的影响。这些不良影响是什么？我们应该做些什么避免这些不良影响？

译文:

随着全球化的发展，媒体在信息传播和通信方面地位越来越重要。然而，一些西方的文化也蔓延到了中国，就像新鲜空气中的苍蝇，并且这些文化对青少年影响很大。

首先，色情电影极大地影响了青少年。色情图片污染了孩子们纯洁的心灵。这对他们可爱的生命来说是毒药。第二，电视上播放的暴力电影引导青少年走上错误的人生道路。在最近几年里，如果你打开电视，很多暴力的电影映入眼帘。因为孩子的感情是脆弱的，所以他们不能够忍受这种强烈的影响。第三，现在看起来坏消息主宰了各种媒体的头条。毫无疑问，那些看了这些杂志的青少年将会有一种错误的世界观。

为了让我们的青少年远离这些不利因素，并且让他们在一个好的环境里生活，政府应该采取以下措施：首先，仔细检查进口电影，严格限制影片的级别，然后告诉人们哪种电影青少年不能看。同时也禁止那些不健康的杂志和书籍。其次，拍摄更多的适合青少年的节目并在电视上播放。他们需要有益于健康的节目，而且他们需要自己的节目。第三，改善青少年的教育不仅教他们在科学和技术方面的知识，而且告诉他们如何去面对困难。让他们成为杰出的有道德的人才。

总之，在我们的社会和媒体中仍然存在着很多不利因素，对于这些问题我们必须高度关注。如果我们用合适的方式去解决这些问题，明天将会更美好。

范文点评:

范文使用了类似于对称式结构的形式，写了四段。开头作者介绍背景，引起了下文；第二段分三点说明不好的信息对年轻人的危害；第三段提出了三个解决方案，最后总结全文。整篇文章结构合理，理由充分，语言丰富，并未拘泥于模板式句型。

90. 负面新闻

Topic:

News editors decide what to broadcast on television and what to print in newspapers. What factors do you think influence these decisions? Do we become used to bad news? Would it be better if more good news were reported?

Sample Answer

The mass media, such as TV and newspapers, are the windows through which the public looks at what changes are taking place around the world. As for editors, it is really an important, but hard job to select the main news events from the hundreds of updated current items on behalf of their audience or readers, when many factors need to be considered in making such choices.

First of all, the news should report the latest developments as soon as possible and editors react accordingly. What most people are concerned about is themselves and their immediate environment rather than events occurring on other distant continents, so editors also tend to present audiences with more local news. Finally, significant and unusual events are most newsworthy in the eyes of editors.

On this last point, editors seem to display a preference for "bad" news over "good" news, because bad news is more uncommon and abnormal. Good weather is just not news, but natural disasters like floods and earthquakes, and their casualties are another selling point. Therefore, editors frequently seek to base their headlines on something appalling, such as disasters. They have done this so much that we audiences have become used to this kind of reporting.

What is presented to audiences and readers directly determines what attitudes they hold towards the world. Reporting too much bad news has many negative effects, such as scaring the public and contributing to their pessimism and sense of insecurity. There is no doubt that increasing the number of good news reports would be advisable and would help to foster a more constructive and optimistic view of the world.

▶考官评分:8

题目:

新闻编辑们决定电视和报纸报道的内容，你认为哪些因素影响他们的决定？我们已经习惯于看坏消息了吗？报道更多的正面消息是不是更好呢？

译文:

大众传媒（如电视和报纸）是公众了解世界变化的窗口。编辑的工作既重要又艰苦。他们要在数以百计的最新事件中为公众和读者选出主要新闻，同时还要考虑许多其他因素。

首先，新闻报道最近发生的事件，编辑也应及时做出反应。大部分人都关心他们身边的事，以及和他们有直接关系的事，不太关心与自己较远的事。所以，编辑要呈现给读者更多的当地新闻。最后，在编辑眼中大事和异常事件的新闻价值更大。

最后一点，编辑似乎对“坏”消息而非“好”消息情有独钟。因为坏消息更不正常，好天气不是消息，但是自然灾害（像洪水、地震和伤亡）就是热点。因此，编辑经常将标题定为令人恐惧的事情，如灾难性的事件。编辑们基本上都是这样做的，作为读者我们已经习惯了这种报道。

读者读到的内容直接决定了他们对相应事件所持有的观点。报道过多的负面新闻，就让大家感到悲观和不安全。毫无疑问，增加正面新闻的数量会让人有一种乐观的建设性的世界观，这也是应该被鼓励的。

范文点评:

范文使用了类似于一边倒结构的形式，写了四段。开头作者介绍背景，引起了下文，后面用两段说明影响编辑决定的因素，每段都有一个主题句，并用三到四个支持句进行阐述。并在第三段末回答了题目的第二个问题。最后一段对第三个问题进行回答，并给出了理由。整篇文章结构合理，理由充分，语言丰富，并未拘泥于模板式句型。

91. 媒体报道犯罪细节

Topic:

Some people think the media should not report details of crimes to the public. To what extent do you agree or disagree?

Sample Answer

With the crime rate hovering at high levels, the print media as well as the electronic media dedicate large proportions of their space or airtime to detailed crime coverage. Whether the media should present detailed accounts of crimes has caused serious debate. Many people believe that the news media should stop giving details of crimes. I totally agree with their view.

In the first place, given the mercenary motives behind most detailed crime coverage, it is imperative that we discourage such coverage. The principal purpose of reporters covering criminal acts is to boost newspaper circulations or television ratings. Consequently, much detailed crime coverage is biased or exaggerated. It only serves to leave a multitude of citizens constantly fearful about crime.

In the second place, detailed reports of crimes by the press afford the potential criminals very useful learning materials. Reporting crimes in graphic detail helps those who are in the process of planning some criminal act to perfect their plans. Drawing on the well-documented crime stories in the media, would-be criminals learn how to avoid the mistakes in their crime, which may aggravate the already soaring crime rate.

In the third place, detailed reports of heinous crimes may traumatize the victims of the reported crimes. **The reporters rarely consult the victims before they describe details of horrific crimes to the public.** Hence, such reports become nothing more than an attempt to satisfy the curiosity of some base minds. Without the victims' consent, graphic accounts of crimes may become nightmares to them.

In summary, detailed crime coverage in the media undermines our lives in several ways. I firmly believe if such reports continue to go uncontrolled, it will exert even more baneful influence on individuals, communities and societies.

▶考官评分:8

题目:

一些人认为媒体不能报道犯罪的细节给公众。对此观点你是否同意?

译文:

伴随着犯罪率的居高不下，平面媒体和电子媒体都用大量版面或者时间来报道犯罪的细节。媒体是否应该报道犯罪的细节引发了激烈的争论。许多人认为新闻媒体必须停止报道犯罪的细节。我完全同意这种观点。

首先，考虑到深度报道犯罪细节的牟利动机，我们就必须制止这类报道。报道犯罪行为的人最主要的目的是促进报纸的销量或者提高电视的收视率，结果很多细节报道都有失偏颇或者夸大其辞。它只会使众多的市民对犯罪越来越恐惧。

第二，新闻的细致报道会给潜在的犯罪分子提供有用的学习材料。对犯罪进行生动细致的报道有助于正在计划犯罪行为的人完善他们的犯罪计划。借鉴在媒体上充分报道的犯罪故事，想犯罪的人可能学到了如何避免犯罪中的失误，可能会使已经很高的犯罪率更高。

第三，对于滔天罪行的详细报道可能给报道中的受害者造成精神上的伤害。记者在向公众详细描述了可怕的罪行之前很少征求受害者的意见。因此，这些报道除了尝试满足一些普通人的好奇心之外，什么都不是。如果没有受害者的同意，犯罪的生动记载可能成为他们的噩梦。

总的来说，媒体对于犯罪的详细报道在很多方面影响了我们的生活。我坚信如果这样的报道仍不禁止，这将会对个人、团体和社会造成更严重的影响。

92. 媒体报道名人私生活

Topic:

Many newspapers and magazines feature stories about the private lives of famous people. We know what they eat, where they buy their clothes and who they love. We also often see pictures of them in private situations. Is it appropriate for a magazine or newspaper to give this kind of private information about people?

Sample Answer

Generally, people read newspapers to find out about world current affairs and they read magazines to be entertained. Therefore, one would expect to find articles that feature the private lives of famous people in magazines rather than newspapers. However, nowadays, more and more newspapers include stories like these which are neither informative nor useful.

In my opinion, this type of gossip about people's private lives should not be in newspapers for several reasons. Firstly, for example, the fact that Princess Diana is going out with a sportsman is not important news. Secondly, if newspapers want to publish articles about famous people they should focus on their public events and achievements. In other words, if there is an article about Princess Diana it should be about her works of charity, which will increase public awareness of important problems. In addition, journalists should make sure that they write about the facts only, not rumours. One should be able to rely on newspapers for the actual truth.

Magazines, on the other hand, focus on social news. But I feel it is more acceptable for them to contain some features about famous personalities. In addition to being popular reading, these stories often benefit the stars by giving free publicity to them, thereby helping their careers. However, I also believe that magazine stories should not mention things that are too embarrassing or untrue just to attract people to buy the magazine. Sensational stories, such as these, cause great unhappiness to the people concerned.

In conclusion, I think newspapers should concentrate on real news but magazines can feature some articles on people's private lives.

▶考官评分:8

题目:

一些报纸和杂志报道明星的私生活。我们知道了他们吃什么，去哪儿购物，他们的恋爱情况。我们还经常看到他们的生活照。你认为报纸或杂志应不应该报道明星的私生活?

译文：

一般来说，人们阅读报纸是为了解世界时事，阅读杂志是为了娱乐。因此，人们更希望找到那些报道名人私生活的杂志文章而不是报纸。然而，如今，越来越多的报纸选择刊登明星趣事，从而使报纸失去了信息性和实用性。

在我看来，这种有关私生活的闲话不应该出现在报纸上的原因有以下几个。首先，例如，戴安娜王妃和某个运动员一起外出并不是重要新闻。其次，如果报纸要发布有关名人的文章，就应把重点放在他们的公共活动和取得的成就上。换句话说，如果有一篇关于戴安娜王妃的文章便应该是和她的慈善事业有关的，这将提高公众对重要问题的公共意识。此外，记者应确保他们写的仅仅是事实，而不是谣言。以使人们应该更信赖报纸，因其所报道的是事实。

另一方面，杂志注重社会新闻。但我觉得杂志更适于做一些关于知名人士的专题报道。除了通俗读物外，通过免费宣传这些故事往往使众多明星受益匪浅，从而有助于他们的事业。然而，我还认为，杂志的文章不应该为了吸引人们购买杂志而提及那些令人太过尴尬或不真实的东西。比如说，一些耸人听闻的故事就造成了有关人士的极大不满。

总之，我认为报纸应专注于真正的消息，但杂志可以报道一些关于人们私生活的文章。

93. 电视中的暴力

Topic:

Some programs on TV are full of violence. This is having quite some negative influences on individuals and even on society. How far do you agree or disagree with the statement? Give your reasons.

Sample Answer

With the rapid development of science and technology, television, as a powerful invention in the 20th century, is becoming an indispensable tool in people's life. People can learn about what is happening around the world simultaneously by watching TV. However, at the same time, some programs with shots or scenes of violence begin to flood the TV screens. Young individuals, as well as the whole society, are unavoidably affected. In my point of view, most of these impacts are negative.

To begin with, youngsters will imitate the scenes and actions of violence and crimes in TV programs, thus becoming criminals. No one would ever deny the inclination and ability of the youth to imitate. Seeing such kind of shots, especially when they are exposed to too much of such scenes, they would think that these are commonplace things in real life. As they know little about the law, they won't be able to know that these are crime committing and hence, they will just copy what they see and eventually break the law. There are simply too many such kind of examples in our actual life that we can just save the trouble to list any here.

Likewise, such kinds of programs have negative influence on adults as well. Although adults possess higher ability to distinguish right from wrong and they have a stronger awareness of law, to any person, once he or she is exposed to something too much, he or she will just become numb and will only take it too much for granted. In this way, the seed of danger is sowed. Indeed, many cases of adult crimes were the result of film or TV influences.

After we have discussed the negative influences of such programs on people, their impact on our society is all but too obvious. Because society is made up of people who are negatively influenced, we simply cannot bear to imagine what the entire society will be like. In fact, many real-life cases reveal that a lot of criminals learned how to rob a bank, burglarize a household and even commit a murder from TV. To prevent such things from happening, security department of the government has to hire more policemen to maintain order, thus aggravating the financial burden of the country and the government.

Apparently, scenes and shots of violence in TV programs are indeed harmful to individuals and society; therefore, they should be strictly censored and controlled.

▶考官评分:8

题目:

一些电视节目充满了暴力。这对个人甚至社会造成了很多负面影响。你是否同意这种观点?给出理由。

译文:

随着科学技术的发展，电视作为20世纪的重大发明，正在成为人们生活中不可或缺的工具。通过看电视，人们可以同步知道世界正在发生的事情。但与此同时，带有暴力镜头的节目充斥整个电视屏幕。年轻人以及整个社会不可避免会受此影响。就我而言，多数情况下，这种影响是消极的。

首先，青少年会去模仿电视节目中的暴力与犯罪行为，从而沦为罪犯。谁都不会否认青少年的模仿倾向和能力。他们看到这类镜头，特别是经常看到这类镜头，就会认为这是生活中很普通的事情，加之他们的法律意识淡薄，所以就不会想到这是犯罪，因而就会去模仿，从而触犯法律。现实生活中上有太多此类例子，我们自然不必多说了。

这类节目对成年人也同样具有消极影响。成年人虽然比青少年具有更强的明辨是非的能力和法律意识，然而，对任何人来讲，任何事情，一旦经常接触便会令人变得麻木、不以为然，危害的种子也就悄然埋下了。事实上，很多成年犯罪也是受到了电影或电视节目的影响。

在谈过了此类节目对人的消极影响之后，其对社的影响也就不言而喻了。因为社会是由人组成的。当社会上的人都被消极影响后，整个社会是一个什么状况就不堪想象了。现实的例子显示：许多罪犯就是从电视上了解到如何抢劫银行、如何入室盗窃，甚至如何谋杀的。为了防止此类事情发生，政府安全部门不得不雇佣更多的警察来维持秩序，从而也增加了国家和政府的经济负担。

可见，电视节目里的暴力镜头确实会对个人与社会造成消极影响，因此，应该予以严格审查和控制。

94. 电视影响孩子的创造力

Topic:

Some British families decide not to buy televisions because they influence the development of the creativity of children. What do you think?

Sample Answer

With the rapid development of science and technology, television, as a new invention in the 20th century is becoming very popular in people's life. People can be informed of the latest news and enjoy the colorful programs at home. In my opinion, television will not affect children's creativity as exaggerated.

Firstly, television is the most effective tool to inform children of the latest news and scientific development over the world. Television tells us the recent development of some researches, such as clone technology, genetic breakthroughs, the new computing technology and so on, which can stimulate the imagination of children and encourage them to carry out relevant experiments, making new findings and breakthroughs in their study.

Secondly, some programs like adventures and geography can enlarge children's knowledge of scope. With the emergence of information technology, the knowledge in textbooks cannot satisfy children's curiosity any more. Children need to learn wider knowledge and know more about our world. Programs like adventures can cultivate children's creativity and the ability to tackle difficulty; programs like geography can teach children knowledge about different countries in the world and initiate their aspiration to know about the nature; programs about science can inspire children's interest in science and technology.

However, the improper programs on television sometimes play a negative role in the growth of children. The shots about violence, crimes and pornography contents are making children walk on the criminal road.

To sum up, I believe that television will not influence children's creativity. But meanwhile, the government and the whole society should do their utmost to prohibit the unhealthy contents on TV and provide the children with a clean growing environment.

▶考官评分:8

题目:

一些英国家庭决定不买电视，因为他们认为电视会影响孩子的创造力。你怎么认为?

译文：

随着科技的迅速发展，电视机作为20世纪的新发明现在已经非常普及了。人们可以在家了解到最新的资讯和享受有趣的娱乐。我认为，电视机不会如此夸张地影响到孩子的创造力。

首先，电视机是一种非常有效的工具，它可以告诉孩子们最新的资讯和世界科技的发展。电视告诉我们最新的研究发展，例如克隆技术，遗传学的突破，新的计算机技术等等。这些资讯可以刺激孩子们的想象力以及鼓励他们进行相关的试验，发明新的东西和突破他们自己的学业。

第二，一些像冒险和地理之类的节目可以拓展孩子的知识范围。随着信息技术的出现，书本上的知识就无法满足孩子的好奇心了。孩子需要学习更广泛的知识以便更多的了解这个世界。冒险类的节目可以培养孩子的创造力和解决困难的能力；地理类的节目可以教给孩子们世界上不同国家的知识以及启发他们对大自然的渴望；科学类的节目可以激发孩子对自然科学和工艺技术的兴趣。

然而，一些不适宜的电视节目在孩子的成长过程中产生了消极影响。暴力，犯罪和色情的画面使孩子走向犯罪道路。

总而言之，我认为电视不会影响孩子们的创造力。但与此同时，政府和社会人士都应竭力阻止电视中不健康的节目，以给孩子提供一个健康的成长环境。

95. 电视和网络取代收音机

Topic:

Internet and TV technology develop very quickly nowadays. Some people say that they will take the place of radio. What's your opinion?

Sample Answer

Internet and TV, as the mainstream of media, play a very important role in information transformation. They present a colorful and vivid world in front of us. Some people assert that Internet and TV would take the place of radio in a couple of years. However, facts tell us that each medium has its own advantages and disadvantages. Radio will not retreat from our life.

Admittedly, Internet and TV bring about many conveniences to us. Firstly, Internet and TV can transform information instantly. They can tell us what happened in the world right away with very impressive dynamic pictures. During the 17th World Football Cup, many people watched the games on TV or Internet live. Internet and TV can also tell us the latest development of science and technology and the fashion trend nowadays, which can keep us abreast with the world. Secondly, Internet and TV also play an important educational role. For instance, people can study history, culture, language and cooking skills from some educational programs. Lastly, people can get entertainment from Internet and TV, which are abundant in interesting and exciting electronic games and adventures.

However, we should not neglect the advantages of radio, which is the traditional but efficient medium to the public. **Radio can be installed in various kinds of places, such as bus, car, train, plane and other public places, which can transform information extensively.** Radio only occupies a small space. You can even put your radio in your pocket and listen to it conveniently. Once you turn on your radio, you can always choose the favorite channel. Compared with radio, Internet and television are not so convenient. If you have no access to Internet, maybe, the best choice for you to get information is from radio. Radio is also employed as the main communication facility in wars.

In conclusion, I don't think Internet and TV will take the place of radio, though they enjoy more advantages over radio. Radio is the complementation to Internet, TV and other media. It will play an important role in the future.

▶考官评分:8

题目:

现在网络和电视技术飞速发展，一些人认为他们将取代收音机。你如何认为?

译文:

网络和电视作为主要媒体在信息传递中起着非常重要的作用。网络和电视呈现在我们面前一个多彩而生动的世界。有些人声称，在几年后网络和电视将取代收音机。然而，事实告诉我们，每种媒体都有自己的优点和缺点。收音机是不会从我们的生活中退出的。

不可否认，网络和电视给我们带来了很多的便利。首先，网络和电视能够迅速地传递信息。网络和电视能够迅速地用非常生动的、印象深刻的图片告诉我们世界上发生的事情。在17届世纪杯期间，许多人用电视或网络看到了比赛的现场直播。网络和电视还能够告诉我们科技的最近发展和当代的流行趋势，这能使我们跟上世界的步伐。第二，网络和电视也起到了非常重要的教育作用。比如，人们从一些教育节目中能够学习历史，文化，语言和烹饪技巧。最后，人们能够从网络和电脑上获得娱乐，因为网络和电视上有很多有趣和令人兴奋的电子游戏和冒险故事。

但是，我们不应该忽视收音机的优点，它是传统但是有效的公共传媒。收音机能够被安在各种各样的地方，比如公共汽车上，小汽车上，火车上，飞机上以及其他的一些公共场所，它能够广泛地传递信息。收音机体积小。你甚至可以把收音机放在你的衣兜里非常方便地收听。一旦你打开收音机，你总是能够选择你喜欢的频道。和收音机比较起来，网络和电视就不是这么方便了。如果你不能上网，也许，你最好的获得信息的方式就是从收音机里获得。在战争期间收音机也被用作主要的通讯工具。

总之，我认为尽管网络和电视比收音机有更多的优点，但它们不会取代收音机。收音机是网络，电视和其他媒体的补充。收音机在未来将起到非常重要的作用。

96. 电视和网络取代书籍

Topic:

TV, Internet and radio are very popular nowadays. Some people say that they will replace books and written words as the main sources of information. To what degree do you agree or disagree to this position?

Sample Answer

Internet and TV, as the mainstream of media, play a very important role in information transformation. They present a colourful and vivid world in front of us. Some people assert that Internet and TV would take the place of books in a couple of years. However, facts tell us that each medium has its own advantages and disadvantages. Books will not retreat from our life.

Admittedly, Internet and TV bring many conveniences to us. Firstly, Internet and TV can transform information instantly. They can tell us what happened in the world right away with very impressive dynamic pictures. During the 27th World Football Cup, many people watched the games on TV or Internet live. Internet and TV can also tell us the latest development of science and technology and the fashion trend nowadays, which can keep us abreast with the world. Secondly, Internet and TV also play an important educational role. For instance, people can study history, culture, language and cooking skills from some educational programs on TV or Internet. Lastly, People can get entertainment from Internet and TV, which are abundant in interesting and exciting electronic games and adventures.

However, we should not neglect the importance of books which are very convenient to carry and easy to get. Books are available everywhere, such as in the library, in the book stores, in your pocket or beside your pillow. After a day's work, we can lay on bed relaxing by reading some novels or newspaper. You can read a very interesting story on a train or on plane. TV and Internet would not be that convenient and further, they could cause tiredness sometimes if you sit in front of TV and computer for a very long time.

In conclusion, books are one of the main sources of information and they are very convenient for people to read. Books will not disappear from our life in the future, though TV and Internet have so profound influences in our life.

▶考官评分:8

题目:

现在网络、电视和收音机非常流行，一些人认为它们将取代书籍成为传播信息的主流。你是否同意这种观点?

译文：

因特网和电视，作为媒体的主流，在信息传递中扮演着非常有意义的角色。他们在我们眼前呈现了一个色彩丰富而且生动的世界。有些人声称因特网和电视会在几年之内代替书籍。然而，事实告诉我们每一种媒体都有他们自己的优点和缺点。书籍不会从我们的生活中退出。

不可否认，因特网和电视给我们带来了很多方便。首先，因特网和电视可以在很短的时间里传递信息。他们可以立刻用给人留下深刻印象的生动画面告诉我们世界上发生了什么。在第27届世界杯期间，很多人通过电视或因特网在线来观看比赛。因特网和电视还可以告诉我们最近科学和工业技术的发展以及当今流行趋向，可以让我们与时俱进。其次，因特网和电视还扮演着重要的教育角色。例如，人们可以通过一些电视或因特网上的教育节目学习历史、文化、语言和烹饪技能。最后，人们可以通过使用拥有许多有趣而且刺激的电子游戏和冒险活动的电视与因特网来进行娱乐。

但是，我们不应该忽略书籍非常方便搬运并且在任何地方易于获得的重要性，书籍到处都可以获得，比如在图书馆、在书店、在你的口袋里或在你枕头旁边。完成一天的工作后，我们可以躺在床上读一些小说或报纸来放松。你可以在火车上或在飞机上读到一个非常有趣的故事。电视和因特网不能实现这种便利，如果你长时间地坐在电视或电脑前有些时候会使你疲劳。

综上所述，书籍是一个主要的信息来源，并且它们非常方便让人们去阅读。书籍将来不会从我们的生活中消失，尽管电视和因特网对我们的生活有着非常深远的影响。

第五大类:动物类题目

97. 动物实验

Topic:

Some people hold that we should not use animals in medical experiments. Do you agree or disagree?

Sample Answer

Since human beings existed in the world, animals have always been accompanying us. They are of great help to humans in many aspects. For example, they help a lot in medical experiments. Many people argue that animals should not be used for testing medical techniques and drugs. Others, on the other hand, claim that without animal testing, some patients would suffer or even die from their diseases. Before rendering my opinion, I think it is more important to take a glance at the arguments on both sides.

Those people who strongly believe that we should use animals in experiments have cogent reasons for it. For one thing, animal testing allows scientists to test and create new drugs. It would be cruel that some people die of a disease because there is not enough information about it. For another, at present there are no other better methods to replace animal tests. Therefore, animal tests are still regarded as the only reliable and feasible method. More importantly, animals such as monkeys or rabbits which are used in experiments are easily bred. Furthermore, most countries set standards for animal treatment in tests, and laboratories have regulations to prevent cruelty.

However, further analysis would make it clear that animal testing should be halted. First and foremost, animal tests violate animals' rights. Nothing seems more brutal than taking away a life, no matter it belongs to a man or an animal. Moreover, not all the experiments are reliable. The treatment and drugs which are effective to animals sometimes are useless and even have negative effects on humans. Thirdly, not all the experiments are necessary.

With the development of technology, computer simulation can achieve similar results.

From the above comparison and contrast, anyone can obviously conclude that animals should not be used for testing medical techniques and drugs. As creatures, animals enjoy the same rights as humans. Information from animals does not apply to humans. What is more, other better methods have been discovered to replace animal tests.

▶考官评分:7

题目:

有些人认为我们不应该在医疗实验中使用动物，你是否赞同?

译文:

自人类生活在这个世界上以来，动物就一直陪伴着我们。它们在许多方面对人类有很大帮助。例如，它们在医学实验方面帮助很大。很多人认为动物不应该被用于测试医疗技术和药物。然而，另外一些人认为，没有动物实验，一些病人就会遭罪甚至死于他们所患的疾病。在我发表意见前，我认为先看一下双方的观点更为重要。

那些强烈主张我们应该使用动物实验的人有着令人信服的理由。一则，动物实验能让科学家们测试和发明新药物。一些人死于因对某种疾病没有足够的了解，这是多么残忍的事情。二则，现在还没有更好的方法来替代动物实验。因此，动物试验仍被视为是惟一可靠且可行的方法。更重要的是，在实验中用到的动物像猴子、兔子等很容易饲养。此外，大多数国家都为动物试验制定标准，实验室也有相关规定来防止残忍事情的发生。

然而，进一步的分析使下面观点更加清楚：动物试验应该停止。首先，动物试验侵犯了动物的权利。没有什么比夺走一个生命更加残忍的了，不管它是一个人还是一个动物。而且，不是所有的实验都是必要或可靠的。那些对动物有效的药物和疗法对人有时是没用的，甚至有负作用。第三，不是所有的实验都有必要进行。随着技术的发展，用计算机模拟可以得到相似的结果。

通过比较，任何人都能明显地得出结论：动物不应该被用于医疗实验。做为生物，动物和人享有相同的权利。用动物做实验所获得的信息不一定适用于人类。而且，已经有更好的办法来取代动物实验。

98. 是否应该投资于野生动物的保护

Topic:

Some people think that the amount of time and money spent on the protection of wild animals would be better spent in improving the well-being of humans. To what extent do you agree or disagree?

Sample Answer

Ecology is attracting more attention from a growing number of people in recent years, while some people claim that time and money should be better spent on the human beings instead of wild animals. I disagree with this viewpoint for the following reasons.

First of all, wild animals have equal rights to live better in the world. The whole earth is not lived alone by human beings. Many wild animals might have lived longer than human beings have appeared. With the development of the human economy, the whole environment of the wild animals is deteriorating, which is partially due to humans' intentional catch of the wild animals to make clothing, medicine, decoration or even food. Furthermore, the expansion of the land development reduced the habitat of the wild animals and the emission and pollution of the chemical substances spoiled the normal living conditions of the wild animals. Owing to the above reasons, human beings should be responsible for the wild animals to remedy the harm brought by us, rather than save the time and money for our own use.

In the second place, wild animals are an indispensable part of the balanced nature. To spend time and money on them is for our benefit. On one hand, many wild animals, such as frogs and birds, eat pests to provide a more agreeable environment for humanity; on the other hand, wild animals are crucial part of our food chain. The absence of wild animals will endanger the lives of human beings. In addition, the research into wild animals will make us know more about ourselves and the changes of the ecology.

It's wise to spend time and money on wild animals. Reasonable investment on the wild life will bring lots of knowledge even profits for human beings. Many people visit wild life conservation zones to gain knowledge, to teach their kids, etc, which is advantageous for both wild life and human beings.

▶考官评分:8

题目:

一些人认为将花在保护野生动物上的金钱和时间，用于提高人类的福利，效果将会更好。你是否赞同此观点?

译文:

最近几年，越来越多的人把更多的注意力转移到生态平衡这方面来，然而有些人主张把投入到野生动物上的时间和金钱投入到为人类谋福利方面。我不同意这种观点，原因有以下几点。

首先，在这个世界上野生动物有平等的权力去活得更好。整个地球上不是只有人类单独的生存着。很多野生动物在人类出现之前就已经生活很长时间了。随着社会经济的发展，整个野生动物生存的环境恶化了，一部分原因是由于人们故意捕捉野生动物用来做衣服、药材、装饰品、甚至食用。此外，土地的扩张发展使野生动物的栖息地减少了，并且排放出有污染的化学物质破坏了野生动物正常的生活环境。由于以上的原因，人类应该对自己给野生动物所造成的伤害而担负起补救的责任，而不是将时间和金钱投入到我们自己身上。

其次，野生动物是生态平衡中不可或缺的一部分。花费时间和金钱在它们身上对我们是有益的。一方面，许多野生动物，例如青蛙和鸟类，消灭害虫从而给人类提供了惬意的生活环境。另一方面，野生动物是食物链中至关紧要的一部分。没有野生动物将会威胁到人类的生存。另外，通过对野生动物的研究会让我们对自己和生态环境的变化有更多的了解。

投入时间和金钱在野生动物上是明智的。对保护野生动物进行合理的投资会使人们学到很多知识，甚至受益。许多人到野生动物保护区参观调查来获取知识，再教给他们的孩子等等，这对于野生动物和人类双方都是有益的。

99. 保护野生动物是否浪费

Topic:

Wild animals have no place in the 21st century, and the protection is a waste of resource. To what extent do you agree or disagree?

Sample Answer

As is known to all, the big contradiction between the limitation of land and the rapidly increasing demand for it escalates an alarming headache of human beings. To improve the situation, some people suggest we instantly give up protecting wild animals, the reason for which, according to them, is simply that they believe there will be no spare places for the wild animals as their shelters or habitats in the 21st century, and thus it is nothing but a waste of resources to carry out the protection. As far as I am concerned, the so-called "suggestion" is extremely ridiculous and has no point at all.

On one hand, wild animals are part of nature around us and to be exact a most necessary part. They are destined to become extinct without our protection, as a consequence of which, the balance of nature will undoubtedly be destroyed and it won't be long before we receive the great punishment that resulted from that. Since the old hurt on us is to be healed, why do some of us still prefer to run risk of being revenged again to break the balance of nature? Never stumble by a single stone twice, never! Remember wild animals are our intimate and faithful friends, and we humankind ought to get along with them under any circumstances.

On the other hand, we have been trying every effort to settle the annoying problem, or at least to prevent the situation from deteriorating. And we have sufficient confidence and capability to fulfill the task, no matter how difficult or sophisticated it may be. Therefore, we can ensure that wild animals will not lose their shelters or habitats, even if in the 21st century.

In general, I stick to the position that it's everybody's responsibility to enforce the protection of wild animals instead of reducing or even stopping it. Similarly, we should deal with such a crucial problem actively and bravely, instead of in a negative way.

▶考官评分:8

题目:

在21世纪，野生动物没有足够的生存空间，保护野生动物是一种资源浪费。你是否同意这种观点?

译文:

众所周知，有限的土地和对土地需求的日益增长之间的矛盾使人们变得越发地担忧。为了改善这种状况，一些人建议我们应该立即停止对野生动物的保护。因为他们认为在21世纪将不会有多余的空间来当作野生动物的庇护所或栖息地，所以对野生动物实施保护只是浪费资源。而对于我来说，这些所谓的建议是极其地荒谬，没有任何意义。

一方面，野生动物是我们所生存的自然界中的一部分，甚至可以说是必不可少的一部分。如果没有人类的保护，它们注定会灭绝，毫无疑问世界平衡将遭到破坏，人类不久也会因此受到很大的惩罚。既然旧伤将愈合，我们为什么还要冒着被报复的危险去破坏生态平衡呢? 永远不要被同一块石头绊倒两次! 切忌，野生动物是我们亲密和忠实的朋友，无论在任何情况下我们都应该与它们和谐相处。

另一方面，我们已经尽力去解决这个令人烦恼的问题或者至少防止情况恶化 。不管问题多复杂和困难，我们都有足够的信心和能力去完成这项任务。因此我们可以确保即使到了21世纪，野生动物都不会失去它们的家园。

总之，我坚持认为每个人都有责任去加强对野生动物的保护，而不是去减少或是不保护它们。同样，我们应该积极勇敢地去处理这个至关紧要的问题，而不应该采取消极的做法。

100. 动物园是否有用

Topic:

A zoo has no useful purpose. Do you agree or disagree?

Sample Answer

Perhaps one of the most blameworthy factors that make some people raise their eyebrows to zoos and criticize that "A zoo has no useful purpose" is the exorbitant price of maintaining them. However, it is too hasty to say so, since most zoos have their significance, both educational and scientific.

Modern zoos are designed to make learning about animals an interesting and enjoyable experience. They provide visitors with the chance to see rare creatures from many different parts of the globe, offering a valuable learning experience in an urban world. Meanwhile, most zoos provide educational programs for a wide range of ages. A visit to a zoo provides opportunity for children to see and touch animals. For schoolchildren, many zoos conduct classes or day trips that focus on different aspects of animal biology and the impacts of humans on animal life.

Modern zoos can also function as a sanctuary for endangered animals, therefore helping maintain ecosystem. An example of a successful reintroduction to the wild is a kind of Asian deer which was native to marshlands in northeast China before its habitat was destroyed more than 800 years ago. Since that time the species has been bred in zoos in China and later in Europe. In 1985 four deer were released to the wild where they are now breeding successfully.

On the other hand, experts warn against placing too much reliance on zoos as biological "arks". More significantly, the number of species that zoos can protect is strictly limited. Today's zoos are home to no more than a few thousand species. During the 21st century, zoo experts will face even harder decisions about which species they can afford to save.

▶考官评分:8

题目:

动物园没什么用，你是否同意这个观点?

译文:

一些人对动物园持有怀疑的态度，而且批评“动物园基本没什么用”，可能动物园最应该接受谴责的一个因素是它需要高价来维持。无论如何，这样说还是太草率了，因为大多数的动物园仍然具备教育和科学的重要意义。

现代动物园的建立旨在使了解动物成为一次有趣且愉快的经历。动物园为游览者提供了一个机会来认识世界各地的珍稀物种，为在城市生活的人们提供了宝贵的学习经历。同时，大多数的动物园还为各年龄段的人提供教育节目。游览动物园给孩子们提供一个观看并触摸动物的机会。很多动物园为那些不同年龄段的中小学生举办讲座，或者组织那些以关注动物生物学的不同方面和人类对动物生活的影响为主题的一日游。

现代的动物园还能够成为那些濒临灭绝动物的一个避难所，从而保护生态系统。一个成功的例子是一种亚洲鹿重返家园，在800年前，也就是它们的栖息地被毁坏以前，它们原产于中国东北的沼泽地区。从那以后，这个物种就在中国以及随后在欧洲的动物园中繁育。在1985年有四头这种鹿放归自然，现在它们在野外已经成功繁衍生息了。

另一方面，科学家们也警告不要在动物园上寄予太大的希望，或把它看成是生物的“方舟”。更值得关注的是，能在动物园被保护的动物毕竟是非常有限的。今天的动物园只是不足一千种动物的家。在21世纪，动物园的专家们将会在他们到底能保护多少动物物种的问题上做出一个艰难的抉择。

101. 动物园是否应关闭

Topic:

Many people believe that zoos should be closed because it is cruel to keep animals locked up. Moreover, zoos do not play a positive role in society. Do you agree or disagree?

Sample Answer

There are two sides to every story, and that includes zoos. We must admit that to imprison animals in such small spaces is something that goes against their nature. We can also say that zoos, unlike big shopping malls that can make large amounts of cash flow all the time, are burning money every day. But you imagine a decent city without a zoo?

On one hand, zoos provide recreation and refreshment for fatigued urban dwellers. People relax when appreciating an elegant swan or a playful chimpanzee. This kind of relaxation is something that can not be obtained through modern entertainment means, such as karaoke or discos. It's a purely natural sensation.

On the other hand, zoos are important to small children. If zoos are places of recreation for adults, then they must be dreamland for small children. Do you remember the first time you were taken to a zoo? I'm sure it was something you'll remember all your life. Small children learn how to protect animals through observing them and this will also add to their knowledge something they will never acquire in the classroom.

Finally, viewed from the scientific aspect, zoos are crucial for protecting certain rare species from extinction. For instance, the survival rate of babies of giant pandas increases when they are raised in advanced facilities in zoos. Zoos also assist research facilities to carry out harmless scientific research on animals' living patterns.

In a word, we should pay more attention to our zoos instead of closing them. This will be beneficial for our planet, our descendants and ourselves.

▶考官评分:9

题目:

许多人认为动物园应该关闭，因为把动物关起来是非常残忍的，并且动物园在社会上并没有起到积极的作用。你是否同意这个观点？

译文:

任何事物都具有双面性，包括动物园。我们必须承认把动物关在如此狭小的空间里是有违它们的自然习性。我们也可以说动物园不像大商场可以一直有大量的现金流动。但是你能想象一个大城市里没有动物园行吗?

一方面，动物园是为城市居民提供娱乐和消除疲劳的场所。人们在欣赏优美的天鹅或者可爱的黑猩猩时会感到放松。这种放松是不能通过现代娱乐方式获得的，例如卡拉OK或者迪斯科。这是一种纯粹的自然感受。

另一方面，动物园对小朋友的意义非同小可。如果动物园是成年人的娱乐场所，那么对小朋友而言一定是梦幻境界。你还记得第一次跟大人去动物园吗？我敢肯定你一生都会记得这件事。小孩子通过观察动物学会如何去保护它们，也能丰富他们的知识，而这样的知识是他们在课堂上学不到的。

最后，依据科学的观点，动物园在保护濒临灭亡的稀有物种方面确实起到了至关重要的作用。例如，大熊猫出生在有着先进设备的动物园里，存活率上升。动物园有助于研究机构对动物的生活习性进行无害的科学研究。

总之，我们应该更加关注动物园而不是将其关闭。这将对我们的地球、子孙后代和我们自己都有益。

102. 动物作为食物

Topic:

Some people think killing animals for food is cruel and unnecessary while other people think it is essential for daily diet. What do you think about the both issues?

Sample Answer

Speaking of the attitude towards killing animals, different individuals may have different reactions and their personal opinions also vary from person to person.

Some people stand against the cruel behaviour, which is not only rather foolish but also quite unnecessary to them. From my point of view, killing animals for human needs is indeed an unmerciful thing and may sound a little bit selfish. Every coin has two sides, however, as is often the case with this stupid-appearing attitude we referred to above. Obviously killing animals can bring us large amounts of useful things to satisfy our basic requirements, such as shoes made of animals' skin, food made from their flesh, etc. So it is incorrect to deny the necessity of the behaviour thoroughly and completely.

Nevertheless, neither do I agree with others whose attitude is just opposite and based on the saying that animals' flesh is necessary to human beings. Frankly speaking, I feel sick of this view because it reveals that the view-holders are likely to commit anything for their own interests regardless of its bad influences. We should not kill animals for the only aim of enjoying meat, for it sounds to me more an excuse than a reasonable explanation. As technology has been developing rapidly, artificial meat becomes available, which makes the excuse sound more insensible.

To sum up, I suggest we keep the killing of animals under strict and tight control, and more importantly try to turn out more products to replace using animals for our daily needs.

▶考官评分:8

题目:

一些人认为杀死动物作为人类的食物非常残忍，并且没有必要，而也有些人认为这是日常饮食必不可少的，从这两个方面谈谈你的想法。

译文:

说到对于杀死动物的态度，不同的人可能会有不同的反应，他们个人的观点也会因人而异。

一些人反对这种残忍的行为，他们认为这种方式不仅相当愚蠢而且没有必要。按照我的观点来看，为了人类的需要而杀死动物，确实是不慈悲的事情，并且可能听起来有点自私。凡事都有利必有弊，然而，我们经常可以看到上面提到的这种愚蠢外衣下的态度表现。很显然杀死动物能够带给我们很多有用的东西，以便满足我们基本的需求，例如：用动物的外皮制造的鞋子、用动物的肉做食品等等。所以，彻底完全地否定这种行为的必要性是不正确的。

然而，我也不同意其他那些态度正好相反的人的观点，因为他们说动物的肉是人类的必需品。坦率地讲，我对这种观点很反感，因为它揭示出这种观点的人倾向于为了他们自己的利益可以牺牲任何东西，而不顾因此所带来的不良影响。我们不应该仅仅以为了享用它们的肉为由来杀死动物，因为这对我来说听起来更像一个借口，而不是一个合理的解释。随着科技的迅速发展，有可能生产人造肉，这就使得这种理由更讲不通。

总之，我建议我们对所杀动物的数量进行严格紧密的控制，更重要的是开发更多的产品代替动物来满足我们的日常需求。

103. 动物是衣服和食物的来源

Topic:

Some people think that animals should be treated as friends. Yet others only consider animals as sources of food and clothing. What is your opinion?

Sample Answer

There is a growing tendency nowadays for some people to treat animals as living meat and walking fur. This leads to the cruel slaughter of animals all over the world every year. Yet, in my opinion, instead of killing animals human beings should treat them as their friends.

In the first place, it is an undeniable fact that animals play a vital role in maintaining the subtle balance of the earth's ecosystem. The lack of this essential part will bring about the destruction of the whole world. Therefore, to some extent, killing animals is equal to digging our own graves.

Secondly, for thousands of years, many animals have given loyal service to humans. Pigeons convey messages in wartime, and dogs help to detect crime. Even pigs, which many people think are the most stupid animals, are used in the battle against drugs. There is no doubt that our lives would be far less convenient without a little help from our animal friends.

Last but not least, animals also help humans in a spiritual way. There is nothing better than keeping a cat or a dog if you want your kids to be more independent and responsible. It is also noted that senior citizens live longer if they keep pets after their retirement.

To sum up, animals are human beings' friends. Those who regard animals as merely a source of food and clothing should at least bear one thing in mind: Being kind to animals is being kind to ourselves. Therefore, for our own future benefits, please treat animals with love and care.

▶考官评分:8

题目:

一些人认为动物是人类的朋友，然而其他人却认为动物是人类的衣食来源，你的观点是什么?

译文:

现在越来越多的人把动物看作是鲜活的肉和会行走的皮毛。这就导致了每年在世界各地都会有残忍猎杀动物事件的发生。然而，我认为，人们不应该杀戮动物，而应当像朋友般对待他们。

首先，动物在维护地球生态系统微妙的平衡上扮演着至关重要的角色，这是一个不可否认的事实。缺乏这个重要的部分将致使整个世界遭到破坏。因此，在一定程度上，杀害动物就好似在自掘坟墓一样。

其次，数千年以来，动物都为人类提供忠实的服务。鸽子在战争时期传递信息，狗帮助人们侦查犯罪。甚至猪，很多人认为是最愚蠢的动物，都可以在战争的时候对抗药物。毫无疑问，如果没有我们的动物朋友，我们生活的便利程度将会大打折扣。

最后，动物也可以在精神上帮助人类。如果你希望你的孩子更加独立和负有责任感，没有比养小猫、小狗更好的方法了。而且据说退休的老年人饲养宠物可以长寿。

总而言之，动物是人类的朋友。那些把动物仅仅看作是食物和衣服来源的人至少应该记住：善待动物就是善待自己。因此，为了我们将来自身的利益着想，请给予动物爱和关怀。

104. 饲养宠物对居民的利与弊

Topic:

Some people are of the opinion that keeping pets such as cats and dogs is beneficial to city dwellers. What do you think?

Sample Answer

Some people are critical of keeping pets, such as cats and dogs in cities, claiming that there are simply not even open spaces for them to roam freely. They also argue that pets pollute living environments. However, I am of the opinion that owning pets is rewarding to city dwellers.

First of all, they could act as companions and stress relievers and in some cases help to foster family cohesion. While they are traditionally associated with family-type households, pets are just as important to households without children; indeed they are often surrogates for children in childless families. **This applies particularly to the elderly, who usually form every close associations with their pets. In an era when the population is aging and more people are living alone, pets can provide valuable relief from loneliness.**

In addition, pets are particularly important for children. A pet in the family keeps kids in touch with a more natural, animal world. Seeing a pet give birth brings understanding of the naturalness of childbirth, and seeing a pet die helps a child to cope with sorrow. **Learning to care for a pet helps a child to grow up into a loving adult who feels responsible towards those dependent on him.** Rightly we teach children to be kind to their pets. They should learn, too, that pets are good for human beings.

People living in the countryside may have access to many types of domestic animals such as cows, horses, and sheep. This is simply not true in cities. Pets can provide a limited opportunity for city dwellers to get in touch with nature. This helps people to become more environmentally conscious.

All in all, I strongly feel that those living in cities can benefit from having pets.

▶考官评分:8

题目:

有些人认为饲养宠物，比如猫和狗，对城市居民有好处，你的观点是什么?

译文:

有些人不赞成在城市里饲养宠物，比如猫和狗。他们认为没有空地让这些宠物自由地溜达，而且这些宠物会污染生活环境。然而，我认为饲养宠物对市民有好处。

首先，宠物可以陪伴人们，减轻人们的压力，有时还可以增进家庭的团结。在传统观念上，宠物被看作是家庭的一员。对没有孩子的家庭来说，宠物就是孩子的替代者，它和孩子一样重要。尤其是对老年人，他们和宠物非常亲密。在老龄化日益严重的时代，更多的人都得独自生活，宠物可以把他们从孤独中解脱出来 。

此外，宠物对孩子而言也很重要。家里养宠物可以让孩子们和更自然的动物世界接触。看到宠物生产可以帮助孩子了解宝宝的自然出生，看到宠物死亡也能帮助孩子应对悲伤。通过照顾宠物可以让孩子在长大后变成一个有爱心的人，也让他们懂得对每一个依赖于他们的人都要有责任心。我们应该教育孩子好好对待宠物，也应该让他们懂得宠物对人类是有好处的。

在乡村生活的人会更容易接触到各种家禽，如牛、马、羊。在城市中却并非如此。饲养宠物是城市居民接触自然的一个有限的机会。这也会帮助人们树立环保意识。

总之，我坚决认为饲养宠物对城市居民是非常有好处的。

范文点评：

典型的辩论型题目，文章运用"一边倒"结构，写了五段，开头段使用"欲扬先抑"的写法，先陈述了对方的观点及两个理由，然后提出自己的观点："我认为饲养宠物对市民有好处"，文章分三个理由段论证，前两个理由段由1句概述和4个支持句组成，层层递进，理由充分，从家庭成员关系和孩子的教育两个方面论证自己的观点，第四段又从客观上——城市居民接触自然机会有限再次阐述自己的观点，结尾段再次重申观点。在语言上，多次使用高分词汇，句型变换多样，表达恰如其分。

105. 饲养宠物是否浪费

Topic:

In Western countries, people spend a lot of money on their pets. Some people think this is a waste of money, and argue that pets are dirty and dangerous. Do you agree or disagree?

Sample Answer

In many Western homes people keep dogs or cats or some other kinds of pets. While this does involve some expense in terms of good food and medical treatment, there are still many advantages to keeping a pet.

First of all, pets are good companions. This is especially important for people who live alone and for older people who do not go out much. Some pets can also help to protect the house from thieves. Secondly, dogs and cats like to play and can give hours of amusement to children and adults. Taking care of a pet also helps children to develop responsible attitudes and to learn about nature. Finally, the actual expense of keeping a pet is not that high, and they can eat the leftovers of family meals.

Some people claim pets are dirty. I don't think this is totally true. Responsible pet owners keep their pets clean and healthy so they are not smelly. People also say that certain pets, like large dogs, can be dangerous. There have been cases of dogs attacking and seriously injuring small children. However, these cases are uncommon and are the result of bad owners. These people either don't train their dogs properly or actually encourage them to be aggressive. So, the problems of pets being unclean or dangerous are in fact the problems of the owners, not the pets themselves.

To sum up, there are more advantages than disadvantages to keeping a pet, especially for lonely people and children. In most cases, therefore, the cost is justified.

▶考官评分:8

题目:

在西方国家，人们花大量的金钱在宠物上，一些人认为这样做是一种浪费，并认为宠物很脏，很危险。你是否同意这种观点?

译文:

在很多西方人的家里，人们经常养狗养猫或是其他种类的宠物。尽管用在食物和医疗方面的费用很昂贵，然而养宠物仍然有很多好处。

首先，宠物是人们很好的伙伴。这一点对于那些独居或年迈而不能经常出门的人来说特别重要。宠物还能看家防盗。第二，狗和猫喜欢玩耍，还会给小孩和成人带来一些快乐。照顾小动物可以培养孩子的责任感，同时认识自然。最后，养宠物的费用可以不必花费太多，因为宠物可以吃家里的剩菜剩饭。

有些人坚称宠物很脏。我认为这不完全正确。负责任的宠物主人会坚持管理宠物使其清洁健康，所以宠物不会发出臭味。人们也指出某些宠物，比如某些大型犬可能很危险。其例证是大型犬攻击小孩使其受到重伤。然而，这些情况很罕见，主要是由一些不负责任的主人造成的。这些人要么没有适当地训练它们，要么鼓励它们养成好斗的本性。所以宠物不干净或是很危险，其实问题在于宠物的主人，而不是宠物本身。

概括起来，养宠物是利大于弊，尤其是对孤独的人和小孩。因此，在大多数情况下，养宠物的花费还算合理。

范文点评:

典型的辩论型题目，文章采用“一边倒”结构，开头段简单介绍背景，提出自己的观点：养宠物有很多好处。分两个理由段论证，第一个理由段作者从正面阐述了养宠物有好处的三个理由，第二个理由段作者采用反驳对方观点的写法再次论证自己的观点，这是一个加分点，结尾段作者重申理由，整篇文章，结构合理，有理有据，句型多样化，很少使用模板句型。

第六大类：环境资源交通类题目

106. 交通拥挤

Topic:

Traffic jam is a problem in most cities all around the world at present. What causes the problem? Make some recommendations.

Sample Answer

Along with the rapid development of urban traffic, certain problems have arisen, one of which is the traffic jam. It has become common to see passengers and drivers having to wait in long lines of buses and cars during the rush hours. From my own perspective, there are several reasons for this problem.

First, the number of vehicles is increasing much more rapidly than the building of roads. In big metropolitan cities, as the number of traffic vehicles is soaring up recently, the development of road system seems rather slow relatively. No sooner has a new road been completed and opened to public traffic than it is crowded with all kinds of vehicles. In addition, there seem to be too many private cars and not enough public buses. In most cases, a car carries only one or two people, while it occupies almost half the space a bus does.

Another reason is that many people, including drivers, pedestrians and cyclists do not obey traffic rules properly, especially at busy intersections. For example, some people drive after drinking, some drive without a license, some run the red light and some surpass the speed limit. All these things undoubtedly worsen the grave situation.

In view of the seriousness of this problem, effective measures must be taken before things get worse. On one hand, there is a need for the government to invest more money in the building of new roads. On the other hand, we should give priority to the development of public transportation and impose restrictions on the use of private cars in urban areas. At the same time, it is of great importance that stricter traffic rules and regulations should be issued to strengthen traffic control.

▶考官评分:8

题目:

交通拥堵是当今世界很多城市存在的问题。造成这个问题的原因是什么？给出一些建议。

译文:

随着城市交通的迅速发展，出现了某些问题，其中之一就是交通堵塞。在高峰期，乘客和司机不得不在排着长队的公交车和小汽车里等候，这已变得司空见惯。在我看来，出现这个问题有以下几个原因。

首先，交通工具数量增长的速度比道路建设的速度更快。在一些大城市，近年来交通车辆的数量急剧增加，而道路交通系统的发展就相对比较缓慢了。一条新公路刚一建完就向公共交通开放，各种各样的交通工具便蜂拥而至。而且，私家车似乎太多而公交车却没那么多。在多数情况下，一个小汽车仅仅载一、两个人，而它却占用了几乎半个公交车的空间。

另外一个原因是，许多人包括司机、行人和骑自行车的人并不完全遵守交通规则，尤其是在拥挤的十字路口。例如，有些人酒后驾驶，有些人无照驾驶，有些人闯红灯，有些人超速行驶。这些无疑使已经很严峻的形势进一步恶化了。

考虑到这个问题的严峻性，在事情进一步恶化前必须采取有效的措施。一方面，政府应该投入更多的资金修建新的公路。另一方面，我们应该优先发展公共交通，限制城市中私家车的使用。同时，发布更严格的交通规章制度以加强对交通的控制是非常重要的。

107. 现代科技污染环境且消耗能源

Topic:

Some people hold that the development of modern technology leads to environmental pollution and energy shortage. Do you agree or disagree?

Sample Answer

Science and technology have been developing rapidly during the past ten years. Their development has brought lots of benefits to mankind. Science has changed so much of today's world. Due to the development of technology, we now live safer, more comfortable and convenient lives. However, it seems quite clear to me that while progress has brought us many time-saving machines, it has also brought us environmental pollution and energy shortage.

The development of technology has been responsible for pollution. **Modern industry, as well as modern traffic conveniences, has created a serious problem of air contamination.** The "green house effect" is now threatening the existence of mankind. Since the population of the earth is increasing very fast, humans must make the earth support the increasing population. This has made it necessary for agriculture and industry to develop rapidly. Such a rapid development produces more and more waste, which goes into the water, the soil and the air. Some of it is made harmless. However, where there is too much of it, the poisonous waste may do great harm to the things around the people.

With the development of technology, the amount and range of materials taken has increased. It is estimated that this trend will continue in the years to come. However, natural resources are not inexhaustible and some resources are already nearly used up. For example, the end of the world's fuel is already within sight. Such essential daily items as water is in short supply in many parts of the world. With the expansion of industrialization, requirement for energy all over the world is on the rise. Consequently, we have a great need for energy because of the rapid growth of our economy.

From what I mentioned above, I believe that it is the development of science and technology that leads to the pollution of environment and shortage of energy.

▶考官评分:7

题目:

有些人认为技术进步导致了环境污染与能源紧缺。你是否赞同此观点?

译文:

在过去十年中科学技术迅速发展。它的发展给人们带来了很多好处。科学在很大程度上已经改变了当今世界。因为科技的发展,我们现在过着更安全、更舒适、更方便的生活。然而,我认为虽然科技进步带给我们很多省时的机器,它同时也造成了环境污染和能源短缺。

科技的发展要对污染负责。现代工业和现代交通便利已经造成了严重的空气污染。"温室效应"正威胁着人类的生存。地球人口增长非常迅速,人类必须使地球能够承受不断增加的人口。这使农业和工业必须迅速发展,而这样的快速发展产生了越来越多的废物,它们被排进了水、土壤和空气中。有些废物并不会造成危害。但在废物太多的地方,有毒废物就可能会对周围的人们造成极大的伤害。

随着科技的发展,所使用材料的数量和种类都有所增加。据估计这种趋势在未来还会继续下去。然而,自然资源是有限的。有些资源已几乎耗尽。例如,人们已经预见到世界燃料即将耗尽。在世界的很多地方,像水这样的日常生活必需品非常紧缺。随着工业化的扩大,世界各地对能源需求日益增长。因为经济的快速增长,我们对能源的需求更大。

正如上文所述,我认为是科学技术的发展导致了环境污染和能源短缺。

108. 人类活动与地球

Topic:

Some people believe that the earth is being harmed by human activities. Others feel that human activities make the Earth a better place to live. What is your opinion?

Sample Answer

The quality of human life has improved greatly over the past few centuries, but Earth is being harmed more and more by human activities. As we develop our technologies, we demand more from our planet. Eventually, this will harm people as well.

Our planet gives us everything we need, but natural resources are not endless. Strip mining devastates whole regions, leaving bare and useless ground. Deforestation removes old-growth trees that cannot be replaced. Too much fishing may harm fish populations to the point where they cannot recover. We are too careless in taking what we want without giving anything back.

There are more people than ever, living longer than ever. So it is no wonder that living areas suffer from too much development. Anyone living in or near a city has experienced "urban sprawl". There is a new shopping area on every corner and new houses, townhouses and apartments everywhere. Traffic gets worse and worse because planners can't keep up with growth. Keeping up with human demand is hard enough. Environmental concerns come last with the growth of pollution. Companies and communities dump waste into water. Landfills are full of trash. Emissions from factories pollute the air with industrial waste, what is worse, radioactive waste have made there no safe place to go. If we are not careful, we will harm our planet beyond repair.

People need to respect the Earth and try to preserve it. If we do not, what kind of future will we have?

▶考官评分:8

题目:

一些人认为人类的活动正在破坏着地球，另一些人则认为人类正将地球变为一个更适合居住的地方。你怎么看?

译文:

在过去几个世纪人类生活的质量有了巨大的改变，可是人们的活动对地球的伤害越来越严重了。在我们发展科技的今天，我们对我们星球的索取越来越多。最后，这也会伤害到人类自己。

我们的星球给予我们所需要的一切，但是自然资源不是无尽的。所有地方的露天矿都遭到了破坏，留下光秃秃且无用的土地。采伐森林破坏了无法取代的原始森林。过量捕鱼可能导致鱼的数量降至难以恢复的水平。我们太疏忽，只想着得到我们所需要的而不给予任何东西。

现今人口数量达到之最，人们的寿命也更长。所以人类的生活区域遭受过度发展的恶果也就不足为奇。任何生活在城市或市郊的人都经历过“城市扩张”。新的购物中心、居民区、市政厅、公寓遍布了每个角落。交通越来越差，因为城市设计者跟不上发展的速度。很难去满足人们日益增长的需要。随着污染的不断增加，环境危害最终会到来。工厂和社区把垃圾倾倒在水里，废物掩埋场被垃圾填满。工厂工业废品排泄物污染了空气，更糟的是，放射性污染物使得我们没有安全的地方可去。如果我们不认真对待，我们就会把这颗星球破坏得难以补救。

人们应该尊敬地球并尝试保护它。假如我们不这样做，我们还会拥有什么样的未来呢？

109. 环境问题

Topic:

Technological development causes a lot of environmental problems. As for the issue, some people think a simple life style can protect environment while others argue that technology itself can solve it. Discuss both sides and give your own opinion.

Sample Answer

As the symbol of 21st century, technology has transformed nearly every aspect of our life, such as communications, traffic, and housing. Environmental pollution, however, haunts technological advance up until now. Greenhouse gas emissions from popular private cars, poisonous pollutants from modern factories, and even noise pollution from air flights have promoted us to doubt whether we have paid too much for what we have enjoyed.

On one hand, if less technological applications in our life are harnessed, environmental pollution will be alleviated. There is no doubt that our life becomes comfortable and convenient with the help of advanced technology, for example, private cars and air planes, which facilitate travel substantially and enhance our working efficiency considerably. Living in one country while working in another turns out to be a common practice for employees in some multinational companies. Nevertheless, from the perspectives of climate change and noise pollution, cars and planes are the main culprits. If we can live a simple life without those conveniences, then it is greatly conducive to safeguarding our surrounding.

On the other hand, perhaps with the development of technology, the harms caused will be lessened. More countries begin to realize that a deteriorating environment accompanies a comprehensive growth in people's living standards and further affects economic development. If natural environment is in a mess, no other countries will be willing to invest there, so a harmonious surrounding is the foundation for a sound development of a country. Under such circumstances, green technology is the future direction for every country, and the balance between technology and environment is the top priority for national policy. As for me, however, I doubt that technological leap can be really compatible with the environment, and, honestly, the possibility is slim.

Taking into account our poor environment, I hope that our life can return to nature, and every one of us drives less, away from those modern inventions detrimental to environment. After all, it is easy to pollute while formidable to improve.

▶考官评分:8

题目:

科技的发展导致了许多环境问题。对于这一问题，有些人认为简单的生活方式能够保护环境，然而还有人认为科技自己能够解决环境问题。讨论这两个方面并给出你自己的意见。

译文:

作为21世纪的象征，科技几乎改变了我们生活中的方方面面。例如通讯、交通和住房。然而，环境污染直到现在还阻碍着科技的发展。私家车排放的温室气体，现代工厂的有毒污染物，甚至空中飞行所带来的噪音污染也促使我们去怀疑我们是否为了享受而付出了太多。

一方面，如果在我们生活中更少的应用技术，环境污染将有所缓和。毫无疑问我们的生活通过借助先进的技术将会更舒适和更方便，例如私家车和飞机，极大地方便了旅行，并且大大地提高了我们的工作效率。对于一个居住在一个国家而工作在另一个国家的跨国公司员工来说这是很常见的事。然而，从气候变化和噪音污染的角度来看，汽车和飞机是罪魁祸首。如果我们可以过没有那些便利工具的普通生活，这将非常有助于保护我们周围的环境。

另一方面，或许随着科技的发展，这些危害将被减少。随着人民生活水平的全面提高许多国家已经开始意识到不断恶化的环境影响着经济的发展。如果自然环境一片混乱，将不会有其他的国家愿意投资那里。因此，一个和谐的环境是一个国家健全发展的基础。在这样的客观环境下，绿色科技是每个国家将来的发展方向，保持科技与环境之间的平衡是一个国家当务之急的政策。然而，对于我来说，我怀疑技术性如此飞跃能否真的与环境兼容，并且诚实地说，这个可能性十分渺小。

考虑到我们的恶劣环境，我希望我们的生活可以回归自然。我们少开车，远离那些不利于环境的现代发明。毕竟环境很容易污染却难以改善。

110. 环境污染

Topic:

We are now living in a throw-away society. What causes the problem? Make some recommendations.

Sample Answer

With the rapid development of society, mankind has entered a throw-away society. We can find metal tins, plastic bags and all kinds of packages thrown away everywhere. It seems that we are addicted to a habit of throwing away anything around us as soon as it is thought useless, which is a threatening social ailment.

As for me, two contributing factors can be identified. Initially, modern technology renders it possible to replace the old with the new at a faster pace. It is a fact that because great strides are achieved in science, one-off products have permeated every corner of our life. Accordingly, this so-called convenience leads to the phenomenon that the used chopsticks, shopping bags, and water bottles are littered randomly. Moreover, lack of the awareness of environmental protection exacerbates the serious problem. It is highly probable that we throw away articles not on the purpose of contaminating the environment, but involuntarily and we are blind to the relevant detriment. Therefore, gradually rubbish accumulates at an alarming rate, while environment becomes the victim to this ugly behaviour.

Before our society becomes a waste dump, it is high time that relevant measures should be taken. Firstly, one-off products should be strictly controlled or abandoned, if possible. As we know, easy access to those products is the main culprit of the popularity of this headaching practice. Secondly, the environmentally friendly education should top the agenda of the government. Obviously, if everyone is fully informed of preciousness but fragility of environment, he or she will think twice next time as for throwing away anything.

Inevitably, the satisfactory solution to the throw-away society calls for cooperation and coordination between government and individuals. In the future, it is hoped that the society will turn from a throw-away one to a recycling-oriented society.

▶考官评分:8

题目:

我们现在生活在一个丢弃型社会中，是什么造成这种现象？并给出你的建议。

译文:

随着社会的飞速发展，人类进入丢弃型社会。我们可以看到四处乱扔的易拉罐、塑料袋和各种包装。我们似乎养成了一个只要是身边没用的东西就随手乱扔的习惯，这是个令人担忧的社会问题。

在我看来，这个问题的形成存在两个重要因素。首先，现代科技促使新事物能够以较快的速度代替旧事物。事实上，由于科学方面取得了巨大进步，一次性制品已经渗透到我们生活的每个角落。因此，这个所谓的便利条件导致用过的筷子、购物袋以及水瓶被随意乱扔的现象。此外，环境保护意识淡薄也使这个严峻问题更加恶化。很可能我们不是出于破坏环境的目的，而只是不由自主地乱扔杂物，并且对于相关的危害后果也不知情。因此渐渐地，垃圾以一个惊人的速度被堆积起来，但环境却成为这种丑陋行为的受害者。

在我们的社会变成一个垃圾场之前，是时候应采取相关措施了。第一，如果可能，一次性制品必须被严格控制或废弃。正如我们所知，这个头疼事件盛行的主要罪魁祸首便是一次性制品的轻松获得。第二，政府应该将环保教育作为政府的首要议程。很显然，如果每个人都能充分意识到环境珍贵且脆弱的话，那么人人都会在下次再扔之前考虑再三的。

不可避免地，对于乱扔杂物的社会，理想的解决方式便需要政府和个人之间的协调合作。希望在未来能够从一个丢弃型社会转变为一个循环型社会。

111. 减少垃圾

Topic:

Nowadays we are producing more and more rubbish. Why do you think this is happening? What can government do to help reduce the amount of rubbish produced?

Sample Answer

The more developed the region is, the more rubbish there is, which is perhaps the never-failing wisdom in modern civilized world. Who is the director in such a black humour?

Firstly, the comfortable and convenient life accompanied by the fantastic growth of science and technology can account for the overwhelming rubbish. As we know, the pride-taking symbol of 21st century is the unbelievable technology, which provides a multitude of one-off products enjoyed avariciously by indolent people, such as chopsticks, shopping bags, and purified water bottles, some of which are non-biodegradable for ages. Accordingly, wastes have been produced and accumulated at an amazing rate. Furthermore, the awareness of environment protection is alarmingly scarce. We are addicted to entertainment of life but often refer to environment as others. In our perspective, pollution combating and nature conserving are far from our essential jobs, and government should take all the responsibility. So we can drop litter without even a grain of shame.

If we hate to witness our earth is transformed into a large rubbish dump, government and individuals should take immediate steps to curb that terrible situation. The authority has to invest more money in efficient disposal of trash, and the large-scale campaign against ugly phenomenon such as random garbage-throwing and spitting should be launched without any delay. As for individuals, behaving themselves and saying no to possible environmental-unfriendly deeds are strongly recommended.

Rubbish-handling is a quite complex issue, and it needs cooperative efforts from people and society as a whole. Since we were capable of turning the world into a splendid wonderland long ago, we have good reasons to believe that a clean, wonderful homeland is not far behind.

▶考官评分:8

题目:

现在我们正制造越来越多的垃圾。你认为这种现象为什么会发生?政府应该做些什么来减少各类垃圾的产生?

译文:

越发达的地方,垃圾越多,这在现代的文明世界中可以说是至理名言。是谁导演了这场黑色幽默呢?

首先,飞速发展的科技带来了舒适且方便的生活,而同时导致了大量垃圾产生。众所周知,21世纪引以为傲的标志是不可思议的科技,它为那些贪婪且懒惰的人们提供了大量的一次性产品,例如,筷子、购物袋和塑料水瓶,其中一些制品是不可降解的。相应地,废品以一种不可思议的速度产生和增长。而且,人们对环境保护的意识惊人的淡薄。我们沉迷于娱乐却忽略了环境。从我们的角度来看,减少污染和自然保护与我们至关重要的工作无关,政府应该负全部责任,而且我们扔垃圾也一点都不感到羞耻。

如果我们不想目睹我们的地球变成一个巨大的垃圾场,政府和个人应该立即采取措施控制这糟糕的情况。当权者应该投入更多的资金来高效地清理垃圾,大规模抵制丑陋的现象就像随地乱扔垃圾和吐痰的行为一样应该即刻发起。至于个人,自我约束和对环境有害的行为坚持抵制。

垃圾处理是一个相当复杂的问题,它需要个人与社会一起努力。既然很早以前我们有能力把我们的世界变成一个奇妙的仙境,那么我们就有充分的理由去相信一个干净美好的家园离我们不远了。

112. 改善环境

Topic:

Individuals have nothing to do to improve the environment. Governments and large companies can do something to improve the environment. Do you agree or disagree?

Sample Answer

It is an undeniable fact that in recent years, environmental pollution, which becomes increasingly serious, has aroused the shared concern of countries around the world. A group of people hold the viewpoint that governments and big companies, rather than individuals, should be mainly responsible for the improvement of the environment. Nevertheless, I am inclined to believe that governments, large companies, as well as individuals should actively shoulder the responsibility of beautifying the environment. In this essay, I will demonstrate my point of view from the following aspects.

Firstly, it is the responsibility of the government, representative of the people, to spare no efforts to ameliorate the environment. To be more specific, government should stage some relevant laws and regulations to severely punish factories which produce a great number of pollutants and those who litter or spit deliberately. Furthermore, large sums of money should be invested in the improvement of the environment, such as the treatment of waste water, trash recycling and so on.

In addition, large companies, on the other hand, should establish the self-consciousness to minimize the possibility of creating pollutants, which may not only be beneficial to the whole country but also to the companies themselves. As an illustration, some transnational corporations are striving to explore some newly-burgeoned industries of high-tech content, high additional value and low energy consumption, taking the place of some high contaminative industries.

Last but not least, it is the top priority of individuals to improve their living space. There is a popular saying which goes like this: "It is everyone's obligation to protect the environment." Most importantly, we should strengthen the consciousness of environmental protection, not only strictly being self-disciplined but also supervising people around. So to speak, it is unreasonable to claim that individuals have nothing to do with environmental protection.

From what has been discussed above, we can safely draw the conclusion that government, big companies and individuals should make their due contribution to salvage the deteriorating environment.

▶考官评分:8

题目:

个人对于环境的改善无能为力，政府和大公司才能改善环境。你是否同意这种观点?

译文:

不可否认，近年来，日益严重的环境污染问题引起了世界各国的共同关注。一些人认为政府和大公司应担负起改善环境的主要责任，而不是个人。然而，我认为政府、大公司和个人都应积极主动地担负起美化环境的责任。在这篇文章中，我将从以下几个方面论述我的观点。

首先，政府作为人民的代表有责任竭尽所能地去改善环境。具体来说，政府应该出台相关法律法规对制造大量污染物的工厂及故意乱扔垃圾、随地吐痰的人进行严惩。另外，应投入大笔资金来改善环境，比如污水的治理，垃圾的回收等。

此外，大公司应该自觉把制造污染物的可能性降到最小化，这对国家和公司本身都有很大的好处。例如，一些跨国公司正大力开发一些高技术含量、高附加值和低消耗的新兴产业来代替那些高污染的产业。

最后，个人应把改善我们赖以生存的环境作为头等大事来看待。就像一句很流行的话所说的那样:"保护环境，人人有责。"最重要的是，我们应该加强自身的环境保护意识，不仅要严格约束自己的行为，同时还要监督身边他人的行为。因此，认为个人与环境保护毫无关系的想法是毫无道理的。

通过以上的论述，我们可以得出这样的结论:政府、大公司和个人都应做出应有的贡献来拯救日益恶化的环境。

113. 水资源短缺

Topic:

What are the causes of water shortage? Please offer some solutions to deal with this problem.

Sample Answer

Since the beginning of time, water has been shaping the face of the Earth. Water sustains human life, our environment and our cultures. But the global demand for water is increasing and the destruction of water-dependent ecosystem has accelerated.

From my point of view, the main reason of scarcity of water resource is the rapid population growth, especially in developing countries. In order to meet the great demand for water, people exploit water resource in various ways. Water supply sources are being stretched to their limits. And surface and groundwater pollution is increasing rapidly. Research indicates that over 1 billion people still do not have access to safe water supplies and over 1.7 billion do not have access to adequate sanitation facilities.

Another reason is the development of industry and agriculture. In some developing countries, some private factories make use of water resource low-efficiently and make much pollution. Irrigated agriculture also contributes to water scarcity. Despite the high yield, irrigation is extremely water intensive. It takes about 1,000 tons of water to grow one ton of grain and 2,000 tons to grow one ton of rice.

Finding solutions of the problem involves the increase of worldwide awareness and international cooperation. Every individual should realize water crisis and save water. As to the government some effective measures should be taken, including erecting modern irrigation systems and increasing the number of sewage water recycling plants. Building more dams can also be an effective solution. Dams play an important role in detaining the surface rain water flowing from the mountains and would prevent the loss of rainwater straight into the sea.

▶考官评分:8

题目:

说说水资源短缺的原因是什么？并且提出一些方案来解决这个问题。

译文:

有史以来，水一直在塑造着地球的表面。水支撑着人类的生命、我们的环境和我们的文化。但是全球水资源的需求量在不断增长，对依赖水资源的生态系统的破坏也不断加剧。

在我看来，水资源缺乏的主要原因是人口的迅速增长，尤其是在发展中国家。为了满足对水的大量需求，人们以各种方式开采水资源。水源将近枯竭。同时，地表水和地下水的污染在加剧。研究表明，超过10亿人仍然未能使用上安全的供水系统，超过17亿人没有合理的卫生设施。

另一个原因就是工农业的迅速发展。在一些发展中国家，一些私人工厂低效率地使用水资源并且产生了大量的污染。农业灌溉也导致水资源的缺乏。尽管灌溉可以高产，但它要用很多水。种植一吨的谷物大约需要1000吨的水，种植一吨的稻米大约需要2000吨的水。

寻找解决这个问题的办法需要全世界人对这个问题更加关注和密切合作。每个人都应该意识到水资源的危机并节约用水。至于政府，则应采取一些有效的措施，包括建立现代灌溉体系，增加污水循环利用的工厂。建造更多的大坝也是一个有效的解决办法。大坝在截流从山脉流下的地表水方面起着重要作用，它将防止雨水直接流到海里造成流失。

114. 提高道路安全

Topic:

The only way to improve the safety on the roads is to give much stricter punishments for driving offences. To what extent do you agree or disagree?

Sample Answer

Traffic has taken the place of cancer and become the main factor in causing death. How to solve this problem is a big headache of government. The usual way is to give strict punishment for driving offence. Personally I think it is one solution, but in no way the only one.

First, we have to admit that, apart from subjective factors, there are objective factors deteriorating road safety. For example, in some third world countries traffic systems are not so developed: roads are narrow and rough. All these make driving extremely difficult and thus increase the unsafe factors in traffic. Or in big metropolitan cities, as the number of traffic vehicles is roaring up recently, the development of road system seems rather slow relatively. It is common to be trapped in traffic jams. When people have to hurry to work, driving offence is unavoidable.

Second, just as the proverb goes, an ounce of prevention is better than a pound of cure. It is better to prevent driving offence than to give strict punishment for it. There should be more effective measures. For example, the driving test should be standardized and made far more difficult than it is. All drivers should take the test every three years. The age at which people are allowed to drive any vehicle should be raised to at least 21. All advertising stressing power and performance of cars should be banned. The government should distribute more capital in improving the road condition. We should strengthen the people's education of the sense of road safety.

Strict punishment is a neither only nor good way to improve the safety on the roads. Only in the condition that other solutions cannot be exercised' should punishment be chosen.

▶考官评分:8

题目:

改善公路安全的惟一办法是更严厉的惩罚违规行为，在某种程度上你同意这个观点吗?

译文:

交通已经取代了癌症成为导致死亡的主要因素。怎样解决这个问题也令政府十分头疼。通常的做法是给予交通肇事者严厉的处罚。我个人认为这是一个解决办法，但绝不是惟一的。

首先，我们必须承认，除去主观因素，还有一些客观因素也在恶化道路安全。例如，在一些第三世界国家交通系统并不是很发达：道路粗糙又狭窄。这些因素导致驾驶变得非常困难，从而给交通增加了不安全因素。而在一些大城市，当最近交通车辆的数量急剧增加时，道路交通系统的发展就相对比较缓慢了。陷入交通拥堵中是很普遍的事情。当人们急着去上班时，违规驾驶是不可避免的。

其次，正像谚语所说的，"防患于未然"。预防违规驾驶要比给予严厉惩罚好。我们应该可以找到更为有效的措施，例如，驾驶考试应该规范化并且增加难度。所有的司机都应该每三年测试一次。允许驾驶任何车辆的年龄应至少提高到21岁。所有大张旗鼓宣传汽车力量和性能的广告都应该禁止。政府应该投入更多资金来改善道路状况。我们应该加强人们的交通安全意识教育。

严惩并不好也不是惟一的办法来改善道路交通安全。只有在其他方法都不能实施的情况下才应选择惩罚。

115. 交通拥挤

Topic:

Traffic is a very serious problem. The pedestrians and bicycle riders are more and more in danger. Many gardens become sacrifices to highways. What are the best ways to make the citizens satisfied?

Sample Answer

Traffic problem becomes the biggest concern of many countries in the world, not only because of the environmental pollution caused by the exhausted gas and irritating noise, but also the menace it takes to the bicycle riders and pedestrians. Furthermore, many gardens and grasslands give way to the rapid development of traffic facilities like highway, flyovers and avenues, leaving less and less space for the citizens.

Admittedly, the development of road construction stimulates the prosperity of economy. For example, the increasing employment rate, the sales of the private cars and the high taxes levied on car owners are what a government expects. But as a responsible government, it should have a long-term development plan instead of the pursuit of a short-term profit. A responsible government should always give priority to people's appeal.

To make the citizens satisfied, firstly, the government should preserve for the citizens more gardens and meadows, where people can spend weekends with their friends and family. Gardens and meadows can also purify the polluted air, creating a good environment for the citizens. Secondly, the government should encourage the use of public transport and limit the ownership of private cars. Due to the economic development, many citizens can afford a private car. Take Shenzhen as an example, the sales of private cars increase by 5,000 every month. It is hard to imagine if the current roads can accommodate so large a number of cars five or ten years later. Finally, the government should consider the relation between economic development and environmental protection, leaving more green lands to our descendants.

To sum up, economic development and environmental protection do not contradict each other. If a government is responsible, it should make no efforts to give people a comfortable living environment and dedicate itself to economic development as well.

▶考官评分:8

题目:

交通拥挤成为严重的问题，使行人和骑自行车的人处于危险当中，公园也成了公路的牺牲品。怎样做才能使市民感到满意呢?

译文:

交通问题成为世界上许多国家最为关注的事情，这不仅因为恼人的噪音和废气所造成的环境污染，也是因为它给骑自行车的人和行人带来了威胁。再者，快速发展的交通设施，诸如高速公路、立交桥和大街等侵占了许多公园和绿地，使得城市居民的生活空间变得越来越小。

诚然，道路建设的发展促进了经济的繁荣，例如，政府所期待的是它可以提高就业率，私家车的销售量以及从车主那征收的高额税收。但是，作为一个负责任的政府，必须要有长期的发展计划而不是短期的利益追求。一个负责任的政府总是应该将民众的诉求放在首位。

为了满足城市居民的需求，政府首先应该为他们保留可以与家人和朋友一起过周末的公园和草地。而这些公园和草地也能够净化被污染的空气，从而为居民创造一个良好的环境。再次，政府应该鼓励居民乘坐公共交通工具并限制私家车的数量。随着经济的发展，许多市民都买得起私家车。以深圳为例，私家车的销量以每个月5,000辆的速度增加。很难想象在未来的5到10年里，目前的道路是否能容纳数量如此多的车辆。最后，政府应该考虑到经济发展与环境保护之间的关系，为子孙后代留下更多的绿地。

总而言之，经济发展与环境保护之间并不矛盾。一个负责任的政府，应该不遗余力地为人们创造舒适的生活环境并致力于经济发展。

116. 迁移大公司到乡村

Topic:

Moving large companies and factories with their employees to the countryside could solve traffic and housing problems in major cities. To what extent do you agree or disagree?

Sample Answer

Like a disease that troubles the patients, traffic and housing problems in almost every metropolis are what governments must address without any delay. But, how? One theory claims big companies and factories should be moved to the hinterland. Although it sounds plausible, the theory is not essentially flawless.

To begin with, it is entirely wrong to attribute city housing and traffic problems to big companies and factories. Why? The area that big companies and factories occupy usually accounts for the less than 15% of the whole city state. Hence, big companies and factories contribute little to housing and traffic problems. Moreover, the number of the employees of big companies and factories is not large enough to give rise to traffic and housing problems.

Next, to move big companies and factories does not solve the housing and traffic problems completely. In fact, it harms rather than helps city economic development by shifting the problems from city to countryside. Once the big companies and factories are moved to the suburb, schools, banks, hospitals, raw material supplies and the like will also stream into the countries. When the system becomes a flood, a new city comes into being. Then, the old problems reappear in the “new cities”. In addition, these big companies and factories trigger and lead the city economic development. To remove them, product and services are expensive. Hence, to move them to the countryside makes little sense.

To sum up, I do not agree that big companies and factories should be moved to the countryside. To solve the problem more effectively and efficiently, the government and scholars should consider more insightfully and seriously.

▶考官评分:7

题目:

把公司迁移到乡村以缓解城市住房和交通压力，你同意这种观点吗?

译文:

如同困扰患者的疾病一样，政府对于城市交通及住房问题的解决刻不容缓。但这些问题应如何解决呢？一种观点认为，大型公司及工厂应该移至城市腹地。这种观点虽然听上去不错，事实上却并不完美。

首先，将城市的住房和交通问题归咎于大型公司及工厂是完全错误的。为什么呢?大型公司及工厂的占地面积通常小于整个城市面积的15%。因此，大型公司及工厂对于住房及交通的影响是很小的。另外，大型公司及工厂的员工人数并不足以加剧交通及住房问题。

再者，转移大型公司及工厂并不能完全解决住房和交通问题。事实上，将城市问题转移至农村不但不会带动城市经济的发展，反而会对经济的发展带来负面影响。一旦大型公司和工厂移至郊区，那么像学校、银行、医院、原材料供应这样的机构都会涌进农村。当一个完整的体系形成时，一座新的城市就诞生了。然后，老问题就会在“新城市”中再次上演了。另外，正是这些大型公司及工厂引领着城市经济的快速发展。它们的转移，将使产品和服务的经济负担加重。因此，将它们移至农村几乎没有任何意义。

总之，我反对将大型公司及工厂转移到农村的观点。如果要有效地解决目前这些问题，政府和学者就需要进行更深刻、更认真的思考。

第七大类：传统与发展变化类题目

117. 资助传统艺术

Topic:

In some countries, the national traditional arts are facing extinction. Some people think that the government should support them. Do you agree or disagree? What should the government do?

Sample Answer

Traditional arts, as valuable cultural relics of a nation, are disappearing far away from the modern society. Some people hold the view that the government should not subsidize the traditional arts. They point out that supporting traditional arts will definitely lay a great financial burden on the government. As for me, I can hardly share this point of view. I believe that I have found some solid reasons.

One of the most attractive points is that traditional arts are national treasures. They are the precious heritage of our ancestors. As the offspring, it is our responsibilities and obligations to inherit them and carry them down to the next generation. China, as one of the highly-civilized countries in the world, abounds in various forms of traditional arts, such as Beijing Opera, Chinese painting, and calligraphy, which are not only our national cultural treasures, but also a rich fortune of the world.

There is another factor that deserves some words here. Traditional arts are the foundation of modern ones. In other words, the development of modern arts depends upon the traditional ones. For example, compared with movie, drama is a traditional art. Many famous movie stars have ever studied in drama institutions.

Some people may say that supporting traditional arts is to sink money. In fact, these traditional arts are certainly not a money waster. They are potentially profitable. There are also a lot of traditional art fans who are willing to pay and even donate for them. In addition, the profits can last a longer time.

Taking all these factors into consideration, we may reasonably come to the conclusion that the government should support traditional arts. Firstly, there is a need for the government to invest more funds on the research of traditional arts. Secondly, the government should organize activities to promote public awareness of the importance of traditional arts.

▶考官评分:7

题目:

在一些国家，传统艺术即将消失。一些人认为政府应该进行资助。你是否同意？政府应怎样做呢？

译文:

传统艺术作为一个民族有价值的文化遗产正在从我们的现代社会逐渐消失。一些人认为政府不应该资助传统艺术。他们指出资助传统艺术将给政府带来沉重的经济负担。我不同意这种观点。我认为我有充分的理由。

最有吸引力的一点是传统艺术是民族瑰宝。它们是我们祖先的宝贵遗产。作为后代，我们有责任和义务继承下来并传到下一代。中国，作为世界上高度文明化的国家之一，拥有各种形式的传统艺术，如京剧、国画和书法。这不仅是我国的文化财产，也是世界的巨大财富。

还有一个因素值得关注。传统艺术是现代艺术的基础。换句话说，现代艺术的发展依赖于传统艺术，例如，相对于电影，戏剧是一种传统艺术。很多著名电影明星都曾经在戏剧学院学习过。

有人可能会说，资助传统艺术浪费钱。实际上，这些传统艺术当然不会浪费钱财。它们是有潜在效益的。也有很多传统艺术爱好者愿意为此付费甚至捐赠。而且，这种效益会持续更长时间。

考虑这些因素，我们可能会有理由得出结论：政府应该资助传统艺术。首先，政府应该拨出更多的资金用于传统艺术的研究。其次，政府应该组织活动来提升公众对传统艺术重要性的认识。

118. 21世纪会带来什么?

Topic:

The 21st century has begun. What changes do you think this new century will bring?

Sample Answer

Mankind has made great progress since scientific exploration began, and this progress seems to be accelerating. In the last hundred years we have seen inventions that have not only greatly improved our lives but changed our lifestyles. There is no reason to believe that this rapid progress will not continue in the 21st century. While there is no way to predict exactly what our scientists and entrepreneurs will come up with, there are indications that advances will be made in certain areas. The following are some examples.

First, advances will continue to be made in the field of medicine that will allow people to live longer and healthier lives. In developed countries today most people already have a lifespan that would have been unusually long a hundred years ago. Steady progress has been made in the eradication of disease and this should continue in the next 100 years. In addition, biotechnology in the field of genetics may someday allow us to develop bodies that are stronger and free of inherited defects. Perhaps we will even be able to clone ourselves. No matter what form these advances take, it is highly likely that we will greatly extend our lifespan in the new century.

Second, new technology has already brought people around the world closer. This trend will continue in the 21st century as communication becomes more efficient and affordable. Countries and their peoples have formed stronger bonds both economically and politically, as in the recent development of the European Union. Perhaps some day in the future there will cease to be national boundaries. However, one side effect of this globalization is that many characteristics of individual cultures will be lost. Sadly, by the end of the century, some languages and art forms may only be found in museums.

Third, we can expect a growing population and demands for a higher standard of living to put increasing pressure on the earth's resources. We have already seen some of the effects of this pressure in the form of pollution and global warming. (It is likely that these trends will also continue and that more damage to the environment will be done.) On the other hand, perhaps we will find more efficient ways to make use of the available resources or develop alternative forms of energy. In that case, we may live in better harmony with nature.

The scenarios above are just three of the many possible changes that this new century will bring. We can expect to see great advances in many fields, including medicine, communications, trade, transportation and production. Although there may be problems in the future, our ingenuity and inventiveness will help us to deal with them.

▶考官评分:8

题目:

21世纪已经来临，你认为它会带来什么？

译文:

从科学探索开始以来，人类就已经取得了巨大的进步，而且进步的速度似乎越来越快。在过去的100年中，我们见证了许多发明的出现。这些发明不仅大大地改善了我们的生活，而且也改变了我们的生活方式。我们没有理由不相信，以这样速度的进步会持续到21世纪。虽然我们没有办法去精确地预测到科学家和企业家想出了什么新点子，但有迹象显示，某些领域仍将会有进步。以下是一些例子。

第一，医学领域会持续发展，从而使人类寿命更长，而且更健康。在现今的发达国家里，大多数人的寿命跟100年前的人比起来，已经算是很长寿了。在疾病的治愈方面，医学已经有了稳定的进步，而且未来的一百年应该还会持续进步。此外，也许有一天，遗传学这项生物科技会使人类的身体更强壮，而且没有遗传上的缺陷。或许我们将来甚至能够复制自己。不管是哪一种形式的进步，非常可能的是，在新的世纪里我们的寿命将大大延长。

第二，新科技已经使世界上的人彼此更靠近。这个趋势会持续到21世纪，因为通讯变得越来越有效率，越来越多的人能够负担得起。国与国之间以及人民与人民之间在经济上和政治上会更紧密地结合，就像欧盟最近的发展一样。或许将来有一天，世界上将没有国界。但是，全球化有一个副作用，那就是各种文化的特性将会消失。遗憾的是，在21世纪末，有一些语言和艺术形式或许只能在博物馆里才能找到。

第三，我们可以预计人口会增加，人类会追求更高的生活水准，因而导致地球资源承受不断增长的压力。我们已经看到了这种压力所导致的一些后果，如污染和全球变暖。这种趋势可能会持续下去，而且可能会对环境造成更大的破坏。可是就另一方面来说，或许我们会找到更有效的方法来利用可获得的资源，或是开发出其他形式的资源。唯有如此，我们才能更和谐地与大自然和平共处。

以上设想只是新世纪可能会带来的变化中的三项。我们预期在许多领域都会有很大的进步，包括医学、通讯、贸易、交通和生产。虽然未来可能会有难题产生，但是我们的创造力和发明力将会帮助我们解决这些问题。

119. 新世纪

Topic:

Many people are optimistic about the 21st century, and they see it as an opportunity to bring about positive changes in the world. To what extent do you agree? What kind of changes would you like to see?

Sample Answer

We having entered the 21st century, the world is witnessing many earth-shaking changes. However, some severe problems have attracted our attention. Frankly speaking, I am always amazed when I hear people say that we should be optimistic about the 21st century. From my point of view, there is much to be done to make the world better.

The dazzling development of technology is a good case in point. With technology accelerating, advances and challenges go side by side. Computers have relieved people from hard manual work, but they have also encouraged people to live in a virtual world. The Internet has provided people with a colourful world, but it has also given risen to new types of crimes. Media have reshaped the way people obtain information, but they have also been responsible for people's laziness and inactive thinking. Mobile phones have promoted people's communication and connection, but they have also invaded people's privacy. Private cars have made it easy for us to move from one place to another, thus saving our precious time, but they have also polluted the environment and killed millions of people. The utilization of nuclear power has to a considerable degree relieved energy crisis, but it has also posed a threat to the world peace.

If I were asked what changes should be in the 21st century, my answers would go as follows. In the first place, I hope that there will be long-lasting peace rather than war. Second of all, I hope that there will be less pollution and starvation. In addition, I hope that everybody can enjoy high-quality education and be oneself. Finally, I hope that cultural differences should be respected and discrimination will be eliminated thoroughly.

As Charles Dickens once wrote,"It was the best of times, it was the worst of times."Maybe, this is the real world in which we live.

▶考官评分:8

题目:

许多人对于21世纪持有积极的态度，并且将其视为积极改变世界的机会。你对于他们的乐观的态度持有同意还是不同意的观点呢？你希望在新的世纪里能够看见哪些变化呢？

译文:

我们已经进入了21世纪，全世界正在见证翻天覆地的变化。然而，一些严重的问题同样引起了我们的注意。坦白地说，当我听说人们对于21世纪保持乐观的态度时我感觉非常的惊讶。在我看来，要使世界变得更好，还有很多事情需要去做。

炫目的技术发展就是一个很好的例子。随着技术的快速发展，进步和挑战共存。电脑已经减轻了人们艰苦的体力活动，但是同时鼓励着人们生活在一个虚拟的世界。因特网已经提供了一个多彩的世界，但是同样增加了新式的犯罪。媒体改造了人们获得信息的渠道，但是同时也应该为人们的懒惰和被动的思考负责。手机促进了人们的交流和联系，但是却同时侵犯了人们的隐私。私家车让我们从一个地方到另外一个地方变得很容易，因此节省了我们宝贵的时间，但是却污染了环境并且害死了数以百万的人们。核能的利用在很大程度上缓解了能源危机，但是却威胁着世界和平。

如果问我21世纪应该改变什么的话，我的回答是这样的。第一，我希望应该是维护持久的和平而不是发动战争。第二，我希望未来将会有更少的污染和饥饿。此外，我希望所有人都能够享受高质量的教育并做自己。最后，我希望尊重文化差异，彻底消除歧视问题。

正如查尔斯·狄更斯曾经写的：“这是最好的时代，也是最糟糕的时代。”或许这就是我们真实生活的世界。

120. 变化

Topic:

Some people prefer to spend their lives doing the same things and avoiding changes. Others, however, think that change is always a good thing. Discuss both views and give your own opinion.

Sample Answer

Over the last half century the pace of changes in the life of human beings has increased beyond our wildest expectations. This has been driven by technological and scientific breakthroughs that change the whole way we view the world on an almost daily basis. This means that change is not always a personal option, but an inescapable fact of life, and we need to constantly adapt to keep pace with it.

Those people who believe they have achieved some security by doing the same, familiar things are living in denial. Even when people believe they are resisting changes themselves, they cannot stop the world around them from changing. Sooner or later they will find that familiar jobs no longer exist, or that the safe patterns of behaviour are no longer appropriate.

However, reaching the conclusion that change is inevitable is not the same as assuming that changing is always for the better. Unfortunately, it is not always the case that new things are promoted because they have good impacts for the majority of people. A lot of innovations are made with the aim of making money for a few. This is because it is the rich and powerful people in our society who are able to impose changes(such as working conditions or property development) that are in their own interests.

In conclusion, I would say that change can be stimulating and energizing for individuals when they pursue it themselves, but that all changes, including that which are imposed on people, do not necessarily have good outcomes.

▶考官评分:8

题目:

有些人喜欢用自己的一生做同样的事情，拒绝改变。然而其他人认为变化是一件好事。讨论两种观点并给出你自己的看法。

译文:

在过去的半个世纪以来，人类生活变化速度的提高超出了我们的最大期望。这是技术驱动和科学突破所带来的成果，使我们所看到的这个世界发生日新月异的变化。这意味着这种变化并不总是个人的选择，而是一种不可避免的生活事实，我们需要不断地适应，跟上它的步伐。

有些人相信他们做同样熟悉的事情时，已经得到了某些安全感，但这些人是生活在自我否定中的。即使当人们开始相信他们自己拒绝改变，但他们无法阻止来自周边世界的改变。迟早他们会发现，熟悉的工作已经不存在，或者说，安全的行为模式已不再适用。

然而，变化是不可避免的这个结论和变化总是更好的这个假设是不同的。不幸的是，并不是因为新事物对大多数人有益，所以新事物才能被推广。许多新事物对一些人来说是以赚钱为目的的。这是因为我们社会只有富人和有权势的人能够施加变化（如工作条件或房地产开发），而且这些都是为了他们自己的利益。

总之，我要说的变化是当个人想要变化时，这种变化是有促进作用和激励作用的，但所有变化，包括强加于人的未必都会有好的结果。

121. 改变习惯

Topic:

Some people enjoy changes, and they look forward to new experiences. Others like their lives to stay the same, and they do not change their usual habits. Which approach do you prefer?

Sample Answer

I believe that life is a river, with every destination having a unique purpose. Change is but a minor part of life and whatever the change, it will be for the best.

People vary, and that is why you often find various approaches to life. For those who are content with the direction their life is heading, the idea of change would probably send shivers through them. This is due to the fact that they are at a point where they are satisfied with the way they have maximized their God-given potential. That is a positive reason for dreading change.

Others dread change due to the fact that they are too scared to try or adapt to new experiences. Taking into consideration the fact that we are all human, fear is a normal feeling. The only disadvantage is the fact that unless you try, you will never know what you could have accomplished, or how well and capable you are to move on. No chance to discover the courage you have within to accept defeat but never stop trying. This is a negative reason for dreading change.

Habits can be addictive, and so the main question here is whether they are positive, beneficial habits or negative ones. By that, I mean that the choice is up to the individual. If the change is from the negative to the positive, then there is no reason whatsoever that one should dread making a change. Doing right is never wrong.

In conclusion, change can either mould you or break you. I would rather try and change for the better, than live my life knowing that I never tried. Within every human being, there is a hidden potential that only change can help maximize. The question however is, whether we will give change a chance. It is all up to you, the individual!

▶考官评分:8

题目：

一些人喜欢改变，他们期待新经历。另一些人却不愿意改变自己的习惯。你同意哪一方的观点？

译文：

我认为生活就像一条河，每个终点都有独一无二的目的。虽然改变是生活中的一小部分，但是不论改变了什么，它都是为了变得最好而改变。

因人而异，这就是为什么你经常发现各种各样的生活方式。改变的想法对于那些满意自己目前生活的人来说，可能是一种打击。这是因为他们对自己目前使天赋的潜力最大化的方式感到满意。这是惧怕改变的积极原因。

另一些人惧怕改变，因为他们害怕尝试或适应新的生活。事实上我们都是活生生的人，恐惧是一种很正常的感觉。惟一的不足是除非你去尝试，否则你永远都不知道你能成就什么，或者你有多大能力能做得多好。没有机会发现你内心面对失败时永不放弃的勇气有多大。这是惧怕改变的消极原因。

习惯是会上瘾的，所以这里的主要问题就是它们是积极的、有益的习惯，还是消极的习惯。我这么说的意思是，选择权在自己手中。如果改变是从消极到积极，那就没有任何理由惧怕做出改变。做正确的事永远不会错。

总之，改变可以成就你，也可以毁掉你。比起从不尝试改变地度过一生，我更愿意尝试为了变得更好而改变。每个人都有潜力，潜力只有改变才能最优化。无论如何，关键问题是，我们是不是应该抓住一次机会去改变。这完全取决于你，由你自己来决定！

122. 习惯与改变

Topic:

Some people enjoy changes, and they look forward to new experiences. Others like their lives to stay the same, and they do not change their usual habits. Compare these two approaches to life. Which approach do you prefer? Explain why.

Sample Answer

It has been said that man is largely a creature of habit. We all develop routines and habits in our everyday lives, whether we are aware of it or not. To some people these routines are very important and even a small change, such as missing the morning paper, can affect the way they feel all day. Other people dislike routines and change their habits often in order to ward off boredom. They may even go so far as to change their residence or job frequently. These two different approaches to life are extremes, but each has advantages and disadvantages.

In the first case, for people who dislike changes, a dependency on routines and habits can provide a sense of security and convenience, but it can also be limiting. Routines provide security because people do not have to wonder what will happen. In this rapidly changing world, it is sometimes reassuring to have a schedule to follow. Habits also make life more convenient because people do not have to think about what they must do next and do not need to worry about forgetting something. They can go through their daily routines automatically. However, this way of life is limiting when people are too dependent on their routine. They may not only be upset when things do not go according to plan, but also miss many good opportunities to try new things.

In the second case, for people who seem to thrive on changes, there are also advantages and disadvantages. First of all, this kind of person is usually more open to new ideas. He can, therefore, learn more and experience more. In addition, because he is not afraid to make changes in his life and take risks, he is more willing to take advantage of unexpected opportunities. This may lead him to a previously unforeseen success. But if a person is always seeking ways to change his life, he may not stick with things long enough to gain the most benefits from them. If he lacks the necessary determination and perseverance, it will be difficult for him to succeed by any means other than luck.

In my opinion, both of these lifestyles are too extreme. Most people are not so dependent on their habits, nor are they addicted to change. For me, a lifestyle somewhere between these two is ideal. I find some habits and routines comforting and convenient, yet I do not want to be afraid to face changes or take advantage of unforeseen chances to improve my life. Therefore, I will continue to follow my routine in daily life, but keep my eyes open for opportunities.

▶考官评分:8

题目:

一些人喜欢改变，他们期待新经历。另一些人却喜欢保持和从前一样，不愿意改变自己的习惯。比较这两种观点，你更倾向哪一方？解释原因。

译文:

人类一直以来被说成是墨守成规。不论我们有没有意识到，在日常生活中，我们一直在例行公事并且养成了习惯。对某些人而言，这些例行公事非常重要，就算像是没有看到早报这种微小的改变也会影响到他们整天的心情。而有些人则讨厌公式化，而且为了避免无聊，经常改变习惯，甚至有些人还会经常变换居住地点或工作。这两种生活态度都很极端，但也各有其优缺点。

第一种人不喜欢改变，依赖固定工作与习惯带给他们安全感与便利，但这样也有所限制。例行公事给他们安全感，因为不需要猜想会发生什么事。在这个快速变迁的世界中，有时预先知道要做什么事情会让人安心。习惯也让人觉得生活更方便，因为这样就不必去想下一步要做什么以及担心会忘掉什么，如此他们就能每天习惯性地过相同的生活。然而，当人们过于依赖例行公事时，其生活方式就会受限。如果事情不按计划进行，他们会不高兴，而且也会错失很多尝试新事物的良机。

第二种人乐于改变，但也是有利有弊。首先，这种人通常比较能接受新的想法。因此，他们能学得更多，而且见识更广。此外，这种人因为不怕改变生活与敢于冒险，所以就更愿意利用意想不到的机会，这也许能让他们获得出乎意料的成功。但如果这种人不断地寻求改变生活的方法，他们也许就因为不能长久坚持而无法从中获得最大的利益。如果缺乏必要的决心与毅力，那么除了靠运气之外，是很难有所成就的。

依我之见，这两种生活方式都过于极端。大部分人既不会过于依赖习惯，也不会执着于改变。对我来说，介于这两者之间的生活方式是最理想的。我认为有些习惯与例行公事能让人觉得舒适而便利，但我面对改变时也不会害怕，或利用意想不到的机会去改善我的生活。因此，虽然我会继续在日常生活中墨守成规，但还是会张大眼睛寻觅机会。

123. 学习过去

Topic:

Learning about the past has no value for those of us living in the present. Do you agree or disagree?

Sample Answer

People live in the present. They plan for and worry about the future. History, however, is the study of the past. It is undeniable that learning about past has its value. It will help us understand people and societies, and it will help us understand changes and how the society we live in came to be.

In the first place, history offers tons of information about how people and societies behave. For example, how can we evaluate war at peace time without historical materials? How can we understand the influence of technological innovation, or the role that beliefs play in shaping family life, without using the experiences? Consequently, history as our laboratory, and data from the past must serve as our most vital evidence to figure out why our complex species behaves as it does in social settings. That is why we cannot stay without history: it offers evidential base for the contemplation of how societies function, and people need to have some sense of how societies function to run in own lives.

The second reason why history is inescapable as a subject of study follows closely on the first. The past causes the present, and so does the future. Any time we try to know why something happened—whether a shift in political party, a major change in suicide rate, or a war in the Balkans or the Middle East—we have to look for factors that took shape earlier. Only through studying history can we grasp how things change. Only through history can we begin to comprehend changes; and only through history can we understand what elements of an institution or a society persist despite change.

In conclusion, I totally disagree with the argument that learning about the past has no value for those of us living in the present.

▶考官评分:8

题目:

对于生活在现在社会的人来说学习历史是没有意义的，你是否赞同此观点?

译文:

人们生活在现在，他们计划着并且忧虑着未来。然而，历史是对过去的研究。不可否认的是，学习过去是很有价值的，可以帮助我们了解人类和社会，帮助我们懂得改变，并了解我们所生活的社会是怎么形成的。

首先，历史提供大量关于人和社会行为的信息。例如，如果没有历史资料，我们如何在和平的年代评价战争?没有经验可以利用，我们如何去了解科技创新的影响，或是信仰在家庭生活中起到的作用?因此，历史作为实验室和来自过去的数据能够帮助我们理解为什么我们在社会中会有如此行为的重要证据。这就是为什么我们不能没有历史：它为我们提供去审视社会功能的基本证据，而且人们需要了解社会在人们生活中是如何发挥作用的。

历史是必不可少的学习科目的第二个原因是直接从第一个原因得来的。现在来自于过去，未来也是如此。任何时间我们尝试着去了解为什么有些事情会发生——不论是政治团体的轮换，自杀率的大幅改变，或者是巴尔干半岛和中东的战争——我们必须寻找早期促成它们的因素。只有通过学习历史，我们才能掌握事物是怎么变化的。只有通过历史，我们才能领会变化。只有通过历史，我们才能了解一种制度或一个社会持久不变的元素。

总之，对于生活在现在的我们来说，我完全不同意学习历史是没有价值的这种观点。

范文点评:

辩论型题目。范文使用一边倒结构，第一段就提出观点，中间用两段阐述作者观点，结尾用一句话再次陈述观点。整个结构非常严谨，值得一提的是，范文使用了反问句和一些例子支持作者观点，相比较模版式句型，显得比较新颖。

124. 保存习俗与入乡随俗

Topic:

When people move to another country, some of them decide to follow the customs of the new country. Others prefer to keep their own customs. Compare these two choices. Which one do you prefer?

Sample Answer

When people move to another country, they not only face a different environment and language, but also different customs. Every culture has its own customs, and all of them are valuable. However, deciding how to deal with the problems of unfamiliar customs is a challenge for many immigrants. Some choose to follow the customs of their new country, while others prefer to adhere to their own customs. Each of these choices has some advantages as explained below.

When people choose to follow the customs of their adopted country, they may find that it helps them to adapt more quickly to the new society. They have something to discuss and share with their new neighbours, and sharing customs is one way for people to feel closer to one another. Thus, following the new customs may help immigrants feel more at home. It may also help them to see the positive things in their new environment and to forget their feelings of homesickness.

On the other hand, those who choose to continue following their own customs may also find that it helps them feel more at home. There are many things to adjust to in another country, and following their traditional customs may help people feel more secure in the new surroundings. More importantly, our customs are a part of us. They are an expression of the culture that has shaped us. This is something that most of us would like to pass down to our children and share with others. Sharing our old customs can also bring us closer to our new neighbours.

To sum up, our customs have value and are an important part of our culture. Therefore, I don't believe that we should abandon our traditional customs when we move to another country. At the same time, I believe that we should learn about the customs of our new home and follow those that appeal to us. In this way, we can remember and celebrate our old culture while adapting to our new one.

▶考官评分:8

题目:

当人们搬到另一个国家后，一些人决定入乡随俗，另一些人则决定坚守自己国家的风俗习惯。比较这两种选择。你更倾向哪一种?

译文:

当人们搬到另一个国家后，不仅要面对不同的环境和语言，还要面对不同的风俗习惯。每种文化都有其风俗习惯，而且都非常宝贵。然而，如何应付因不熟悉习俗所产生的问题，对许多移民而言都是一种挑战。有些人选择入乡随俗，有些人则宁愿坚守自己国家的风俗习惯。如以下所解释的，这两种选择都有一些优点。

当人们选择遵循他们移入国家的风俗习惯时，他们可能会觉得这样有助于更快地适应新的社会。和新邻居有话题可聊，有东西可以分享，同时拥有相同的风俗习惯是能让人们觉得更亲近的一种方式。因此，入乡随俗，有助于使移民感到更舒服自在，也会帮助他们看到新环境的优点，忘掉思乡的情绪。

另一方面，那些选择坚持自己本国风俗习惯的人是因为觉得这样做有助于让他们觉得更自在。要适应另一个国家，有很多事要做，而传统的风俗习惯会让人在陌生的环境中觉得更有安全感。更重要的是，风俗习惯是我们的一部分，能体现出塑造我们的文化原貌，这是我们大多数人都想传承给后代并和他人分享的东西。和新邻居分享我们的传统习俗也可以使我们和新邻居更亲近。

总之，风俗习惯极具价值，并且是我们文化中很重要的一部分。因此，我认为当我们搬到新的国家时不应该抛弃传统习俗。同时，我认为我们应该学习新的风俗习惯，选择我们所喜爱的风俗。如此一来，我们一方面能够适应新的文化，同时也能保持并颂扬自己原有的文化。

范文点评：

辩论型题目。范文使用了对称式结构，第一段解释题目并引入下文。中间用两段分别分析了两种选择各自的优点，最后一段提出自己观点。范文结构思路清晰，使用了如宾语从句等加分句型，并用一些连词使作者观点非常具有层次感。

125. 保存习俗与入乡随俗

Topic:

Some people think visitors to others countries should imitate local customs and behaviours. Some people disagree; they think the host country should welcome cultural differences. What do you think?

Sample Answer

The tourist trade is booming. Systems of communication by air, sea and land make it possible for us to visit each other's countries at a moderate cost. Some people think that, when we are in a foreign country, we should maintain our own cultural custom. Others hold that we should try our best to communicate with the local people. As far as I am able to judge, I am for the latter opinion.

The aim of travel is not only for relaxation and sightseeing but also for understanding. With the frequent contact between people from different places and different nations, the exchange of culture and science is sure to be promoted. It may lead to a better understanding of people all over the world.

Unfortunately many tourists deliberately protect themselves from too much contact with the local people. They live at international hotels and a strict schedule makes it impossible for them to wander off on their own; and anyway, language is always a barrier, so they are only too happy to be protected in this way.

The sad thing about this situation is that it leads to the persistence of national stereotypes. We do not see the people of other nations as they really are, but as we have been brought up to believe they are. When we travel abroad, we should make as many friends as possible with local people, learn the local culture and respect the local custom. Then we will find how absurd and harmful national stereotypes are.

Stereotypes can be positively dangerous. They stir up racial discrimination and blind us to the basic fact that all people are human. We are all similar to each other and at the same time all unique.

▶考官评分:8

题目:

一些人认为当人们到国外的时候，应该入乡随俗，另外一些人则不同意，他们认为东道国应该欢迎这些文化差异，你的意见是什么?

译文:

旅游业正在繁荣兴旺地发展。海、陆、空等交通通信系统的发展使我们能够花费合适的费用去拜访其他国家。一些人认为，当我们到外国的时候，我们应该保持自己的文化习俗。其他人认为我们应该尽力地和当地人交流。就我而言，我赞成后一观点。

旅游的目的不仅是放松和观光，而且是为了更好地了解别人。随着不同地区和不同民族的频繁接触，注定要促进文化和自然科学的交流，这将会促进全世界的人能更好地相互理解。

不幸的是，很多旅行者故意地自我保护，而不愿意和当地的居民过多接触。他们住在国际饭店，有一个严格的时间表使他们没有时间自己单独出去散步，而且无论如何，语言总是一个障碍，所以他们总是非常喜欢以这种方式来保护自己。

糟糕的是，这种情况导致了民族陈旧观念的持续。我们不能够看到其他民族真实的面目，而只是想当然地认为他们的生活是什么状态。但我们出国旅游的时候，我们应该尽可能地和当地人交朋友，学习当地的文化，尊重当地的习俗。然后，我们会发现民族封闭是多么的荒谬和有害。

封闭非常有害。民族的自我封闭激起了种族的歧视，甚至使我们忽视了所有的人种、民族都是人类这一基本事实。我们彼此都是很相似的，并且都很独特。

范文点评:

辩论型题目。范文使用的是对称式结构，第一段解释了题目并提出自己观点，中间三段深入分析了两种观点的优缺点，最后一段总结并再次强调自己支持的观点。范文使用了表语从句等加分句型，结构清晰。

126. 传统科技

Topic:

Some people believe that when a country begins to develop its science and technology, the traditional technology and methods are bound to die out. Therefore, the maintenance of the traditional technology and methods is futile. What do you think?

Sample Answer

Recently, the issue regarding the future of traditional technology and methods in the midst of the rapid development of science and technology has been in the limelight. Some people argue that the traditional technology and methods are bound to die out, hence the futility of maintaining them. On the other hand, some people firmly believe that the traditional technology and method will survive the technological revolution. As far as I am concerned, the latter opinion carries more weight.

For one thing, being traditional is quite different from being out of date or obsolete. Tradition is what we inherit from our forefathers, and its being handed down from generation to generation itself proves its capacity to survive. Only those things that have weathered arduous trials time after time can be called tradition; otherwise, they are something obsolete.

For another, the survival of traditional technology and methods does not mean that they linger on in a steadily worsening condition. On the contrary, their existence tends to propel and even accelerate the development of science and technology. If we compare the development of science and technology to the construction of a modern building, the traditional technology and methods can be likened to the foundation. Without a solid foundation, the building is destined to collapse.

In addition, the development of science and technology originates in traditional technology and methods. Thus, development itself does not exclude tradition, but requires its assistance.

In a word, development and technological renovation can only be accomplished on the basis of traditional technology and methods. From what has been discussed above, we may safely arrive at the conclusion that traditional technology and methods are far from obsolete, and are bound to contribute more to the development of science and technology.

▶考官评分:8

题目:

一些人认为当一个国家发展科学技术的时候，传统技术方法必定会消失。而且，保留传统技术方法是没有用的。你的观点是什么?

译文:

当今科学技术飞速发展，其中传统技术方法的未来发展问题最近成为人们争论的焦点。有些人认为传统的技术方法必定会消失，因此，保留它们是没有任何价值的。另一方面，有些人坚信传统的技术方法将在技术革命后继续存在。据我所知，后者的观点更可靠。

首先，传统并不意味着过时和陈旧。传统是我们从祖先那里继承而来的，然后通过世世代代的验证而流传至今的，它的存在本身就证明其价值。只有那些经历一次次严峻考验的事物才能称之为传统，反之，只能被人们遗弃。

其次，现存的传统技术方法并没有每况愈下，反而能推进、甚至加速科学技术的发展。如果我们把科学技术的发展比作现代建筑的构建，那么传统技术方法就是地基，没有坚实的地基，建筑终会倒塌。

而且，科学技术就是从传统技术方法发展而来的，所以它的自身发展并不会和传统相抵触，相反还需要传统的帮助。

总之，发展和技术革新只有通过传统技术方法才能得以实现。基于上述讨论，我们完全可以得出结论：传统技术方法完全不会被淘汰，一定会为科学技术的发展做出更多贡献。

范文点评：

辩论型题目。范文使用了典型的一边倒结构，第一段解释题目并提出自己观点引出下文，中间三段论述了自己支持的观点，每一段并用了二至三句支持句作为观点解释，最后一段整体论述总结。范文结构非常典型，思路流畅，语言上用了一些8分词汇和宾语从句等加分句型。

127. 传统风俗习惯

Topic:

With the development of society, customs and habits have changed a lot. Is it a good or bad phenomenon? What's your opinion?

Sample Answer

With the development of society, customs and habits have changed a lot. For example, Chinese people used to have the habit of calling on each other or exchanging presents during festivals, but with the modern conveniences and facilities such as the telephone and the computer and people's greater concern for privacy, they would choose to communicate by telephone or e-mail now. Are these changes good or bad?

People who oppose the changes hold that some long-cherished precious traditions are lost with the changes of customs and habits such as the above-mentioned examples. Despite the conveniences, modern technology also brings side effects. Modern people are more and more isolated and indifferent to each other. Furthermore, these people are worried that changes of customs and habits imply the betrayal of our forefathers, our past, and our history. They also point out that people are morally deteriorating with the loss of tradition. Material gains are much valued than spiritual ones, which may eventually give rise to a national crisis.

Indeed, the changes of customs and habits have many disadvantages, but in the meantime there exist advantages to these changes. Firstly, some customs and habits came into being only because of people's superstition and ignorance. This kind of customs has brought more harm than good to the society and the nation. The customs of giving lucky money in the Spring Festival and holding large dinner parties at wedding lay a heavy economic burden on people. Secondly, many old-fashioned customs do not respect human rights and distort human nature. Even today some Arabic countries still keep the customs of killing the female family members who are sexually abused by villains, for the disgrace they bring to the family.

In conclusion, I think it is a good phenomenon that customs and habits have changed. New customs and habits can make people's communication more efficient, and they allow people to communicate with each other in an equal, natural and simple manner. New customs and habits have created more opportunities for women such as education, employment and management. With the advance of society, all people will enjoy a better life.

▶考官评分:8

题目:

随着社会的发展，风俗习惯改变了许多。这是一个好现象还是坏现象？你的意见是什么？

译文:

随着社会的发展，风俗习惯也改变了许多。比如说，中国人过去常常在节日期间相互拜访或者互送礼物，但是有了现代的便利设备和设施，例如电话和电脑，还有人们对个人隐私的更多关注，人们现在会选择通过电话或电子邮件交流了。这些改变是好事还是坏事呢？

反对这些改变的人认为，一些被珍视已久的宝贵传统会随着上述例子中风俗习惯的改变而被遗弃。尽管这些便利设备及现代科技同样带来负面影响，现代人彼此之间越来越孤立和冷漠。此外，这些人担心风俗习惯的改变意味着对我们祖先、过去、历史的背叛。他们同样指出人们会随着传统的丧失而道德败坏。物质利益比精神利益更宝贵，这有可能最终导致民族危机。

确实，风俗习惯的改变有许多不足，但与此同时这些改变也存在着优点。首先来说，一些风俗习惯的产生仅仅是由于人们的迷信和无知。这种风俗带给社会和民族的弊大于利。过春节给压岁钱和举行特大的婚礼宴会的风俗使人们承受一笔沉重的经济负担。其次，许多旧风俗实在不重视人权且扭曲人的天性。甚至现如今一些阿拉伯国家仍然保留着杀掉遭受坏人性侵犯的女性的习俗，因为她们给家族带来了耻辱。

总而言之，我认为风俗习惯的改变是一个好现象。新的风俗习惯可以使人们的交流更便捷，而且使人们平等、自然和朴素地相互交流。新的风俗习惯为女人创造了例如教育、工作和管理等越来越多的机会。随着社会的进步，所有人都将享受到更好的生活。

范文点评:

辩论型题目。范文使用了对称式结构。第一段解释了题目，还引用了一些生活中的例子来论述题目，作者并没有直接提出自己观点，而是提出一个疑问，中间两段分别陈述了风俗习惯改变的好与坏，并且每段用三到四句左右论述了主题句，最后一段提出自己观点。范文引用了一些例子，非常形象的支持了作者观点，结构严谨，语言流畅，生动。

128. 传统服装

Topic:

Now many people are forgetting their history and culture, so some people suggest that we should encourage people to wear their traditional clothing every day. Do you agree?

Sample Answer

Some people suggest that we should wear our traditional clothing every day, since many people are forgetting history and culture. As far as I am concerned, this proposal seems a bit absurd and ridiculous.

Nobody should ignore and forget our brilliant history and gorgeous culture. Without doubt, traditional clothing is part of our cultural heritage as well as a symbol of our civilization. In many people's eyes, the traditional clothing is elegant and graceful, with which I am totally in agreement. But it doesn't mean that old-fashioned dresses are suitable for our work and life in the present-day modern society.

We are living in a brand new era, full of challenges and opportunities. With the tempo of people's living and working speeding up, people have to hurry up to work on weekdays, and go outdoors to exercise or relax themselves on weekends; therefore there are different sorts of clothes for different functions and occasions. Furthermore, it is a superficial way to encourage people to wear traditional clothes with the aim of remembering history and culture. I don't think it works as some advocates expect.

The campaign to make sure not to forget our history and culture calls for long-term efforts. People can be better cultivated through comprehensive education in history and culture. When people are learning more about history and culture, their pride and curiosity will be aroused. I believe that this kind of education will play a crucial role in keeping people remembering the past and benefit the future generations. Moreover, we should adopt a correct attitude toward the past, that is to say, to absorb the essence and reject the dross.

In a word, I can hardly share the proposal that people should be encouraged to wear the traditional clothing every day in order to preserve history and culture. However, on some special occasions such as during Chinese traditional festivals, it is acceptable to wear traditional costumes, which adds colour to the festivity.

▶考官评分:8

题目：

现在很多人正在遗忘他们的历史和文化，因此一些人建议应该鼓励人们每天穿着传统服装，你是否同意此观点？

译文：

鉴于许多人对历史文化的遗忘，一些人建议我们应该每天都穿着传统服饰，在我看来这个提议似乎有点荒唐可笑。

每个人都不应该忽视和忘记我们灿烂的历史和美好的文化。毫无疑问，传统服饰既是我们文化遗产的一部分，又是我们文明的标志。在许多人眼中传统服饰非常典雅大方，对此我完全赞同。但这并不意味着旧时的穿着适合我们现代社会的工作和生活。

我们生活在一个充满挑战和机遇的新时代。随着人们生活和工作节奏的加快，人们不得不在工作日匆忙赶去上班，在周末去户外锻炼或放松自己。因此不同的用途和场合需要穿不同类型的衣服。此外，鼓励人们穿传统服饰来记住历史文化是一种肤浅的方法。我并不认为这样做就能如一些支持者所预期的那么有效。

这项确保铭记我们历史文化的活动需要长久的努力。人们可以通过对历史文化的综合教育而变得更有素养。当人们学习更多的历史文化时，会激起他们的自尊心和好奇心。我相信，这种教育会在使人们铭记过去的历史文化与有益于后代上起到至关重要的作用。况且，我们应该以一种正确的态度对待过去，也就是说，取其精髓去其糟粕。

总之，我实在难以赞同应该鼓励人们每天穿传统服饰以便保护历史文化的提议。然而，诸如中国传统节日等一些特殊场合，穿传统服饰合情合理，得给节日增添了许多色彩。

范文点评：

辩论型题目。范文使用的一边倒结构。第一段使用“欲扬先抑式”，提出自己的观点：旧时的穿着并不适合我们如今现代社会的工作和生活。中间两段分析作者观点，每段使用两至三句支持句，最后一段，重申自己的观点。整篇文章结构合理，理由充分。

129. 时尚服装和舒适服装

Topic:

Nowadays, the trend of fashion changes very rapidly, and gradually people become the slaves of it. Some people think that a person should choose comfortable clothes, which he or she likes, regardless of fashion, do you agree? Write an essay to state your opinion.

Sample Answer

One of the most fickle things in modern society is fashion. Fashion leaders are constantly inventing new trends in clothing and decoration, and consequently a great amount of time and money is spent on this endless pursuit. To correct this human feeling, some people advocate that one should wear comfortable clothes which are in line with one's personal taste. To me, this is a very sensible idea.

We all admit that clothing should be able to illustrate a person's individual characteristics. Everyone has the right to seek his or her unique style, instead of surrendering to the latest fashion. If you want to be different from others, you should not follow the fashion; you should have your own style. Following the latest fashion trend only makes you a tiny drop in an ocean of people.

At the same time, we should be clear that the basic function of clothing is to keep us warm and comfortable; therefore, it is stupid to choose clothes which may be pleasant to our eyes, but are tortured to wear. The impression we make on others is often important, but it can never be important enough to make us willingly undergo discomfort.

In a word, it is unwise to follow the trend of fashion aimlessly. **To be relaxed, modern people, we should form our own style and wear clothes that make us comfortable and self-confident.**

▶考官评分:8

题目:

如今，时尚改变的趋势非常迅速并且为人们所追求。一些人认为人们应该穿舒适的衣服，只要是他/她喜欢的，即使不是时尚的也好，你是否同意？写一篇文章陈述观点。

译文:

在现代社会中，时尚变幻无常。时尚达人总是在服装和装饰方面不断引领新潮流。因此，大量的时间和金钱都花在这无休止的追求上。有些人认为，要想纠正这些人的观念，应穿符合个人品味的舒适衣服。对我来说，这是一个非常明智的想法。

我们都承认，服装应该能够体现一个人的个性特征。每个人都有权要求他或她拥有独特的风格，而不是盲目跟随最新的时尚。如果你想与众不同，你不应该只是跟随潮流，你应该有自己的风格。跟随最新的潮流只会使你在人潮人海中变得更加渺小。

与此同时，我们应该清楚衣服的基本功能是能让我们保持温暖和舒适，因此，如果只是为了满足我们眼睛的需求，但是却穿得不舒服，这是愚蠢的选择，我们给人的印象的确重要，但是绝不能重要到足以使我们心甘情愿地接受不适。

总之，盲目地跟随潮流是不明智的。现代人应该放松些，我们应该形成我们自己的风格，让我们自己感到舒适和自信。

130. 传统建筑与现代建筑

Topic:

Modern buildings are appearing in large numbers, some people believe that we should build our buildings in traditional styles. To what extent do you agree or disagree?

Sample Answer

Large cities in the world are just construction sites all year round and many modern buildings, especially skyscrapers with glass walls, are being erected here and there. Buildings in traditional styles have given way to all these modern giants. From my own perspective, this is an avoidable trend if we wish to house more people and host more offices as more and more people are swarming into cities.

In the first place, modern buildings can house more people and host more offices. We know that a modern building can be as high as over 100 stories, thus, with the same land base, far more rooms are created by directing the construction upward. This is particularly necessary when we take into consideration the fact that the population explosion has made large cities more crowded than ever before and land prices are rocketing to ever broken records with each passing year.

In the second place, modern buildings can make valuable tourist resources. In fact, many skyscrapers have become the symbols of some metropolis around the world and a visit to them becomes a must. For example, the Oriental Pearl Television Tower and the Jinmao Tower, two symbols of Shanghai with a height of over 400 meters, have attracted millions of visitors every year, bring in a huge amount of money.

Admittedly, traditional buildings have their own advantages when compared with modern concrete structures. They are more like homes, cozier and more convenient. There is no need for one to press a button and then wait for a long time in order to be elevated to a certain story or vice versa. And people don't have to worry about a power failure which will bring so much trouble to going up and down. However, it would be a mere fantasy to expect large cities to develop in such a way with available land areas shrinking at amazing rates nowadays.

Therefore, building more modern buildings in our cities seems to be the only way out in providing more rooms for city dwellers and all kinds of business firms and offices.

▶考官评分:8

题目:

现代化建筑物的数量在不断增加，一些人认为我们应该建造传统建筑物，你是否同意此观点?

译文:

世界上的各大城市一年到头简直就是建筑工地。许多现代化的建筑，尤其是带玻璃幕墙的摩天大楼在各个地方拔地而起。传统风格的建筑已让位于这些现代化的建筑。从我个人的角度来看，随着越来越多的人涌入城市，如果我们想建造更多的办公室来容纳更多的人，这样做就是一个不可避免的趋势。

首先，现在建筑可以容纳更多人和办公室。我们知道，一座现代化的建筑可以高达100多层，因此，在同样面积的地基上，通过建高层便可建造出更多的房间来。当我们考虑到人口爆炸已使得大城市比以往任何时候都更加拥挤不堪以及土地价格也逐年蹿升、不断创出新高这些事实时，这样做就尤为必要了。

其次，现代化的建筑可以成为宝贵的旅游资源。事实上，很多摩天大楼已经成为世界上一些大都市的象征，从而成为人们游览的必去之处。比如，上海的两座象征性建筑：东方明珠和金茂大厦，高度都超过400米，每年要吸引数百万的游客，给上海带来了很可观的收入。

诚然，与现代混凝土建筑相比，传统建筑有其自身的优势：他们更有家的感觉、更温馨和方便。人们没有必要为了上到某个楼层或下降至某个楼层而去按动一个按钮，然后等上好半天。人们无需担心停电而给上上下下所带来的巨大麻烦。然而，随着当今可用土地面积以惊人的速度在缩小，期盼大城市如此发展只能是妄想。

因此，在我们的城市中建造更多的现代化高楼似乎是为城市居民和各种各样的商务公司、办事处提供更多空间的惟一出路。

范文点评:

辩论型题目。范文使用一边倒结构，第一段用三句话介绍了背景，中间写了两个理由段，并且用二至三句话支持了自己的观点，最后一段只用一句话总结了观点。范文结构合理，语言上除了使用定语从句等加分句型外，还用一些例子支持自己观点，非常生动。

131. 传统食品

Topic:

What are your opinions about the advantages and disadvantages of "fast food" and "traditional food"?

Sample Answer

When we talk about fast food, we are referring to food such as hamburgers, chips, etc., that can be cooked easily, and is generally sold by restaurants to be eaten quickly or taken away, while "traditional food" is elaborately prepared, usually at home, using traditional methods.

Fast food, as its name implies, is usually quick to prepare. When making sandwiches, for example, you take a slice of ham plus two pieces of bread and put them together-that's all there is to it. This presents a great advantage in this fast-moving modern society. It saves you a lot of time, so that you can devote more energy to your work and gain a competitive edge. Moreover, sandwiches are easy to make, and you don't have to be a good cook to prepare your lunch or dinner. The ingredients are ready-made, and all you have to do is to put them together. However, some people frown on fast food, believing that it is less tasty and less nutritious. Some people even call fast food "junk food."

On the other hand, traditional foods generally involve elaborate preparations. Because of all the efforts you invest in the preparation of such meals, they usually look and taste better, which may enhance your appetite. The cooking of traditional food accommodates a number of factors, such as color, smell and taste, and most importantly, nutrition. Besides, the cuisine that is related to traditional food is part of any culture. But the cooking of traditional food tends to be time-consuming, involves the use of utensils and takes time to learn. On top of all this, traditional meals are usually much more expensive than fast food.

Fast food started out as an expedient to cater to those who can't afford the time to cook or the expense of traditional food. Now it has become part of our life. Like it or not, it is here to stay. On the other hand, traditional food is an inalienable part of our culture, which we can't afford to give up. So, all in all, the co-existence of the two kinds of foods only makes our life more colorful.

▶考官评分:8

题目:

你认为快餐和传统饮食的优点与缺点是什么?

译文:

每当谈起快餐，我们就会提及汉堡包、薯条这类食物，因为它们制作简便，食用方便而且还可以外带，并且在餐厅都普遍有售，然而传统饮食就需要精心的准备，一般都是在家采用一些传统的制作方法。

速食，正如其名，食物可以快捷地被准备好。比如当你要做一个三明治，你只需要拿两片面包再夹上一片火腿就可以完成了，如此而已。这个对于当今高速发展的社会是很有利的。它能为你节省很多时间，这样你就能有更多的精力投入到你的工作上来，从而更具有竞争优势。此外，三明治很容易制作，你不需要成为一个好的厨师就能烹饪你的午餐或晚餐。这些配料都是现成的，你需要做的只是把它们组合在一起。而有些人对速食反感，因为他们觉得速食缺乏营养，不好吃，甚至有的人还把速食叫做“垃圾食品”。

另一个方面，传统食物的制作总是会涉及复杂的准备工作。因为你投入了所有的精力来准备这种菜肴，当然它们在外观和味道上都更胜一筹，也可以提高你的食欲。在传统食物的制作工艺上要注重几点因素，比如色、香、味，还有最重要的就是营养。此外，料理都与一部分文化有关。但是烹饪传统食物是很费时的，要用到很多器皿，并且需要花费大量的时间去学习。最重要的一点，传统食物通常都要比速食昂贵很多。

速食的起源主要是为了迎合那些没时间做饭或者说消费不起传统食物的群体。现在却已成了我们生活的一部分。不管你喜不喜欢，它确实已经存在了。另外，传统食物是我们文化中不可分割的一部分，我们不能把它放弃。所以，总而言之，只有这两种食物的共同存在才让我们的生活变得更加丰富多彩。

范文点评：

由于涉及到需要分析“优点”与“缺点”，所以这是一个解释型题目，必须使用对称式结构。第一段简单陈述了快餐与传统食品的定义及区别。中间的理由段有两段，各用一段分析了快餐与传统食品的优点和缺点，最后一段再次重申观点及其理由。整篇文章结构合理，理由充分。语言上模版句型使用较少，语言流畅。

132. 语言消失

Topic:

Several languages are dying out every year. However, some people do not think it is important and claim that our life will be simpler with fewer languages. To what extent do you agree or disagree?

Sample Answer

Language extinction is so alarming that it has elicited a heated discussion. As for me, I doubt that our life will be simplified and beautified as some languages lose popularity.

Admittedly, various communication tools have inevitably posed a severe threat to a smooth and harmonious exchange among distinct countries where languages are differentiated. As a result, maybe misunderstanding or even conflict will ensue due to lack of a thorough understanding. However, resorting to depriving some languages of existence to solve that problem of communication is far from a perfect methodology.

As we know, language is the representative of a nation's particular culture, so the disappearance of the former will lead to a void culture. A language, no matter oral or written, is a definite carrier of fantastic and shimmery civilization accumulated after a series of generations of a country, hence certifying the substantial power of culture. How can we tolerate the extinction of language, or specifically culture? Moreover, what culture signifies is the characteristic root of a nation. Language dying gradually out means a rootless culture, so a nation will be not an entity in a true sense.

Furthermore, if there are only a small number of languages in the world, how monotonous it is! Each language is the embodiment of the essence of a race, which is absolutely distinctive from others. **It is the charismatic attraction of various languages that spice up the whole world and thus traveling to the different is the favorite to modern people.** Let us imagine what will happen if several or only one language can be heard wherever we go. It is terrible indeed.

From the above-mentioned discussion, it is conceded that language dying out is beneficial to our life to some extent, yet I am convinced that the drawbacks of the phenomenon have overshadowed the advantages offered. It is not, or will not be reasonable to sacrifice language to attain a smooth communication.

▶考官评分:8

题目:

每年都有好几种语言消失。然而，一些人并不认为它们是重要的并且声称更少的语言会让我们的生活变得简单。在多大程度上你赞同或者反对此观点?

译文:

语言灭绝是如此的令人担忧，以至于引起了激烈的讨论。对于我来说，我怀疑我们的生活会由于一些语言的流行性消失而更简单、更美好。

大家一致认为各种通讯工具不可避免地对不同语言国家之间的顺畅和谐交流构成了严重的威胁。因此，由于缺乏一个全面的了解而误解甚至导致冲突。然而，通过剥夺一些语言的存在这种方法去解决沟通的问题远远不是一个完美的方法。

众所周知，语言是一个国家特有文化的代表，所以前者的消失会导致空无的文化。一种语言，无论是口头的或者是书面的，绝对是神奇和闪亮的，并且是经过几代人积累的文明载体，因此证明了文化的巨大力量。我们怎么能忍受语言或者尤其是文化的消失呢？此外，文化是一个国家最有特征的根基。语言的逐步消亡意味着文化没有根基，所以一个国家在真正的意义上不会成为一个整体。

此外，如果世界上只有少数的几种语言根基，那是多么的单调！每一种语言都是一个国家民族本性的体现，是绝对不同于其他的。这就是语言的吸引力所在，不同的语言使整个世界充满趣味性，因此去不同的地方旅游是现代人最喜欢的事情。让我们想象无论我们去哪儿如果我们只能听到几种或一种语言，那确实太可怕了。

从以上的讨论中，我们承认语言消失在某种程度上有利于我们的生活，但我深信它的弊端超过了它的优势。为了能够顺利的沟通，牺牲语言不是，或不会是合理的。

133. 语言文化多样性

Topic:

What are the reasons for losing a variety of languages and cultures?

Sample Answer

Nowadays people all over the world, especially the young people seem to live in the same way. They drink Coco-Cola, eat McDonald's hamburgers, and see the movies such as Star Wars, made by Hollywood. Instead of their own country's traditional festivals, they even celebrate the Christmas. It is an undeniable fact that we are losing the variety of language and culture. In my opinion, there are two main reasons.

The alarming increase of people's enthusiasm of learning English accounts mainly for this issue. In China, the number of people who study English is on the rise. For going abroad or seeking for a good career, some university students even spend more than half of their studying time on this foreign language. As a result, they neglect the learning of their own country's language and culture. They have little time to read books, magazines and newspapers written in Chinese, their own national language. No matter whether their English is fluent or not, they cannot express their ideas in Chinese very well. I am one of them. When I prepare for IELSTS writing, faced with some topics, within 40 minutes, I even fail to write them in Chinese.

The loss of variety of language and culture also attributes to the development of tourism. The tourist trade is booming. Superb systems of communication by air, sea and land make it possible for us to visit each other's countries at a moderate cost. What was once the "grand tour", reserved for only the very rich, is now within everybody's grasp.Therefore, a greater understanding develops between the nations of the world. That is to say, while the foreign ways introduced by travelers have a deep influence on the local people, the visitors are also deeply influenced by the local culture.

Flowers with different colors make a garden more beautiful. Thus, effective measures must be taken to deal with the loss of variety of language and culture.

▶考官评分:8

题目:

遗失各种语言和文化的原因是什么?

译文:

现今世界上所有的人，尤其是年轻人都在以看似相同的方式生活。他们喝可口可乐，吃麦当劳的汉堡包，看着例如好莱坞制作的《星际争霸》之类的电影。这些已经取代了他们国家传统的节日，他们甚至庆祝圣诞节。这是一个不可否认的事实：我们正在遗失各种各样的语言和文化。在我看来，主要有两个主要原因。

人们对英语学习热情的急剧增加是主要原因。在中国，学习英语的人数在不断增加。由于希望出国寻求更好的职业，一些大学生甚至花费一大半的学习时间来学习英语。所以，导致他们忽略了学习自己国家的语言和传统。他们很少有时间来读用中文（他们母语）写的书，杂志和报纸。无论他们的英语是否流利，他们都不能很好地用中文表达他们的思想。我就是他们当中的一员，当我准备雅思写作的时候，面对一些话题，在四十分钟以内，我甚至不能用中文写出来。

各种语言和文化的流失也同样归结于旅游业的发展。旅游业正在蓬勃发展。在优质的通讯系统中通过空中，海上，陆地（交通工具）我们可以以一个适当的成本访问其他国家。曾经所谓的“大旅游”（只为非常富有的人而保留），如今每个人都能做到。因此，加深了世界上各个国家之间的了解。也就是说，当游客带来的外国方式对本地人有很深的影响时，而旅游者也会同样受当地文化很深的影响。

不同颜色的花使花园更加美丽。因此，必须用有效的方法来处理各种语言和文化流失的现象。

范文点评：

此题是解释型题目，所以范文使用的是对称式结构。范文共四段，开头段使用四句话介绍背景，没有使用任何模板式句型，是本篇文章的一个加分点。中间用两个理由段说明了各种语言和文化遗失的原因，最后一段使用了比喻句陈述了需要用有效方法处理这种现象的必要性。整篇文章结构合理，理由充分。在语言上，全篇文章使用了的模板式句型比较少。

134. 创造一个全球通用的语言是否必要

Topic:

Do you think there is the necessity of creating a new global language? Give specific reasons and examples.

Sample Answer

Maybe there are people who believe that there is the necessity of creating a new world language. They may also give all kinds of reasons for doing so. However, no matter how sound these reasons are, I'm convinced I won't accept them. Let me convey my mind more clearly: I don't think there's any necessity to create a global language.

First of all, English has, in fact, become a global language. Nowadays, English-speaking countries are the most developed in almost every aspect and English has accordingly become the most influential language in the world. Statistics show that English accounts for

80% of the world's entertainment language such as movies, television and music. It also takes up 75% of the world's IT language. It can be said that there are a large proportion of people in almost every country around the world who are learning English for reasons ranging from job hunting considerations to international-exchange necessities. There's no exaggeration that people who don't know English will find it increasingly difficult to survive.

Moreover, facts have proved that it is extremely time and energy consuming to learn a new language. In fact, someone has long created one and has made great efforts for people to learn to use it. It is Esperanto. However, this effort has turned out to be in vain because not too many people really learnt it or used it. Why so? The reason is simple: any foreign language needs years of industrious efforts to learn well with the only exception of one's mother tongue, which is usually acquired in a natural manner and in a natural environment.

All in all, it is just unwise to create a new world language.

▶考官评分:8

题目:

你认为有必要创造一种新的全球语言吗？给出具体的理由和例子。

译文:

也许有人会认为创造一门新的全球语言是必要的，而且会给出多种多样的理由，但是，不管这些理由多么充分，我相信自己肯定是不会接受的。让我表述得更清楚明了些：我认为没有任何必要再去创造一门新的世界性语言。

首先，英语事实上已经成为一门世界性的语言。如今，说英语的国家是世界上各方面都最为发达的国家，英语从而也就相应地成为最具影响力的语言。据统计，英语占据了比如电影、电视和音乐等80%的娱乐界语言和75%的IT语言。可以说，世界上任何一个国家都有相当比例的人因为工作、国际交流等各方面的原因在学习这门语言。毫不夸张地讲：不会英语的人会越来越发现生存变得愈发困难。

再者，事实证明：学好任何一门语言都是件极为费时费力的事情。而且，历史上也的确有人尝试过创造并推广一门新的世界语言，那就是世界语，但是，最终并没有多少人去学习或学会，这个努力最终也就徒劳了。为什么会这样呢？因为除了母语是在自然环境下学会的之外，学习任何一门外语都要经过多年的努力付出。

综上所述，重新创造一种全球性语言绝非明智之举。

范文点评:

范文共四段，第一段解释题目并引出作者观点，中间两个理由段，论述了作者认为的没有必要再去创造一门新的世界性语言的观点，最后一段一句话重申了观点。范文结构清晰，语言上除了使用定语从句等加分语言，还用一些例子使观点更具有说服力。

135. 同一语言

Topic:

At present many people think that one language should be used as the common language, but others think that by doing so the cultures of different nations will be lost. What do you think of these two opinions?

Sample Answer

These days, there is an increasing number of scholars who hold the opinion that, with the development of globalization, we need a common language to be spoken by all the people in the world, however other scholars are afraid that this will weaken other languages and cultures at the same time. As for me, I am not in favor of the viewpoint that one language should replace others as the common one.

In the first place, nowadays it is universally acknowledged that language is not only a tool of communication but also a kind of art. Each language, no matter what kind of language it is, it has its unique pronunciation, grammar and expressions, which contribute to the diversity of the world. So, if the diverse languages are diminished, our world will become less colorful.

In the second place, we can say that language is a part of culture, and plays a considerably important role in it. Indeed, some social scientists consider it the keystone of culture. Without language, so the argument goes, culture would not be possible. On the other hand, language is influenced and shaped by culture; it reflects culture. In the broadest sense, language is the symbolic representation of a people, and it comprises their historical and cultural backgrounds as well as their approach to life and their ways of living and thinking. Cultures differ from one another, and each culture is unique. There is no denying the fact it will be a disaster for us to see the world's diverse cultures disappear one by one.

When all the factors are examined, we may safely come to the conclusion that although we are convinced that, no matter what our career choice is, a command of foreign languages is an important skill to acquire, yet we should protect our own language, the carrier of our culture.

▶考官评分:8

题目:

如今一些人认为应该使用一种通用语言，但另一些人认为如果这样做将遗失其他语言和文化。你怎样看待这两种观点?

译文：

最近，随着全球化的发展，越来越多的学者支持世界上的所有人使用相同的语言表达观点，但是也有学者担心这样将同时削弱其他语言和文化。就我而言，我不赞成以一种语言替代其他所有语言作为共同语言。

首先，现在人们普遍认识到，语言不仅仅是一种交流的工具，同时也是一种艺术。每一种语言，不论是什么样的语言，都有其独特的发音、语法和表达方式，都对世界的多样性做出了贡献。因此，如果减少语言的种类，我们的世界也会因此失色，变得不那么丰富多彩。

第二，我们可以说，语言是文化的一部分，在文化中扮演着相当重要的角色。事实上，一些社会科学家认为，语言是文化的基石。依据论据而言，没有语言谈何文化。另一方面，文化影响和塑造了语言，语言又反映着文化。从广义上讲，语言是民族的象征，它包括人们的历史和文化背景以及他们的生活态度、生活方式和思维。文化互有不同，独一无二。事实上，如果我们看到世界上各种不同的文化逐渐消失，那将是一场不容否认的灾难。

综上所述，我们可以肯定地得出结论，虽然我们相信无论我们选择何种职业，掌握一门外语是一项重要的技能。但是，我们应该保护自己的语言，因为它是我们的文化载体。

范文点评：

辩论型题目。范文使用了一边倒结构。第一段解释了题目直接引出观点。中间用两段分析了作者观点，最后一段重申自己观点。范文结构完整清晰，语言上较少的使用了模版句型，还使用了一些如主语从句，宾语从句等加分句型。

136. 全球一体化

Topic:

Differences between countries have become less evident. For example, nowadays the same films, fashions, brands and TV programs are found worldwide. To what extent do you think the disadvantages of this outweigh its advantages?

Sample Answer

Globalization creates conditions for widening international exchanges and strengthening mutual understanding between nations. It expands cultural, educational, and scientific cooperation between countries. It encourages the process of modernization and the enrichment of national culture. However, I believe the disadvantages of this outweigh its advantages.

Globalization creates the possible danger of diminishing the national culture and exerts a negative impact on the preservation of national identity. Through globalization and an open door policy, erroneous concepts and a lowering of ethical standards, a selfish and individualistic lifestyle and harmful cultural products can easily be imported into the country. At present, modern information technology which in the main is controlled by US is hourly and intensively disseminating US ideology, way of life, and culture across the world. Even US food is promoted so that some people consider globalization as global Americanization.

During the process of economic globalization, inequality between developed and developing countries has been increasing and the gap between the rich and the poor has become wider. Globalization goes to assist developed countries. Globalization does not pose equal interests and risks to all nations. With an overwhelming advantage compared with most of the developing countries in terms of finance and the level of science and technology, developed capitalist countries control the situation of economic globalization.

For these reasons, globalization is a fierce and complicated struggle in both cultural and ideological fields. As the proverb says, fire is a good servant, but a bad master. We take the initiative in international economic integration but also have to take the initiative in fighting to prevent our distinct culture from cross-bred phenomena.

▶考官评分:8

题目:

国家之间的差异已经不那么明显了。举例来说，同样的电影、时尚、品牌和电视在全世界范围内都能找到，你认为这样弊大于利吗?

译文:

全球化为扩大国际合作创造了条件，加强了国家之间的相互理解。这也扩大了国家之间在文化、教育和科技领域的合作。它促进了现代化的进程、丰富了民族文化。然而，我认为，这一进程的不利之处超过了它的优点。

全球化可能导致民族文化消失，并且在保持民族特色方面有负面的影响。通过全球化和对外开放政策，错误的观念和低劣的伦理标准、自私和个人主义的生活方式以及有害的文化产品能够很容易地被传入本国。当前，主要由美国控制的现代信息技术时刻在世界范围内集中地散布美国的意识形态、生活方式和文化甚至宣传美国的食品，以至于一些人认为全球化就是全球美国化。

在经济全球化的过程中，发达国家和发展中国家的不平等在加剧，贫富差距在扩大。全球化进程确实对发达国家帮助很大。全球化并没有为所有的国家带来同等的利益和风险。与大多数的发展中国家相比，发达国家在经济和科技水平方面占据着绝对优势，发达的资本主义国家控制了经济全球化的局势。

基于这些原因，全球化在文化和意识形态领域进行着激烈而复杂的斗争。谚语云，火是一把双刃剑。我们在经济全球化的过程中应采取主动，在努力防止我们的文化被同化方面要采取主动。

137. 英语的普及和旅游业的发展是否伤害了少数民族和小语种？

Topic:

Will the popularity of English and tourism harm the minorities and minor languages?

Sample Answer

Economic globalization benefits the world immensely, especially the prosperity of tourism. As a result, the cultures, languages and customs in the minorities are not mysterious to the world any more, which should be attributed to the popularity of tourism.

It is a consensus that tourism can stimulate the economic development in a region, since tourism plays an important role in the acceleration of the improvement of service, such as transportation, accommodation, catering and other marginal business. With a view to attracting more tourists, the minority regions have to consider how to improve their image and service, during the course of which they can have an overall plan to promote the status of their region. Nowadays, many people travel for minority regions to satisfy their curiosity, where they can have unexpected findings.

Furthermore, tourism can strengthen the interflow of cultures and traditions between the people in different regions. Trips to minority countries and regions render people a lot of new cultures and customs, which, presumably, have been handed down from old ages and enjoyed very splendid history. Formerly, people can only get some segments about the minorities from videos, films and other incomplete descriptions on books. Now, tourists have more opportunities to communicate or even live with the minority people and acquire first-hand knowledge about them, which provides the researchers with a lot of authentic information.

Admittedly, tourism damages the natural environment in some minority regions and spoils the peaceful life of them to some degree due to their frequent activities in the minority regions, the environment being deteriorated in some regions, which is not what we expected.

Generally, the popularity of English and tourism brings more advantages than damage to the minority regions, since it has enriched people's knowledge and widened their horizons. But meanwhile, we should be on the alert for the damage to the minority regions and take effective means to tackle the problems tourism arouses.

▶考官评分:8

题目:

英语的普及和旅游业的发展是否会伤害少数民族和小语种?

译文:

经济全球化进程极大地有利于世界的发展，特别是旅游业的发展。正因为如此，少数民族的文化、语言和风俗对世人已不再神秘，这都要归功于旅游业的发展。

人们已经普遍认为由于旅游业在加速服务业发展的过程中起到了极为重要的作用，如交通，住宿，餐饮及其他与商务有关业务，所以它能够刺激一个地区经济的发展。因此，为了吸引更多 的游客，少数民族地区需要考虑到如何提升他们的形象和提高他们的服务水平，在这一过程中，他们可以有一个整体性的计划用以提高本地区的地位优势。如今，很多人到少数民族地区去旅游，那里意料之外的发现可以满足他们的好奇心。

此外，旅游业可以加强不同地区人民之间的文化和传统交流。去少数民族国家和地区旅游使人们接触到许多新的文化和习俗。据推测这些文化和习俗是在古代产生并流传下来的，并有非常辉煌的历史。从前，人们只能从影像资料，电影和一些书籍的部分描述中了解少数民族的掠影。而现如今，游客有了更多的机会和少数民族的人们交流、甚至可以和他们共同居住来了解有关于他们的第一手资料，这也为我们的研究人员提供了大量真实的信息。

诚然，在一些少数民族地区，旅游业的发展破坏了他们的自然环境，游客们频繁的观光在一定程度上破坏了当地人平静的日常生活。某些地区环境正在恶化，所有的这些都不是我们所期望看到的。

总的来说，英语的普及和旅游业的发展对少数民族地区来说是利大于弊的，它们不仅丰富了人们的知识，更拓宽了人们的视野。但与此同时，人们应该警惕自己对少数民族地区所带来的破害，并采取相应有效的措施解决旅游业发展引起的问题。

138. 国际旅游业是否促进国家间的了解

Topic:

International tourism has become one of the biggest industries in the world. Some people think it unfortunately causes a lot of tension rather than understanding between people from different cultures. To what extent do you agree or disagree?

Sample Answer

The ever-increasing living standards make it possible that people can travel abroad, appreciating fascinating exotic cultures. Some people, however, point out that this exchange exerts a more negative impact on the relationship among people with different cultures and people tend to be more hostile towards each other. As for this assertion, I am rather doubtful.

It is generally agreed that the booming tourist industry can boost local economic development considerably. When people travel to a place of attraction, they will visit local shops, dine in restaurants and seek accommodations, which not only provides opportunities of making money, but also improves employment rate. If tourists can bring such benefits to host countries, then there is no doubt that they are warmly welcome, and a mutual understanding is likely to be established.

Moreover, through international travel, the platform of exchange can further tolerate feelings among different people. For example, when foreigners come to China, perhaps they will be startled when people greet each other with "Have you dined?", but gradually they know the true meaning is nothing more than a common concern showing social politeness. If similar phenomena occur frequently, so-called misunderstanding or culture shock will definitely come into non-existence.

Granted, international travel contains the potential threats such as environmental pollution and violation of cultural tattoos, which maybe tarnish tourist images. It is true that some travelers lack the awareness of environmental protection, throwing away rubbish anywhere they go. Meanwhile, due to being blind to local traditional customs, some people even arouse strong enmity from people in destination. Those undesirable practices, nevertheless, can be corrected through suitable education.

Overall, with the need to know more about the rest of the world and the high mobility modern transportation ensures, more people love international tourism. After all, travel is an indispensable part of human life.

▶考官评分:8

题目:

国际旅游业已经成为世界上最大的产业。一些人认为它在两国之间引起的关系紧张多于理解，在某种程度上你是否同意这种观点？

译文:

生活标准越来越高使人们出国去欣赏迷人的异国文化成为可能。然而一些人指出，这种交流对于来自不同文化之间人们的友谊有负面的影响，让人们更加敌视对方。就这种论断而言，我感到很怀疑。

人们普遍认为，旅游业的蓬勃发展能极大地促进当地的经济发展。当人们被一个地方吸引而去旅游，他们会去当地的商店买东西，去饭店吃饭，找地方住宿。这不仅为当地的人提供了赚钱的机会，而且提高了就业率。假如游客可以为东道国提供如此多的好处，毫无疑问他们会热烈欢迎，那么他们中间就能更加理解对方。

此外，通过国际旅行，这种交流平台可以更进一步地容忍不同人之间的分歧。例如，当外国人来到中国时，他们或许会因为中国人用“吃了吗？”互相问候而吃惊，但是他们逐渐知道了这样做的真正的含义无非是社会礼节中的一种普遍的关心而已。如果相似的现象时有发生，就不会出现所谓的误解或是文化冲击了。

但是，国际旅行也有潜在的威胁，例如，环境污染和文化渗透，从而玷污了旅游者的形象。确实一些旅游者缺乏环境保护意识，他们走到哪儿，垃圾扔到哪儿。由于无视当地习俗，一些人甚者引起了当地人的强烈不满。不过那些不良行为可以通过适当的教育改正。

总的来说，由于想了解世界其他地方和高机动性的现代交通保障，更多的人喜欢国际旅游。毕竟，旅游是人生不可或缺的一部分。

139. 世界杯缓解国家关系

Topic:

Sports events such as the World Cup may help reduce the tension between and bias towards countries. Discuss.

Sample Answer

There is no doubt in my mind that sports events which pit one country's athletes against another's can promote world peace. For one thing, they channel aggressive instincts into harmless competitions. For another, the spirit of sportsmanship dictates that one's opponent is not one's enemy, but a partner whose opposition helps to raise the level of one's skill. Moreover, a defeated opponent is not to be despised but to be honored, so long as he or she has played the game fairly and made every effort to win.

However, there is a dark side to international sports events these days. Many such competitions are funded by giant corporations, who regard them simply as advertising vehicles for their products. In addition, the pressure on top-class athletes to win is so great that they frequently resort to taking stimulants and other illegal drugs to enhance their performance. Another unfortunate result of this domination of sports by big money is that athletes from the poorer countries are seldom represented at the major world competitions.

This leads me to the conclusion that we should strongly support the Olympic Games, and make sure that money does not corrupt this international goodwill sports gathering. Everyone agrees that the Olympics are a shining example of how friendly rivalry can dissolve tensions between countries and promote harmony between their peoples. In this regard, it is important that the Games should be distributed more fairly among the countries of the world.

▶考官评分:8

题目:

体育赛事如世界杯可以减少两国之间的冲突和偏见，试讨论一下。

译文:

在我看来，毫无疑问，体育赛事中国与国之间运动员的对抗能促进世界和平。一方面，他们引入积极无害的竞赛项目。另一方面，体育精神决定对手不是敌人，而是有助于提高自己技能的合作伙伴。而且，参赛者只要他（她）公正地参加比赛并且在比赛中为获胜作出了努力，就算成为失败者也不会被藐视，而是被尊重。

然而，如今在国际赛事期间也有黑暗的一面。许多大公司以是否将他们的产品进行广告宣传作为资助比赛的条件。另外，由于顶级运动员因承受着要赢得比赛的压力而常常使用兴奋剂及其他非法药物以提高自己的比赛成绩。同时，由于比赛需要大量的资金投入，所以部分贫穷国家不能派代表参加这种世界赛事。

总之，我的结论是，我们应该坚决支持奥运会，并确保不会因资金而滋生这一国际友好体育聚会的腐败问题。大家一致认同，奥运会是一个能够证明友好竞争并且可以解决国家之间紧张关系和促进两国人民关系和谐的典范。鉴于此，奥运会在全球各国举行是相当重要的。

第八大类：政府类话题

140. 禁止吸烟

Topic:

Some people propose that smoking should be banned. Do you agree or disagree?

Sample Answer

Smoking is a social problem we are trying to solve. Some people suggest that the government should ban smoking. Indeed, smoking is detrimental to people's health and it violates the rights and freedom of nonsmokers. However, in my opinion, smoking should not be banned for the following reasons.

First of all, tobacco is a wonderful commodity to tax. It contributes much to the government's revenue. For example, the government of Britain collects enough from smokers to pay for its entire educational facilities. If smoking is banned, there will be a great drop in the government's income. In addition, more serious social problems will arise, such as unemployment, because tobacco industry employs a lot of workers.

Those who strongly approve of the ban lay too much emphasis on the rights of nonsmokers. They ignore smokers' rights. Smoking is just a personal hobby and amusement. It is a kind of lifestyle. It is a stress reliever and can bring great pleasure to smokers. On the contrary, for smokers, nothing seems more difficult and painful than giving up the habit.

We must admit that smoking is harmful to people's health. However, the harm that smoking brings to people's health is exaggerated. As long as we smoke in moderation, it will not cause great harm to our body. Take Mr. Churchill as an example. He both smoked and enjoyed a long life.

To sum up, I do not think that smoking should be banned. The tobacco industry makes a large contribution to the government's economy. Smoking also brings smokers many psychological benefits. Moreover, there is no evidence showing the direct link between smoking and any fatal diseases.

▶考官评分:8

题目:

有些人提倡禁止吸烟，你是否同意此观点 ?

译文:

吸烟是我们正在想办法解决的一个社会问题。有些人建议政府应该颁布禁烟令。确实，吸烟危害人们的健康，并且它侵犯了不吸烟人的权利和自由。然而，我认为，由于以下原因吸烟不应该被完全禁止。

烟草是一种很好的征税商品。它会为政府带来很可观的收入。例如，英国政府从吸烟者身上征税用于支付全部的教育设施。如果吸烟被禁止了，这对政府收入将会是一个很大的损失。另外，更严重的社会问题会由此产生，如失业，因为烟草行业雇用了很多的工人。

强烈赞成这个禁令的人过分强调不吸烟者的权利。他们忽视了吸烟者的权利。吸烟仅仅是一个人的爱好和消遣。它是一种生活方式。它是一种压力的释放，而且可以给吸烟者带来极大的快乐。相反，对于吸烟者来说，戒烟是最困难、最痛苦的事情。

我们必须承认吸烟对于人们的健康是有害的。然而，吸烟带给人们健康的这种伤害被夸大了。只要我们吸烟适度，就不会对身体造成很大的伤害。以丘吉尔先生为例，他既吸烟又长寿。

总而言之，我认为吸烟不应该被禁止。烟草工业对于政府的财政有很大的贡献。吸烟带给吸烟者很多心理上的安慰。而且，没有证据显示吸烟和致命疾病之间的任何联系。

141. 公共场所禁止吸烟

Topic:

Some businesses now say that no one can smoke cigarettes in any of their offices. Some governments have banned smoking in all public paces. This is a good idea but it also takes away some of our freedom. Do you agree or disagree?

Sample Answer

Currently, many governments have taken the lead in campaigns to eliminate smoking by banning smoking in public places, including restaurants, buses and trains. Now, an ever-growing number of private businesses are issuing regulations forbidding smoking by their employees in their offices. However, some sections of the populace say that, although they approve of the antismoking drive, the banning of smoking in offices is an attack on their freedom.

It must be borne in mind that smoking is a health hazard which affects not only the smoker himself, but also all the people around them. In fact, doctors tell us that almost as many people contract diseases—even fatal ones—from breathing "second-hand" smoke, as smokers do.

I am sure that I am not alone in stating that the hallmark of a civilized society is the willingness of citizens to give up some of their freedom for the common good. We all give up our freedom to walk in the roads which vehicles use, and the freedom to make loud noises at midnight which might disturb our neighbors. How much more sensible it is to give up the freedom of polluting the air that we must all breathe!

The critics may be right, but is it necessarily a bad thing to surrender some of our freedom in this case? To my mind, the ban on smoking must be made as total as possible to have a positive impact on the health of the general public. Therefore, although the critics of the office smoking ban may be right logically, they are certainly wrong morally.

▶考官评分:8

题目:

一些公司禁止员工在办公室吸烟，一些政府也出台政策禁止在公共场所吸烟。禁止在公共场所吸烟是好事，可是却剥夺了吸烟者的自由。你同意这种说法吗?

译文:

目前，许多政府率先通过在公共场所包括餐馆、公共汽车和火车上禁止吸烟来发起禁烟运动。现在，越来越多的私企制定禁止他们的员工在办公室吸烟的制度。然而，有些人说，虽然他们赞同反吸烟运动，但是在办公室禁止吸烟是对他们自由的一种攻击。

必须明确的是吸烟是危害健康的，它影响的不仅是吸烟者自已，而是影响周边所有的人。实际上，医生告诉我们，许多人从吸烟者那里吸到的二手烟几乎都会染病，甚至是致命的疾病。

我可以肯定的是我不是仅仅在阐明一个文明社会的标志是公民为了大众的利益自愿放弃他们的一些自由。我们全部放弃了我们在机动车道上行走的自由，放弃在午夜制造巨大噪音的自由，因为这会干扰我们的邻居。我们放弃了污染空气的自由因为我们要呼吸！还有更加明智的吗?

评论家也许是对的，但是在这件事情上我们放弃一些自由一定是坏事吗？我认为，必须要尽可能完全禁止吸烟，这样才能对公众的健康有积极的影响。所以，虽然对于办公室禁烟令的评论家来说也许理论上是正确的，但他们在道德上一定是错误的。

142. 投资艺术还是投资基础设施

Topic:

Some people say the government should not put money in the arts, such as music, opera and paintings, but instead should spend more money on construction of infrastructure. Discuss.

Sample Answer

Nowadays, the government is planning to allocate more funds on the construction of artistic projects such as museums, art galleries and parks. However, critics complain that this money should be spent more wisely, say, for building up basic infrastructure. This has aroused a heated debate among the citizens.

Some people contend that artistic and cultural projects will surely bring many advantages to the whole society. First of all, the projects can help people to cultivate a better taste for arts and enhance the sensitivity to beauty, thus enriching their spiritual life and upgrading their quality. A man does not live only by bread. Furthermore, these artistic projects are certainly not a money waster. They are potentially profitable. A beautiful city will attract more tourists, thereby boosting its economy. And the money so earned can be further used for the improvement of our standard of living, as well as for the construction of basic infrastructure.

However, views on this issue vary from person to person. Some people hold that priority should be given to basic infrastructure. Nowadays many countries are still struggling to achieve modernization and many people are still living below the poverty line. It is without saying that it is difficult to enjoy cultural and leisure pursuits if one's physical needs are not satisfied. So, surely no one would disagree that it is unreasonable to spend government revenue on cultural projects while millions of people still do not have enough food and clothing.

Personally I agree that more money should be spent on artistic and cultural projects. They contribute substantially to the landscaping of cities. It is shortsighted not to build them in our cities in the interest of saving money. They make good business sense.

▶考官评分:8

题目:

有些人认为政府应该把钱用于加强艺术文化建设，如音乐，雕塑和绘画，而不是花在提高基础建设水平。试讨论一下。

译文:

如今，政府正在计划拨更多的资金用在艺术事业的建设上，比如博物馆，画廊和公园。但是，批评家抱怨说这些钱应该花得更明智一点，比如用来建设基础设施。这在市民中引起了一场激烈的辩论。

有些人认为这些艺术文化工程的确会给整个社会带来很多好处。首先，这些工程能帮助人们培养一种对艺术更高的品位，增强人们对美的敏感度，因此丰富了他们的精神生活，也提高了他们的素质。人并不只是靠面包活着。而且，这些艺术工程当然不会浪费钱财。他们是有潜在利益价值的。一个美丽的城市会吸引更多的游客，进而推动经济的发展，而且这样赚来的钱可以进一步用来提高我们的生活质量以及基础设施建设。

不过，对于这个问题，人与人的观点是不同的。有些人认为应该优先考虑基础设施建设。如今很多国家仍然在追求现代化的路上挣扎，还有很多人仍然生活在贫困线以下。毫无疑问，一个连生理需求都不能满足的人去享受对文化和休闲的追求是很困难的。所以大家都认为在有上百万人仍然吃不饱穿不暖的情况下把政府收入投在文化项目上是不合理的。

我个人赞成把更多的钱花在艺术和文化工程上。他们对城市风景的美化做出了很大的贡献。为了省钱而不在我们的城市里去建造这些设施是种目光短浅的行为。它们有很好的商业意义。

143. 投资艺术还是投资医疗教育

Topic:

Some people said the government should not put money on building theatres and sports stadiums, and they should spend more money on medical care and education. Do you agree or disagree?

Sample Answer

Some people are of the opinion that with the limited budget the government should invest money in medical care and education. As I see it, theatres and sports stadiums are as important as, if not more important than medical care and education. So I believe that it is sagacious to spend money on the construction of theatres and sports stadiums.

Theatres can also play an important role in education. There are various forms of education and according to a survey people especially young children are more likely to receive education in the form of amusement. By watching plays, they are able to gradually learn how to adapt themselves to the society and how to communicate with others.

Investment in sports stadiums is an active measure to improve people's health. If people's health is improved, we need not spend too much money on medical care and the money to be saved each year can be considerably great, considering the large number of people. So investing money in sports stadiums can save a lot of money in the long run.

Theatres and sports stadiums have other practical uses. By watching plays in theatres, people can cultivate a better taste for arts and enhance the sensitivity to beauty, thus enriching their spiritual life and upgrading their quality. Do remember that a man does not live only by bread. Theatres also provide a kind of place of entertainment and recreation for common people to spend their leisure hours. Through sports activities, people can benefit both physically and mentally.

Of course, medical care and education are also essential. However, with our current limited budget, I prefer the choice of investment in theatres and sports stadiums.

▶考官评分:7

题目:

有些人认为政府应该把钱投在医疗教育上而不是艺术体育上，你同意这种观点吗?

译文:

有些人认为，政府应该把有限的资金投在医疗保健和教育上。在我看来，与医疗保健和教育相比，剧院和体育场即使不是更重要，也一样重要。所以，我认为应当把钱明智地花在建设剧院和体育场上。

戏院也可以在教育中发挥重要的作用。教育的形式有很多，根据调查，尤其是儿童更有可能接受寓教于乐的教育形式。通过观看戏剧，他们逐渐能够学会如何适应社会，以及如何与他人沟通。

投资体育场也是一个改善人民健康状况的积极措施。如果人民的健康得到改善，我们就不需要花太多的钱在医疗保健上，而且考虑到人口数量之多每年可节省许多钱。因此，从长远来看，投资体育场可以节省很多钱。

剧院和体育场也有其他许多实际用途。在影院看电影，人们可以培养出更好的艺术品味，加强对美的感知，从而丰富他们的精神生活并提高其素质。一个人的生活里并不是只有面包。剧院还提供了一种娱乐场所，可以使百姓度过闲暇时光。体育活动有益于人们的身体和精神的健康。

当然，医疗保健和教育也是必不可少的。然而我国目前的预算有限，那我宁愿选择投资于剧院和体育场。

144. 在资金上政府应该支持理科生还是应该支持文科生

Topic:

Science and technology develops very fast in the current society. Some people think that the government should give financial support to the students who study science and technology; some others think the government should support the students who study arts, language and business. What's your opinion?

Sample Answer

Our society owes a lot to the development of science and technology. The invention of automobiles shortens the distance of people's travel; the invention of airplanes makes the world become smaller; the invention of computers makes our work and study more efficient. All these should attribute to modern science and technology. But should the government only support the students in science financially and abandon the investment in study and research of other fields like arts, business administration and other humanity subjects? Personally, I don't agree to this opinion.

Firstly, the development of arts and other humanity subjects helps us understand our society and gives people spiritual enjoyment. For example, philosophy helps us know our world and think in right ways; arts cultivate people's aesthetic talents and abilities and help people understand what is beautiful and what is ugly; literature gives people joys and sorrows, rendering people abundant imagination.

Secondly, the development of arts and humanity subjects can help the development of science and technology. Facts prove that many scientists are also great artists. For example, Albert Einstein, the greatest scientist in the scientific history, was also a very good and professional violinist. Arts can help to cultivate people's thinking and imagination. That's the reason why the students in middle schools and universities are encouraged to develop artistic and literary interest.

Thirdly, if the government only gives financial support to the students in science and technology, the students will look down upon arts and humanity subjects and choose to study science and technology. Then, no one will be interested in arts.

To sum up, science and arts are complementary to each other. The government should put emphasis on both and encourage the students to choose what they like as their subject.

▶考官评分:8

题目:

当今世界科技飞速发展，一些人认为政府应该给予理科生财政支援，一些人却认为政府应该给文科生财政支援。你怎么看待这个问题?

译文:

我们社会要感谢科学技术的发展。汽车的发明缩短了人们旅行的距离。飞机的发明，使世界变得小了很多。计算机的发明使我们的工作效率更高。所有的这些都归功于现代科学技术的进步。但是政府怎么能仅仅在财政上支持理科生，同时放弃在其他领域或科研投资（像艺术、商业、管理、和其他人文科目）呢？我个人不同意这种观点。

首先，艺术和其他人文科学的发展帮助我们了解社会，带给人们精神上的享受，例如：哲学可以帮助我们认识世界和提供正确的思考方法；艺术培养人们的美学天赋和能力，并且帮助人们知道美丑之分；文学带给人们欢乐和悲伤，丰富人们的想象力。

其次，艺术和其他人文科学也有助于其他科学和技术的发展。事实证明许多科学家同时也是伟大的艺术家。例如：阿尔伯特·爱因斯坦这位在科学历史上不仅是伟大的科学家而且还是一位专业的小提琴家；艺术能培养人们的思考和想象力，这就是为什么在中学和大学时代鼓励学生发展艺术和文学的兴趣。

最后，如果政府在财政上仅仅支持理科生，这些学生将看不起艺术及其他人文科学，这样就不会有人对艺术感兴趣了。

总而言之，艺术和科学是相辅相成的，政府应该两者都重视，鼓励学生选择他们喜欢的科目。

145. 政府负责医疗和教育

Topic:

Some people say that the government should pay for the health care and education of its citizens, but other people say that it is not the government's responsibility. What is your opinion?

Sample Answer

There has long been a heated discussion about whether the government should shoulder the responsibilities for its people's basic expenses such as health care and education. Some people argue that yes, it's the government's unshakeable duty to do so. Others, by contrast, hold the opposite opinion. Personally, I choose to stand on the former side.

To commence with, let's make clear what "the government" means. It is an institution representing its people's interest and benefits. A democratic government is, in Jefferson's words, "of the people, for the people and by the people". Apparently, health care and education both fall into the ring of people's fundamental interest, benefits and rights, thus for sure making a part of the unshakable duties of any government.

Furthermore, to guarantee these two benefits is actually crucial to every nation's stability. This is because they are both long-lasting and are extremely costly. If one has to afford them independently, he or she will be forced to do a lot of savings, and will thus live in anxiety for a lengthy period until the day when bank saving is considered "secure", which is very likely to be in one's sixties. Therefore, if without these rudimentary benefits, our society will be running under tremendous pressure and insecurity. How can we expect it to develop smoothly and stably?

Admittedly, it is also comprehensible for some people to hold the opposite view. They suppose that too much expenditure on these two fields will slow down a country's advancement and people will enjoy fewer benefits as a further consequence. True as it seems to be, these people still ignore one issue, that is, the existence of the government is to ensure that people live a better life. If some basic investment shrinks, it has undoubtedly to be considered negative regardless of whatever potential benefit it may bring about.

All in all, it's the government's due and inescapable responsibility to bear people's health care and education expenses, both currently and in the longer term.

▶考官评分:8

题目:

一些人说政府应该负担其公民的医疗费用，一些人认为这些不是政府的责任，因为政府没有这样的义务，你的观点是什么?

译文:

政府是否应该为人民承担诸如医疗、教育等方面的基本费用，长期以来一直是一个引发激烈争论的问题。对此，有些人认为毫无疑问政府有这个责任，而其他人却不这么认为。就我个人来讲，我同意前者的观点。

首先，让我们搞清楚“政府”的含义。政府就是代表其人民利益的机构。按照杰弗逊的说法，一个民主的政府是“民主、民享、民治”。显然，医疗和教育属于人民的基本利益和权利范畴，所以属于政府不可推卸的责任。

另外，这两方面利益的保障对国家的稳定起着至关重要的作用。因为它们不仅持续时间很长，也非常耗费钱财。任何人如果被迫要独立承担起那么大的费用，他就将不得已去大量储蓄，并且将在很长一段时间里生活在焦虑中，直到所存储蓄足够对未来有保障的一天。而那时，他可能已经60多了。所以，离开了这些最基本的保障，我们的社会将会处在巨大的压力和不安定之下。我们怎么能够指望这样的社会长期稳定地发展呢?

诚然，有些人持反对意见也是可以理解的。他们认为，在这两个领域花费太多的资金将会阻碍社会发展，从而使人们的社会福利不好。虽然说得有理，但是这些人还是忽略了一个问题，即：政府的存在就是为了人民更好地生活。如果这些基本花费缩水，那么不论在将来可能会有何种益处，在当下仍是一个负面的举措。

综上所述，无论是短期还是长期，承担人民最基本的医疗和教育费用是政府不可推卸的责任。

146. 私立医疗机构的利弊

Topic:

Some people that think good health is very important to every person, so medical services should not be run by profit-making companies. Do the disadvantages of private health care outweigh the advantages?

Sample Answer

As an increasing number of people are aware of the importance of good health, the conflict between the ever-growing demand for high quality medical service and the insufficient public medical facilities has been worsened and this issue has been receiving much more attention than ever before. Most of us may thereby form an unrealistic picture about private health care which has been advocated as the best solution so far. However, I firmly believe the disadvantages of private health care outweigh its advantages.

Most private health care centers are profit-oriented and indifferent to others' sufferings. It is universally agreed that the prime goal of a hospital is to save lives and cure those in need. However, most owners of private health care centers, just like shop-owners, just aim at making as much money as possible and this runs against the basic principles of hospitals. Newspapers have reported repeatedly cases of some private hospitals refusing to save the lives of poverty-stricken patients, manifesting that some private health care centers are indeed problematic in nature.

Furthermore, contrary to what the general public believe, a large number of private health care centers are not qualified enough to practice medical service. In some private hospitals, though the cost of treatment is higher than that in most public hospitals, patients often cannot receive the service promised in advertisements. What is more terrifying is that some so-called doctors in those hospitals have no work experience at all and even their diplomas are fake ones.

Last but not least, the government's administration and supervision over private hospitals are often inadequate. Once obtaining the license, some private hospitals would do anything only if it is profitable. Aggravated by inadequate and inefficient inspections and evaluations from the government, many severe consequences have resulted from time to time.

To sum up, though nowadays private health care centers are playing an indispensable role, they are not without their inborn shortcomings. Before those problems mentioned above can be solved, it is still too early to talk about transferring most of the medical service to profit-making hospitals.

▶考官评分:8

题目:

一些人认为健康很重要，所以医疗机构不应该是以盈利为目的，你认为私立医疗机构的弊大于利吗？

译文:

由于越来越多的人意识到保持健康的重要性，对高质量医疗服务日益增长的需求与供应不足的公用医疗设施之间的矛盾不断加剧，这个问题备受关注。私立医疗机构由此被看作是这一问题的最佳解决方案。我们中很多人就此抱有一种不切实际的想法。然而，我坚决相信私立医疗的缺点远远大于它的优点。

大部分私立医护中心是利润至上，对他人的疾苦冷漠无情。众所周知，医院的首要目标是救死扶伤。然而，大部分私立医疗中心的老板就像商店老板一样，竭尽所能赚钱，这便与医院的基本原则背道而驰。报纸上已经重复报道了很多私立医院拒绝救治穷人的案例，这说明有的私立医院从本质上讲就是有问题的。

不仅如此，与大部分人的想法相反，众多私立医疗中心并不具备从事医疗服务的资格。在某些私立医院里，尽管医疗费用比大部分公立医院高出很多，病人往往得不到广告中承诺的服务。更为耸人听闻的是这些医院的某些所谓医生根本没有什么工作经验，甚至某些医生的文凭也是假的。

最后，这些私立医院的管理和监控存在不足。一旦拿到营业执照，只要有利益，某些私立医院便开始为所欲为，加之政府的检查和评估一直都不足、无效，由此造成了许多严重后果。

总的来说，尽管现在私立医疗机构发挥着不可或缺的作用，它们还是有很多与生俱来的缺点。在上面提到的问题得到解决以前，谈论将大部分的医疗服务使命交给营利性机构恐怕还为时尚早。

147. 政府的作用

Topic:

A government's role is only to provide defence capability and urban infrastructure (roads, water supplies, etc.). All other services (education, health, social security) should be provided by private groups or individuals in the community. To what extent do you agree or disagree with this opinion?

Sample Answer

Government can only provide a limited range of services for citizens. Certain types of service, however, must be provided by governments, whereas both governments and private groups or individuals can share the responsibility to provide other services.

Government must provide those services which are essential to a country. These include defence capabilities and social security. Private enterprise and the profit motive should not form part of these essential services. On the other hand, some services could be provided by either governments or private groups or both. Education and health care are examples of such services. A government must provide at least a basic level of education and health care so all citizens can have access to them. Private enterprise, though, could also provide services in these areas for those who wish to pay for them.

Urban infrastructure is another area where government and private groups or individuals can share responsibility. Governments must build and maintain a system of roads, but toll roads can be built and road maintenance can be carried out by private contractors. Similarly, other infrastructure, such as water or electricity supply, can be operated by private companies.

To sum up, there are some services such as defence and social security which must be provided by government. Other services, for example water supply or education, could be provided by both. A government's role is only to provide some services while others should be provided by the private sector. In fact, both government and private groups can share in the provision of most services.

▶考官评分:8

题目：

政府的作用只是在于维护国家安全和提供基础设施（道路、公路、水资源供给等等），而其他服务（教育、健康、社会保障）则应该由私立机构或社区里的个人提供。你是否同意这种观点？

译文：

政府只能为民众提供有限的服务。某些类型的服务无论如何必须由各国政府提供，但是各国政府和私人团体或个人可以分担责任，以提供其他服务。

政府必须提供那些本国所必需的服务。这些服务包括国防力和社会保障。私营企业和利润激励机制不应成为这些基本服务的组成部分。另一方面，一些服务可以由政府或私人团体提供或两者兼施。教育和卫生保健便是这方面的例子。政府必须至少提供最基本的教育和医疗保健，以使所有公民可以平等地享有它们。然而，私营企业也可以为那些愿意支付费用的人们提供与这些领域相关的服务。

城市基础设施建设是由政府和私人团体或个人分担责任的另一领域。各国政府必须建立和维护道路系统，但可由私人承包商进行收费公路的建设及相关道路的修建。同样，诸如水或电力供应等基础设施可由私营公司经营。

概括起来，有一些服务，如国防和社会保障必须由政府提供。其他服务，例如供水或教育，可以以政府的名义提供其中一些服务，而其他应由私立机构提供。事实上，政府和私人团体可以共同提供大部分服务。

148. 是否应该强制退休

Topic:

In some countries the average worker is obliged to retire at the age of 60 to 65. Some people agree this practice, while others do not. What do you think?

Sample Answer

At what age should seniors withdraw from permanent work? One practice in some countries is to require them by law to retire at the age of 60 to 65. However, such policy will bring about some serious social problems.

The first reason against the compulsory practice is that it restricts personal choice. Having pursued a career for years, some older employees regard it as part of their lives, the basis for their happiness. This compulsory policy would make them feel useless and depressed. There would even be a greater likelihood of their suffering from certain mental problems.

The social effects of asking some seniors to retire by law are more alarming. One of its negative impacts is a strain on the labour market. Among people nearing retirement age are some experts in their various fields. With knowledge and experience accumulated over many years, they may indeed be more productive and valuable than young people. In some circumstances, the role they play in their own areas cannot even be replaced, so forcing them to retire means losing a significant part of the organization's labour resource and even leads to labour shortage.

Having seniors retire by force not only means stopping them from being productive, but also implies a social welfare cost. The more retirees, the more pensions a government has to pay. This may hinder economic progress, as pensions could cost a significant part of the country's wealth. Worst of all, when the burden becomes too heavy to shoulder, serious social and economic problems will arise. There is no doubt that the burden of social security payments is lower when seniors remain at work.

These are only some of the reasons against compulsory retirement. All in all, it is not appropriate for a government to impose compulsory retirement on the aged. What it can do is to suggest an age when old people may choose to retire.

▶考官评分:8

题目:

一些国家的法定退休年龄是60到65岁，一些人同意这个规定，另一些不同意。你同意这种规定吗?

译文:

老人究竟应该在多大岁数退休呢?一些国家的法定退休年龄在60至65岁之间。然而这种强制性的政策可能会带来一些严重的社会问题。

反对强制退休的第一个理由是它限制了个人的选择。由于在某个行业工作了很多年，一些老员工视工作为生活的一部分，工作是他们幸福的基础。强制退休政策让他们觉得自己无用并感到沮丧，甚至在很大程度上可能会患上某种精神疾病。

强制老人退休所引起的社会问题也需要引起我们更多的注意。其负面影响之一是会使劳动力市场紧张。接近退休年龄的人常常是不同领域的专家。他们积累了多年的知识和经验，而且的确比年轻人有创造力，也更有价值。在很多情况下，临退休人员在他们自己的领域内有着不可替代的作用。所以强迫老人退休意味着这个机构大量宝贵的劳动力资源将流失甚至会导致劳动力短缺。

强迫老年人退休不仅意味着不让他们继续工作，而且意味着会增加惊人的社会福利成本。退休的人越多，政府需要支付的退休金就越多。由于退休金开支占据了国家财政的很大一部分，经济发展受到了阻碍。最糟糕的是，一旦这项开支超负荷了，就会引起严重的社会和经济问题。勿庸置疑，如果老年人继续工作，社会保障费用就会降低。

这只是反对强制退休政策的部分理由。总之，政府强迫老年人退休是不正确的。我们只能建议老人在何时退休。

149. 新闻审查

Topic:

Some people say that censorship should be cancelled completely. Do you agree or disagree with the statement? Give your specific reasons for your answer.

Sample Answer

As to whether it is worthwhile for a modern civilized society to retain the practice of censorship, there is a long-running controversial debate. It is quite natural that people from different backgrounds may have divergent attitudes towards it.

Some critics insist that we should abolish this practice. They claim that this is a violation of freedom. As society progresses, democracy should develop, too. We should enjoy more freedom than before. We should be allowed to do whatever we like to. And news reporters should have the right to report what they want to cover. All of us have the basic human rights such as freedom of speech and freedom of press. Moreover, the practice may more often than not be abused and applied to all aspects of life. Some artists even say that the practice of censorship will ineluctably interfere with their creation. Therefore, they hold that any efforts to restrict people's freedom of speech and press should be condemned.

Inevitably, on the other side, there are others who strongly advocate the practice of censorship. Democracy can not go to extremes. They think that it's essential to exercise this practice because they believe that too much liberty spoils all. They have several reasons for this. Firstly, with this practice, we can guarantee the positive influence of the mass media. We can make sure that what is reported is true and that the effects are good. If people are given the reins to report whatever they like to, there is possibility that some news items are nothing true but sensational in order to grab the public attention and make profits. Secondly, the responsibility of society of mass media is strengthened. They will think over what kind of results their articles will bring about every time they write. And they will aim to collect writing materials which will exert beneficial and positive influence on the public. Thirdly, we can have a clean cultural environment, which is essential and crucial to the smooth and healthy development of our society.

With views of both sides considered, I think that it's necessary to exercise the practice of censorship for the good of our society, and for the good of our younger generations.

▶考官评分:8

题目:

有些人认为应该完全取消审查制度，你同意这种观点吗？并说明理由。

译文:

关于现代文明社会保留审查制度是否有价值，长久以来都是一个有争议的话题。很自然不同背景的人对此持有不同的态度。

一些评论家坚持认为我们应该废除这种制度。他们认为这是对自由的违背。随着社会的进步，民主也应该随之发展。我们应该享有比以前更多的自由。我们应该被允许做我们喜欢做的事情。新闻记者有权利报道他们想报道的事情。我们大家都有基本的人权，例如，言论自由和新闻出版自由。而且，这个惯例可能更经常地被滥用到生活各方面。一些评论家甚至认为审查制度不可避免地影响到了他们的创造力。因此，他们认为任何限制人们言论自由的行为都应受到谴责。

不可避免的是，另一方面，其他人强烈提倡审查制度。民主不能走向极端。他们认为有必要实行这一制度，因为他们坚信太多的自由会毁掉一切。对此他们有若干理由。第一，有了这一制度，我们可以保证大众媒体的积极影响。我们能够确保报道属实、影响良好。如果人们有权报道任何他们喜欢的事情，就有可能出现一些失实的新闻，以抓住公众的注意力并以获取利润为目的。第二，大众媒体的社会责任增强了。每当他们写作时他们会思考他们的文章所带来的结果。他们会致力于写对公众产生有益和积极影响的文章。第三，我们能有一个干净的文化环境，这对社会平稳健康发展是有必要且至关重要的。

考虑到双方观点，我认为有必要为了我们社会和年轻一代的利益而保留审查制度。

150. 博物馆

Topic:

What are the purposes of places such as museums and how should they be funded?

Sample Answer

Over the past several years, through the painstaking joint efforts by the government and citizens, our city has taken on a new look. People praise highly the beautiful environment and cityscape. Currently, the city government is planning to allocate more funds on the construction of museums, with an aim to upgrade the artistic taste of the citizens.

Museums can enrich people's cultural life. First, by visiting museums, people can cultivate a better taste for arts and enhance the sensitivity to beauty, thus enriching their spiritual life and upgrading their quality. Second, museums provide a kind of place of entertainment and recreation for common people to spend their leisure hours. Most important of all, they are an essential part of spiritual civilization construction. Do remember that a man does not live only by bread.

Museums help boost the local tourism. Most museums are symbols of the city as well as the country, which appeal to visitors from home and abroad. For instance, when foreign friends are visiting Beijing, apart from the Great Wall, they are bound to have a tour in the Forbidden City, the most famous museum in China. Visiting a museum is one of the best ways to learn the local culture and touring through a museum provides visitors with a pleasant experience.

Museums also play a vital role in education especially to students and children who will learn a lot of knowledge from them. By visiting the historical museum, they can learn the tradition, history and culture of the country and the world. The natural museum can arouse their interest of science. By visiting it, they can find how interesting the nature is. These activities are much more meaningful and valuable than playing video games.

Museums are indispensable for the people as well as the country. Therefore, the whole society should take effective efforts to subsidize the construction of museums. It is the government's duty to invest more money in the building and maintenance of museums. Sometimes the government's budget is limited, so attracting the foreign investment is also a sensible way. The profitable enterprises and wealthy individuals should also give their hands.

▶考官评分:7

题目:

建造博物馆的目的是什么呢？它又应该由谁助资呢？

译文:

在过去的几年里，通过政府和市民的通力合作，我们的城市已经焕然一新。人们对美丽的环境和优美的城市景色给予高度的评价。现在，政府将投入更多的资金来建设博物馆，以提升市民的艺术品味。

博物馆能够丰富人们的文化生活。首先，通过游览博物馆，人们能够培养更好的艺术品味，提高对美的感知，从而丰富他们的精神生活，提高生活质量。其次，博物馆提供了娱乐消遣的场所，使得老百姓能够在那里度过空闲时间。最重要的是，这都是精神文明建设的重要部分。确实要记住人不单单是靠吃面包活着的。

博物馆有助于当地旅游业的发展。很多博物馆作为国家象征的同时，也是城市的标志。这就有助于吸引国内外的游客。例如，当外宾游览北京的时候，除了长城，他们也很喜欢去游览紫禁城——中国最著名的博物馆。游览博物馆是了解当地文化的最好途径，也能够带给游客非常美好的体验。

博物馆在教育中也起到很重要的作用，特别是对那些学生和孩子，他们从中学到很多知识。通过游览历史博物馆，他们学到了本国乃至世界的传统，历史和文化。自然博物馆能够激发他们对科学的兴趣。通过参观游览，他们能够发现自然是多么有趣。这些活动比玩电子游戏要有意义和有价值得多。

博物馆不仅对人民很重要，而且对国家也很重要。因此，全社会应该采取有效的措施来资助博物馆的建设。修建和维护博物馆是政府的职责。有时候，政府的预算有限，因此吸引外资也是一个很明智的办法。效益好的企业和富裕的个人也应该出一把力。

范文点评:

作者开头通过举自己的例子说明建造博物馆有改变市容的作用。接下来的三段分别叙述出博物馆有丰富人们文化生活，促进当地旅游业发展和教育的作用。结尾段提出全民资助建设博物馆。

151. 投资武器

Topic:

Should a country invest huge amounts of money on the research of weapons?

Sample Answer

With the development of world peace and the process of globalization, the aspiration for peace becomes very keen. But there are still some countries, which carry out experiments with advanced and mass-destructive weapons. From my point, it is against the trend of our world and people's will.

Firstly, the development of weapons can cause instability and chaos of our world. The people who love peace are keeping an eye on the conflicts between India and Pakistan. Many people and soldiers become cannon fodders every day. Many soldiers and civilians are wounded in the battlefields, which is a misery in the current world.

Secondly, large amounts of investment on the research of weapons will decelerate the development of other aspects, such as education, economy, industry and infrastructure. The arms race between USA and former USSR is a very vivid illustration. Now, the economy of both countries is seriously affected by the Arms Race, especially the former USSR. Finally, some weapons are mass destructive and catastrophic, one of which is atom bombs. People in Japan still remember the nightmare when two atom bombs exploded over Japan. Many people died and disabled, which is a tragedy of our world.

Of course, it is understandable and reasonable for a country to keep some weapons for the purpose of self-defense rather than invasion.

We are in favor of peaceful solutions to the disputes between countries, because every country enjoys independent sovereignty and equal rights with others. Any invasion and threats to a country are against the international laws and people's aspiration.

►考官评分:8

题目:

一个国家应该把大量的钱投资在武器制造上吗?

译文:

随着世界和平的发展以及全球化的进程，人们对和平的渴望变得非常热切。但是仍然有一些国家在用高级的杀伤力强的武器做试验。在我看来，这是违反世界潮流和人类意愿的。

首先，武器的发展会造成世界的不稳定以及混乱。热爱和平的人都会密切关注印度和巴基斯坦的冲突。每天都有许多平民和士兵成为炮灰。许多士兵和百姓在战场上受伤，这是当今世界的不幸。

第二，在研究武器方面的大量投资将减缓其他方面的发展，例如教育、经济、工业以及基础建设。美国和前苏联之间的军备竞赛就是非常鲜活的例子。现在，两个国家的经济都受到军备竞赛的严重影响，特别是前苏联。最后，一些武器是具有大规模破坏性和灾难性的，原子弹就是其中之一。日本的人们依然记得两颗原子弹在日本爆炸的梦魇。很多人死去或残疾，酿成世界的惨剧。

当然，国家持有一些武器用来正当防卫而不是入侵是可以理解的，也是合情合理的。

我们赞同和平地解决两国之间的争论，因为每个国家享有独立主权和与他国一样的平等权利。对任何国家的入侵和恐吓都是违反国际法律和人类意愿的。

152. 帮助穷国

Topic:

Many people think that countries have a moral obligation to help each other, while others argue that the aid money is misspent by the governments that receive it, so the international aid should not be given to the poor countries in the world. What do you think?

Sample Answer

With the process of economic globalization, many countries and regions have strengthened cooperation and liaison in the fields of industry, agriculture, trade and finance. In order to dedicate themselves to the mutual development, many developed countries spare no efforts to help the poor countries by means of technological, medical and financial aid, which, to my mind, is quite essential to the development of the world.

Firstly, aids from developed countries optimize people's living standard and eradicate poverty in the poor countries. Due to the backwardness of science and technology, people in some undeveloped countries and regions such as Africa, Latin America and Asia suffer a great deal from poverty, hunger and the scarcity of water. International aids from developed countries have improved their living environment and helped them with the development of agriculture, industry and economy.

Secondly, international aids give good medical care and help promote hygienic condition in the poor countries. Malaria, cholera and smallpox were once severe threats to people's health. With the help of the World Health Organization and some developed countries, these diseases have been eliminated soon and the residents in the infected areas survived these deadly diseases, which would have devoured millions of lives without international aid.

Finally, aids to the undeveloped countries in turn benefit the donators. Due to the limitation of natural and human resources, the production cost rises sharply in the developed countries. With a view to reducing cost, many countries transferred their assembly lines and production bases to the developing countries, which not only solves the problem of low rate of employment in the developing countries but also make full use of the local resources.

Nevertheless, some countries are showing great concern about the mal-expense of their aid aroused by bureaucracy and corruption of some governments. Therefore, the governments should take effective measures to utilize international aids reasonably and prevent abuse. Only with the help of international aids, can our world develop more quickly and prosperously.

▶考官评分:8

题目:

很多人认为出于道德责任，各国之间应该互相帮助，但是其他人认为得到援助的国家会把钱用到不正确的地方，因此不应该给予贫困国家援助，你怎么认为?

译文:

随着经济全球化进程的发展，许多国家和地区在工业，农业，贸易及金融领域都加强了合作和联系。为了共同发展，许多发达国家通过科技，医疗和财政援助不遗余力地帮助贫穷国家。我认为，这对于世界发展是极其重要的。

首先，来自发达国家的救助能够提高人们的生活标准并消灭贫困。由于科学技术的落后，一些不发达国家和地区的人们，例如非洲，拉丁美洲和亚洲，长期饱受贫困，饥饿及淡水缺乏之苦。发达国家的国际援助已经改善了他们的生活环境并帮助他们发展农业、工业和经济。

第二，国际援助给予贫穷国家良好的医疗救助并帮助他们改善了卫生条件。疟疾，霍乱和天花一度是人们健康的严重威胁。但在世界卫生组织和一些发达国家的帮助下，这些疾病很快被根治了，而受感染地区的居民也从这些致命的疾病中幸存下来。如果没有国际援助，数百万的生命将已被这些疾病吞噬。

最后，给予不发达国家的援助反过来也使捐赠者受益。由于自然资源和人力资源有限，发达国家的生产成本急剧上升。出于降低成本考虑，许多国家都把他们的装配线和生产基地转移到了发展中国家。这不仅解决了发展中国家就业率低的问题而且充分利用了当地资源。

尽管如此，许多国家都对一些政府的官僚主义和贪污腐败所引起的滥用援助费用表示极大关注。因此，政府应采取有效措施合理利用国际援助和防止滥用。只有通过国际援助，我们的世界才会发展得更快，更加繁荣。

153. 政府解决住房问题

Topic:

Housing shortage in big cities can cause severe consequences. Only government action can solve this problem. To what extent do you agree or disagree?

Sample Answer

There is no denying that housing shortage in metropolitan cities has already become an extremely serious problem over the last decades. The severe consequences caused by housing shortage have also become an issue that has drawn wide public concerns. Some people claim that proper actions should be taken by the government without any delay in view of the severity of the problem, but others are in high favor that, in addition to the government, both individuals and big enterprises should also take on the responsibilities to deal with this problem. Thus, a controversial discussion has arisen on this issue.

People who side with the former opinion point out that only the government has the obligation and ability to make out policies to standardize the behaviors in house construction and purchasing. In addition, only the government can provide sufficient fund and necessary facilities in the process of problem solving.

People who agree with the latter viewpoint believe that joint efforts from both the government and big enterprises are needed to better solve this problem. For one thing, big enterprises, especially real estate companies, have more professional insights into this issue. For another, it is impossible for the government to focus only on solving housing problems because it has a lot more issues to address. Besides, housing problem is closely related to the overpopulation in big cities and the problem of overpopulation can not be solved in the short term.

Based on the foregoing discussion, I would argue that the government, enterprises and individuals should join their efforts in order to effectively cope with this problem.

►考官评分:8

题目:

大城市的住房紧缺将会造成严重的后果，只有政府出面才能解决这个问题，你同意此观点吗?

译文:

毫无疑问，最近几十年里大城市住房紧缺已成为一个非常严峻的问题，而住房紧缺所造成的其他问题也逐渐引起整个社会的广泛关注。有人认为，由于此问题相当严重，政府必须立即采取相应措施予以解决；而有些人却坚持认为，除政府之外，个人以及大的公司机构也有责任来解决这一问题。由此引发了就此话题的争议和探讨。

同意前一种观点的人指出只有政府才有责任及能力出台相关政策来规范建房及购房行为。另外，只有政府能够在解决问题的过程中提供足够的资金及必要的设施。

同意后一种观点的人认为政府与大公司机构应当共同努力才能更好地解决问题。第一，大的公司，尤其是房地产公司对此问题有更专业的见解。第二，政府不可能集中所有注意力来解决住房这一问题，因为还有其他很多问题需要解决。另外，住房问题与大城市的人口过剩有直接关系，而大城市人口过剩问题也不可能在短期内解决。

基于以上论证，我认为想要更有效地解决这一问题必须依靠政府、公司及个人共同努力。

154. 公民纳税

Topic:

People believe that they should be able to keep all the money they earn and should not pay tax to the state. To what extent do you agree or disagree?

Sample Answer

To work and get paid is a well accepted social practice, but to pay part of salary to the government as tax has been challenged by quite a few opponents who believe that their salary is their own money and nobody can take it away without their consent. In my opinion, people should pay tax to the state for the following three reasons.

The first reason is that people get paid in different ways. For those industrial workers, the salary comes from part of the profits they create themselves. But for those who do not manufacture products, policemen for example, there is no direct profit from their work. Therefore, part of the profit made by industrial workers need to go to this latter group of people, whose work is equally important to the entire society.

The second reason is that the tax paid to the state is partly used to build and maintain public works which in return benefit the people themselves. The convenient transportation network like airlines or railways has made the world smaller and travel over long distance has become a commonplace experience. Without the contribution of taxpayers, there would be no such kind of things to speak of.

The last reason is that poor people can be helped by the tax paid to the government. For various reasons, some people are not as fortunate as others in finding a job or even shelter to keep themselves from starvation, diseases and even death. At his time, the tax money works. It offers these people the most basic foods and clothes to survive the difficulty and enjoy their right to live as a human at the least.

All in all, taxation is an important way of redistributing the GDP. It is beneficial not only to the whole country and society, but also to every individual.

▶考官评分:8

题目:

人们认为他们应该存上自己赚的钱不需要向国家纳税，你同意这种观点吗?

译文:

按劳取酬是众所周知的常理，但要向政府纳税却遭到相当一部分人的反对。他们认为工资仅仅属于他们自己，任何人都不能无故拿走。我认为，人们应该向政府纳税，原因有以下三个方面。

首先，人民获得劳动报酬的方式是不同的。产业工人的工资直接来自于他们创造的利润。但是对并不直接参与生产的人来说（比如警察），他们的工作并不直接产生利润。事实上，产业工人创造的利润一部分要分配给上述这样的群体。他们的工作对于整个社会同样至关重要。

第二，国家所获得的税收有一部分用于建设和维护造福人类的公共工程。像航空和铁路这样的便捷交通网络使得世界变得越来越小，从而使人们在遥远的两地之间穿梭成为平常事。如果没有纳税人的贡献，这一切就无从谈起。

最后，政府的税收也会造福穷人。出于种种原因，有些人没能够幸运地找到工作，只能风餐露宿、食不果腹，深受疾病和死亡的困扰和威胁。这时候，政府的税收就可以发挥作用了。它使得穷人能够解决基本的温饱问题，渡过难关，从而享受到最起码的做人的权力。

总而言之，税收是国民收入再分配的一个重要途径，它不但有利于整个国家和社会，还有利于我们每个人。

155. 旅游业

Topic:

Many developing countries are currently expanding their tourist industries. Why is the case? Is it a positive development?

Sample Answer

Currently, there is a hot discussion about the reasons why there are developing countries in growing numbers expanding tourist industries and whether it is a positive development or not. As far as I am concerned, I am convinced that it is a positive development. In this essay, I will make an analysis of the reasons in the following paragraphs.

The first and foremost reason is that, tourism, which becomes the principal source of financial revenue in many developing countries, is financially beneficial to the economic development. For instance, China needs an increasing amount of foreign currencies for its modernization drive. Tourism is one of the most crucial channels to obtain such currencies. Furthermore, tourism facilitates the development of the catering business and transportation service as well. Additionally, tourist industries make primary contribution to the national income and tax revenue.

In the second place, tourism provides local habitants in tourist attractions with more opportunities of employment, which has eliminated some social problems to some extent. In the scenic spots, it is common that even the uneducated people can make a living simply by selling souvenirs, local specialties and so on, which relieves the pressure of the local government.

Last but not least, it is true that tourism contributes a great deal to the friendship and mutual understanding between people from different countries, which will unquestionably enhance the future cooperation in international affairs. Tourism provides people with a good opportunity to have a better understanding of the culture, history and customs in foreign countries.

All in all, it is of great benefit for developing countries to promote the tourist industry, for it will play a positive role in both the economic and political development of a country.

▶考官评分:8

题目:

很多发展中国家开始发展旅游业，为什么会这样呢？这是一个好的发展吗？

译文:

当前，人们对发展中国家大力发展旅游业的原因以及这是否有利展开了热烈的讨论。在我看来，我确信它是积极的发展。在这篇文章中，我将在以下段落对其原因进行分析。

首先，旅游业是很多发展中国家财政收入的主要来源，在财政上对这些国家的经济发展很有利。例如，中国需要大量的外汇用于现代化建设。旅游业是获得外汇的重要渠道之一。此外，旅游也能促进餐饮业和交通运输业的发展。另外，旅游业还对国民收入和税收做出不可或缺的贡献。

其次，旅游业给当地居民提供了更多的就业机会，这在某种程度上消除了一些社会问题。甚至是一些没有接受过教育的人也能靠卖纪念品或当地特产等谋生，这种现象在旅游景点相当常见，这减轻了当地政府的压力。

最后，旅游业极大地增进了各个国家以及人民之间的友谊和相互了解，这毫无疑问将促进各国间今后在国际事务中的合作。旅游业给人们提供了一个更好的了解国外文化、历史以及习俗的机会。

总之，发展中国家发展旅游业有相当大的益处，因为它不仅在经济上发展，同时也会在政治发展方面起到积极的作用。

156. 发展旅游业的利与弊

Topic:

Tourism is a multibillion-dollar industry that supports economic development. However, some people think that it causes too much damage to the local environment and culture. What do you think?

Sample Answer

Tourism, as a multibillion-dollar business, is booming everywhere. Some people, laboring under the belief that tourism serves as an engine of economic growth, seem to ignore its negative effects on the environment and culture. But I think that these are not concerns that we can shrug off lightly.

Over the past century, with the development of new transportation means, travel has become easier than ever. Many popular places are flooded with visitors, who spoil the beauty of nature by creating and leaving behind God-knows-how-much trash. In addition, a lot of unsightly artificial facilities have been and continue to be built in order to promote tourism, with disastrous effects on the environment.

Another drawback of tourism is the conducted tour, which greatly restricts the exposure of tourists to local culture, and contributes little to mutual understanding between nations and cultures. On the contrary, the superficial impressions tourists get during such tours only intensify their stereotyped ideas about other cultures. On the other hand, the foreign ways introduced by travelers may well have an adverse impact on the local people, who tend to be susceptible to the influence of more advanced cultures. In the long run, the uniqueness of individual cultures will be wiped out by such homogenization.

But don't get me wrong. I am not saying that the tourism industry shall be banned in any country, as it does help to shore up the economy in places which offer few sources of income. The significant point is that the unchecked growth of the travel business may render the development of an economy unsustainable. So steps have to be taken to prevent the local culture from being "contaminated" or even engulfed by other cultures. It is high time that we did something to rectify this by taking the environment and cultural protection into account.

▶考官评分：8

题目：

旅游业是个通过盈利数亿来支持经济发展的产业，然而，有些人认为它会破坏当地文化和环境。你同意这种观点吗？

译文：

旅游业作为一项价值数十亿美元的产业正在世界各地迅速发展。一些人坚信旅游业是推动经济发展的引擎，似乎却忽视了它在环境和文化上所能造成的负面影响。然而我想这个烦恼不是我们轻易就可以摆脱的。

在上个世纪，伴随着新型运输工具的发展，旅行比以往容易多了。许多著名的景点都吸引了各地的游客，他们破坏了大自然的美丽并且留下了只有老天才知道不计其数的垃圾。另外，为了旅游业的发展而不断建造的一些不美观的人工设施，正在严重地破坏我们的环境。

旅游业的另外一个缺点就是旅行中导游的引导，极大地约束了旅客对当地文化的接触，对于国家与文化之间的相互认识作用甚微。相反，观光者在这种旅行环境下，对别的文化产生肤浅的印象只会强化他们对古老传统的认识。在另一方面，游客带来的外来方式可能会对本地居民产生不良的影响，因为本地的居民对外来先进文化的影响很敏感。从长远来看，每个独立的文化特性都将会被这种国际一体化所同化。

请不要误会。我并不是说旅游业在任何一个国家都应当被禁止。因为它确实支撑住了一些收入来源缺少的国家的经济。重要的是未经审核就发展旅游业务可能会使经济发展不可持续化，所以我们必须采取相应的步骤去防止本地文化被外来文化“污染”或者甚至是吞噬。在重视环境和文化保护的同时，我们早该采取措施进行整顿。

157. 彩票

Topic:

The lottery does more good than harm. Discuss.

Sample Answer

For better or worse, the lottery has become a part of our life. There are, it is true, people who worry about the negative effects the lottery may have, but I believe it does more good than harm.

First of all, the lottery is an effective way of raising money for welfare programs and other public projects. Although taxes have traditionally been the main source for such undertakings, people pay taxes grudgingly, and increasing taxes is time-consuming and may result in increasing popular discontent. However, people eagerly buy lottery tickets, and so, so long as it is well regulated, the lottery can serve as an important source of state revenue.

For average people, especially those who have no salable skills, the lottery might be the only opportunity for them to get rich-even to become a millionaire overnight. For instance, a friend of mine has been in financial trouble for many years. The other day, he hit the jackpot by selecting the winning number in the lottery. Now he is the richest guy in our community, and is leading a life he never even dreamed of before.

With some people, their enthusiasm for the lottery is not about money but about fun. They don't care about winning or losing; they just like to choose numbers and watch the results. They enjoy the excitement of analyzing the possibilities. For them, buying lottery tickets is just one of their hobbies.

Some people are concerned that the lottery may encourage laziness and gambling. But evidence from the countries where public lotteries are legal does not justify this worry. In fact, in China the lottery has turned out not to be a monster but something beneficial. In conclusion, experience has shown that the advantages far outweigh the disadvantages.

▶考官评分：8

题目:

彩票利大于弊，讨论。

译文:

不论好坏，彩票已成为我们日常生活的一部分。的确有一部分人担心彩票会引起负面影响，但是我相信它的利大于弊。

首先，彩票是一种筹集资金用于社会福利事业和其他公共项目的有效方式。虽然税收是这些项目历来的主要资金来源，人民很勉强地缴税，并且增加税收是耗时的，而且可能会导致越来越多的人不满。然而，人们急切地购买彩票，所以，只要它能被良好地管理，彩票可以作为一个国家收入的重要来源。

对于普通人，特别是那些没有一技之长的人，彩票可能是他们惟一的可以在一夜之间成为百万富翁的机会。举例来说，我的朋友多年一直处在经济危机之中。有一天，他中了彩票的大奖。现在，他是我们交际圈中最富有的人，过着他从来没有梦想过的生活。

有一些人，他们热衷于彩票不光是为了钱而还是一种乐趣。他们不太在乎输赢，而是通过观察，找出规律，他们在分析中奖概率的同时享受着快乐。对于他们来说，买彩票只是他们的一种爱好而已。

有些人担心，彩票会催生懒惰和赌博。但是国家合法的彩票并不能为这种担心作辩护。事实上，我国彩票催生出来的并不是一种怪物，相反却是对大家都有利的。最后，经验表明彩票的优势远远大于它的弊端。

第九大类：平等类话题

158. 女子是否应该参军

Topic:

Many females join the army in some countries. Some people think women should not join the army. Do you agree or disagree?

Sample Answer

This is a world of gender equality, or, at least, a world calling for so. Many people are confident that we should not allow women to join the army as soldiers. On the other hand, other people stand on a very different ground. They advocate that women should be entitled to joining the army.

Some arguments can be made that women should be allowed to serve as soldiers in army. In the first place, it is the rights and obligations for every citizen to defend his motherland. We cannot deprive women of such rights. In the second place, allowing women in the army is beneficial to soldiers' psychological health. As this society is made up of males and females, the environment consisting only of members of the same sex will definitely lead to mental problems. Finally, the war in modern times uses largely hi-tech weapons. In other words, although women are physically weak, they can still become qualified soldiers.

However, further analysis would make it clear that women should not join the army. To begin with, female soldiers would reduce the efficiency of military operations. They are more likely to get wounded. As a result, it can, when real battle occurs, put the whole troop in danger. Moreover, women's joining the army would inevitably boost the military budget. The uniforms and weapons such as tanks or helicopters have to be redesigned for the convenience of women soldiers, which takes a good sum of money. Last but not least, female soldiers' stay in the army is shorter than the male soldiers, as they have another profession waiting for them: mother. Consequently, the country, in the light of training cost, incurs losses.

In summary, I do not think it a good idea to have females in the army. Females are physically weaker than males and therefore it is difficult for women to be soldiers. In addition, the government would have to invest more money on military facilities for the sake of women soldiers.

▶考官评分：7

题目：

在一些国家有很多女性参军。有些人认为女性不应该被允许参军？你同意还是不同意？

译文：

这是一个男女平等的世界，至少是提倡男女平等的世界。很多人认为我们不应该允许女性参军。另一方面，一些人持有完全不同的看法。他们认为女性有资格参军。

有些理由指出女性应该参军。第一，保卫国家是每个公民的权利和义务。我们不能剥夺女性这种权利。第二，允许女性参军对士兵的心理健康有好处。因为社会是由男性和女性组成的，只包含一个性别成员的环境一定会导致心理问题。最后，现代战争大量使用高科技武器。换句话说，虽然女性身体瘦弱，她们还是能成为合格的士兵。

然而，进一步的分析指出：不应该允许女性参军。一方面，女性士兵会降低军事行动的效率。她们更容易受伤，因次，当真的战斗打响，可能会使部队处于危险之中。而且，女性参军会不可避免地增加军事预算。为了女性的方便，诸如坦克或直升飞机的军服和武器需要重新设计。这要花很多钱。最后，女性在军队服役的时间少于男性，因为有个重要的职业等待着她们：母亲。因此，国家在培训费用上，会造成损失。

总之，我们不能否认双方都有道理。在我看来，让女性参军不是一个好主意。女性在身体上比男性瘦弱，因此，对女性来说，当兵是很困难的。而且，因为女兵，政府将不得不投入更多的钱在军事设施上。

159. 大学招收相同数目的男生和女生

Topic:

The university should accept equal numbers of male and female students in every subject. Do you agree or disagree?

Sample Answer

Whether the university should accept equal numbers of male and female students in every subject is a commonly discussed topic and still in debate. Some people claim that it should be the policy; otherwise it will raise a discrimination based on gender. But from the point of my view, the ratio of man and woman students in college ought to be different depending on different areas.

First of all, let us talk about the so-called first nature. In general, boys love machines much more than girls do from their early childhood. Boys like playing with cars and games, while girls love Babe Dolls and decorating their bedrooms. It can certainly be expected that more boys are interested in engineering, and more girls intend to choose literature or education when they grow up.

Secondly, psychologically speaking, men are more logical and women are more sensitive and careful. That is why you see dominant party of girls in nursing school. At the same time, dealing with mathematics is a piece of cake to boys but a big disaster to most of girls. To choose a subject depends on the individual's personality, so it will be unreasonable for the university to take equal numbers of males and females in every subject.

At last, in today's society, there are still different social responsibilities to males and females. Even though in more and more fields, for example, biological research or computer science, you can see no big difference between the two genders and boys or girls are doing equally well, there are certain areas preferring one gender but not the other one. We are all used to meeting a sweet nurse in white at hospital but may feel weird to see a big guy injecting flu shot to you.

From discussed above, we can easily see the truth that males and females have physiological differences and are interested in different fields. So I can not see a convincing reason to urge the university to accept equal numbers on male and female.

▶考官评分:8

题目:

大学在每一个学科应招收同等数量的男生和女生。你同意还是不同意?

译文:

大学在每一个学科招收的男女同学数量是否都应该相等，这是一个热门话题并且一直颇受争议。一些人声称“相等”应该成为政策规定，否则将导致性别歧视。但在我看来，大学里男女学生的比例在不同的领域里应该有所不同。

首先，我们来说说所谓的天性。一般来说，在早期的儿童时代，男孩比女孩更喜欢机动车辆。男孩喜欢玩小汽车和游戏，而女孩喜欢芭比娃娃和装饰她们的卧室。当然我们可以预期，当他们长大的时候，更多的男孩会对工程学感兴趣，更多的女孩当她们长大后往往选择文学或者是教育。

第二，从心理学上讲，男人更理性而女人更敏感细腻。那就是为什么在护士学校你会发现绝大部分都是女生。同时，做数学题对于男生来说不过是小菜一碟，而对大多数女孩来说则是灾难。选择某一学科要取决于个人的特征，因此对于大学来说，在每一学科都招收同等数量的男生和女生是不合理的。

最后，当今社会，男女仍然要承担不同的社会责任。尽管在越来越多的领域，如生物学研究和计算机科学领域，你可能看到男孩和女孩之间没有太大的差别，他（她）们做得同样好，但仍有一些领域更需要某种性别的人而不是另一种性别的人。我们在医院都习惯于看见一个穿着白大褂的美丽护士，而看见一个大个子家伙给你打针则会感到惊慌。

通过上面的讨论，我们很容易看出，男女之间有生理上的差别是事实，他（她）们各自对不同的领域感兴趣。因此我不认同大学招收同等数量男女学生。

160. 男女分校

Topic:

Should children be educated in single-sex schools? What is your opinion?

Sample Answer

Which form of education is more desirable for children—co-education, where boys and girls attend school together, or single-sex schools? To answer this, one should first think about the aim of education at school. Cramming children's heads full of knowledge is by no means the main purpose. The more important goal is to prepare them to take their place in adult society. As this society is made up of males and females, a segregated school consisting only of members of the same sex cannot serve this purpose well.

By contrast, a co-educational school is far preferable in achieving this aim, offering students nothing less than a true version of society in miniature. Boys and girls are given the opportunity to get to know each other, and to learn to live together from their earliest years. They are in a position to compare themselves with each other in terms of academic ability, athletic achievement and many of the extra-curricular activities which are part of school life. In this way, boys don't grow up imagining that women are mysterious creatures and girls don't grow up scared of men. Years of associating with each other at school dispel illusions of this kind.

Those against co-education hold that the environment will probably lead children to puppy love which will then serve as an obstacle to their academic achievement. They believe segregated schools will prevent such things from happening. In fact, it is likely to make matter worse. Love is a normal physical and emotional need in the process of one's growing-up. Such a desire can not be effectively suppressed. As a matter of fact, when you try to suppress it by separating boys from girls, you achieve the exact opposite. Alternatively, members of the same sex spend all their time together as they will seek to satisfy their need for intimacy. As a result, segregated schools may breed sexual deviation.

In co-educational schools, it cannot be denied that the flower of love between boys and girls may blossom too early. But this is not necessarily as harmful as many educators may think. What we need to do is to teach them how to deal with problems about love when they occur.

In conclusion, co-educational schools, rather than segregated schools offer the proper place for children to become well-adjusted citizens in society.

▶考官评分:8

题目:

孩子是否应该在单性学校接受教育，你的观点是什么？

译文:

对于孩子们来说，哪一种教育模式更让人满意，是男女合校（让男孩和女孩一起上学），还是建立单性学校？如果要回答这个问题，就必须先考虑学校教育的目的。在孩子们的头脑里填满知识绝不是主要目的。更重要的目标是帮助他们在成人世界里找到合适的位置。由于社会是由男性和女性组成的，只由同性组成的学校不能够很好地满足这方面的需要。

比较而言，男女同校能够很好地满足这方面的要求。男女同校为学生们提供了一个真实社会的缩微图。男孩和女孩都有机会彼此了解，并在他们小的时候试图一起生活。他们在学习能力，体育成绩和许多课外的课程上相互比较，而这也是学校生活的一部分。这样，男孩在长大之后不会觉得女孩很神秘，而女孩也不会对男孩产生恐惧。在学校，彼此间常年的相互合作能够驱散这方面的幻想。

那些反对男女同校的人认为这样会导致早恋，对他们的学习有害。他们相信单性学校会防止这类事情的发生。事实上，这样会更糟。爱情是一个人在成长过程中的一个自然的生理和心理需要。这种渴求不能被有效压制。实际上，你越压制，就越会取得相反的效果。相反地，同性的伙伴会花所有的时间呆在一起去满足他们亲密的需求，结果会造成性别偏离。

不可否认，男女同校容易面对早恋。但这个问题并不像很多教育工作者所想象的那么严重。我们需要做的是教他们在面对爱情时如何处理这类问题。

总之，男女同校比分校能够为孩子们提供一个更为合适的空间，使孩子们能够成为社会的有用人才。

161. 男性领导和女性领导

Topic:

Throughout the history, male leaders often made society more violent and conflicting. If women governed the world, it would be a more peaceful world? To what extent do you agree or disagree?

Sample Answer

Sometimes while looking back on the way we have come along, one may find that seemingly the road is always bumpy and muddy and sadly, the driver happens to be a man most of the time. Some people may thereby form a misunderstanding that it is the male driver who has made the voyage uncomfortable and full of suffering. It is the same case when it comes to history. I firmly believe that whether society is more violent and conflicting does not have a close relationship with the gender of the leader.

Throughout the history, it is indisputable that the number of male leaders far surpasses that of female ones. However, this can't serve as the prerequisite of the saying that it is the existence of male leader who created more violence and conflicts in society. On the one hand, most of the time, when male leaders were in power, society remained peaceful and the time of peace was much longer than that of war. On the other hand, it is unreasonable and unacceptable to blame everything on male leaders.

Even if the world had been dominated mostly by female leaders, nobody could be sure that the world would have been more peaceful. One could never reverse the wheels of the history and assume that everything could have been changed for the better. In fact, it could have been worse. Therefore, to make such an assumption is groundless and valueless. Furthermore, not all women are peaceful and graceful. There were in world history quite a few women who were aggressive and impetuous, especially when they came into power.

To summarize, male leaders don't prevail over female ones when it comes to governing society and vice versa. No matter who seizes the throne, the orbit of society would never be changed. To exaggerate the function of the gender of the leader does not hold any water.

▶考官评分:8

题目:

在历史上，男性领导人往往使社会有更多暴力和冲突。如果妇女统治世界，这将是一个更加和平的世界吗？你是否同意？

译文:

有时回首旅程，我们会发现好像这条道路总是坎坷泥泞，遗憾的是驾驶员往往又都是一位男士。因此就有了一些人的误解：是这个男驾驶员使得旅途不舒适甚至痛苦。谈到人类的历史其实也是一样的道理。所以，我认为社会是否更加暴力和动荡与领导者的性别没有密切联系。

纵观历史，毫无疑问，男性领导者远多于女性领导者。然而，这一点不能说明男性领导者的存在催生了社会上更多的暴力和冲突。一方面，在大部分男性领导者掌权的时间里，社会还是安定的，而且安定的时间比战争的时间要长很多。另一方面，将一切都怪罪在男性领导者身上是没有道理，也是不能接受的。

即使世界真的由女性领导，没有人能够确定世界会更和平。首先，没有人可以反转历史的车轮，认定一切都会变好。事实上，结果可能会更加糟糕。所以，这种假设没有任何根据和意义。另外，不是所有的女性都是优雅和安静的。历史上有相当一批女性争强好胜、冲动鲁莽，尤其是当她们掌权以后。

总的来说，男性领导者不比女性领导者在管理社会上有任何优势，反之亦然。不管是谁掌权，社会的轨迹不会因此而改变。夸大领导者性别的作用是不能成立的。

162. 保留高级职位给女性

Topic:

Most high level jobs are done by men. Should the government encourage a certain percentage of these jobs to be reserved for women?

Sample Answer

Now, most of the jobs in society that are high-paying, powerful, and demand a lot of responsibility are held by men. I think the government should reserve a percentage of these jobs for females.

Firstly, the problem of unfair employment distribution comes from social convention. At a young age most girls are not encouraged to pursue political office, business success, or professional prestige. On the other hand, boys are told to do these things. As a result, men hold the high level jobs but this does not mean they are very good at what they do. If the government set a quota for hiring women to do high level work, such as working in the government itself, then perhaps women would be more inspired to be ambitious in their life plans.

Furthermore, to legislate a percentage of high level jobs for women would work to fight the unwritten sexist rules of the workplace. For instance, if a man and a woman both compete for a managerial position of a company, and both are equally qualified and have the same experience and background, there is little doubt who would get the job. Even more, if the man is less qualified and less experienced than the woman, the man would still probably get the job because of his sex. Therefore, the government should reserve a certain percentage of high level jobs to ensure that some highly trained women could be hired.

On the other hand, there are many arguments against the use of a quota system for women. It is true that the injustice and discrimination could be reversed. This is to say that some qualified men might be denied a job while some unqualified women would be given one. Nevertheless, a quota system would break down some barriers between the men and the women. With the help of this practice, the sexism in the workplace will disappear gradually.

To sum up, from what I have mentioned above, it is not difficult to get to the conclusion that the government should reserve a percentage of these jobs for females.

▶考官评分:7

题目:

现在大部分高级职业工作是男人在做，政府应该鼓励预留一定比例的这类工作给女性吗？

译文:

如今，大多数社会中的高收入，有权利的，并且需要承担很多责任的工作被男人占据。我认为政府应该为女性提供一定的从事这些工作（的比例）。

首先，雇佣歧视的问题来源于社会习俗。大多数女孩在小时候不被鼓励去追求政治工作，商业成就，或者是职业影响力。另一方面，男孩被叫做这些事。结果，男人掌握了高级的工作，但是这并不意味着他们擅长于他们所做的。如果政府对于雇佣女性做高等工作发出一个号召，比如在政府部门工作，那时也许女性将会被鼓励而对她们的生活计划更加有雄心。

此外，为女性立法制定一定比例的高级工作会打击工作性别潜规则。比如，如果一个男人和一个女人都竞争一个公司的管理职位，并且都有相同的品质，工作经验和背景，几乎毫无疑问到底谁会胜任。即使这个男的的品质和工作经验不如那个女的，这个男的还是有可能得到这个工作，因为他的性别。因此，政府应该对高级工作规定一个确切的比例，来确保一些受高等教育的女性从事这样的工作。

另一方面，对于女性的一定份额的制度还有很多争论。的确不公平和歧视可能会反过来加在男性身上，也就是说，一些有能力的男性或许会被拒绝从事某项工作，然而没有能力的女性会被给予这项工作。不过，一定份额的制度将会瓦解男人和女人之间的障碍。通过这个举措，工作场合的性别问题会逐渐消失。

总之，通过我之前所提的，不难得出结论：政府应该为女性保留这类工作的(性别)一定比例。

163. 运动员娱乐人士的高薪

Topic:

Some people feel that entertainment workers (e.g. film stars, pop musicians or sports stars) are paid too much money.Do you agree or disagree? Which other types should be highly paid?

Sample Answer

I agree with the view that stars in the entertainment business are usually overpaid. This is true whether we are considering stars of films, sports or popular music, and it often seems that the amount of money they are able to earn in a short time cannot possibly be justified by the amount of work they do.

However, it is also true that it is only those who reach the very top of their profession who can get these huge salaries. So the size of salary that stars expect is closely linked to the competition they have to overcome in order to reach success.

Furthermore, the majority of stars do not hold their top positions long. Sport stars and pop stars , for example, are soon replaced by the next younger, more energetic, generation, while the good looks of most films stars quickly fade. So this relatively short working life may be some justification for the very high pay.

Unfortunately, professionals from the other fields, who make a much greater contribution to human society, are paid so much less that it is hard to disagree with the statement. Teachers, nurses, laboratory researchers etc. are never listed among the best-paid professionals, yet, they are more important to our well-being and our future than the stars who earn their fortune so quickly.

In conclusion, I think there may be some reasons why entertainment stars earn high salaries but overall I agree that they are overpaid. The gaps between their earnings and those of people who work less selfishly for the good of society cannot be justified. Such professionals should be much better appreciated and better paid.

▶考官评分:7

题目:

一些人认为娱乐人员（例如电影明星，流行音乐人或者体育明星）应高薪。你是否认同？哪些其他的行业也应该获得高薪？

译文:

在娱乐业的明星们都有可观的收入，我同意这点。每当我们想到电影明星，体育明星或者流行音乐人，就会觉得通常看上去他们在短时间内会获得更多的的收入，对于他们的工作量来说是不公平的。

然而，事实上只有那些在他们的专业上达到极高水平的人会得到颇丰的收入。明星们希望的薪水的多少和竞争有关，这样他们为了成功就会去克服。

此外，大多数的明星不能长期保持他们的首要位置。体育明星和流行歌手，例如，很快就会被年轻人，更有活力的一代取代，与此同时许多电影明星的容颜也会很快老去。所以这个相对短暂的工作生涯可能是一些高薪的理由。

不幸的是，其他领域的专业人士，那些为人类社会做出很大贡献的却获得的很少，很难不同意这种说法。教师，护士，搞研究的工作人员等，从来没有名列到收入最高的职业中。但是，对于我们的福利和未来，他们比起那些迅速获得财富的明星来说更重要。

总之，我认为这里也许有些原因使明星获得颇丰的收入，但是整体来说他们获得的过于多了。他们的收入与无私为社会公益服务的人的收入的差距是不公平的，这样的专业人员应该更好地被赏识并且获得更高的收入。

164. 运动员娱乐人士的高薪

Topic:

In some countries, sports and entertainment personalities earn higher salaries than professionals like doctors, nurses and teachers. Why do you think this happens in some societies and do you consider it is good or bad?

Sample Answer

Nowadays, sports and entertainment personalities have increasingly higher value than professional workers. As society progresses, consumers will place higher value on leisure and fitness, and they spend more money on entertainment and sports, which is the major reason for those people to enjoy higher salary and more popularity. In addition, the media and advertising industry give them great publicity to bring them even higher value. However, in my opinion, the escalation of the high value on sports and entertainment personalities is not a good development.

Some professional workers actually create more value than the sports and entertaining personalities. The teachers will educate many individuals; perhaps through their influence, some students may change the destiny of mankind. The doctors will save the lives of hundreds of people. A physicist will gain a better understanding of the nature of reality, and perhaps contributes to the advancement of technology in order to make life better for all the humanity. However, those professional workers might receive only 1/10, or 1/100 of the money that sports or entertaining personalities obtained and they attract only slight attention from people.

If professional workers achieve higher value than sports and entertaining personalities, it will motivate young people into making science a career choice and drive human knowledge to new heights. Sports and entertaining programs, on the other hand, are quite inadequate for people who want to meditate and look for deeper meanings of life.

The destiny of our children and ourselves is a concern that requires foresight. There is something lacking in our culture. It is time that we value more of the professional workers for the well-being of the society.

▶考官评分:7

题目:

在一些国家，体育和娱乐人士比起像医生、护士、教师这些专业工作者有着更高的收入，你认为原因是什么，这一现象好还是不好？

译文：

如今，体育和娱乐人士比起专业工作者有着越来越高的价值。随着社会的进步，消费者很看重休闲和健康，他们在娱乐和体育上花费更多的钱，这也是那些人享有高收入和更受欢迎的主要原因。此外，媒体和广告业给予他们的极大关注也使他们的价值更高。然而，在我看来，对体育和娱乐界人士的过高重视不是一件好事。

事实上，一些专业工作者能比那些体育和娱乐人士创造更多价值。老师能教育很多人；也许通过他们的影响，有些学生可能会改变人类的命运。医生可挽救数百人的生命。物理学家会对事物的本质有更好的理解，这可能有助于技术的进步，使人类生活得更加美好。然而，这些专业工作者可能只能得到体育或娱乐人物所获得收入的1/10或1/100，而且只能稍微引起人们的注意。

如果专业工作者能比体育和娱乐人士获得更高的价值，它将鼓励年轻人把科学作为他们的职业选择并推动人类的知识到达一个新的高度。从另一方面来讲，体育和娱乐节目对那些想深入思考和寻找生命深层意义的人们来说是很不够的。

我们孩子和我们自己的命运是需要远见。我们的文化缺少一些东西。为了社会的福祉，现在是我们更尊崇专业工作者的时候了。

165. 运动员的高薪

Topic:

Successful sports professionals can earn a great deal more money than people in other important professions. Some people think this is fully justified while others think it is unfair. Discuss both views and give your own opinion.

Sample Answer

As a result of constant media attention, sports professionals in my country have become stars and celebrities, and those at the top are paid huge salaries. Just like movie stars, they live extravagant lifestyles with huge houses and cars.

Many people find their rewards unfair, especially when comparing these super salaries with those of top surgeons or research scientists, or even leading politicians who have the responsibility of governing the country. However, sports stars' salaries are not determined by considering the contribution to society a person makes, or the level of responsibility he or she holds. Instead, they reflect the public popularity of sport in general and the level of public support that successful stars can generate. So the notion of "fairness" is not the issue.

Those who feel that sports stars' salaries are justified might argue that the number of professionals with real talent is very small, and the money is a recognition of the skills and dedication a person needs to be successful. Competition is constant and a player is tested every time they perform in their relatively short career. The pressure from the media is intense and there is little privacy out of the spotlight. So all of these factors may justify the huge earnings.

Personally, I think that the amount of money such sports stars make is more justified than the huge earnings of movie stars, but at the same time, it indicates that our society places more value on sport than on more essential professions and achievements.

▶考官评分:8

题目:

成功的运动员比其他重要职业的人挣得多很多。一些人认为这很公正，另外一些人认为不公平。讨论双方并给出你的观点。

译文:

由于媒体不断的推波助澜，我国的许多职业运动员已成为了明星和名人。那些顶尖的运动员收入颇丰。像一些电影明星一样，他（她）们生活奢华，拥有豪宅香车。

许多人觉得这些运动员的回报是极为不公的，尤其将他们的高薪与那些顶级的外科医生，从事研究的科学家或有管理国家责任的高官的工资相比。然而，运动员的薪水并不是由一个人对社会所做出的贡献或者其责任水平所决定的。相反，从整体上来说它们反映的是体育运动在大众眼中的普及性以及那些成功的体育明星获得人们支持的程度。所以，“公平”的概念并不是问题关键之所在。

那些认为体育明星拿高薪无可厚非的人争辩说那些有天赋的体育运动员实属凤毛麟角，高薪是对他（她）们的娴熟技能和为成功所付出的努力的承认。竞争持续不断，运动员在他（她）们相对较短的运动生涯中每次参赛必须面临检验与挑战。同时，来自于媒体的压力令人窒息，他（她）们必须生活在镁光灯下，几乎没有隐私可言。这一切都证明了他（她）们无愧获得高薪。

在我个人看来，比起电影明星的高薪，体育明星的高薪更受之无愧。但与此同时，这种现象也表明我们的社会更关注体育而非其他一些更重要的领域和成就。

166. 关注名人的意见

Topic:

When famous people such as actors, athletes and rock stars give their opinions, many people listen. Do you think we should pay attention to these opinions?

Sample Answer

Famous people, such as athletes, actors, and other entertainers, are often interviewed by the press. They not only answer questions about their careers and personal lives, but also often give their opinions on issues of the day. The public tend to give more consideration to the views of the famous than it does to the opinions of more ordinary people. Should we give greater weight to these opinions? In my opinion, we should not, for the following reasons.

First, famous people are not necessarily well informed about the issues under discussion. While everyone has a right to express his opinion, a willingness to speak does not imply knowledge. Furthermore, a famous person may be an authority in his field, but that does not mean he is also an expert in others. For example, an actor who plays a doctor on TV is probably not a true authority on medical matters.

Second, a famous person may not be impartial. Rather, he may have financial or other motives for the opinions he espouses. **This is particularly true when some type of product endorsement is involved.** A good example of this would be an entertainer who proclaims the benefits of a certain product when he has, in fact, never even tried it.

Third, a reliance on the opinions of famous people may prevent us from thinking for ourselves. We should all develop the ability to evaluate facts and reach our own conclusions. While there is no harm in listening to the opinions of others, we must realize that our situations are often very different. What may be true or beneficial for one person, may not be so for another. This is especially true in the case of famous people who, due to their wealth and fame, live in circumstances that are very different from those of ordinary people.

To sum up, we would be better off learning to evaluate situations and reach our own conclusions than relying on the opinions of others, no matter how well-known. **Listening to the views of other people is a good way to gather information and come to our own decisions.** However, we should not accept the opinions of others blindly. Instead, we must consider their knowledge and motivation. Famous people have the power to draw attention to a certain message that might not otherwise be heard, but we must still determine the validity of the message for ourselves.

▶考官评分:8

题目:

像演员、运动员、摇滚明星这类名人提出自己的看法，很多人都会听。你认为我们是否应该注意这些看法?

译文:

媒体常会采访像运动员、演员以及其他的艺人这样的名人。这些名人不仅会回答有关他们的工作以及个人生活的问题，而且通常还会对时下的一些话题提出自己的看法。与一般人所提的意见相比，大众对名人的意见会进行更加认真的思考。我们是否应该比较重视名人的意见呢?就我的观点而言，大可不必如此，我的理由如下。

首先，名人不见得会对所讨论的议题有充分的了解。尽管每个人都有发表意见的权利，但有表达的意愿不代表就具备了这方面的知识。此外，名人也许在他的专业领域是权威，但这并不表示他在其他领域也是专家。举个例子，一个在电视上扮演医生的演员在医学领域内可能就不是真的权威。

第二，名人不见得会保持公正。相反，他可能会因为金钱或其他动机而支持某种意见，这一点特别适用于对某种产品的支持。艺人可能从来没用过某种产品，却宣称使用之后好处很多，这就是一个很好的例子。

第三，依赖名人的意见可能会使我们无法独立思考。我们应该培养自己评估事实并得出结论的能力。虽然听别人的意见没有什么坏处，但我们必须了解，每个人的情况通常都不尽相同。对某人而言是正确的或有利的，不见得就适用于其他人，这点在名人的身上尤其贴切。因为他们拥有一般人所没有的财富与名声，其生活环境更是和一般人大不相同。

总之，我们最好学会如何评估情况并得出自己的结论，而不是只依赖别人的意见，不论那个人多有名。听取别人的意见是获取信息并做出决定的一个很好的方法，但我们不应该盲目地接受别人的意见。相反，我们必须考虑他们的知识与动机。名人有能力可以吸引人们注意原本不会被注意的信息，但我们仍必须自己判断这些信息是否正确。

167. 不同职业享有相同假期

Topic:

The length of the holiday that an employee receives per-year varies from job to job. Do you think people should have the same amount of holidays regardless of their occupations? Give reasons for your answer.

Sample Answer

Nowadays, people are enjoying more and longer holidays and some people advocate that people should have the same length of holiday regardless of their occupations. They hold that it is unfair for people not to rest for the same length of time even though they have worked as hard. They even regard this as a human rights issue, just like women's right to vote. But taking into account the characteristics of different professions, we may examine this issue from another angle.

As we know, jobs vary from one another in their labor intensity, so that people in different occupations may have a different kind and amount of leisure time to refresh themselves. For example, blue-collar workers may work longer hours and physically tired, while white-collar workers such as doctors and teachers are more mentally stressed. Therefore they can not work continuously as long as those physical labor workers. Generally speaking, it needs more time to pull through the mental weariness than physical tiredness.

Secondly, different tasks and duties are required for different professions, which results in the varieties of holiday periods for people in different walks of life. Some employees cannot have their legal holidays and even have to work overtime, such as policemen, construction workers and people in the service line. This kind of professions just can't be interrupted for a moment; otherwise the society will be in a mess. Even for some people in the same occupations, they can not have the same holidays entitled to them due to many factors out of human control, such as special assignments, and health conditions etc, then not to say people in different fields.

Thirdly, with the development of science and technology, the ways people work are gradually changing. Computer experts make their programs, doctors give patients diagnosis and tutors give students instructions at home through optical-fabric cable connections, which saves them much time. Consequently, it may be quite natural for these people to have more leisure than their colleagues who still have to take buses to go to work. In another word, the way people work is not fixed so that they need different holiday phases.

All the above suggest that we can not come to the simple conclusion that the different length of holiday time indicates unfairness. We may discover that is it neither possible nor reasonable to apply this belief to practice.

▶考官评分:8

题目:

各行各业的人每年假期的长度是完全不同的，你认为人们不论什么工作都应该享受同样多的假期吗？请给出你的理由。

译文:

如今，人们正享受着更多和更长的假期。一些人主张不论其职业，每个人都应该享有同样长度的假期。他们认为对于那些即使努力工作也不能享有相同的休息时间的人来说是不公平。他们甚至认为这是一个和妇女投票权很类似的人权问题。但是，考虑到不同职业的特点，我们应从另一个角度研究这个问题。

众所周知，不同职位的人的劳动强度是不同的，这使得从事不同职业的人根据不同种类和不同的休假时间来调整自己。例如，蓝领可能长时间工作并且身体疲劳，而白领如医生和教师则承受较大的心理压力。因此，他们不能和那些体力劳动者一样长时间的工作。一般来说，调整心理疲劳比调整身体疲劳所需的时间更多。

其次，不同的职业有不同的任务和责任，从而导致了不同行业的人拥有不同长度的假期。有些人不能拥有法定节假日甚至超时工作，如警察，建筑工人和从事服务行业的人。这些职业是不能被中断的，否则社会将混乱。甚至有些在相同职业的人们，由于人为因素的影响他们不能享有相同的假期，如特殊任务和医疗卫生等，更何况不同的领域的人呢。

第三，随着科学技术的进步，人们的工作方式也在逐渐变化。电脑专家编写电脑程序，医生给病人诊断和导师给学生留作业都可以在家里通过光纤上网来完成的，这大大节省了他们的时间。因此，很自然这些人比那些仍然坐汽车去上班的同事有更多的休闲时间。换句话说，由于人们的工作方式不固定，他们需要的假期也不同。

综上所述，我们不能根据假期长度不同来简单给出结论说这件事情就是不公平的。我们会发现把这种观点运用到实践是既不可能实现也不合理的。

168. 大学生挣钱多

Topic:

A great number of people think that those with university education should get higher pay than those without, for they believe that the former have sweated and sacrificed more. To what extent do you agree with this point of view?

Sample Answer

Many people believe that those who have received higher education should earn far more than those who have not, because the former have exerted more efforts than the latter. Personally I do not agree with this opinion, for the following reasons.

In the first place, one's individual income does not wholly reflect the extent to which one's self-value and social value are realized. A person who has received higher education may offer more social value than one who has not. Economists and merchants may serve as perfect examples to verify this point. Both are engaged in the economic sphere.

Nevertheless, the former might create more economic returns for society, while the latter might bring himself more economic profits. Although the economist may not be as wealthy as the merchant, his work is more meaningful to the society he lives in.

In the second place, some people who have admirable capabilities have not had the opportunity to receive higher education. Then, after years of exertions and hard struggle, they secure a proper place for themselves in society and realize their own self-value. Such people have received no college education. However, they deserve what they have earned.

All in all, it is ridiculous to rack one's brains about who, a man with a higher education or another one without it, should earn more money than the other. One's earnings cannot be solely determined by his or her educational background. We should observe what kind of effort a person has made and decide how we are to define "personal income" before finally judging who should earn more.

▶考官评分:8

题目:

许多人认为受过大学教育的人应该比没有受过大学教育的人得到更高的报酬，因为他们相信前者付出的更多。你同意这种看法吗?

译文:

许多人相信获得良好教育的人能比没有获得良好教育的人赚到更多的钱，是因为前者会比后者更加的努力。就个人而言，我不同意这个观点，有以下几个理由。

首先，个人收入并不能完全反应一个人的自身价值和社会价值。一个获得良好教育的人也许能比没有获得良好教育的人贡献更多的社会价值。经济学家和商人作为例子就可以很好地证明这一点。两者都是从事于经济领域。

然而，当前者给社会创造了更多经济价值的同时，后者则给自己带来了更多的经济效益。虽然经济学家可能不会像商人一样富有，但是他的工作对于他生活的这个社会来说却是更有意义的。

其次，一些人拥有令人称赞的资质却没有机会去接受更好的教育。然后，经过若干年的努力和艰苦的奋斗，他们在社会上为自己找到了一个合适的领域并且实现了自身价值。这些人没有接受大学教育，但是，他们获得了他们应该得到的。

总而言之，绞尽脑汁去关心到底是接受了高等教育的人还是没接受高等教育的人能赚得更多的钱是很荒谬的。一个人的收入并不只是他的教育背景就可以决定的。在判断谁赚得多之前，我们更应该关注一个人所付出的努力，以及如何定义“个人收入”的概念。

第十大类：社会问题类话题

169. 如何对待罪犯

Topic:

Some people hold that criminals should be sent to prison. Some others think they should do something else outside prison as the punishment. What is your opinion?

Sample Answer

In recent years, the record of crime rate has been constantly renewed. A growing number of people have begun to challenge against the existing practice of sending criminals to prison. They argue that the law offenders should be punished to do something for the public. It is quite natural that people seldom reach a total agreement on such a controversial issue.

Some people advocate that we should let criminals do something else as punishment. In the first place, they can get better reclamation in this way. Doing something for society is a good measure, which not only punishes the criminals but also encourages them to begin a new life as well. Another reason is due to the limited jail space. Letting criminals do something outside jails decreases the cost of the government. Finally, the imprisonment of criminals cannot scare off the criminals. Up to now, there is no evidence showing the direct link between the implementation of imprisoning criminals and the decline of crime rate.

Some others approve of the imprisonment of criminals. First of all, it can ensure a safe living environment to the law-abiding citizens. For criminals like thieves, robbers, rapists or even murderers, it is improper or even dangerous to let them out of jails, because they still pose threats to our society. Second, it is the best deterrent to those potential criminals. It will make would-be criminals think twice before they commit a crime. Last but not least, it is a great spiritual consolation to the victims. Those who suggest setting criminals free lay too much emphasis on the rights of criminals. They ignore the rights of victims.

All the above opinions make sense. After careful consideration, I am in favor of the latter view that we should retain the practice of sending criminals to prison. It can guarantee the safety of citizens. It can reduce the crime rate. Furthermore, it serves a punishment for the merciless offenders while a comfort to the innocent victims.

▶考官评分:7

题目:

有人认为罪犯应该被关进监狱,有人认为他们应该被惩罚做一些别的事情，说明你的观点。

译文:

近年来，犯罪率屡创新高。越来越多的人开始对于送罪犯去监狱的做法持反对意见。他们认为那些违法者应该通过为社会多做些贡献来接受惩罚。在这样一个颇有争议的问题上，人们很少能达成完全的一致，这是很自然的。

一些人倾向于让罪犯做其他事作为惩罚。首先，这可以让他们得到更好的改造。为社会做些公益事业就是个办法，既对罪犯进行了惩罚，还能够鼓励他们开始新的生活。另一个原因是监狱的有限空间，可以降低政府的开支。最后，对罪犯的监禁丝毫也不会威慑到其他罪犯。到目前为止，没有任何证据表明在监禁罪犯和犯罪率的降低之间存在联系。

另外一些人主张把罪犯关进监狱。首先，这可以为守法者营造一个安全舒适的环境。像小偷、抢劫犯、强奸犯甚至杀人犯，释放他们是不合理甚至非常危险的，因为他们仍然对社会构成威胁。其次，这是对罪犯最好的威慑。这可以让想要犯罪的人在犯罪之前再三考虑。最后一点，这是对受害者的一种精神上的抚慰。那些不同意关押罪犯的人过度强调了罪犯的权利，而忽视了受害者的权利。

以上的观点都很有道理。经过谨慎的考虑，我倾向于后一个观点，即继续保留关押罪犯的做法。这可以保证老百姓的安全，还可以降低犯罪率。而且，这是对无情的罪犯的惩罚，同时也是对无辜的受害者的安慰。

170. 城市和乡村

Topic:

Some people prefer to live in the countryside. Others prefer to live in a big city. What is your opinion?

Sample Answer

An increasing number of people are pouring into the city and looking for a nest there. Some people hold the opinion that we should live in the countryside. However, some others strongly argue that city is a better place for us to live in. It is quite natural that people from different backgrounds may have divergent attitudes towards it.

Those people who strongly believe that living in a big city has several benefits have cogent reasons for it. To begin with, there are more job opportunities readily available in big cities than in the countryside. Furthermore, not merely there are more job positions in big cities, the pay is more decent. Besides, children are supposed to be able to receive an education with a higher quality compared with their counterparts who live in the countryside. For most families, children's education is always put first. More importantly, shopping, a necessary activity in everyday life is more convenient in the city than in the country. Urban citizens can buy what they want at any time of a day.

However, there are a large number of people who hold a different view concerning this case. They believe that living in the countryside also has some advantages. First of all, people who live in the countryside often have a much comfortable lifestyle. Most of them are immune from the suffering of high work stress. In addition, although the average pay is much less than that of big cities, the price of daily necessities, such as vegetables or meat, is usually more inexpensive. Therefore, the cheap life in the country appeals to many city-dwellers. What is more, instead of suffering loneliness which is prevalent in big cities, children might grow up healthier because of harmonious relationship among residents in the countryside. A country allows children to experience a more natural environment without all the distractions of entertainment places in the city.

Both sides make sense. Therefore it is really hard for me to draw a definite conclusion. To my mind, the countryside is a better place for people to live in. Country life is featured in the fresh air, the peaceful night, and the friendly people. Wherever the city may be, the life there is much more expensive than in the countryside. Furthermore, without all the dangers and distractions of city life, children will grow up healthier.

▶考官评分:7

题目:

有人喜欢住在乡下，也有人偏爱住在大城市。你的观点是什么？

译文:

越来越多的人涌入城市，在那里寻找安身之处。有些人认为我们应该居住在乡村。然而，另外一些人强烈地认为城市是更适合我们居住的地方。来自不同背景的人对于这个问题有着不同的态度，这是很自然的。

强烈认为居住在大城市有很多好处的人有充实的理由。首先，大城市比乡村有更多现成的工作机会。此外，在大城市不仅有更多的工作岗位，而且收入也更体面。第二点，大城市的孩子有望能够比居住在乡下的孩子受到更高质量的教育。对于大多数的家庭来说，孩子的教育永远是第一位的。最重要的是，购物作为日常生活必要的活动在城市中就更为便利了。都市的人可以在一天的任何时间购买想要的东西。

然而，对于这个问题，很多人持不同的看法。他们认为，生活在乡下也有一些好处。第一，生活在乡下的人经常过着一种很舒服的生活。他们当中的绝大多数人无需承受高强度的工作压力。而且，尽管平均收入比大城市少很多，但日常必需品如蔬菜和肉的价格通常会更便宜。所以，便宜的生活方式吸引着很多都市人。再者，与大城市中人们普遍承受着孤独不同，乡下的人们之间相处和谐，因此儿童能够更健康地成长。在乡下长大的孩子能够体验更自然的环境，而不会因都市里各种娱乐场所而分心。

双方都有道理，因此我很难得出一个明确的结论。在我看来，乡村更适合人们居住。因为乡村生活意味着清新的空气、宁静的夜晚、友善的乡亲。无论哪个城市，生活费用都要比农村高。而且，没有都市的各种危险和令人分心的事情，孩子们可以更健康地成长。

171. 找工作考虑什么因素和谁的建议

Topic:

When we seek a future career, what factors should we consider? Whose suggestions should we consider?

Sample Answer

Choosing the right career is regarded as a turning point in one's life. It is so crucial that we cannot afford to make a single mistake. However, it is always not easy to make a satisfying choice. Sometimes we find ourselves involved in dilemmas. To my mind, when we seek a job, the following factors need to be taken into consideration.

The first factor that can be seen by every person is that the salary should not be too low. Most people will be married and have children, so they need a stable income because of their family responsibilities even if they are not satisfied with their job. In addition, to live a more comfortable life is a part of human nature. All these things need a certain amount of money.

Another factor that we must consider is that we should have an objective understanding of our ability so that we will know which occupation is suitable for us. In other words, the job should allow us to live a balanced life. It should not be so time-consuming that we have no time for family, friends and personal interests. Nor should it give us so much pressure that we cannot relax in our free time.

As the proverb goes, two heads are better than one. When we choose a job, always remember to talk with parents, teachers or anyone we trust. They possess rich experience and knowledge from which we are sure to benefit. They know us best and can offer us most sincere advice. Keep in mind the old saying that it is good to learn at another man's cost. Furthermore, we may also seek advice from the career advisory office that is always ready to provide professional suggestion.

▶考官评分:8

题目:

当我们选择未来的职业时，应该考虑什么因素?应该听取谁的意见?

译文:

选择一个对口的工作被认为是一个人生命中的转折点。它至关重要，所以不允许我们犯任何错误。然而，做出一个满意的决定通常不太容易。有的时候我们发现自己进退两难。我认为，在找工作的时候，以下的因素需要考虑在内。

每个人都能看到的第一个因素是薪水不应该太低。大多数都将结婚生子，所以因为他们的家庭责任他们需要稳定的收入。而且，要过一个更舒适的生活也是人的本性，这些都需要一定数量的钱。

我们必须考虑的另一个因素是我们应该对自己的能力有一个客观的评价，这样才能知道什么样的工作适合我们。也就是说，这个工作应该能让我们过着均衡的生活。我们的时间不应该被工作完全占据，让我们没有时间跟家人和朋友相处，或无法发展个人兴趣。工作也不能有过大的压力，使我们连在空闲时间也无法放松。

俗话说，三个臭皮匠顶过一个诸葛亮。在选择工作的时候，记着和父母、老师或者任何我们信任的人商量一下。他们拥有丰富的经验和知识，这必定使我们从中受益。他们最了解我们，可以给我们提供最诚挚的建议。记住一句老话，从他人的教训中吸取经验是明智的。此外，我们也可以到职业咨询事务所寻求帮助，他们随时会给你专业的建议。

172. 警察佩带枪支

Topic:

Unlike other countries, the police in the UK do not carry guns. Some think this leaves citizens unprotected, while others consider it reduces the overall level of violence in society. Give reasons for both sides of this argument and state your own opinion.

Sample Answer

As opposed to the extensive use of weapons in the US, people in UK, even the police are not allowed to take guns. Some people argue that it may trigger off insecurity of city dwellers, whereas others assert that it can eliminate the whole violence in the society. Hereby, I would like to discuss both perspectives in the following paragraphs.

Some people believe that the absence of carrying guns is disadvantageous in many aspects in any nations. It has been a trend that the violence is increasing in various parts of the world. More and more criminals these days carry guns and other dangerous weapons, but our police force only have pepper spray and batons for protection (as well as bullet proof vests). This is not enough, not enough of a deterrent, not enough in today's society. If the police have proper equipment, i.e carrying a gun, they would hopefully not lose their lives and the residents will feel safer and better protected.

Others, however, hold the opinion that police should not be allowed to carry guns. There have been plenty of cases that some robbers or thieves who commit crime but do not deserve death were shot down by police. Furthermore, some unqualified and irresponsible policemen may hurt some innocent citizens even to death when they are pursuing some culprits. Additionally, guns of police may often be lost and will touch off an even worse situation. And thus, it will reduce the overall violence in our society by not allowing guns to the police.

In conclusion, both opponents and proponents of such a practice have their respective reasons and justifications. However, as a person always expecting a peaceful life, I personally agree with the latter view. If the guns and some of other weapons would be totally restricted in the modern globe, the serious phenomenon of violence and other relevant behaviors would vanish. Hence, it is my sincere wish that governments of other countries would follow the example of UK to avoid the whole violence in the world.

▶考官评分:8

题目:

英国的警察不像其他一些国家可以带枪。一些人认为这样会让公民缺乏保护，而另一些人认为这样减少了社会上总体的暴力水平。给出双方的理由并且陈述自己的观点。

译文:

与美国广泛使用武器不同，在英国，市民甚至是警察都不允许带抢。一些人认为，这将引起城市居民的不安全感，而另一些人声称，这将消除整个社会的暴力。因此，我将在下面两段讨论这两个方面。

一些人认为，在任何一个国家，警察不带枪在很多方面都是不利的。在世界的每一个角落，暴力上升是一个趋势。当今社会，越来越多的犯罪分子带枪或其他危险武器。但是我们的警察却只有胡椒粉喷雾剂和警棍作为防护（以及防弹衣）。这是不够的，没有威摄力，在我们这个社会中是不够的。如果警察有相应的配备，如带一支枪，他们就有望不会牺牲，市民也会感到更安全，从而能够被很好的保护。

然而，另一些人坚持认为警察不应该带枪。有太多的例子，一些强盗或小偷犯了罪，但罪不致死，结果却被警察枪毙。而且，一些不够格或不负责任的警察在追捕犯人的过程中可能会伤害无辜的人，甚至导致死亡。此外，警察的枪经常被丢失，这将引发更严重的后果。因此，不允许警察带枪将会减少社会上的暴力。

总之，反对或支持警察带枪的人都有他们的原因和理由。然而，作为一个一直企盼和平生活的人，我个人同意反对警察带枪者的观点。如果枪支和一些其他的武器在当今全球被彻底限制，严重的暴力现象和其他的一些相关行为将会消失。因此，我衷心希望其他国家的政府以英国为榜样,在整个世界避免暴力。

173. 废除死刑

Topic:

Should capital punishment be abolished? What is your opinion?

Sample Answer

In recent years, an increasing number of people have begun to challenge against the existing practice of capital punishment. They argue that in a civilized and enlightened society, such a barbaric and cruel practice should be abolished. But, on the other side, there are also many people who strongly advocate the remaining of capital punishment, saying that the world would be in great chaos and full of blood and violence without death penalty. It is quite natural that people seldom reach a total agreement on such a long-running controversy.

Those people who approve of the practice of death penalty hold that it is the best deterrent to crime. It will always remind would-be criminals that crime does not pay so that they will think twice before they commit a crime. The decline of heinous crime has a direct correlation with the implementation of capital punishment. Secondly, it serves a just reward for the heartless and merciless malefactors while a great spiritual comfort to the victim's family. The third merit lies in that it is very economical to end the life of a person guilty of crimes for which even death is an insufficient punishment. The practice helps lessen the prison crowding and thus cuts down on government budget.

Towards the same issue, many others who advocate the abolition, however, argue that in a highly modernized world, it is inhuman and barbaric to take away one's life on any pretext. They believe in that life is precious and irreversible and that only God can take away one's life. Moreover, capital punishment can not scare off the criminals. Up to now, there is no evidence showing the direct correlation between the practice and the declining incidence of felony. We should offer the offender a chance to mend his/her way and take over a new life. The criminals can be safely locked up in prisons and receive education through labour.

Both sides of the argument have very strong feelings and sound reasons. After a thorough consideration, for my part, I am in favor of the former view that we should retain the time-honored catholicon to ensure a safe and comfortable living environment to all these law-abiding citizens. An old saying best expresses my attitude: "Mercy to the criminal may be cruelty to the people."

▶考官评分:8

题目:

是否应该废除死刑？你的意见是什么？

译文:

最近几年，越来越多的人开始对死刑这种现行制度进行挑战。他们表明在一个文明和民主的社会，如此一种野蛮残酷的行为应该被制止。不过，相反，也有很大部分的人强烈提倡保持死刑制度，在没有死刑的条件下世界会陷入混乱甚至充满血腥和暴力。很自然，在这长期的论战中人们很少能达成一致。

那些支持死刑的人认为这是对犯罪最好的威慑。这总会想起那些要成为罪犯的人，犯罪无利可图，所以在实施犯罪前他们会三思而后行。执行死刑直接导致重罪犯罪率的减少。第二，这是那些无情残暴的歹徒应得的惩罚同时也会给受害者的家人精神上极大的安慰。第三，它是结束一个罪人非常经济的方式，甚至有些人被判死刑来作为他们的惩罚都不足够。这种方式有助于缓解监狱的拥挤并且减少了政府的预算。

关于同样的问题，其余许多提倡废除（死刑）的人，无论如何，坚决主张在这个非常现代化的世界，无论什么借口夺走一个人的生命，死刑都是没人性的残酷的。他们信仰生命是宝贵而且不可逆转的，只有上帝才能剥夺人的生命。此外，死刑也并不能吓跑罪犯，到目前为止，没有证据可以证明采取死刑和减少重罪犯罪率两者之间有必然的联系。我们应该给罪犯一个机会去改善自己的行为并引导他们过上新的生活。罪犯能安全的被关押在监狱中并在劳动中接受教育。

辩论的双方都拥有非常强烈的感情和有判断力的理由。通过全面的考虑，对于我而言，我支持前者的观点，即保留这个历史悠久的万灵药来确保给我们所有的这些守法的公民一个安全舒适的生活环境。一句古话能很好的阐述我的态度：“对罪犯的仁慈，就是对人民的残忍。”

范文点评:

典型的辩论型题目。作者采用对称式结构，写了四段。开头段介绍了大致背景以及双方观点。接下来的两段分别说明双方观点，第一个理由段用三个理由说明死刑的好处，第二个理由段说明了死刑的缺点并提出了取代死刑的方法，每个理由都有支持句，论证充分。最后一段说明自己的观点：认为还是应该对罪犯严厉一些——即不可废除死刑。语言虽然使用了一些模板句型，但不是很多，正确灵活运用了其他加分句型，因此考官评分8分。

174. 年轻女性犯罪

Topic:

The rate of young women crimes is rising in the current society. What are the causes and how to solve it?

Sample Answer

Juvenile delinquency is a very serious problem confronting us in modern society. At the same time, the rate of young women crimes spearheads very fast. Some sociologists and educationists show great concern about this problem. In this essay, I will find out the causes for this issue and explore some possible solutions.

First of all, the rapid development of society and the changes of people's value of the world account mainly for the issue. In the old days, women were confined to housework and baby-sitting, which barricaded women's steps. Now, with the eye-catching development of economy, many young women go out to find a job, which renders them more opportunities to contact the outside world. As a consequence, young women are apt to be influenced by the malfeasance in the society.

Secondly, the rise of criminal rate attributes to the lack of education of women. The prosperity and luxury in some metropolises are very attractive to some young women. Some of them leave the countryside in the hope that they can make a good fortune in the cities, where they often find themselves disappointed for lack of good education or skills. Therefore, some of them felt despaired and embark on the criminal road.

The last factor is the over-description of violence on the media. TV is the most powerful medium, which transforms abundant information around the world. However, some programs are full of violent description, sexual alluring and bloody contents, which are easy to make young women astray.

In order to solve the problem, people think up various solutions. From my point of view, I think the following are worth mentioning. On one hand, the government should pay more attention to the problem and issue relevant laws to crack down young women crimes. Meanwhile, we should strengthen education and raise the quality of people, helping them set up a correct outlook of the world. Only when the government and the society join hands in solving the problem, will the rate of young women crimes fall down.

▶考官评分:8

题目:

当今年轻女性的犯罪率正在增加，这是什么原因并且有什么解决方法?

译文:

青少年犯罪是现代社会面临的一个严重问题。与此同时，青年女性的犯罪率快速上升。一些社会学家和教育学家非常关注这个问题。在这篇文章中，我将找出引起这个问题的原因并探讨一些合适的解决办法。

首先，社会的快速发展及人们世界观的变化是引起该问题的主要原因。以前，女性被限制在家做家务活和看护孩子，这些都阻碍了女性接触外面社会的步伐。而现在，随着经济得到引人注目的发展，许多年轻女性都出去找工作，这就为她们提供更多机会接触外部世界。而结果也使她们易于受到社会中不法行为的影响。

第二，女性所受教育的不足造成了犯罪率的上升。对于许多女性来说，大都市的繁荣和奢华是非常具有吸引力的。她们中的一些人离开农村，梦想着能够在城市中赚大钱。而现实往往是她们经常由于自身缺乏良好的教育和技能而沮丧失望。因此，一些人就丧失了信心而走上了犯罪的道路。

最后一个原因就是媒体中对暴力的过多描述。电视是最具影响力的传播媒介，它可以传播世界各地的丰富信息。然而，一些电视节目中充斥着暴力场面，色情诱惑和血腥内容，这些都有可能使年轻女性误入歧途。

为了解决这个问题，人们想出了各种各样的办法。就我个人而言，我认为以下方法还是值得一提。一方面，政府应该更多关注女性犯罪问题并出台相关法律予以惩治。同时，我们应该加强对女性的教育，提高女性的道德品质，帮助她们树立正确的世界观。在这个问题的解决上，只有政府与社会携起手才能使年轻女性的犯罪率降低。

175. 青少年犯罪

Topic:

Juvenile delinquency is increasingly common. Discuss the reasons and make some suggestions.

Sample Answer

Pistols shooting, gun flashes, people screaming hysterically and running in panic, confusion everywhere. This was not a scene from a Hollywood movie, but a recent shooting incident at an American school. The most appalling thing was that the emotionless and brutal killer was a teenager boy. This is a typical example of the increasingly disturbing panorama of juvenile crimes plaguing our society.

In the first place, the juvenile delinquency can be attributable to the rising divorce rate and family violence. It is reported that the juvenile delinquency is proportional to the high divorce rate. In such families, children are usually not properly taken care of, and to make things worse, their psychology may probably be distorted. Also, living in a family full of violence, children take it for granted that violence is the best way to resolve problems and they are likely to adopt the measure of "an eye for an eye and a tooth for a tooth". Thus, it is likely that such children may easily be led astray and even worse, they may embark on the criminal road.

What is more, the over-description of violence on the media is another vital cause to be considered. Nowadays, many programs are full of crime, violence, pornography and bloody contents; they are often glorified and polished to attract youngsters' eyes and to be conveniently imitated. Watching too many these programs, children may become isolated, violent and aggressive. Thus, their committing crime seems easy to be understood.

Given the seriousness of this problem, we have no alternatives but to adopt some feasible and effective measures. To begin with, relevant laws should be set down and implemented to crack down youth crimes. What is more, the families should be reinforced and proper guidance and support should be given to the youth. Finally, crime, violence, pornography and bloody contents shown in media should be banned and the measures to reduce stress from both education and society should be rendered to youngsters. **Only when these measures are taken will the rate of juvenile delinquency fall down.**

▶考官评分:8

题目:

现在青少年犯罪越来越普遍，阐述原因并提出解决办法。

译文:

手枪扣响，火光闪过，人们发出歇斯底里的尖叫，惊慌逃跑，到处是一片混乱。这不是好莱坞的大片中的情形，而是最近在美国的一所中学里发生的枪击事件。最令人震惊的是残忍无情的杀人犯居然是一个十几岁的孩子。这是困扰着我们社会的青少年犯罪所造成的日益混乱的场景中的一幕。

首先，青少年犯罪应归因于持续上升的离婚率和家庭暴力。据报道，青少年犯罪和高离婚率成正比。在这样的家庭，孩子们通常不会被细心照顾，更糟糕的是还会使他们的心理扭曲。并且，生活在一个充满暴力的家庭，孩子们会理所当然的认为暴力是解决问题的最好方式，他们也更愿意接受以牙还牙这种方式。因此，这样的孩子似乎更容易误入歧途，更糟糕的是，他们也许还会走上犯罪的道路。

另外，媒体上对暴力的过度报道描述，是另一个应该考虑的重要原因。现如今，许多犯罪，暴力，色情，血腥内容被美化鼓吹来吸引青少年的注意力，并被轻易模仿。孩子们看了太多这样的节目以至于很孤僻，暴力，好斗。因此，他们的犯罪行为便可以被理解了。

考虑到问题的严重性，我们没有选择，必须采取一些可行并有效的办法。首先，应该制定相关的法律并实施来减少青少年犯罪。另外，家庭需要被巩固并且应该给青少年提供合理的保证和支持。最后，犯罪，暴力，色情，血腥等场景应该在媒体上禁止播放，并且采取措施减少教育和社会给青少年带来的压力。只有采取这些办法，青少年犯罪才会下降。

176. 年轻人药品滥用

Topic:

Today's youth are experimenting with illegal drugs, and at an increasingly early age. Discuss the causes and some effects of widespread drug use by young people in modern society. Make any recommendations you feel are necessary to help fight youth drug abuse.

Sample Answer

Thanks to China's reform and opening-up policy, there has been earth shaking economic and social progress in the past two decades and people's living standard has improved, but at the same time it gives rise to a host of serious social problems like drug abuse, the causes of which may be inner and outer influence.

Some people become rich materially but spiritually barren and search for new excitement, and some start with ignorance and curiosity because they think drugs can ease stress and renew energy, which may be considered the inner causes of drug abuse. On the other hand, some young people like to follow the fashions and are easily influenced by their companions and cannot resist the temptation of taking up new things like drugs, and more importantly, they can get drugs through different channels, which may be the outer causes of drug abuse.

Today's youth are experimenting with drugs at an increasingly early age, which has been brought to public concern. The widespread drug abuse by young people has far-reaching adverse effects on the drug users, their families and even the society. The drug users themselves suffer from different symptoms and at last easily contract AIDS. Since taking drugs costs a huge sum of money, it brings bankruptcy to many families, and even those millionaires. As a result, many families are broken down.

The following suggestions should be taken into consideration when the government is seeking solutions to youth drug abuse. First of all, the government should promote the public awareness of the great harm brought by drugs. We can invite some ex-drug-addicts to show the destructive power of drugs by using their own experience. Secondly, the government should strike hard against drug-trafficking and impose heavier penalty on drug-related crimes and drug smugglers.

▶考官评分:8

题目:

现在的年轻人不仅使用违禁药品，而且年龄趋向于年轻化。试讨论原因以及青少年滥用药品的影响，并且提出可以改善这一现象的建议和意见。

译文:

由于中国改革开放的政策，在过去的二十年间经济、社会和人们的生活水平发生了翻天覆地的变化，但是同时，也引起了许多一系列严重的社会问题，比如吸毒，其原因可能是内部和外部因素的影响。

一些人很有钱但是精神空虚，所以去寻找新的刺激。一些人开始是因为无知和好奇而吸毒，他们觉得毒品能帮助他们缓解压力和恢复活力，这也许被认为是造成吸毒的内在原因。另一方面，一些年轻人喜欢追求潮流而且特别容易受到同伴的影响，不能抵制一些新事物的诱惑，就像毒品。而更重要的，他们能从不同渠道获得毒品，这也许是造成吸毒的外在原因。

现在年轻人尝试毒品的年龄越来越小，这使公众更加焦虑。年轻人广泛的吸毒给自己、他们的家庭甚至社会造成了更深远的影响。吸毒的人患有不同的症状，最后很容易感染上艾滋病。由于吸毒耗费巨资，以至于很多家庭破产，即使是那些百万富翁。最后，很多家庭破裂了。

当政府正在寻找解决年轻人吸毒问题的方法时，以下的建议可以提供参考。首先，政府需要提升公众对于毒品危害的警觉意识。我们可以邀请一些戒了毒瘾的人用他们的亲身经历来给人们讲述毒品的危害。其次，政府需要加大打击毒品的力度并且对贩卖和走私毒品的人进行严厉的惩罚。

177. 安乐死该不该合法化

Topic:

Should euthanasia be legalized? What is your opinion ?

Sample Answer

In the last several decades, advances in medical technology have made it possible for people to enjoy longer life span than in the past. Yet when it comes to the desirability of extending the life of the terminally ill and the legalization of the practice of euthanasia, people from different backgrounds have very different opinions.

Some people, including some doctors, claim that the practice of euthanasia has merits. First of all, the quality of life is as important as life itself. It is meaningless to maintain the life of a terminally ill patient, which will only prolong his/her agony and sufferings. Secondly, euthanasia will bring emotional and financial release to the patient, the family and to society, thus saving money, and the unnecessary labour of doctors and nurses. Moreover, it is also a human's basic right to choose when, where, and how to die. In a sense, a mercy killing enables one to die with dignity and peace.

However, people rarely reach an absolute consensus on such a controversial issue. The opponents argue that the practice of mercy killing is just another kind of killing and killing is always wrong and a sin. No one is entitled to take away another human beings' life—only God can. Life is precious and we all should respect it. Anyway, life under any circumstances is better than death. Besides there is always the chance that some cure may be discovered for the particular disease.

Undeniably, there are good points on both sides of the argument. But after careful consideration of the above reasons, I, personally, stand on the side of the advocates, because I firmly believe that the legalization of euthanasia will not only bring mental and physical release to the terminally ill, but also benefit the family and the whole society. The practice of euthanasia is a symbol of the advancement of civilization.

▶考官评分:8

题目：

安乐死是否应该合法化？你的建议是什么？

译文：

最近几十年，医疗技术的进步使得人们的寿命比过去更长了。但当谈到延长绝症晚期病人的生命和实施安乐死的合法化时，不同背景的人有着非常不同的观点。

有些人（包括一些医生）声称实施安乐死有其优点。首先，生活质量与生命本身同等重要。挽留一个绝症晚期病人的生命是毫无意义的，这只会延长他或她的精神上和生理上的痛苦。第二，安乐死会给病人及其家人以及社会带来精神上和物质上的解脱，包括节省金钱和不必要的医生和护士的劳动力。再者，选择何时死、在哪儿死以及怎样死也是一个人的基本权利。在某种意义上，实施安乐死能让人死得平和、体面。

然而，人们在这样一个具有争议性的话题上很少能达到完全一致。反对者争辩说实施安乐死只是用另外一种方式杀人，而杀人始终是错误的，是罪过。任何人都没有资格夺走其他人的生命——除了上帝。生命是珍贵的，我们都应该尊重生命。无论如何，好死不如赖活着。而且总是有机会能治好某些特殊的疾病。

不可否认，争论的双方都有能支持自己的理由，但当我对上述理由进行了详细的考虑之后，我个人还是站在倡导者的一方，因为我坚信安乐死的合法化不仅能够给绝症晚期病人带来精神上和生理上的解脱，而且对病人的家庭和整个社会也是有益处的。实施安乐死是文明进步的一种标志。

178. 枪击闯入者

Topic:

A burglar was shot dead by the owner of the house being broken into. Do you think the owner's action was justified?

Sample Answer

Ever since this incident was reported in the newspapers, there has been much controversy about it. After weighing all the pros and cons, I find that I agree that the owner's action was justified. I support my point of view with three arguments: self-defense, the sanctity of property and the need to deter criminals.

First, everyone has the right of self-defense. When a burglar breaks into somebody else's house, he is a potential threat to the lives of the people who live there. Therefore, the house owner has the right to defend himself and his family with any weapon he can lay his hands on. If that weapon happens to be a gun, the burglar only has himself to blame.

Second, it is a principle of law that private property is inviolable. A person's home is probably the most precious thing he has, and usually contains most of the things that the house owner considers valuable. He has the right to protect the things he has worked hard to accumulate, especially against a thief.

Third, there is far too much crime nowadays, and many people think that the courts are too lenient with burglars when they are caught. By shooting the burglar dead, the house owner did a great service for society. In fact, his action sent a warning to other burglars that if they break into other people's houses, they are risking their lives.

All in all, I think that the house owner's action was a good one in three aspects. He benefited himself, by preventing the burglar harming him. He benefited the rule of law by asserting the right of a person to safeguard his own property. And, last but not least, he benefited society by deterring would-be burglars.

▶考官评分:8

题目:

窃贼被潜入房子的房主持枪打死，你认为房主的行为是否正确?

译文:

自从这件事在报纸上一报道就引起了很大的争议。经过权衡所有利弊，我觉得我坚信房主的行为是正当的。我有三个理由支持我的观点：自卫，个人财产神圣不可侵犯和遏制犯罪。

首先，每个公民都有权利自卫。当窃贼闯入别人的房子，他就潜在地威胁了住在那里的人的生命安全。因此，房主有权用他手中的任何武器保卫自己和他的家人。如果手上拿的正好是一把枪，那么窃贼只能为自己的行为负责。

第二，根据法律原则私有财产是不可侵犯的。一个人最珍贵的财产可能就是他的房屋，通常房间里还有一些房主认为价值连城的物品。他有权保护这些通过多年努力工作所积累的财产，特别是当窃贼进行偷盗时。

第三，现今窃贼频繁作案，很多人认为法院对于被抓住的窃贼过于仁慈。开枪杀死窃贼，应当说，房主为社会做了很大贡献。事实上，他的行为还对其他窃贼起到警告作用。如果他们企图闯入他人家里就要冒着生命危险。

总之，从这三个方面来看我认为房主的行为是正当的。这利于房主自己，防止窃贼伤害。同时不仅有利于捍卫法规，维护人民生命和财产的安全，而且有利于社会的安定，阻止窃贼犯罪。

179. 小城镇与大城市

Topic:

Some people prefer to live in a small town. Others prefer to live in a big city. Which place would you prefer to live in?

Sample Answer

People seldom agree with each other, even in such trivial issues as preference between big cities and small towns. It's a little bit hasty to say that it is better to live in a big city than to live in a small town, or vice versa.

Living in a big city has several benefits. First, there are more job opportunities readily available in big cities than in a small town. Furthermore, the qualities of the position are much higher as well. In addition, the pay is more decent. **Second, children are supposed to be able to receive an education with a higher quality compared with their counterparts who live in a small town.** Finally, living in a big city has a superior overall living standard to that in a small town. There are more commodities and services in city markets and there are even much more television channels in big cities.

However, living in a small town also has some advantages. People who live in a small town often have a much comfortable life style. Most of them are immune from the suffering of high work stress. **Although the average pay is much less than that of big cities, the price of daily necessities is usually more inexpensive.** Instead of suffering loneliness which is prevalent in big cities, children might grow up more healthy because of harmonious relationship among residents in small town. **They might have fewer channels in television, but they have more friends readily available to chat or entertain with.**

According to my current situation, although I am longing for the cozy atmosphere and relationship among neighbors and friends which almost only exist in small towns, I have chosen to live in one of the biggest cities in my country – Beijing, since I have found a pretty good job here, and decent pay. I think I would prefer living in a small town when I retire one day.

▶考官评分:8

题目:

有些人喜欢住在大城市而有一些人则喜欢居住在小城镇，你更喜欢哪个？

译文:

人们之间存在着不同见解，即使像喜欢大城市还是小城镇这样微不足道的问题，也存在不同见解。简单说住在大城市比住在小镇好是草率的，反之亦然。

在大城市住着有几个好处。首先，大城市比小城镇有着更多的工作机会，此外，工作的质量也比小城镇要高，并且薪水更可观。其次，在同等条件下城市里的孩子能比小城镇在的孩子得到更好的教育。最后，大城市比小城镇的生活水平更高。市场里有更多的日用品和服务，甚至还能收看更多频道的电视节目。

但是，生活在小城镇里也有一些优势。在小城镇中的人常常拥有更舒适的生活。大部分人不用承受高度的工作压力。尽管平均薪水比大城市低，但是生活必需品的价格也比大城市低多了。与大城市孩子要遭受孤独寂寞相比，小城镇里的孩子因为和谐的居民关系能更健康地成长。他们能收看的电视节目比大城市的要少，但是他们拥有更多的可以交谈和娱乐的朋友。

就我目前情况来说，虽然我更渴望小城镇中才有的惬意生活和邻居朋友间的和谐关系，我却不得不选择我们国家最大城市之一——北京，因为我已经在这里找到了一份不错的工作，薪水也不错。我想，当我退休的时候，我会选择居住在一个小城镇。

180. 城市存在的问题

Topic:

While people flood into big cities to seek jobs and a happy life, there is a tendency for people to move out. What problems do big cities have?

Sample Answer

Every year men and women crowed into cities in search of employment, a decent living, and the excitement and stimulation of urban life. According to a research, the population in Shanghai alone has increased 26% in the last three years. With the rise in urban population, many big cities have met problems of their own.

One big problem is the ever-increasing pressure produced by over-crowding. As more and more people flood into cities, city services and facilities have been strained to a breaking point. Cities have been exposed not only to the problem of traffic and housing, but to the problem of education, sanitation, employment and so on.

A second problem is the physical environment. One is the rise in the concentration of high buildings, stripping people of contact with sun and trees and grass—condemning them to a life among stone and concrete, neon lights and endless flow of traffic. Another is the growing number of cars and buses, whose exhaust sends huge quantities of carbon dioxide into the atmosphere, making the air of cities unbreathable.

But of all our problems, the most serious and pressing, the one which threatens to paralyze the city is the widespread crime. Bank robberies which were unheard of in the past now occur more frequently. Not a single day passes without the reports of somebody being mugged, being kidnapped or being murdered. Today, even walking in the street in broad daylight will make you nervous, let alone in the late night.

All these problems make big cities no longer attractive to people as years before. The tendency to move to the edge of the city, the suburban areas reflects this mentality. Unless there is some improvement, more and more people will seek to live in suburbs.

▶考官评分:8

题目:

在越来越多的人涌入大城市寻找工作和幸福生活的同时，又有一种离开城市的趋势，大城市有什么问题?

译文:

每年成群人涌入城市寻找工作，寻找一种不错的生活，一种令人兴奋和刺激的城市生活。根据调查，仅在上海的人口就在近三年内增长了26%。随着城市人口的增长，许多城市都出现了问题。

一个大的问题就是由于过度拥挤导致的不断上升的压力。随着越来越多的人涌入城市，城市服务设施已经到了紧张的临界点。城市不仅暴露出交通和住房的问题，同时也暴露出了教育，卫生，就业等方面的问题。

第二个就是自然环境的问题。一方面高楼的高度集中，剥夺了人们接触阳光、树木、草地的机会——迫使他们生活在钢筋混凝土，霓虹灯和无休止的交通堵塞之中。另一方面私家车和公交车数量的增长，排放出大量的二氧化碳到大气中，让城市的空气变得令人窒息。

但是在所有问题之中，最严重和紧迫的是威胁着城市的频繁犯罪。以前从未听到的银行抢劫，现在却频繁发生。每一天的报道都充斥着打劫，诱拐，谋杀。今天，甚至大白天走在大街上都会让你紧张，更别说在深夜了。

这些问题让大城市并不像以前那样吸引人了。人们搬向郊区的趋势就反映了这一心理。除非有什么改进，不然会有越来越多的人去寻求在市郊生活。

181. 孩子肥胖

Topic:

Nowadays, more and more children are becoming obese. Give possible reasons and suggestions.

Sample Answer

As some children in poor countries are vastly underweight as a result of poverty, others elsewhere in the world are suffering from another problem—obesity, as a consequence of improved living conditions. A recent study has shown the latter problem is becoming an epidemic, as the number of obese children in the developed world keeps rising alarmingly. I believe there are several factors responsible for this increase.

In some cases, there is a genetic link to obesity. It has been found that the children's weight is related to that of their parents. A child of obese parents is more likely to become overweight, as he may inherit some of genes that control body weight from his mother or father.

Are genetic reasons the only explanation? Other factors must also be at work and among them is a poor diet. Being afraid that their children may not get enough to eat and even suffer from poor health, some parents are too permissive, allowing them to eat too much, with as many as five or six meals a day. The increasing popularity of fast-food and sweets make matters even worse.

It is not just of a question of what young people eat, but also a matter of lifestyles. TV and the Internet have produced sedentary lifestyle. Children who watch TV passively or who use computers for hours every day simply do not get enough physical exercises. Besides, a growing number of preteenagers have come to rely on public transport or lifts from their parents, rather than walking or using bicycles. Lack of activity gradually contributes to overweight.

Obesity may have knock-on effects, especially in the form of such diseases as diabetes and heart problems in children's later lives. Solutions to the problem may vary according to root causes. **Those whose obesity is gene-related should consult doctors.** For others, a better lifestyle, more exercise and a proper diet consisting of more vegetables and fruit and fewer fatty foods may assist.

▶考官评分:8

题目:

现在越来越多的孩子发胖，试给出可能的原因并且提出建议。

译文:

如今，在很多贫穷的国家，许多孩子太瘦；而相反在一些富裕的国家，一些孩子又过胖——这是生活水平提高的结果。最近的一项研究调查表明，肥胖儿的问题非常严重。发达国家肥胖儿数量的持续增长已经为人们敲响了警钟。我认为这种增长的原因有以下几点：

有时候遗传因素会导致肥胖。研究表明，儿童的体重和父母有关。如果父母胖的话，孩子也容易胖，因为他们从父母那里遗传了一些基因，而这些基因会影响孩子的体重。

遗传是造成肥胖儿的惟一原因吗？不，还有其他原因，其中之一就是饮食问题。家长总是怕孩子们吃不饱，影响健康。还有的家长让孩子们吃得太多，甚至一天吃5~6顿饭。快餐和甜食的普及使这种问题更加严重。

不光是孩子们吃的食物引起发胖，生活习惯也会引起发胖。看电视和上网会使人养成久坐的生活习惯。爱看电视和爱上网的孩子往往得不到足够的锻炼。此外，越来越多的不到十来岁的孩子们也学着他们的父母，越来越依赖于公共设施和电梯，而不愿意步行或者骑自行车。缺少运动也会逐渐使他们发胖。

肥胖的后果非常可怕，将来容易诱发糖尿病和心脏病。解决这个问题需要从根本上做起。由于遗传造成的肥胖儿需要去看医生。而由于其他原因造成的肥胖儿则需要改变生活方式，多做锻炼，注意饮食，多吃蔬菜和水果，少吃高脂肪的食物。

182. 幸福的定义

Topic:

It is hard for people to agree on the definition of happiness. Why? How do people achieve happiness?

Sample Answer

The responses of people around the world will paint a varied picture, as a result of difference in their living conditions, their sex, as well as different cultural and religious experiences. Ask a beggar what his happiness is, and he may reply "A square meal". However, those who have to attend banquets every day for business may seek more for their happiness. It is very hard to give a definition of happiness that holds true for everyone. Although the definition varies from people to people, the routes to happiness are similar for most of us. Whoever you are, follow the strategies below and you may find happiness within a week.

Take care of your health. A good physical condition is the best thing God can give us. Poor health will spoil everything. To achieve good health, you should get enough sleep, take time for fun, exercise, and relax and be free from work stress from time to time.

You should count your blessings and find the good in each situation. Focus on the good things in your life and start a gratitude journal if possible. To do this, make a point each day of writing down five things for which you're grateful. You'll be amazed at how happy you are.

Give something nice for someone else. Reaching out to other people increases our sense of self-worth, and also brightens someone else's day. Moreover, such actions will be rewarded with others' respect and friendliness. You make someone happy, and at the same time, are made happy.

You need to find balance. All too often we involve ourselves disproportionately with the same type of activities throughout a week. Variety will help us find a more balanced outlook on life. If you work alone all day, spend your evening hours on a group activity. If meetings occupy your day, explore your creative side in an activity of solitude such as enjoying light music. The more interests you have, the more colourful your life becomes, and the more balanced it is.

If you are now feeling unhappy and seeking help to get out of it, why not try these steps to make your world a better and happier place? You'll win emotionally and professionally.

▶考官评分:8

题目:

对“幸福”的定义人们很难达成一致。你认为这是什么原因造成的？人们如何寻找幸福？

译文:

世界各地的人们对这个问题的回答必将构成一幅多姿多彩的画面。这是由于人们的生活环境不同，性别有差异，并受不同的文化和宗教信仰的影响。问一个乞丐“幸福是什么”，他可能回答“一顿丰盛的晚餐”。然而，对于那些为了生意每天都不得不参加宴席的人来说，幸福的内容就可能更多。每一个人的想法都是正确的，因此很难对幸福下定义。虽然幸福的定义有很多，但通向幸福的途径对大多数人来说却是相似的。不管你是谁，只要采取以下的策略，你就可以在一周之内找到幸福。

注意身体的健康。一个好的身体是上帝所能赐予我们的最大财富。如果身体不好，一切事情将无从谈起。要想有好身体，人们应该保证充足的睡眠、一定时间的娱乐、锻炼和放松，不断地从工作压力中解脱出来。

你应该积累你的福气，发现在每个环境中的好的事物。注意你生活中的好的事物，从而开始你心存感激的生命之旅。去做这些，每天记下让你高兴的五件事，你就会惊讶地发现你是如此幸福。

要学会给予，对别人施以援手会增强我们的自我价值意识，也会给别人的生活带来光明。此外，通过这一行动也会得到尊重，友谊等奖励，你使别人幸福的同时也使自己幸福。

你需要求得平衡——我们在每个星期里总是过于忙于某件工作。丰富多彩的生活使我们对生活前景找到更好的平衡点。如果你整天独自工作，那么你应该在晚上参加一些集体活动。如果你开了一整天的会，那么独处（如听听轻音乐）能够激发你的创造力。你拥有的兴趣越多，你的生活就会变得越丰富多彩，你获得的平衡也就越多。

如果你感到不快乐，希望能够解脱，为什么不采用这些方法使你的世界变得更加美好、幸福呢？你会感到身心愉快。

183. 幸福与经济的关系

Topic:

Some people believe that personal happiness is directly related to economic success. Others believe there are other factors. What do you think?

Sample Answer

The pursuit of happiness has long been the dream of generations of human beings. They have always been puzzled by the essence of happiness. What is happiness? Is it closely related to one's economic success? Will one's financial success lead to happiness directly? Personally, I don't agree that one's economic success is the only prerequisite of one's happiness in life.

One's materialistic happiness is dependant on one's economic success, though not completely. Without a strong and steady economic background, one could never imagine an easy and simple life, let alone an affluent and luxurious one. If you aren't able to afford a house, a car, or even a book, anybody would be horrified at the mere mention of this kind of life. Definitely, some people will feel happy right away if their basic demands for life are satisfied. However, we have to admit that these people still need to be successful materialistically to some degree.

On the other hand, one's success in economy may not necessarily lead to one's spiritual happiness. As we all know, money doesn't get you everything and some even say that money is the root of all evils. One's financial success may be built on the sacrifice of time, health and love, which are the three most essential elements of spiritual happiness. All of us are not new to this picture: a successful businessman tasting loneliness alone with a broken heart.

In my point of view, one's economic success is only one of the key factors of happiness, but never the only one. To be happy, one needs to be both spiritually and materially satisfied though each of us may have a totally different picture of happiness.

▶考官评分:8

题目:

有些人认为一个人的幸福与他经济上的成就是直接相关的，而另外一些人则不这么认为，你怎么看待这个问题?

译文:

对幸福的追求一直都是人类世世代代的梦想，尽管人类一直困惑于幸福的真谛。幸福是什么?幸福和经济的成功有密切联系吗?个人经济上的成功能够直接带来幸福吗?就个人而言，我不认为经济上的成功是人类幸福的惟一前提。

一方面，一个人的物质幸福依赖于经济上的成功，尽管不是完全依赖。没有稳定的经济后盾，很难想象如何过上轻松简单的生活，更不用说富裕奢侈的生活了。如果买不起房子、车，甚至是一本书，任何人提到这种生活都会害怕。当然，有一些人只要基本的生活需求得到满足就可以立刻感到很幸福。但是我们仍然必须承认，这些人也需要某种意义上的经济成功。

另一方面，一个人的成功不见得能带来精神层面的幸福。众所周知，金钱不能带来一切，甚至有人说金钱是万恶之源。经济上的成功可能就是建立在牺牲时间、健康和爱情的基础之上，而这三件事情是个人精神层面幸福的基本要素。我们对于这个画面并不陌生：一位职场成功的男士带着一颗破碎的心独自品味孤独。

我认为，经济上的成功只是幸福的一个重要因素，但绝对不是惟一因素。尽管我们每一个人对于幸福有完全不同的理解，要幸福就要精神上和物质上都能得到满足。

184. 永不说谎

Topic:

Should people always tell the truth? Give your opinion and reasons to support it.

Sample Answer

Honesty has always been considered to be a worthy character trait in whatever culture. Indeed, it is often thought of as the most important human value. Generally speaking, it is therefore not a good idea to tell lies. However, there may be some circumstances when telling lies might be necessary and could even be justified.

Providing one makes sure the lie is for the benefits of others, not one's own, it can perhaps be justified. For example, doctors may lie to benefit their patients when they wish to speed recovery or to conceal the approach of death. The requirement of honesty also seems dwarfed when there is a greater need to shelter aging parents from heart-attack in the case of the brutal news that their son has died accidentally. To put his wife at ease and to guarantee a promise of top secrecy, a husband may claim that a life-threatening assignment is just a business trip. All these are benevolent deceptions and are understandable.

When you make deceptions with good intention, there is one more thing you have to be sure about—that you do it well. Lying is a great art, and you need to be very careful about it, until practice and life experience give you the confidence, elegance and precision to do it gracefully and beneficially. If you don't, you are almost certainly going to get caught. Once caught, you can never again be, in the eyes of the good and the pure, what you were before. Many a young person has ruined his reputation permanently through a single clumsy and ill-told lie, the result of carelessness born of incomplete training.

Integrity is desirable, but the opinion that we ought not to lie at all, of course, is putting it rather more strongly than necessary. I maintain that we can practice this art, if it is in others' interest, and if you know how to use it well. Otherwise, you had better be honest rather than risking your integrity and credibility by playing tricks. The more important thing is not to think about telling lies, or slide into those mechanical and untruthful habits of thought.

▶考官评分:8

题目:

人们是否应该一直讲真话？试述你的观点并给出理由。

译文:

在任何一种文化中，诚实都是一种美德。实际上，它被认为是最重要的一种品质。总的说来，说谎并不好。说谎只有在不得不说的时候才说，而且应该有正当的理由。

如果一个人确认谎言对别人有益而不是对自己有益，这就是正当的。例如，医生可能对自己的病人说谎，这是为了病人好。因为医生希望能够加速病人的恢复或者挽救病人的生命。当患有心脏病的老人的儿子意外丧生时，为了病人的需要就不得不隐瞒残酷的真相。为了使妻子放心，并维护最高机密，丈夫不得不把执行有生命危险的任务说成是一次商务外出。这些都是善意的谎言，而且可以理解。

如果是善意的谎言，你需要确信你能够做得很好。说谎是一门艺术，你需要非常小心。只有在你的实践经验和生活阅历都足够的情况下你才能够很好地，准确无误地这样做。如果不是，你会自食其果。如果谎言被揭穿，你在光天化日之下就不能再像以前那样生活了。很多年轻人都是因为一句简单的并不高明的谎言彻底毁了自己的名声，这是经验不够的结果。

正直是理想化的，但是认为“绝对不能说谎”这种观点是走极端了。如果对他人有利，而你也知道如何运用好，那么我们可以采用善意的谎言。否则你还是保持正直，不要玩火。更重要的是不要思考谎言，也不要陷入那些机械的虚伪的思考习惯中。

185. 永不放弃

Topic:

The expression "Never, never give up" means to keep trying and never stop working for your goals. Do you agree or disagree with the statement?

Sample Answer

Near the end of the Second World War, Churchill delivered his famous and shortest speech: "Never, Never Give Up." People in Britain and other countries, were tremendously encouraged, and finally went through the hardest period in human history.

The words represent a strong and positive attitude toward life. Some people are ready to quit when they cannot endure the difficulties, or they cannot find a way to finish the task. Such people usually become upset and lose their self-confidence, although they virtually can do everything well. Most people fail to acquire a second language because they have given up. It might be the easiest task among academic curriculums, because one can be successful only by repetition.

Never give up. Such strong belief often gives us a second chance. The fact that we failed somewhere does not mean to fail everywhere. Many successful people did fail before. Yu Minhong, the founder of New Oriental School, was able to study in Peking University only after three attempts to pass the Entrance Examination of Colleges and Universities. After graduation, almost all his classmates went abroad, while he was refused by officials in visa, yet he never gave up, which made his later success inevitable.

Psychology teaches us that we do get what we want. First of all, we must make sure that our goals are achievable, and our methods are practical. A superficial claim like"I wanna be a millionaire!" or"inventing a perpetual motion machine"are absolutely meaningless. But it is realistic or meaningful to acquire a second language by careful planning, and relevant persistence. Numerous examples tell us that even if the methods are problematic, many still finally attain great achievements. Therefore, "Never, never give up"is really something that we should always bear in mind.

▶考官评分:8

题目:

那句永不放弃的谚语的意思是你要永远努力、永远都不要放弃自己的目标，你是否同意这种观点？

译文:

二战结束前夕，丘吉尔发表了他著名而且最短暂的演讲：“绝不，永不放弃。”英国人民以及世界其他国家的人都受到了巨大的鼓舞，并且最终度过了人类历史上最艰难的时期。

这句话表现出人们有一种强大的力量和积极的态度去对待生命。一些人在不能忍受困难的时候，或是不能找到一种方式去完成任务的时候，他们想要放弃了。这些人通常会变得十分沮丧，并且失去信心，尽管他们实际上能够把每件事都做好。大多数人没能掌握第二语言是因为他们放弃了。学习语言可能是文化课当中最简单的任务，因为它能只通过重复就能成功。

永不放弃。这种强烈的信仰通常给我们第二次机会。事实上，我们在某方面失败了并不等于我们在所有方面都会失败。很多成功人士也曾失败过。俞敏洪，新东方学校的创始人，在连续三年尝试高考后终于能在北京大学就读。毕业之后，他的大部分同学都出国了。但是他一次又一次的被签证官拒绝，然而他没有放弃，这就使他日后成功成为必然。

心理学告诉我们，我们能做到我们想做的。首先，我们必须确定我们的目标是可以达到的，我们的方法是可以实践的。一个肤浅的要求像是“我想成为一个百万富翁！”或是“发明一个永动机”是完全没有任何意义的。但是通过仔细的计划和相应的努力，学习第二语言是现实的而且有意义的。许多例子告诉我们，即使这些方法是有疑问的，但仍旧有许多人能够最终获得成功。因此“绝不，永不放弃”是我们真正应该记在脑海中的话。

186. 年轻人与年老人

Topic:

There is nothing that young people can teach older people. Do you agree or disagree?

Sample Answer

The older generation today always complains that the youth are unmotivated and directionless, that they lack focus and the future is going down because of their behavior. Nonetheless, youth are the product of their upbringing and the representation of their time. Thus what they are and what they know will certainly be different from those of the older generation. Therefore, to say that the youngsters are useless is wrong, as they can also contribute in their own way, and teach the older generation a lesson or two.

As we all know, today's technology moves very fast. With our daily responsibilities, it is almost impossible for us to keep up with every new gadget that comes out. With young people, it is different, new things that interest them. Furthermore, being young, they absorb new knowledge like a sponge. Thus, they can help us to get in tune with new technologies. Young kids, for example, can probably teach their grandparents to use the computers, which in turn, will also be good for their relationships.

In addition to this, by looking at the young, we can learn about the society better. As I've mentioned earlier, youngsters represent their time, hence, by understanding them, we can understand the needs of the society, as this group of age is the most outspoken. A good example would be the hippie movement in the 60s. The movement displayed their dissatisfaction with the system, and their need for more freedom of expression.

As someone once said, "Life is a learning experience". From that, we can deduce that there is no full stop to the process of learning. Instead of being critical and cynical, maybe we can try to understand the youth better by learning from each other. After all, they are the future.

▶考官评分:8

题目:

年轻人不能教会老年人做任何事。你是否同意这种看法?

译文:

今天，老一辈总是抱怨年轻人没有动力没有方向，抱怨他们缺少专注精神，因为他们的所作所为会使未来越来越糟。但是，年轻人是他们培养的结果，也是他们时代的代表。因此他们是什么，他们懂得什么当然会与老一辈不同。因此，说年轻人没有用是不对的，他们也可以以他们自己的方式做出贡献，给老一辈上一课。

我们都知道，现今科技发展得特别快。以我们日常的职责，想把每个新出现的小玩意搞明白是不可能的。对年轻人来讲就不一样了，新东西使他们感兴趣。而且作为年轻人，他们像海绵一样汲取知识。因而，他们能帮助我们跟上新科技的步伐。比如说，小孩子能够教他们的爷爷奶奶使用计算机，反过来这对他们的关系也有好处。

除此之外，通过对年轻人的观察，我们能更好地了解社会。就像我前面提到的年轻人代表了他们的时代，他们这个年龄段的人是说话最直率的，因此通过了解他们，我们就能够了解社会的需要。六十年代的嬉皮士运动就是一个很好的例子。这一运动反映了他们对社会系统的不满，和他们更想表达自由的要求。

就像有人曾经说过的“生活就是学习的过程”。从这句话我们可以知道，学习的过程没有止境。与其批评和讽刺，也许我们还不如试着通过相互学习去更好地了解年轻人。毕竟未来是他们的。

187. 鼓励大龄高管退休

Topic:

Some people think that the company should encourage the employees who are in high positions and over 55 years old to retire, in order to give opportunities to new generation. Do you agree or disagree?

Sample Answer

Some people are of the opinion that the employees in the high executive positions should be encouraged to retire when they are over 55 years old. They claim that, by doing this, young people will be given more opportunities. Others oppose this kind of mandatory retirement. Both sides seem to have their reasons.

Young people are superior to the old in many ways. First, most young people have received formal education in university, where they acquire abundant knowledge and skills. Compared with young people, old people's knowledge is out-dated, which does not fit in the development of the current society. Second, young people are more open-minded than old people who have a tendency of conservation. Young people can adapt themselves to the changeable world more easily. Finally, the young are energetic and vigorous. Old people react more slowly than young people who can always make quick judges and prompt decisions.

Some people who examine this issue from another angle hold that although young people have some predominance they still cannot compete with the old people. First, young people lack adequate experience and skills to deal with sophisticated problems. Some young people, who are very radical when faced with trouble, have a lot of things to learn from old people and most high positions require rich experience and academic achievements. Second, age is not always a true indicator of one's capacities and thanks to the improvement in medical science, people enjoy a much longer life expectancy, so we should redefine the term "old age". Finally, it would be more economical for the company to retain the old hands than to spend more time and money training new ones.

In my opinion, the company should not force the old people to retire to give way to the young. The practice is unfair to the old, hinders the social development and does harm to the young who gain the high positions easily.

▶考官评分:7分

题目:

公司应当鼓励那些高管职员在55岁退休，从而为年轻人留下更多的机会。你是否同意这种观点?

译文:

一些人认为应当鼓励高管在55岁的时候退休。他们声称，这样做将使年轻人有更多的机会。其他一些人则反对这种强制性的退休。双方看起来都有各自的理由。

年轻人在某些方面比年长的人更有优势。首先，大多数年轻人在大学接受过正式的教育。在那里他们获取丰富的知识和技能。相比较年轻人而言，年长的人的知识显得过时了，使其不能适应现代社会的发展。其次，年轻人比那些具有保守意识的年长的人思想更加开放。年轻人可以让自己更轻松地在多变的世界中生存。最后，年轻人具有充沛的精力和活力。年长的人则比那些可以经常做出快速判断和及时决定的年轻人反应慢。

一些人则从另一个角度看待这个问题，他们认为虽然年轻人占主要优势，但他们仍然不能和年长的人竞争。首先，年轻人缺少足够的经验和处理复杂问题的技能。一些年轻人，当他们面对一些麻烦时过于激进，他们有很多东西需要向年长的人学习，许多高层职位需要丰富的经验和学术成就。其次，年龄并不总是一个人能力的真实反映。感谢医药科学的进步，人们可以有更长的寿命，所以我们应该重新定义“年老”这个概念。最后，对于公司而言，雇用老手比花更多的钱和时间来培训新手更加经济实惠。

在我看来，公司不应该强制让老员工退休以便给年轻人让位。这种行为对年长的人不公平，阻碍了社会发展并且对那些可以轻松得到高职位的年轻人不利。

188. 老龄化

Topic:

In many countries, the proportion of older people is steadily increasing. Does this trend have more positive or negative effects on the society?

Sample Answer

The world is getting older. You come across old people everywhere-in restaurants, on airplanes, in hospitals and even in Disneyland! Things were quite different 20 years ago, when young people dominated the world. Is this change in demography good or bad for society? I would say it has more negative effects than positive ones.

Doubtlessly, older people are much experienced in life, so to society, and particularly to the younger generation, they are a valuable treasure. This is because older people can give us constructive suggestions and can assist us in doing many different things, preventing us from making mistakes. So, seen from this perspective, an increasing proportion of older people in the population are not necessarily something bad.

However, I would not be accurate to say that having an older population always benefits us. It also has negative effects on the society. First of all, the aging population is retiring from the working world. That means it does not offer society the labor it needs for its sustained economic growth. Japan has actually been troubled by its aging laborers who are destined to be the pure wealth consumers. Japanese people are even encouraged by their government to give birth to more babies, not for themselves, but for the nation!

Secondly, rapid social development calls for more people with creative and innovative minds and generally speaking, these refer to young people. Electric bulbs and computers would never have come about without groups of young people who were not happy with the status quo and were bold enough to challenge established traditions. It is said more than 80% of the great inventions and literary works are created by people under 40 years old.

In a word, while older people enlighten us with their rich experience, they use up more than what they produce. At the same time, they are more likely to follow rules docilely. Therefore, the demerits of an aged population far outweigh its merits.

▶考官评分:8

题目:

很多国家老年人的比例正在增加，这种趋势对社会的影响是正面的还是负面的?

译文:

世界性的老龄化日益严重，老年人随处可见：在饭店里、在飞机上、在医院里，甚至在迪斯尼乐园里！20年前情形还大为不同，那时候年轻人是世界的主流。这一人口比例的变化对社会来讲究竟是好事呢，还是坏事呢？我认为此状况弊大于利。

毋庸置疑，老年人生活阅历丰富，对社会，特别是对年轻人来讲，这是一笔宝贵的财富。老一辈可以为我们提供富有建设性的意见，可以协助我们做很多事情，可以防止我们犯错误。所以，从这个角度讲，老龄人口比重的增加不见得是件坏事。

但是，如果说老年人给我们带来的都是积极的影响也是不对的。他们的负面影响同样存在。首先，老年人退休后不再工作。这就意味着他们不再能够提供社会经济持续发展所需要的劳动力。实际上，日本就受到日益老龄化的劳动力影响，因为老年人注定会成为纯粹的财富消费者。日本人甚至得到政府的鼓励多生孩子，这样做不是为了他们自己，而是为了他们的国家！

第二，社会要取得快速发展，需要更多的创新人才。从一般意义上讲，就是需要年轻人。如果没有大批不满现状的年轻人勇于挑战传统，就不会有今天的电灯和计算机。据说，80%的伟大发明和文学作品是由40岁以下的人所创造的。

概括来讲，年长的一代给予我们丰富的经验，但却是财富的主要消费者。与此同时，他们更多时候倾向于循规蹈矩而缺乏创新。因此，人口老龄化的弊端远大于其优势。

189. 竞争和合作的重要性

Topic:

Some people say that the best preparation for life is learning to be cooperative. Others take the opposite view and say that learning to be competitive is the best preparation. Tell which one you agree with and explain why.

Sample Answer

Learning to be competitive is clearly the best preparation for life. No one can be trusted. This becomes very clear as one has more experience in the world. Everyone is out to make their own lives better and must do everything they can to succeed. Let me explain.

In the first place everyone knows that man is by nature a competitive, aggressive, and selfish animal. Even Darwin, in "The Origin of the Species", makes it very clear that the weak will die, and only the strong will survive. Since this is our fate; the only intelligent thing to do is to be strong, and be a winner.

Also, in the business world, everyone knows that the most important order of the day is to beat your competitors. This can only be done by competing by any and all means necessary to win. No one wants to go out of business, so you must compete. Also, you must be better than the other employees you are working with, because in this age of downsizing, you do not want to be fired.

Further, in the sports world, the strongest will come out as winners. They become our heroes and they are glorified in every way. In fact, the only way our world rewards people is to give trophies to the winners, not to the losers. Everyone wants glory in life and learning to be competitive is the only path to glory.

Therefore, the only way to survive in this world is to be competitive. To learn to cooperate is a ridiculous way to live one's life. In fact, I know that when I wish to beat someone who is weaker willed than I, I will use their foolish cooperative actions against them in the end.

题目：

有些人认为学会合作是对生活的最好准备，而有些人持反对意见认为竞争才是对生活最好的准备。你同意哪种观点并加以解释。

译文：

学会竞争显然是对生活最好的准备。没有人值得信任。一个人在这个世界上经历得越多对此就会认识得越清。每个人都为活得更好而生，为了成功也一定什么都做得出来。让我来解释一下。

首先，每个人都知道人天生就是一种好强，好斗又自私的动物。连达尔文都在他的《物种起源》里明确表示弱肉强食。因为这是我们的命运，所以最明智的做法就是变得强大，才能成为赢家。

其次，在商界，每个人都知道一天中最重要的日程就是打败竞争对手。这只有用尽一切必要手段去竞争才能做得到。没人想要丢掉饭碗，所以你就必须要去竞争。而且，你还必须做得比你的同事好才行，因为在这样一个裁员的时代，你一定不想被炒鱿鱼。

再次，在体育界，最强的会成为最后的冠军。他们成为我们的英雄并每天被荣耀包围着。实际上，我们的世界奖赏世人的惟一方法就是给胜者而不是失败者战利品。每个人都想在生活中获得荣耀，而学会竞争是通向荣耀的惟一途径。

因此，在这世界生存下去的惟一办法就是学会竞争。学会合作的生活实在是可笑的。实际上，我知道当我想要打败意志没有我坚定的人的时候，我最后会利用他们愚蠢的合作行为打败他们。

190. 竞争与合作

Topic:

Some people think people should learn to compete, but others think that people should be taught to cooperate. What is your opinion?

Sample Answer

Cooperation and competition are both essential to people. They are equally necessary for a person to achieve success in his or her future life. But if I must choose one, I would say that competition is as important as, if not important than, cooperation.

Competition helps enhance individual abilities. Competition makes people creative. Competition is a product of the development of society and it gives people a sense of the pursuit of excellence. This is people' s inborn nature. Without competition, people would remain idle and have no ambition. Many people are fond of competition because it enables them to bring their knowledge or skills into full play. If you want to remain competent in the fierce competition, you have to spend much time reading to make yourself qualified for your present job.

Competition is the guarantee of enterprises' existence. They have to produce better things. Otherwise, they will have no customers. So in fact they produce better things for their own benefit. At the same time, people's various requirements can be satisfied and our society can develop as well.

Society, through competition, has developed a lot. Fair competition promotes progress and renews the looks of our society. Without competition, people would create nothing. They would feel satisfied with their present conditions. With no competition, therefore, there would be no progress.

Cooperation is also indispensable for a better life of the people. Cooperation helps bring individual abilities into full play, make up for each other's inadequacy and enhance the overall quality of the parties concerned. But cooperation without competition may bring about a peaceful life to all but destroy individual's initiative and eventually affect social development.

▶考官评分:7

题目:

有些人认为人们应该学会竞争，另外一些人认为人们应当学会合作。你有什么看法?

译文:

合作和竞争对人们都很重要，它们对一个人在将来的生活中是否成功同等重要。但是如果我必须选择一个的话，我认为竞争如果不比合作重要的话，至少和合作一样重要。

竞争帮助提高个人的能力。竞争使得人们有创造力。竞争是社会发展的产物，并且它给人们一种追求卓越的意识。这是人与生俱来的天性。没有竞争，人们将会仍然懒散，没有雄心壮志。很多人喜欢竞争因为它使得他们能够完全展示自己的知识和技能。如果你想在激烈的竞争中一直获胜，你就不得不花费大量的时间来学习，以使你胜任当前的工作。

竞争是企业存在的保证。他们不得不生产更好的商品。否则，他们就不会有顾客。所以事实上他们为了自己的利益而生产了更好的产品。与此同时，人们的各种需求也得到了满足，我们的社会也得到了很好的发展。

社会通过竞争，有了很大的发展。合理的竞争推动了进步，改变了我们社会的面貌。如果没有竞争，人们什么也创造不了。他们将会满足于当前的条件。因此，没有竞争就没有进步。

合作是人们过更好的生活所不可缺少的，合作使个人的能力得到全面展示，可以相互弥补不足，以增加该团队整体的实力。但是，没有竞争的合作会带给所有人安静的生活，但是会毁灭个人的创造性，甚至最终影响社会的发展。

191. 娱乐与竞争

Topic:

Should children pursue sport for recreation or as a form of competition? Give your opinion and reasons to support your argument.

Sample Answer

Every parent wants their child to have a happy childhood and to grow up as a well-balanced person. To this end, we adults should always present children with a view of a world which is true, good and beautiful. It is therefore easy to answer the question of whether sport for children should be regarded as recreation or as competition. Recreation is clearly the key to future happiness.

When children take part in sport games just for fun, they will gain pleasure from them and cultivate good relationships with others and a sense of cooperation. It also allows children to view each other as collaborators, especially when they get in trouble.

On the other hand, competition is absolutely destructive for children and the psychological damage cannot be over-estimated. Competitive games by definition must produce a loser and a winner. Defeat will undermine self-esteem and cause self-doubt. For winners, it does not build character: winning produces feelings of pride which are short-lived. The more the young compete, the more they need to compete to feel good about themselves. Once they fail to beat others, they will feel very frustrated.

Competitive encounters have an equally toxic effect on children's relationships among children. In a competition, each child inevitably comes to regard others as rivals or as obstacles to his or her own success. It leads children to envy winners and to dismiss losers. Children become suspicious of just about everyone, as nobody would trust a person who may gain from his failure.

The problem is competition itself. If we would like our children to enjoy their childhood and make a friendly world for them, a playing field should not be turned into a battlefield.

▶考官评分:8

题目:

孩子们应当把体育运动作为娱乐还是作为一种竞争?说出你的观点和理由并进行陈述。

译文:

所有的家长都希望自己的孩子有一个快乐的童年,然后成长为一个全面的人才。为此,家长应该给孩子呈现出一个真实的、美好的、靓丽的世界。因此对于体育究竟是消遣还是竞争这类问题就很容易回答了。显而易见,消遣是将来幸福的关键。

如果孩子们参与体育运动是为了娱乐,他们会从中获得快乐并学会和他人之间建立良好的合作关系。这也使得孩子们视他人为合作者。这一点在他们遇到问题的时候就显得更加重要。

另一方面,竞争对于孩子们来说是破坏性的而且会造成难以弥补的心理上的创伤。按照定义来说,竞争性的游戏一定会产生一个胜利者和一个失败者。失败会破坏自尊,而产生自我疑惑。而胜利对于性格培养也没有好处。胜利使人骄傲,而这种骄傲不会持久。年轻人参与竞争越多,为了保持良好的感觉,他们就越希望在竞争中获胜,所需要的就越多。一旦他们不能够战胜其他人,他们就会感到沮丧。

竞争性的比赛对于孩子之间的关系也是有害的。在竞争过程中,每个人都不可避免地视其他人为竞争者或者是成功路上的绊脚石。这使得孩子们嫉妒胜利者,而远离失败者,孩子们会变得多疑,因为没有人相信自己会从失败中有所收获。

这个问题是竞争本身造成的。如果我们希望孩子能够享受童年并给他们创造一个美好的世界，就不要把玩耍的领域变成战场。

192. 仔细规划与自由安排

Topic:

Some people prefer to plan activities for their free time very carefully. Others choose not to make any plans at all for their free time. Compare the benefits for planning free-time activities with the benefits of not making plans. Which do you prefer-planning or not planning for your leisure time?

Sample Answer

In this busy society, our free time is very valuable to us. It is important that we take some time to relax and renew our energy in order to face the challenges ahead of us. Different people like to spend their leisure time in different ways. Some like to plan their activities so that they can make the most of the time available while others prefer not to plan anything. Both schools of thought have their advantages.

When people carefully plan their leisure time, they will not waste any time on decision making or last-minute preparations. This saves them time and, therefore, makes them feel that they have more free time to enjoy. Planning ahead also allows people to take advantages of the opportunity to participate in certain restricted activities. For example, by planning ahead, they can buy tickets for a concert or play that may later be sold out. Finally, being better prepared for an activity not only saves time but can make the outing more fun and more meaningful. It is not much fun to make a spontaneous trip to the beach only to find you have left your swimsuit at home.

However, unplanned leisure time also has its advantages. With no commitment to take part in a certain activity or meet a friend at a certain hour, the non-planner can take advantage of last minute changes and opportunities. Furthermore, he will not be disappointed about his plans, because he has made none. On the other hand, if someone has looked forward to a baseball game all week, it is very disappointing if it is cancelled due to rain. Last but not least, unplanned leisure time can be more relaxing. During the workweek, we must all be punctual and face deadlines. Some people prefer to make their free time as different from that as possible.

Although both planned and unplanned leisure time have their benefits, I still prefer to plan my free time activities. My free time is limited, and so I want to make the best use of it. By planning ahead, I can take part in the activities that I want and spend time with the people I want to see. And in case my plans should be changed by unforeseen circumstances, I can always go to Plan B.

▶考官评分:7分

题目:

一些人喜欢为空闲时间制定详细的计划，另外一些人选择不做任何安排。比较这两种行为的好处，并且说明你更喜欢哪种做法。

译文:

在这个忙碌的社会中，空闲时间对我们而言是非常珍贵的。找个时间放松一下并且恢复精力以面对接踵而来的挑战是很重要的。每个人喜欢的休闲方式各不相同。有些人喜欢做什么事情有计划性以充分利用休闲时间，而有些人却宁愿不做任何计划。这两种想法都各有优点。

当人们仔细规划休闲时间后，就不会浪费时间做决定，或是最后才仓促地准备。这样做能节省时间，因此会让他们觉得可以享有更多的空闲时间。提前计划也让人们可以利用机会去参加某些受限制的活动。例如，假如事先有规划，就可买到晚一点就买不到的音乐会或戏剧演出的门票。最后，为活动做好准备不仅可以节省时间，还能让旅游更有乐趣，更有意义。当你一时兴起去海边玩时，而到达之后才发现泳衣放在家里，可能就太扫兴了。

然而，对休闲时间不做任何计划也有好处。因为不用参加特定的活动，也没有和朋友相约在某个时间见面，所以不做计划的人就能在最后一刻改变主意并利用机会。而且，如果计划落空了，他也不会失望，因为他根本没有计划。另一方面，假使有人整个礼拜都在期待能去看棒球比赛，若球赛因雨取消，这实在是一件非常令人失望的事。最后一项要点是，不做计划的休闲时间能使人更加放松。在工作日，我们必须都很准时，且要面临最后期限的压力。有些人希望空闲时间能尽可能和工作时有所不同。

虽然计划或不计划休闲时间都各有好处，但我还是比较喜欢计划我的休闲活动。我的空闲时间有限，因此要尽量善加利用。事先做好计划，我就能参加想要参加的活动，见我想要见的人。而且假如计划因非预期的情况而有所改变时，我还可以采用另一个替代方案。

193. 第一印象

Topic:

Some people trust their first impressions about a person's character because they believe these judgments are generally correct. Other people do not judge a person's character quickly because they believe first impressions are often wrong. Compare these two attitudes. Which attitude do you agree with?

Sample Answer

When we first meet someone, we know nothing about his or her character. However, we often make some assumptions based on the impression that the person makes. Can these first impressions be trusted? Some people believe that our initial judgment of a person is usually correct, while others think it is often wrong. There are arguments to support both positions.

People who trust their first impressions believe that a person's appearance can be a good indication of not only his character, but also how he views himself and the people around him. It is true that we often send messages about our feelings without being aware of it. Body language is a good example of this. A person's posture, gestures and facial expression can tell us a lot about what he is thinking and feeling. Furthermore, dress and grooming can indicate whether someone cares enough about us to make a good impression.

On the other hand, first impressions can sometimes be misleading. People may be nervous around others they don't know well or in an unfamiliar situation. This may cause them to act in ways that do not reflect their true character. Likewise, some people may give a false impression because they are trying too hard to impress. They may be consciously or unconsciously fooling the other person. In addition, a new acquaintance might simply be in a bad mood or not at his best for other reasons.

Considering the arguments above, I believe that it is better not to judge a person's character too quickly. First impressions are, at best, an indication of how a person is feeling at the moment, and may not indicate his or her true character. However, due to the importance that many people do place on first impressions, we should be aware of the impression that we make on others. To sum up, I think we should not judge people according to first impressions, but we should take care to make a good impression ourselves.

▶考官评分:8分

题目:

一些人相信自己对别人的第一印象，因为他们认为这种判断一般都是正确 的。另外一些人不会很快地对别人进行判断，因为他们认为第一印象一般都是错误的。比较这两种观点并说出自己的看法。

译文:

当我们初识某人时，我们对对方的情况一无所知。然而，我们却经常根据对方给我们留的印象做出一些假设。这些第一印象可靠吗？有人认为，对人最初的判断通常是正确的，而有人却认为，最初的判断通常是错的。这两种立场都有其支持的论点。

相信第一印象的人认为，一个人的外貌可以充分显示其个性，以及他对自己和周围人的看法。的确，我们经常不自觉地透露自己的感觉，肢体语言就是最好的例子。人的姿势、手势及脸部表情可以显示出很多信息，告诉别人他正在想什么，有什么感觉。此外，穿着打扮能说明这个人是否在乎我们，想不想给我们留下好的印象。

另一方面，第一印象有时会让人误解。有人可能会因为跟周围的人不熟或处于不熟悉的环境而心生紧张，这样可能会使他们的表现不符合真实的个性。同样地，有些人可能因为过度想给别人留下深刻的印象而造成不实的印象。他们可能在自觉或不自觉的情况下欺骗对方。此外，初识者可能只是心情不好，或基于某种原因而未能表现出最佳状态。

基于上述论点，我认为最好不要太快评判别人的个性。第一印象充其量只能告诉我们当时某人的感受如何，无法显示其真实的个性。可是，因为很多人非常重视第一印象，所以我们应该注意自己给别人的印象。总之，我认为我们不该凭第一印象来评判别人，而且应该注意自己是否给别人留下好的印象。

194. 团体与组织的重要性

Topic:

Groups or organizations are an important part of some people's lives. Why are groups or organizations important to people?

Sample Answer

Most people belong to at least one group or organization. These groups of people include social clubs, special interest groups, sports teams, classmates and workmates. Such organizations play an important part in people's lives today because they provide both material and personal benefits.

Both formal and informal organizations can provide their members with material benefits. For example, membership in an exercise class offers the benefit of improved health. In addition, organizations which work toward a specific goal, such as passing legislation or improving a neighborhood, allow people to achieve that goal more efficiently by working together. Finally, some organizations provide special benefits that are reserved for members, for example a music or book club in which the members exchange materials or receive special discounts.

Most organizations also provide personal benefits, the most important of which is a sense of belonging. When people choose to ally themselves with a group, that becomes part of their identity. In the group, they can find people of like-minded interests and feel like part of a team. This gives the members both companionship and the opportunity to share their feelings with sympathetic listeners. Moreover, trying out different groups enables people to discover their interests and clarify their goals. Through this process they can find out where they best fit in.

In conclusion, organizations and informal groups of people are important in our lives because they provide us with many advantages. They help us clarify our goals and interests and find the support we need to pursue them effectively. More importantly, they give us companionship and a sense of belonging.

▶考官评分:7分

题目:

团体和组织是人们生活中重要的组成部分，它们为什么重要?

译文:

大部分的人都会隶属于至少一个以上的团体或组织。这些团体包括社交联谊的俱乐部、特殊兴趣的团体、运动团队、同班同学以及同事。这些组织在每个人的生活中都扮演了重要的角色，原因就在于它们能提供物质利益并且给人们带来好处。

正式与非正式的组织都能给会员带来实质性的好处。举例来说，参加运动课程的会员能有增强体质的好处。此外，因某些特定目标而形成的组织能通过团队合作更有效地达到目标，如通过法规或是改善社区。最后，有些组织提供会员独享的好处，例如音乐俱乐部或读书会，其会员可以资源共享，或是享有特别的优惠折扣。

大部分组织也提供给个人一些好处，其中最重要的就是归属感。当人们选择加入某个团体时，这种关系便成了个人身份的一部分。在团体中，他们能够找到志趣相投的人，感觉自己是团体的一分子。会员不但获得友谊，同时也有机会和能够产生共鸣的听众分享自己的感受。此外，经常试着加入不同的团体有助于发现自己的兴趣所在，并认清自己的目标。通过这个过程，每个人都能找到最适合自己的团体。

总之，由于这些组织和非正式团体能带给我们很多好处，所以它们在我们的生活中十分重要。它们能够帮助我们认清自己的目标和兴趣，也使我们能够在追求目标和兴趣时得到必要的支持。更重要的是，团体能使我们获得友谊和归属感。

195. 我们这一代

Topic:

Every generation of people is different in important ways. How is your generation different from your parents' generation?

Sample Answer

The world is constantly changing and so are the people in it. With each generation we see important developments that affect the way we think and live our lives. Therefore, it is not surprising that each generation of people is different from the one before, and my generation is no exception. My peers and I differ from our parents in several important ways, including our view of the world and our expectations of the future.

People my age usually have a more global outlook than their parents. Unlike the previous generation, we have been exposed to a wide variety of information about the world from a very young age. We have benefited from technological advances such as satellite communications and the Internet. **These have truly made the world a global village and we have been greatly influenced as a result.** We are not only concerned about our traditional way of life, but also about our present way of life.

Our expectations of the future are also different. This is due mainly to the greater prosperity and peace that we have known. Few of us have suffered true economic hardship and most take a good education and high standard of living for granted. **Although we are willing to work hard to succeed, we also value our leisure time.** We are more likely to spend money on recreational activities than start saving for our old age in our youth. Our prosperity has made us more materialistic than our parents, but also more carefree.

Given our different circumstances, it is not surprising that we are so different from the previous generation. Our parents may shake their heads and worry over these changes, but no doubt their parents did the same. Rather than worry about what the next generation is coming to, I believe it is smarter to look for and appreciate the advantages in these developments.

▶考官评分:7分

题目:

每代人之间都有很大的不同。试述你这一代与父辈之间有什么不同。

译文:

世界在不断改变，世界上的人也是如此。每一个时代中，我们都可以看到一些重要的发展，它们影响着我们的思维方式和生活方式。因此，每个时代的人和上一代的人大不相同，这一点也不令人惊讶，而我们这一代也不例外。我以及与我同龄的人对于某些重要的事情就和父母的想法不同，其中包括我们的世界观和我们对未来的展望。

我们这一代人通常比父母有更宽广的世界观。不像上一代的人，我们在很年轻的时候就已经接触到不同的世界信息。我们因科技的进步而获益，如卫星通讯和互联网。这些科技确实使世界成为一个地球村，而我们也因此受到很大的影响。我们不仅关心自己传统的生活方式，也关心现今世界的生活方式。

我们对未来的展望也不同。这主要是因为我们经历的是更加繁荣和和平的景况。我们之中很少有人真正经历过经济困难，大部分的人都把良好的教育和高生活水准视为理所当然。虽然我们愿意努力工作以求功成名就，但是我们也很重视休闲时间。我们很有可能把钱花在娱乐活动上，而不会在年轻时就开始储存我们的养老金。富裕的生活使我们比父母更重视物质生活，也使我们更无忧无虑。

如果考虑到我们与父母之间的差异，那么我们这一代和上一代大不相同就没什么可惊讶的了。我们的父母或许会摇头叹气，慨叹这些变化，但毫无疑问，他们的父母也做过同样的事。我认为与其担心下一代会变成什么样子，不如期待并欣赏这些发展所带来的好处，这会是更明智的做法。

196. 人口过剩

Topic:

Describe some of the problems that overpopulation causes, and suggest at least one possible solution.

Sample Answer

In most countries of the world the population is increasing alarmingly. This is especially true in poor, undeveloped countries. Overpopulation causes a considerable number of problems.

In poor countries it is difficult to provide enough food to feed even the present number of people. In addition, education to limit the number of children per family is not always successful. Poorer countries usually have a lot of unemployment too, and an increase in population simply makes the situation worse. The environment also suffers when there are too many people living on the land.

In rich, industrialized and developing countries it is very difficult for governments to provide effective public services in overcrowded cities. Moreover, there is usually a great deal more crime, which is often due to high rates of unemployment. Further large increases in population only cause more overcrowding, unemployment and crime.

There are two main solutions to the overpopulation problem. Firstly, every woman who is pregnant but who does not want to give birth should be allowed by law to have an abortion. Secondly, governments must educate people to limit the size of the family. In China, couples are punished financially if they have more than one child. This may seem cruel, but the "one-child policy" is beginning to have an effect in the world's most populous nation. Eventually, similar policies might also be necessary in other crowded nations, such as India, for example.

To sum up, if the population explosion continues, many more people will die of starvation in poor countries, and life in the cities, even in affluent nations, will become increasingly difficult.

▶考官评分:8

题目:

请描述人口过剩将可能导致的问题，并至少提出一种可行的解决办法。

译文:

世界上大多数国家的人口以令人震惊的速度在增长，特别是在贫困、不发达的国家，人口过剩导致了很多问题。

贫困的国家甚至很难为现有的人口提供足够的粮食。另外，限制每个家庭孩子受教育的数量也不总是成功的。较穷的国家往往有很多失业者，而人口的增加只会使情况更糟。而当有太多人生活在这片土地上，环境也将面临考验。

在富裕的工业化国家和发展中国家，对政府来说拥挤的城市提供有效的公共服务也是相当困难的。此外，大量的犯罪往往要归咎于高失业率。人口的进一步增长只会导致更拥挤、更高失业率和犯罪率。

对人口过剩问题有两种主要解决方案。第一，法律应当允许每个怀孕又不想要孩子的女性堕胎。其次，政府必须教育人们控制每家人口的数量。在中国，如果一对夫妇想要一个以上的孩子，他们将会受到经济惩罚。这看起来或许很残酷，但“计划生育”政策的影响在人口最多的国家已经开始。最终，其他拥挤的国家，例如印度也有必要采取类似的政策。

综上所述，如果人口爆炸继续下去，贫困国家将会有更多的人死于饥饿，而在城市中生活，即使在富裕国家生活也会变得愈加困难。

197. 人们寿命更长的原因

Topic:

In general, people are living longer now. Discuss the causes of this phenomenon.

Sample Answer

People nowadays are living much longer than their counterparts in the past. In China, the average life expectancy has reportedly increased more than 4 years since 1990. Among various factors that contribute to this phenomenon are the continuously advancing food condition, the rapidly developing medical care system, and finally the current stable social and economic circumstance.

The food condition overall is becoming better and better, and is an important factor that makes people live much longer than before. First of all, foods are more hygienic. People today drink untainted mineral water, and sterilized skim milk. Furthermore, foods are more nutritious, not to mention various carefully designed nutritious products.

Of equal importance is the rapidly developing national medical care system. Development of modern technology has always been amazing. Certain diseases such as tuberculosis, pneumonia, and dysentery are now easy to remedy with low expense, but in the past, they are all probably lethal. Dental technology seems developed little except its exorbitantly charged bill, yet the simplest technology contributes to people's longevity most. It is not difficult to imagine that if an individual who lived in the past got a toothache, without certain dental care which is common today, he was certainly in an awful prospect: he might even die of a toothache!

Finally, the current stable economic circumstance is also a great influential factor. Social and economic circumstance has a dramatic effect on people's life expectancy. It was reported that Russian life expectancy dropped from 70 to 58 shortly after the disintegration of the previous Soviet Union. Apparently, people have less pressure in a more stable society, and the less pressure they suffer, the healthier they are. At the same time, various types of insurance are readily available, which make people feel safe, therefore indirectly contributes significantly to longevity of people.

▶考官评分:8

题目:

现在人们的寿命普遍比以前长，试述这一现象的原因。

译文:

今天的人们比过去活得更长。在中国，自1990年以来，据报道人均寿命增长了4年。产生这一现象的各种原因中包括不断改善的食物、快速发展的医疗系统以及当前稳定的社会和经济环境。

食物水平总体上越来越好，这是人们寿命超过过去的一个重要因素。首先，食物变得更卫生。今天人们喝无污染矿泉水，灭菌的脱脂牛奶。另外，食物比以前更有营养，更不用说各种各样精心设计的营养品了。

同样重要的还有快速发展的国家医疗系统。现代科技的发展成果令人惊异。像肺结核、肺炎、痢疾等疾病的治疗费用很低，但是在过去，这些都是致命的。牙科技术看起来没有改变多少，除了它高昂的费用，但是这个最简单的科技使人们寿命更长。不难想象，过去人得了牙病，没有现代的牙科技术，他一定会陷入一种糟糕的境地，甚至因为牙疼而死。

最后，当前稳定的经济环境也是一个重要的影响因素。社会和经济环境在人类平均寿命中产生很大的影响。据报道俄罗斯人的平均寿命在前苏联解体后从70跌落到58。显然，人们在稳定的社会中承受的压力更少。他们承受的压力越少，他们的身体就越健康。同时，现代人还有各种各样的保险，这使得人们感觉安全，因此也间接地为人类的长寿做了巨大贡献。

198. 居民区安装监控器

Topic:

With the increase in security awareness, security monitors are popping up in some places. Some are very useful, like the monitor eyeing the supermarket and the monitor checking traffic flows on roundabouts. But are monitors in the residential areas really necessary?

Sample Answer

Recently, more and more residential districts have been installed with monitor cameras. It's said that the installation can vastly enhance the security of the residents. But some people are against it. The discussion as to whether the surveillance system is a blessing or a curse arouses most people's interests. In my opinion, I support that the monitor camera should be mounted in the residential areas.

Installing monitor cameras is good for residents and the neighborhood. First of all, as what the advocates claim, it is an effective approach to improve the security situation. Consequently the guards can easily know what is going on in the districts from the screens of the monitor cameras, and they will be able to offer a helping hand to residents if it is necessary.

Furthermore, the monitor cameras can be used to keep watch on the specified areas all day, so if something unusual happens, for example, a thief goes into a house and steals some valuable things, the police can review the records to find out some clues. It provides some valuable clues for the police to investigate and solve the case.

Finally, if the monitor cameras have been installed in the residential districts, the people living there don't need to install the expensive security devices that they used to install. So the people living there can be spared lots of money on individual household safety devices.

In conclusion, although installing monitor cameras has its negative effects, it can to a great extent make people feel more secure. That is a very important thing for people nowadays. Therefore I support installing the monitor cameras in the residential districts. The installation will undoubtedly play an increasingly significant role in modern life.

▶考官评分:8

题目:

随着人们对安全的重视，一些地方开始安装监视器。一些监视器非常有用，比如安装在超市里的监视器以及在十字路口监控交通的监视器，但是在居民区安装监视器有必要吗?

译文:

最近，越来越多的住宅区安装上了监视器。据说监视器的安装能够大大地增强居民的安全保障。但是有些人却不这样认为。关于监视系统到底是一件好事还是一个祸根的讨论引起了大多数人的兴趣。以我个人来看，我赞成在住宅区安装监视器。

安装监视器对居民自身以及邻居都是有好处的。首先，正如倡导者所声称的，这是提升安全状况的有效方法，也使得保安通过监视器的屏幕能够很容易地知道居民区正在发生什么事并在需要的时候为居民提供帮助。

此外，监视器能够全天候监视特定区域。这样，如果有什么异常发生，例如，当一个小偷钻进了一所房子并偷了一些值钱的东西时，警察就能够通过审查监视录像去找到一些线索。它为警察调查和破案提供了很多有价值的线索。

最后，如果住宅区安装了监视器，住在那儿的人们就不需要再像以前一样安装一些昂贵的安全设备了。这样，住在那的人就能够在家庭安全设施上省下不少钱了。

总之，虽然安装监视器有它的负面影响，但是它能在很大程度上使人们感觉更安全——对于现在的人来说，这是一件非常重要的事。因此我赞成在居民区安装监视器。监视器的安装无疑将在现代生活中扮演一个越来越有意义的角色。

199. 超市安装监控器

Topic:

Nowadays surveillance cameras are widely used in supermarkets. Some think that this is a violation of human rights, while others insist that they are for the benefit of the supermarkets. Discuss both sides of argument.

Sample Answer

Nowadays supermarkets not only make a lot of money for their owners, but also bring them some trouble. How can they prevent theft without annoying their customers? The use of surveillance cameras seems a good solution. But more and more arguments arise with the increasing use of such cameras. Before giving my opinion, I think it is important to look at the arguments on both sides.

Those who support using surveillance cameras in supermarkets insist that it is the vest way to protect the owners' profits. Firstly, a camera is more effective than security guards. One camera can easily cover an area for which 3 – 4 security guards are needed. Secondly, a camera is much more objective. Sometimes our eyes might deceive us, while a machine can record exactly what happens. It can prevent much unnecessary embarrassment.

On the other hand, some people voice doubts about the installation of surveillance cameras. The most important reason for their disapproval is that such instruments show distrust of customers. Customers should not be watched suspiciously as if they were prisoners. Cameras can become evidence of a serious violation of human rights.

All in all, the best solution is for both sides to respect each other's needs. The shopkeeper should place surveillance cameras in such a way that the customer does not feel that he or she is being spied upon. At the same time, the customer should respect the shopkeeper's concern about theft.

▶考官评分:8

题目：

现在超市普遍安装监视器，一些人认为这种行为侵犯了人权，另一些人认为这是超市的权利。讨论双方观点。

译文：

现代社会，超市不仅使商家赢利而且还带来了很多的麻烦。那么超市商家如何才能既不干扰顾客又能防盗呢？监视器似乎是一个很好的解决办法。但是随着监视器的广泛应用，与之相关的越来越多的争论也在不断出现。在阐明我的观点之前，我认为重要的是从上述两种观点出发来讨论这个问题。

支持超市安装监视系统的人认为，监视器是保护顾客利益的最佳选择。首先，监视器比保安更有效。一部监视器可以很容易地监控到一片需要3-4名保安的范围。其次，监视器更加客观。我们的眼睛在某些情况下很可能会欺骗我们，然而一部监视器却可以精确地记录发生的事情，它可以避免很多不必要的尴尬情况发生。

另一方面，有些人则对这些监视器的设置表示怀疑。他们反对的最重要的原因是这些设备表明他们对顾客的不信任。顾客不应该被有所怀疑地监视，就好像他们是犯人一样。监视器是一项严重侵犯人权的证明。

总而言之，对于双方最好的解决办法就是尊重双方彼此的需求。超市商家可以通过不让顾客感到被监视的方式安装监视器。同时，顾客也要体谅超市商家对于失窃的顾虑。

200. 体育锻炼的好处

Topic:

Participating in sports is important to physical health as well as spiritual health and social development. Do you agree?

Sample Answer

In China, people keep fit by participating in different sports including running, walking, cycling, playing badminton, tennis, table tennis, football, and so on. Most of them think that participating in sports is important to physical health only and has nothing to do with spiritual health and social development. Some even claim that participating in sports has negative effects on spiritual health and social development. However, in my opinion, it is beneficial to physical health as well as spiritual health and social development as a whole despite of some negative effects it has brought.

Firstly, participating in sports can develop one's temperament and character spiritually. For example, if a person goes in for a kind of sport in which a team is involved, he needs to learn how to cooperate with other team members and how to adjust himself in an emergency. In addition, participating in sports can cultivate one's sense of honor and dignity. Athletes taking part in Olympic Games are such examples and those who have won the games are admired as heroes of the nation.

Furthermore, participating in sports can hold people together and thus can indirectly stimulate the social development. Because sports are activities in which all participants enjoy absolute equality without any discrimination in any aspect, they can hold together people of different strata in society. As for professional athletes, it is also important for them to pay attention to their own education or cultural study; otherwise they will become spiritually unhealthy and intellectually barren men. It is not the fault of participating in sports though.

Therefore, it is not difficult for us to come to the conclusion that physical exercises bring us great benefits. People from all walks of life should be encouraged to take up some kind of sports to help maintain a physically and mentally sound body and enrich their lives.

▶考官评分:8

题目:

参加体育锻炼不仅对身体健康有好处，而且还有利于人的心理健康和社会发展。你同意这种观点吗?

译文:

在中国，人们保持身体健康总是喜欢参加不同的体育运动，包括跑步、散步、骑自行车、打羽毛球、网球、桌球、踢足球等等。他们大部分的人认为参加体育运动仅仅对于身体健康很重要，但对于精神健康和社会发展却没有任何作用。一些人甚至认为参加体育运动会对精神健康和社会发展产生消极的影响。不管怎样，依我看来，总体上说尽管体育运动会带来一些消极影响，但是还是会有利于身体健康、精神健康和社会发展。

首先，参加体育运动能陶冶情操和提高人的精神品质。举个例子，如果一个人参加一种需要团队合作的运动，他需要学习如何与团队中的成员合作并且在紧急情况中调整自己的状态。另外，参加体育运动还能培养人的荣誉感和尊严。运动员参加奥林匹克运动正印证了这点，他们因为赢得了比赛而成为国家的英雄。

此外，参加体育运动有利于民族团结，这样能间接地刺激社会的发展。因为体育是参与者不受任何歧视并且完全享受平等的运动，体育可以团结社会中各个阶层的人。对于一个专业的运动员，重视他们自身的教育或者文化的学习是很重要的，否则他们会变成精神不健康，知识匮乏的人，但是这并不是参加体育运动的缺点。

所以，我们不难得出结论体育运动带给我们很多的好处。我们应该鼓励从事不同行业的人参加体育运动，从而有利于帮助他们保持身心健康并且丰富他们的生活。

201. 义务兵役制

Topic:

Along with the amazing development of society, more and more people begin to realize that only peace can ensure human prosperity. In recent years, some people propose that compulsory military service should be abolished. Do you agree or not? Give your reasons.

Sample Answer

In many countries, children are called upon for military service when they are 18 years old nowadays. Meanwhile, in China, especially in lots of universities, freshmen are required to take military training before they begin to study. It seems that it is a must in the growth-process of the young. However, is it proper to maintain military service in an era characterized by peace and development? This question is a very controversial one.

We can't deny that we have benefited a lot from military service. Firstly, it offers a good way to strengthen a person not only physically but also psychologically. No matter how tired he becomes during the difficult training, he must clench his teeth and carry on. Gradually, a strong character can be built up. Secondly, military training arouses people's awareness of discipline and unity. In the army, everything is fixed. One must obey the rules and do what he is scheduled to do promptly. Also, teamwork spirit and unity are very important for soldiers if they want to achieve a task perfectly.

Despite the advantages the military service has, it has some very serious disadvantages. In the army, no one is allowed to say "no" to an order. Such a discipline may possibly lead to bullying and conformity. "Yes Boys" and "Yes Girls" are found everywhere. Their lack of creativity and individuality will eventually turn into lack of vitality of their nation. What's more, it is a step away from peace. If it goes to extremeness, military service will inflict a fear called "MILITARISM" on us. People become militant. The threat of war will lead people all around the world into jeopardy.

All these opinions make sense, and it is consequently hard to decide which one is more reasonable. In my opinion, we'd better popularize the military service properly and restrain its bad effects. We should make it a good way to maintain peace and create a better world for us to live in.

▶考官评分:8

题目:

随着社会的飞速发展，越来越多的人认识到只有和平才能保证人类的繁荣。近几年有些人提出应当废除义务服兵役的传统。你是否同意此观点？请给出理由。

译文：

目前许多国家，年满十八周岁的孩子都被召去服兵役。与此同时，在中国，特别是在许多大学里，大一新生在开学前都要求进行军训。在年轻人成长过程中，这似乎是一件必须做的事情。然而，在一个不断发展的和平时代，保留服兵役的传统还合适吗？这是一个非常有争议的问题。

我们不能否认我们从服兵役中获益良多。首先，无论在心理上，还是在生理上，它都是使一个人更成熟、更强壮的好办法。不管在艰苦的训练中他有多么累，他必须咬紧牙关坚持下去。渐渐地，性格就会更坚强。第二，军训能让人更注重纪律性和团结性。在军队里，任何事都是固定的。你必须遵守那些规则，迅速地做好规定的事。而且，对士兵来说，如果他们想要出色地完成一项任务，团队合作精神和团结是非常重要的。

尽管军训有其优点，但也有许多非常严重的缺点。在军队里，任何人都不能对命令说“不”。这样一种约束可能会导致恃强凌弱和顺从。唯命是从的男孩和女孩到处可见。他们的创造力和个性的缺乏最终会导致他们国家缺乏活力。更可怕的是，这是远离和平的一步。如果达到极致，军训会使我们感到有种“军国主义”的恐慌。人们会变得好战。战争的威胁会让全世界的人陷入危险之中。

所有这些观点都是有意义的。因此，来决定哪个观点更合理是困难的。在我看来，我们最好正确地推广军训并遏制它不良的影响。我们应该用一种好的方式去维持和平，创造一个更好的地球来让自己居住。

202. 帮助别人的方式

Topic:

Nowadays some people like to give help to the local community or provide people with direct help. Other people prefer to give money to national and international organizations. Discuss both of the two ways and present your own opinion.

Sample Answer

Nowadays, people have been attaching more and more attention to charity. However, when it comes to the actual approaches to be adopted to express their caring and loving, their opinions vary considerably. As for me, I believe each approach may have its own advantages and disadvantages and it's really hard to tell which one is the best choice.

First, it is generally agreed that direct help is beneficial to both parties. On one hand, it offers a unique rewarding feeling to those who give help. Whenever they see the smile on the face of those who are helped, those who offer the help will undoubtedly acquire a sense of fulfillment, which will propel them to engage themselves more enthusiastically in the cause of charity. On the other hand, when others do not actually need any financial support, direct help, as a commonly-accepted form, seems to be indispensable. However, this form is usually only restricted to one's neighborhood.

Second, compared with offering direct help, giving money to national and international organizations has been gaining increasing popularity among the public for its high efficiency and great convenience. There are times when people having the intention to help do not happen to have the time to do so. There are also times when people who offer help prefer to be behind the veil. Fortunately, all these problems have been solved with the appearance of many national and international charity organizations, which has made it possible to make the best use of the fund to help as many people as possible in the right way and at the best time. Nevertheless, a lack of administration and supervision over these organizations may trigger misuse of the fund or even corruption of the officials involved.

Clearly, there are various ways to help others. What is the most important is whether one has a loving and sympathetic heart which drives him or her to extend a helping hand o those who await our help.

▶考官评分:8

题目:

现在一些人喜欢帮助地方社区或者直接为别人提供帮助，另一些人宁愿捐款给国家或国际机构，讨论这两种做法并给出自己的观点。

译文:

现在，人们越来越重视慈善事业。但在通过什么方式表达自己的友好和爱心方面人们的分歧很大。对我而言，我相信每一种方式都有其优点和缺点，很难辨别哪一种是更好的选择。

首先，以直接方式给予帮助对于双方都有裨益。一方面，它带给施予帮助的一方独特的回报感受。看到受助者脸上洋溢的微笑，施助者肯定会有一种成就感，这种感觉又会促使他们更加热衷于慈善事业。另一方面，当其他人并不需要金钱方面的帮助时，直接帮助作为广为接受的形式，便显得不可或缺，然而这种帮助往往只能局限在邻里之间。

其次，与直接帮助相比，将钱捐给国家机构或者国际机构的方式因为高效和方便越来越受公众欢迎。有时候，有意愿提供帮助的人碰巧没有时间和精力这么做；有时候，人们希望以匿名的方式提供帮助。所幸随着这些国家机构和国际机构的出现，这些问题都迎刃而解了，在最合适的时间以恰当的方式给尽量多的人提供帮助也成为可能。然而，对于这些机构的管理和监督的缺乏可能会导致资金滥用，甚至导致官员腐败。

可见，帮助他人的方式不止一种，最重要的是人们是否有爱心和同情心去向那些需要帮助的人伸出援助之手。

203. 缓解压力的办法

Topic:

People have various ways of relieving stress. What are some of the ways that you find most effective in relieving stress? Give reasons and examples to support your response.

Sample Answer

The ways in which people relieve their stress are very much different: some cry, some laugh, some overdrink themselves and some dance wildly, and so on and so forth, to name just a few. However, the two most effective ways that work on me are sleeping in and taking long walks.

Now let's look at many advantages of sleeping in. Sleeping in may help ease our nervousness and give our exhausted nerves a break. While under pressure, we tend to be impatient and easily lose our temper, which could only aggravate our feeling of pressure. Sleeping in once there is a chance can help adjust our nerves and this is conducive to getting over nervousness and tiredness. Furthermore, sleeping in can let us forget all about the stress for the time being. Once falling asleep, we would be free from thinking about the stress any longer and everything recedes to temporary tranquility, so when we wake up, the stress is not that strong anymore. Of course, we are unable to sleep in wherever we are and whenever we want to, rather, we need to find time, that is, when work allows us to do so.

Next, let's take a look at some of the positive points of taking long walks. As we know, taking a walk itself is the best form of exercise that can help us keep fit, thus improving our capability to alleviate or eradicate pressure, which in turn makes for our long-term health. Meanwhile, taking long walks provides us with opportunities to enjoy the beauty of the surrounding sceneries and to think over the problems in our mind. Therefore, we are actually doing exercises, feasting our eyes on the sceneries and thinking about things at the same time: all three in one, which means that stress or pressure becomes only a small part of the whole process.

In general, my own experience across the years has proved that the above-mentioned two ways are the most effective in terms of relieving and even eradicating stress, so I highly recommend them to you and hope they would produce the same effect on you.

▶考官评分:8

题目:

人们有各种各样缓解压力的办法。你有什么有效的解压办法？给出理由并举出例子。

译文：

人们缓解压力的方式确实千差万别：有人痛哭，有人大笑，有人狂饮，有人狂舞，凡此种种，不一而足。可我认为对自己来讲最有效的方式是猛睡觉和散长步。

我们先来看看睡大觉的诸多好处。睡大觉可以使我们紧张、疲劳的神经得到休息。压力大时，我们往往会感到烦躁、容易上火，这只会使我们更有压力。一有机会，猛睡一场，我们的神经就会得到相应的调整，从而有助于克服紧张和疲劳。另外，睡大觉可以使我们暂时忘掉压力。进入睡眠状态后，我们便不会再去思考压力的问题，一切的一切都暂时归于平静，等醒来的时候，压力往往会变得小了。当然，睡大觉并非是随时随地都可以做到的，而是要找时间，在工作允许的情况下。

我们再来看看散长步的绝妙好处。散步本身就是最好的体育锻炼，可以使我们保持身体健康，从而提高我们解压的能力和一直保持身体健康。同时，散长步的过程中我们可以一边欣赏周围的景色，一边思考大脑中的问题。这样，我们一边锻炼，一边赏景，一边思考，三合一，压力也就成了很小的一部分了。

总之，经过我多年的实践证明，这两种方式对于缓解，甚至是彻底解压具有极佳的效果，因此，我向朋友们大力推荐，希望它们在你的身上也能产生相同效果。

204. 孩子所承受的压力

Topic:

Today's children are living under more pressure from society than children in the past. To what extent do you agree or disagree with the opinion?

Sample Answer

Nowadays children are growing up in more favorable conditions than ever before. However, they are also faced with much greater pressure than children in the past.

Firstly, the burden with academic learning has become extremely heavy. It has become a trend for kids to take extra courses beyond their normal school curriculum, for parents believe that this can ensure their children a chance to a better university. And only a better university can ensure their kids a good job in the future. This would no doubt bring huge pressure to their children, affecting their health both physically and mentally.

Secondly, the pressure of employment is becoming greater and greater. Statistics show that in 2007 about one million college graduates failed to find jobs. Most of them held bachelor's and even master's degrees. The fact that even well-educated people are confronted with unemployment problems urges children to obtain more skills and become more versatile so as to stay competitive on the job market.

From the above discussion, we can easily come to a conclusion that children do live under more pressure than ever before. Under so much work and pressure, it is difficult for them to develop good personalities and interpersonal communication skills. They may become more solitary and even suffer from certain mental illnesses. Therefore, our government and society should create opportunities and reform our educational mechanism to let our kids enjoy their supposed happy childhood.

▶考官评分:8

题目:

现在孩子所承受的压力要比以前大，你在何种程度上同意或不同意这个想法?

译文:

如今的孩子比以前生活更优越了，但是同时他们所承受的社会压力也越来越大了。

首先，学习上的压力变得极为沉重。孩子在学校正常上课之外上额外的课程辅导也成为一种趋势，因为家长认为只有这样才能保证孩子将来考上好大学。也只有考上好大学，才能够找到好工作。这无疑给孩子带来了巨大的压力，影响他们的身心健康。

第二，就业压力越来越大。数据显示，2007年中国有一百万大学生找不到工作。而他们大部分都持有学士学位甚至硕士学位。受过良好教育的大学生都面临就业困难的问题，这就迫使孩子们尽可能多地掌握技能，变得更加多才多艺，才能够在求职就业方面更有竞争力。

由此，我们很容易得出结论：孩子们确实比以前压力大了。他们在如此大的压力之下很难培养好自己的性格以及与人交往的能力。他们可能会变得性格孤僻，甚至会患上精神疾病。因此，我们的政府和社会应该创造机会，改革教育体制，让我们的孩子享受到自己本该幸福的童年。

205. 工作满意度

Topic:

As most people spend a major part of their adult life at work, job satisfaction is an important element of individual wellbeing. What factors contribute to job satisfaction? How realistic is the expectation of job satisfaction for all the workers?

Sample Answer

Nowadays many adults have full-time jobs and the proportion of their lives spent doing such jobs is very high. So feeling about one's job must reflect how an individual feels about his or her life as a whole, and because of this, job satisfaction is indeed very important for the wellbeing of that person.

Employees get job satisfaction in a number of ways. Firstly, a person needs to feel that they are doing valued and valuable work, so positive feedback from superiors is very important in this respect. A sense of fullfillment is also encouraged if a worker feels the job is worth doing because it contributes to the society or the economy as a whole. Secondly, when someone feels they are improving or developing their skills through training opportunities, for example, then there is a sense of progression and purpose that rewards a worker. The sense of belonging to a team or a working community also contributes to job satisfaction because colleagues help each other to enjoy their working lives. Satisfaction is also increased by the sense of responsibility for and loyalty to a team.

Of course not everybody enjoys their work. Hard economic realities mean that many people have little choice in the kind of job they can get. In some cases an employee is working in a job that suits neither their skills nor their personality. Some jobs are repetitive and boring, and labour relations may be poor and lead to resentment and insecurity rather than to job satisfaction.

However, even though it is unlikely that all workers do feel happy in their work, I think it is not unrealistic to promote more job satisfaction in any job. If the factors identified above are implemented, then any job can be improved and more workers can feel greater degrees of job satisfaction.

▶考官评分:8

题目:

由于大多数人在工作上花了大部分时间，因此工作满意度成为个人幸福感的重要因素。工作满意度是由什么因素组成的呢？对所有员工来说，对于工作满意程度怎样的期望，才算是现实的呢？

译文:

现在大多数成年人都有全职工作，并且工作的时间在生活中的比例非常高，所以一个人对工作的感觉必定反映出这个人对他或她的整体生活的感觉，正因为如此，工作满意度确实对于这个人的幸福感很重要。

员工可以通过很多方式获得工作满意度。首先，一个人需要感受到他们正在做的工作是受重视的和有价值的，那么从上级那里得到积极的反馈在这方面非常重要。总的来说如果一个工人因为他的工作促进了社会和经济的发展而认为它非常值得去做，那么满足感也是受鼓励的。其次，当有人觉得他们通过培训可以改善或提高他们的技能，例如，给工人有种循序渐进的和有目标性的奖励的感觉。一个团队或工作团体的归属感也有利于工作满足度，因为同事们互相帮助，享受他们的工作生活。工作满意度也增加了对团队的责任感和忠诚度。

当然并不是每个人都喜欢他们的工作。严峻的经济形势意味着许多人只能做已经找到的工作，其他的别无选择。在某些情况下，人们所从事的工作并不是他们所学的专业，也不符合自己的个性。有些工作是重复、枯燥的，并且劳资关系也可能很差，这些导致的不满情绪和不安全感，远远超过了对工作的满意度。

不过，尽管所有工人不可能对他们的工作都感到满意，但我认为在任何工作领域，提升更高的工作满意度并不是不切实际的。如果上述问题都得以解决，那么任何工作都可以得到改善，将会有更多的工人对自己的工作越来越满意。

206. 常换工作的原因

Topic:

As society changes, more and more people do not want to stay in one career or job. Many people change their careers and jobs. What is the cause of this phenomenon? Can you give some suggestions to solve this problem?

Sample Answer

With the development of our society, there is a growing discontent among people about a "life-long career". They are seeking experience in more than one field of work. Personally, I believe that there are several incentives contributing to this phenomenon and I will elaborate on them in this essay.

In the first place, social developments have brought about a more flexible work style and work philosophy. It will be really difficult for modern people to see any point of getting retired from the place where their career got initiated. Instead, they are eager to try new things and gain fresh experience from frequent job-hopping, from which their life could be made more colorful and diversified.

In the second place, another imperative motivation is that people, in most cases, change their jobs for a higher salary. Just like a saying goes, "People strive upward." According to statistics, the foremost reason that people change jobs is for a better pay. Consequently, if one can get a more appealing offer from some other employer, what's the point of staying in the original one?

If some measures have to be taken to lessen or even eliminate this phenomenon, I reckon that companies should take up an inescapable responsibility through providing all their employees with a clear and transparent ladder of promotion as well as sufficient benefits in order to alleviate employees' impulses of leaving. What's more, especially in terms of job ethics and a sense of responsibility. In this way, people may form a more precise and mature attitude towards career and thus not being carried away by this ever-changing fickle world.

From all that have been discussed above, we can draw a safe conclusion that there are various causes for people's frequent job-hopping. There is much left to be done if we really want to alter this situation.

▶考官评分:8

题目:

随着社会的变化，越来越多的人不愿只待在一个工作岗位上，很多人常换工作。阐述造成这种现象的原因及提出解决办法。

译文:

随着社会的发展，越来越多的人开始不满于单一的工作经验，他们开始从事各种不同领域的工作。我认为，造成这种现象有多种原因，我将在本文中进行详细阐述。

首先，社会发展带来了一种更为灵活的工作方式和哲学理念。当代人很难理解终身只做一份工作本身有什么意义。相反，他们更倾向于通过频繁地跳槽来尝试各种新鲜事物，并且从中获得不同的感受，同时令生活更为丰富多彩。

其次，在大部分情况下，另一个至关重要的原因是薪酬。正如谚语所说："人往高处走。"相关数据表明，人们换工作的首要动机是为了更高的薪水。所以，如果能从其他公司得到一份更诱人的薪酬，为什么还要待在原公司呢?

如果要采取一些措施来减弱甚至消除这种现象，我想公司首先应该承担起一份不可推卸的责任。公司需要给员工提供一个清晰透明的上升阶梯，以及更好的福利待遇，从而减弱员工离职的冲动。另外，也应该加强相关的职业培训，尤其是在职业伦理与责任感这两方面。这样人们可以对职业有更准确和更成熟的态度，就不会在不断变化的社会中迷失方向。

综上所述，人们的频繁跳槽有多种多样的原因。想要改变这种局面，我们所需做的还有很多。

207. 常换工作的利与弊

Topic:

Some people prefer to stay in the same job for the same company, but others prefer to change jobs frequently. You should use specific reasons to compare the advantages and disadvantages of both sides.

Sample Answer:

In modern society, employment is based on mutual options between companies and individuals rather than unilateral decisions of companies. Therefore, some people are able to change jobs frequently while others still prefer to stay in the same job for the same company. From my point of view, both sides have their own advantages and disadvantages.

Let us have a touch on the former attitude towards career first. The people who prefer to frequently change jobs, usually called "job hoppers", are bound to have more opportunities to develop their personal abilities as well as sociable skills. As a result, they may possess more enthusiasm and ambition when confronted with work, and they may behave more creatively and efficiently when challenged by various tasks. However, due to the instability of their jobs, they are generally suffering great pressure, stress and intolerable mental pains. They have no other choices but to enforce themselves to keep up with the fast-paced jobs so that they even forget how to relax.

On the other hand, there are also people who prefer to stay in the same job for the same company. The advantages of this attitude towards career consist in the relatively stable income and less competitive stress under most circumstances. Besides, as their working experience increases, they are more likely to acquire promotion or have their pay raised. Nevertheless, we all regard it a natural truth that every coin has two sides. Compared with people holding the former attitude, the latter have their own disadvantages, such as the same old routine work and narrow horizon.

As compared and analyzed above, both attitudes towards career have their advantages and disadvantages. In terms of which side you will stand by or which attitude you will adopt, it is none of others' business but really up to you.

题目：

有些人喜欢在同一家公司做同样的事情，但是其他人宁愿不断跳槽。论述从事不同的工作和从事同一种工作的利弊。

译文：

当今社会，工作是以公司和个人共同选择为基础的，而不是公司单方面的选择。因此当别人还在选择在同一家公司做同一件事情时，一些人已经频繁换工作。针对这种现象我认为各有利弊。

首先我们借前者的职业观来说。想经常换工作的人通常叫“工作漏斗”。他们想拥有更多的机会去提高个人能力和社交技能，面对工作可以有更多的热情和抱负。在他们挑战不同工作时，他们将会获得更多的创造力和更高的效率。不过由于脑力劳动通常会给他们带来很大压力以及无法忍受的脑力劳动之苦。他们别无选择，只能强迫自己加快节奏地完成那些工作，甚至忘记如何去放松。

另一方面，也有人更喜欢待在同一家公司做同样的事情。这种职业观的优点是，在大多数情况下能有一个相对稳定的收入和没有太大的竞争压力。此外，他们的工作经验也会有所提高，也更有可能提高自己从而得到更多的薪水。然而，我们要关注这样一个事实，任何事物都具有两面性。相对而言，人们比较支持前者的观点，认为后者有不少缺点。比如说，同样的惯例工作和狭隘的视野。

根据以上的对比和分析，关于职业的两种观点都各有利弊。对于这些说法你可以不在意或采用任何一种，这与别人没关系，还是得自己拿主意。

208. 任何人都可以成为运动员或者音乐家

Topic:

It is generally believed that some people are born with certain talents, for instance for sport or music, and others are not. However, it is sometimes claimed that any child can be taught to become a good sports person or musician. Discuss both views and give your own opinion.

Sample Answer

The relative importance of natural talent and training is a frequent topic of discussion when people try to explain different levels of ability in, for example, sport, art, or music.

Obviously, education systems are based on the belief that all children can effectively be taught to acquire different skills, including those associated with sport, art, or music. So from our own schools experience, we can find plenty of evidence to support the view that a child can acquire these skills with continued teaching and guided practice.

However, some people believe that innate talent is what differentiates a person who has been trained to play a sport or an instrument, from those who become good players. In other words, there is more to the skill than a learned technique, and this extra talent cannot be taught, no matter how good the teacher or how frequently a child practices.

I personally think that some people do have talents that are probably inherited via gene. Such talents can give individuals a facility for certain skills that allow them to excel, while more hard-working students never mange to reach a comparable level. But, as with all questions of nature versus nurture, they are not mutually exclusive. Good musicians or artists and exceptional sport stars have probably succeeded because of both good training and natural talent. Without the natural, continuous training would be neither attractive nor productive, and without the training, the child would not learn how to exploit and develop their talent.

In conclusion, I agree any child can be taught particular skills, but to be really good in areas such as music, art or sport, then some natural talent is required.

▶考官评分:8

题目:

人们普遍认为有些人在体育或音乐方面是有天赋的，而有些人没有。然而，有时候宣称任何孩子都会被教成为一个好的运动员或者音乐家。讨论双方观点并且给出你的个人观点。

译文:

当人们试图解释每个人在体育、艺术或音乐方面的能力时，他们经常会讨论一个人的天赋和后天培养的相对重要性。

显然，教育体制是以孩子们能够通过教育有效的掌握各种技能这个信念为基础的，这些技能包括：与体育，艺术或者音乐，以及与这些相关联的。所以从我们学校的教学经验来看，我们可以找到许多论据来支持这个观点。一个孩子可以通过不断的教学和有指导的实践来掌握这些技能。

然而，一些人认为天赋是区分被训练去进行体育项目或者一种乐器的人和优秀的运动员或音乐家。换句话说，学习技能有更多超越技术层面的东西，并且这种天赋是教不出来的，不管老师有多好或者一个孩子有多勤奋。

我个人认为有些人有天赋可能是通过基因遗传。这些天赋可以使个人在某一确定的技能上擅长，然而即使是更努力的学生也从来不能达到可比的水平。但是，对于有关天生与后天培养的所有问题，它们不是互相排斥。优秀的音乐家，艺术家和体育明星都可能通过刻苦训练和天赋而成功。没有这种天赋，长期的训练会枯燥无效，并且没有这种训练，孩子会不知道学习怎样利用他们的天赋并且发展他们的天赋。

总的来说，我认为任何孩子都可以学习不同的技能，但是在这些音乐，艺术和体育等领域中，还是需要有些天赋。

209. 先天和后天

Topic:

Research indicates that the characteristics we are born with have much more influence on our personality and development than any experiences we may have in our life. Which do you consider to be the major influence?

Sample Answer:

Today the way we consider human psychology and mental development is heavily influenced by the genetic sciences. We now understand the importance of inherited characteristics more than ever before. Yet we are still unable to decide whether an individual's personality and development are more influenced by genetic factors or by the environment.

Research, related to identical twins, has highlighted how significant inherited characteristics can be for an individual's life. But whether these characteristics are able to develop within the personality of an individual surely depends on whether the circumstances allow such a development. It seems that the experiences we have in life are so unpredictable and so powerful that they can boost or over-ride other influences, and there seems to be plenty of research findings to confirm this.

My own view is that there is no one major influence in a person's life. Instead, the traits we inherit from our parents and the situations and experiences that we encounter in life are constantly interacting. It is the interaction of the two that shapes a person's personality and dictates how that personality develops. If this were not true, then we would be able to predict the behavior and character of a person from the moment they were born.

In conclusion, I do not think that either nature or nurture is the major influence on a person, but that both have powerful effects. How these factors interact is still unknown today and they remain largely unpredictable in a person's life.

▶考官评分:8

题目:

研究表明我们与生俱来的特性比我们过去生活中的经历对我们的个性和发展更有影响力。你认为哪种影响更主要?

译文:

如今我们认为遗传学对心理和精神的发展有很大影响。我们比以前任何时候都认识到遗传特性的重要性。然而我们仍然不能确定个性的发展主要受遗传的影响还是受环境的影响。

同卵双胞胎的研究突出了遗传特性对一个人的一生具有重大影响。然而这些遗传特性是否真的能够影响一个人的内在个性，还取决于环境是否适合这样的发展。生命中某些无法预料的强有力的经历能够加强或者推翻某些影响，许多的研究发现支持这一看法。

笔者认为，在人的生命中没有主要的影响。而且，从父母那里遗传来的特征和我们在生命中偶然遇到的情况与经历是相互影响的。形成人的性格和决定人的性格怎样发展是这两方面相互影响的结果。如果不是这样，那么我们在人们出生的那一刻就可以预测每一个人的行为和性格。

总之，我既不认为天性是影响一个人的主要因素也不认为后天培养是主要因素，但是两者都具有强有力的影响。这些因素是如何相互影响的，至今我们仍然不清楚，并且在一个人的生命中这些因素在很大程度上仍然无可预测。

210. 先天和后天

Topic:

Nature and nurture, which plays a major role in the personality and development of children?

Sample Answer:

In children's development of personality, which plays a major part, nature or nurture? As I see it, nurture is as important as, if not more important than nature.

Family does play a significant role in shaping children's inclination and character. After one is born, the first and nearest surroundings is the family in which he will grow up. Parents are the first teachers to their children. Every day, parents' speech and action influence the mental and physical development of their children who tend to follow what their parents do. Because the family is children's most direct source of knowledge and other experience, those who are brought up in good family tend to possess many pleasant characters.

When a child becomes old enough to communicate with other children, he begins having friends who sometimes influence him more rapidly than do families. By associating with friends, one can gradually get into the society and become sociable. To some extent, man is a sociable creature so that children should understand the society, get used to it, and get pleasure out of it. To this point, friends would help. As for me, I have lots of friends who have many different opinions and personalities. Discussing with them enriches my thought, and playing with them builds up my personality.

Some people advocate the role of nature in molding children's characteristics. They take for example some of famous families in the world, which brought up many scientists, such as Bernoullis. But it should be a forceful example to demonstrate the importance of the family's nurture.

If you want to succeed, do not rely on the nature. To achieve your goal needs the efforts of yourself. God helps those who help themselves.

▶考官评分:7分

题目:

天性和后天培养，哪个因素在孩子性格的发展过程中起主要作用?

译文:

在儿童个性发展过程中，什么占据主导地位，是他们的天性还是后天的培养？在我看来，后天如果不能比天性重要，至少也与天性同等重要。

家庭在孩子的爱好和性格的形成中起重要的作用。当一个孩子出生以后，他所面对的第一个和最近的环境就是他即将在那里成长的家庭。家长是孩子的第一位老师。每天，家长的言行都会影响孩子们的身心发展，孩子们也会学父母的行为。因为，家庭是孩子获取知识和经验的最直接源泉，那些在好的家庭里长大的孩子会有很多好品质。

当一个孩子长大到可以与别的孩子交流的时候，他们会交一些朋友，这些朋友有时候会比家庭更快地影响他们的行为。通过结交朋友，他们可以逐渐地步入社会并善于与人交往。在某种程度上，人是喜欢交往的动物，所以孩子们应该学会了解社会，适应社会，并且在其中找到快乐。基于这一点，朋友可以给予一定的帮助。就我而言，我有很多朋友他们都有不同的观点和个性。在和他们讨论的过程中丰富了我的思想，和他们玩乐的时候增强了我的个性。

一些人认为孩子的个性是天生的。他们举了很多世界上著名的家庭的例子，在这些家庭中产生了一些科学家，例如贝努里家族。但是这其实是一个有力的例子来说明家庭教育的重要性。

如果你想成功，不要依赖于天性。要想达到目标需要你自身的努力。天助自助者。

211. 成功与运气

Topic:

"When people succeed, it is because of hard work. Luck has nothing to do with success." Do you agree or disagree with the quotation above? Use specific reasons and examples to explain your position.

Sample Answer:

Success is always what human beings chase. Someone succeeds for his luck while someone succeeds for his hard work. As far as I am concerned, I fully agree with the claim that there is no correlation between success and luck.

First of all, an education is the key factor of success. One wishing to be admitted to the university will have to take several tests. It is doubtful that someone will be so lucky that knowing nothing, he could pass the test with a high score. Therefore, in order to be successful, one should prepare for the tests and work hard, because a good education will provide him with a good job and an opportunity to accomplish some of his goals and dreams. In my lifetime, I have never met a person who could graduate from a college without working hard.

Secondly, it is impossible to make a career if one is lacking knowledge. Luck plays no role in achieving this success. Even if someone was unbelievably lucky enough to become a manager, not being qualified enough, he will be asked to resign in the near future because of his inability due to lack of knowledge and experience to make right decisions. For instance, I used to work for a very small company owned by a friend. Although he had no knowledge or experience in business, the company had been profitable for a short time, which he attributed to his luck. But this company was finally closed because of the wrong strategies and decisions made by him.

On the other hand, it can not be denied that many businessmen become successful only for their new ideas, not for their long time of hard work and many people having done a lot of work still can not be successful men. Sometimes luck may play an important role in success. But it is mainly acting through one's diligent work. It is the hard work that leads us to the front of luck.

In sum, success is every person's pursuit. We always dream that someday we will be successful businessmen, famous scientists, or distinguished politicians. All of these things are simply not possible without hard work. Luck has no place in such a scheme of events.

▶考官评分:7分

题目：

“一种观点认为成功全部取决于一个人是否努力，而与运气毫无关系。”你是否同意这种观点，并用解释和例子来阐述自己的看法。

译文：

人们总是在追逐成功。有些人因为幸运而成功，与此同时，有些人因为努力工作而成功。就我而言，我完全同意成功和幸运完全没有关系的这种说法。

首先，教育是成功最关键的因素。一个人要想进入大学，不得不经历若干考试。值得疑惑的是，一些人太幸运了以至于他们什么都不懂仍能以高分通过考试。因此，为了成功，人们应该为考试做好准备并且努力学习，因为一个好的教育将会给他提供一个好的工作和机会，使他完成他的目标和梦想。一生当中，我从未遇见过没有努力学习就顺利地从大学毕业的人。

第二，一个缺乏知识的人是不可能在事业上有提升的。幸运在实现成功中没有起到作用。即使有人没有足够的资格却成为了一个经理，幸运地令人难以置信，他也将会在不久的将来因无能力被要求辞职。这归因于缺乏知识和经验去做出正确的决定。举个例子来讲，我过去在朋友开的一家小公司工作，即使他在经商方面没有知识或者经验，公司在短时期内仍然是获利的，这要归功于他的幸运。但是因为他错误的策略和决定导致他的公司最终倒闭了。

另一方面，不可否认的是，许多商人成功仅仅因为他们的新想法，而不是因为他们长时间的辛劳工作，还有许多人做了很多工作却没有成功。有时，幸运在成功中起了很重要的作用。但是主要还是由于人们至始至终的辛勤工作起作用。努力工作使我们走在了幸运的面前。

总之，每个人都追求成功。我们总是梦想着终有一天我们能够成为一名成功的商人、著名的科学家或者杰出的政治家。不努力工作不可能就实现所有这些事情。在这些大事件中的计划中，没有幸运的位置。

第二章

图表作文题库全部题目和范文

1. 一个图表

The table below shows the results of a survey which sampled a cross-section of 100,000 people asking if they traveled abroad and why they traveled for the period 1994—1998.

Write a report for a university lecturer describing the information shown below.

VISITS ABROAD BY UK RESIDENTS BY PURPOSE OF VISIT (1994-1998)					
	1994	1995	1996	1997	1998
Holiday	15,246	14,898	17,896	19,703	20,700
Business	3,155	3,188	3,249	3,639	3,957
Visits to friends and relatives	2,689	2,688	2,774	3,051	3,181
Other reasons	982	954	972	967	990

Sample Answer

The table illustrates the results of a survey about the purpose of visit abroad of 100,000 UK residents over 5 years(1994 to 1998).

It can be seen from the table that there was a slight decrease in the number of holiday from 15,246 in 1994 to 14,898 in 1995. After that, the number increased sharply until 1998, peaking at 20,700. However, the 5 years witnessed a gradual rise in the number of business from 3,155 to 3,957.

According to the table, the number of visits to friends and relatives remained stable from 1994 to 1995. However, there was a dramatic growth in the number over the next four years. The period from 1994 to 1998 experienced a fluctuation in the number of other reasons and it reached its lowest point at 954 in 1995

We can see from the table that from 1994 to 1998, holiday had the highest number among the four reasons. Comparatively, the number of business was slightly higher than that of visits to friends and relatives. Other reasons had the smallest number in the four reasons.

▶考官评分:8分

译文:

这个表格显示了有关1994~1998五年间100000英国居民出国旅行目的的一个调查结果。

从表格中可以看到度假的数字从1994年的15246缓慢下降到1995年的14898。从那儿以后，这个数字急剧上升直到1998年，达到最高点20700。然而，商务出行的数字在这五年中从3155逐步增加到3957。

根据这个表格，探亲访友的数字从1994年到1995年基本保持不变。在接下来的四年中急剧上升。从1994年到1998年，由于其他原因旅行的数字经历了一个波动，在1995年达到最低点954。

从表格中，我们可以看到度假在四种原因中占有最大的比例。比较而言，商务出行的数字比探亲访友的稍高。其他原因旅行的数字是最低的。

杨凡老师点评：

此题是最常考的图表作文，占60%左右。它的特点是“既有不同的时间，也有不同的对象”。这样的题目，通常写四段：先写一个开头段，主体段落写三段，先用两段分别描述各个对象在这段时间的变化，再用一段对不同对象进行比较。这篇范文就是这样写的。写了一个开头段，改写题目中的文字说明。主体段落先用两段分别描述四个对象在这五年中的变化规律。然后，再用一段对它们进行比较。

2. 一个图表

The graph below shows radio and television audiences throughout the day in 1992.

Summarise the information by selecting and reporting the main features, and make comparisons where relevant.

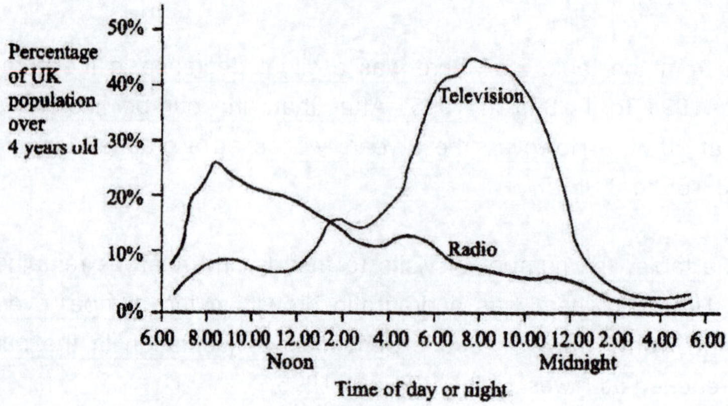

Sample Answer

The graph shows the percentage of the UK population over the age of 4 that listened to radio and watched television throughout the day in 1992.

There was a slight increase in the number of TV audiences from about 3% at 6:00 a.m. to about 7% at 8:00 a.m. From 8:00 a.m. to 12:00 p.m., it remained almost stable. After that, the number of TV audiences rose sharply until 8:00 p.m., peaking at about 45%. From then, the number fell rapidly until around 6:00 a.m. next morning.

Unlike television, the number of radio audiences increased rapidly from 6:00 a.m. to 8:00

a.m. At 8:00 a.m., it reached its highest point at 25%. And then, for the rest of the day, the number dropped gradually, with a slight increase from 4:00 p.m. to 5:00 p.m. and around 11:00 p.m.

Before around 2:00 p.m., the number of people listening to the radio was larger than that of people watching TV. However, for the rest of the day, much more UK audiences chose to watch TV rather than listen to radio. As a whole, throughout the whole day, for UK audiences, TV was more popular than radio.

▶考官评分:7分

译文:

此图显示了1992年英国一天中，年龄在4岁以上的人听收音机和看电视的百分比。

从早上6点到早上8点看电视的人的比例有个小小的增长，从3%增长到7%。从早上8点到12点则基本保持不变。之后看电视的人的数量急速增长，在下午8点的时候达到一个高峰（大约45%）。此后，便迅速下降直到第二天早上6点钟。

与电视不同，听收音机的人数从早上6点到8点增长得很快，并在8点的时候达到了一个顶峰，接近25%。然后在其余的时间里人数开始逐渐下降，但在下午4点到5点和晚上11点的时候有一个小小的回升。

在下午2点以前，听收音机的人数要多于看电视的人数。但在其他的时间里，更多的英国人选择了看电视而不是听收音机。总的来说，从这一整天来看，对于英国观众来说，电视比收音机更受欢迎。

3. 一个图表

The graph shows the demand for energy and the energy available from fossil fuels in Freedonia from 1985 to 2005.

Write a report for a university lecturer describing the information shown below.

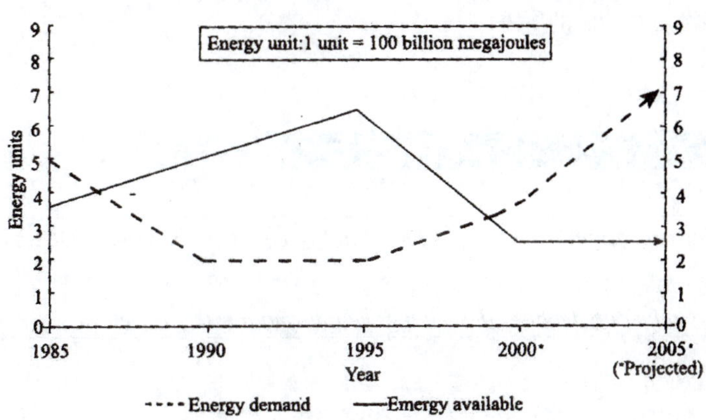

Sample Answer

The line graph indicates the changes of energy demand and the energy available from fossil fuels in Freedonia for 20 years to 2005.

According to the line graph, the amount of energy available from fossil fuels increased significantly from approximately 3.5 units(each unit is equivalent to 100 billion megajoules) in 1985 to 6.5 in 1995, which was its peak. But after that it dropped sharply until 2000 when it remained stable at about 2.5 units until 2005.

On the contrary, between 1985 and 1990, the demand for energy decreased gradually from 5 units to nearly 2 units. There was little change in this number from 1990 to 1995. Since 1995, it jumped suddenly. In 2000, this number increased to less than 4 units but after then it will go up more rapidly and reached 7 units in 2005.

It can be seen from the line graph that energy available was higher than energy demand from 1986 to 1999. However, after 1999, energy available was unable to keep up with energy demand.

▶考官评分:7分

译文:

该线状图显示了到2005年为止的20年间Freedonia地区化石燃料的能量需求和能量供应上的变化。

根据线状图，化石燃料的供应数量从1985年的3.5个单位（每个单位等价于一千亿焦耳）开始显著地增长，并在1995年达到了最多的6.5个单位。但随后该数字快速地下降，在2000年稳定在2.5个单位并一直延续到2005年。

与之相反，在1985年到1990年间，能源的需求从5个单位逐步减少到大约2个单位。从1990年到1995年这个数字有着微小的改变。自从1995年，该数字却陡然增加。到了2000年，增加到稍少于4个单位的水平，但之后又快速地增长，在2005年达到了7个单位。

从线状图能够得出在1986年至1999年间能源的供应量大于能源的需求量。然而，在1999年之后，供应量并不能满足对能源的所需。

4. 一个图表

The table below shows the figures for imprisonment in five countries between 1930 and 1980.

Write a report for a university lecturer describing the information shown below.

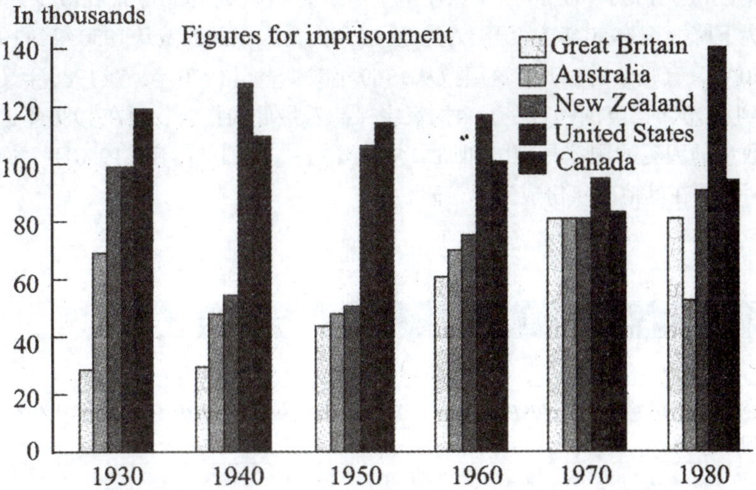

Sample Answer

The bar chart compares the numbers of prisoners in five countries from 1930 to 1980.

The number of prisoners in Great Britain increased from 30,000 in 1930 to 80,000 in 1980. The number of prisoners in Australia fell rapidly from 1930 to 1940, increased gradually to 1970 and then decreased sharply to 1980. The number of prisoners in New Zealand dropped sharply from 1930 to 1940, but then increased gradually to 1980.

The number of prisoners in the United States rose sharply from 1930 to 1940, and then decreased to 1950. The number decreased from 1960 to 1970, and then increased to 1980. The number of prisoners in Canada decreased slightly from 1930 to 1940, and then increased slightly to 1950. The number decreased from 1960 to 1970, and then increased to 1980.

From 1930 to 1970, Great Britain had the lowest figure among the five countries. In 1980, Australia had the lowest number. The country which had the highest number was either the United States or Canada. Canada had the highest number in 1930 and 1950. The United Sates had the highest number in other years.

▶考官评分:7分

译文:

柱状图对比五个国家从1930年至1980年的囚犯数量。

在英国，这个数量从1930年的30000增长到了1980年的80000。而在澳大利亚，囚犯数量从1930年至1940年迅速下滑，之后到1970间呈现出一个逐步上升的态势，而到了1980年这个数字又快速地减少了。这组数字就新西兰而言从1930年到1940年间是一个急剧下降的过程，但又逐渐上增加直至1980年。

美国的囚犯数量从1930年至1940年急剧地上升，之后直到1950年都在减少。而后在1960至1970年间表现为下降，至1980年为上升态势。在加拿大，囚犯的数量从1930年到1940年有轻微的下降，到了1950年又有轻微的上升。这组数从1960年减少直至1970年，在1980年又开始上升。

从1930年到1970年，英国一直在五个国家中保持着最低的指数。而在1980年，澳大利亚成为最低。有最高数量的囚犯的国家是美国和加拿大两国之一。在1930年至1950年，加拿大一直保持最高的数量。而美国在其他的年份成为了最高。

5. 一个图表

The bar chart shows the different modes of transport used to travel to and from work in one city, in 1950, 1970, 1990.

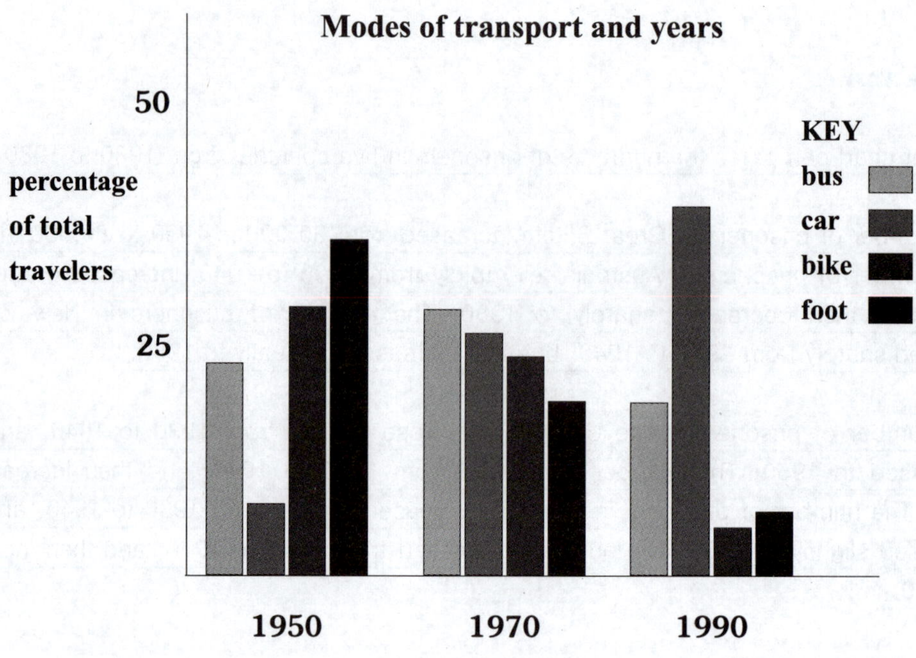

Sample Answer

The bar chart compares the use of different types of transportation for commuters in a city from 1950 to 1990.

The use of cars increased significantly from 1950 to 1990. In 1950, only a few people drove to work. But, in 1970, about one quarter of the people owned a car. By 1990, the number of people who went to work by car jumped to over 30%. The use of bus went up from 1950 to 1970 (approximately 20% and 30% respectively) and went down from 1970 to 1990 (under 20%).

During the same period, there were gradual decline in the use of bicycle and on foot. In 1950, more than half of the people were cycling or walking to work. In 1970, the use of bicycle and on foot still occupied over 40% . But in 1990, the number of these people decreased to less than 20%.

In1950, foot had the highest percentage in the four modes of transport, whereas cars had the lowest percentage. In 1970, bus was the most popular mode of transport, but foot became the least popular. However, in 1990, while automobiles have become the most popular means of transportation, bike was the least popular.

▶考官评分:8分

译文:

此图比较了从1950年到1990年城市上班族使用不同交通工具的情况。

从1950年到1990年，小汽车的使用数量有明显上升。在1950年，只有很少一部分人开车上班。在1970年，大约四分之一的人拥有了小汽车。到了1990年，开车上班的人数跃到了30%以上。公交车的使用从1950年到1970年呈递增趋势（分别是大约20%和30%），从1970年到1990年减少（低于20%）。

同一时期，骑车和步行的人逐步减少。在1950年，超过一半的人都是骑车或者步行上班。在1970年，骑车和步行的人数仍然占据了40%以上。但到了1990年，这些人数降至20%以下。

在1950年，步行在四种交通方式中占最高的比例，但是小汽车占的比例最低。在1970年，公共汽车是最普遍的交通工具，但步行成为了最不普遍的。然而，到了1990年汽车已经成为最普遍的交通工具，但是公共汽车是最不普遍的。

6. 一个图表

The table below shows the number of men and women who are more than 100 years old in 1911, 1941, 1971 and 2001 in UK.

Write a report for a university lecturer describing the information shown below.

	1911	1941	1971	2001
Males	73	131	287	536
Females	100	317	2035	4085
Total	173	449	2,322	4,621

Sample Answer

The table shows the number of men and women who are more than 100 years old in 1911, 1941, 1971 and 2001 in UK.

We can see from the table that the number of males increased gradually from 1911 to

2001. An interesting fact is that for every 30-year period, the number almost doubled. In 1911, 73 men lived more than 100 years, and in 1941, the number increased to 132. In 2001, the number was 536, which was about 8 times as much as in 1911.

It can be seen from the table that the number of females increased dramatically from 1911 to 2001. It increased three times from 1911(100) to 1941(317). Between 1941 and 1971, the number rose even more drastically, from 317 to 2035. It doubled from 1971 to 2001.

According to the table, in every year period, the number of women was larger than that of men, especially in 1971 and 2001, when the number of women was about 10 times greater than that of men.

▶考官评分:7分

译文:

这个表格分别显示出在1911年，1941年，1971年和2001年英国男性和女性百岁老人的数据。

从表格中我们可以看出，从1911年到2001年男性的数字逐步上升。一个有趣的现象是每隔30年，这个数字几乎都翻了一倍。在1911年，有73位男性的百岁老人，而在1941年这个数字增加到了132位。在2001年，这个数字是536位，几乎是1911年的八倍。

从表中还能够看出从1911年到2001年间女性的数量有着戏剧性的增加。从1911年的100人到1941年的317人，几乎是原来的三倍。1941年至1971年间，这个数字更是快速的增加，从317人达到了2035人。2001年又是1971年的两倍。

通过图表，每年女性的数字都要大于男性的数字，特别是在1971年至2001年，在2001年女性百岁老人更是男性的十倍。

7. 一个图表

The following table gives statistics showing the aspects of quality of life in five countries in 1982. Summarise the information by selecting and reporting the main features, and make comparisons where relevant.

Country	GN per head (US dollars)	Daily calorie supply per head	Life expectancy at birth (years)	Infant mortality rates (per 1000 live births)
Bangladesh	140	1,877	40	132
Bolivia	570	2,086	50	124
Egypt	690	2,950	56	97
Indonesia	580	2,296	49	87
USA	13,160	3,652	74	12

Sample Answer

The table illustrates four aspects of quality of life in five countries in 1982.

In terms of “GN per head”, USA had the highest number, which was 13,160 US dollars. Egypt occupied the second place with 690. Comparatively, the number of Indonesia was slightly higher than that of Bolivia(580 and 570 respectively). In the meantime, Bangladesh had the lowest number and the number of USA was about 100 times as much as that of Bangladesh.

As for “Daily calorie supply perhead”, we can see a similar pattern. USA had the highest number, while Bangladesh had the lowest. Although the number of Indonesia was much lower than that of Egypt, it was slightly higher than that of Bolivia.

In the area of “Life expectancy at birth”, USA ranked the first position, which was followed by Egypt. As to “Infant mortality rates”, the number of Bangladesh was about 10 times more than that of USA.

It can be seen from the table that American citizens enjoyed the highest quality of life in the five countries in 1982, whereas Bangladesh was the country which had the lowest quality of life.

▶考官评分:8分

译文:

这个表格显示了1982年五个国家生活质量的四个方面。

在GN per head这个项目上，美国占首位，是13160美元。埃及占据第二位，是690。比较而言，印度尼西亚的数字比玻利维亚的略高（分别是580和570）。同时，孟加拉国最低。美国的数字大约是孟加拉国的100倍。

至于每日卡路里摄入量这个项目，我们看到相似的规律。美国有着最高的数字，而孟加拉国有着最低的数字。虽然，印度尼西亚的数字比埃及的低很多，但它比玻利维亚的略高。

在寿命这个项目上，美国占据首位，埃及紧随其后。至于婴儿死亡率，孟加拉国比美国多10倍。

从表格中可以看到，美国公民1982年在五个国家中的生活质量最高，孟加拉国是这五个国家中生活质量最低的。

杨凡老师点评:

一个图的第二类典型题目，即“只有不同的对象，没有不同的时间”，占30%。写一个开头段，主体段落按项目分段，但最多写三段。在每段中对五个对象(五个国家)进行比较。最后可以写个结尾段，指出从图表中得出的结论。

8. 一个图表

The table below summarizes some data collected by a college bookshop for the month of February 1998.

Write a report describing the sales figures of various types of publications, based on the information shown in the table.

	Non - Book Club Members			Book Club Members	Total
	College Staff	College Students	Members of Public		
Fiction	44	31	0	76	151
Non-Fiction	29	194	122	942	1287
Magazines	332	1249	82	33	1696
Total	405	1474	204	1051	3134

Sample Answer

The table shows the sales figures of fiction books, non-fiction books, and magazines in a college bookshop for February 1995.

In terms of "Fiction", book club members had the highest number, which was 76. Comparatively, the number of college staff was slightly higher than that of college students (44 and 31 respectively). It is notable that no fiction books were sold to members of the public.

As for "Non-Fiction", book club members had the highest number, while college staff had the lowest. The number of book club members was about 30 times as much as that of college staff. In the meantime, the number of college students, which was 194, was slightly higher than that of members of the public, which was 122.

In the area of "Magazines", college students ranked the first position, which was followed by college staff. As to "Total", the number of college students was the highest and it was about 7 times as much as that of members of the public, which was the lowest.

▶考官评分:8分

译文:

这张表格显示了一所大学书店在1995年2月期间小说、非小说类书籍和杂志的销量情况。

对于"小说类"书籍，销售给图书俱乐部会员的数量为76，占据最多。相比较而言，大学教职工的购买量略多于大学生的（分别为44和31）。很明显，社会人群并没有购买小说类书籍。

至于"非小说类"图书，俱乐部成员拥有的数量最多，而大学教职工的则最低。俱乐部成员的数量是教职工的将近30倍。与此同时，大学生的是194，其数量略高于社会人群的122。

“杂志”部分，大学生排名第一，紧随教职工。关于“总量”，大学生拥有的数量最多，大约是数量最低的社会人群的七倍。

9. 一个图表

The table below summarizes some data about underground railway systems in 6 cities.

Write a report describing the information shown in the table.

Underground Railway Systems

City	Date opened	Kilometres of route	Passengers per year (in millions)
London	1863	394	775
Paris	1900	199	1191
Tokyo	1927	155	1927
Washington DC	1976	126	144
Kyoto	1981	11	45
Los Angeles	2001	28	50

Sample Answer

The table shows the details regarding the underground railway system in six cities.

London has the oldest underground railway system among the six cities. It was opened in the year 1863, and it is already 140 years old. Paris is the second oldest , in which it was opened in the year 1900. This is then followed by the opening of the railway system in Tokyo, Washington DC and Kyoto. Los Angles has the newest underground railway system and was only opened in the year 2001.

In terms of the size of the railway system, London, for certain, has the largest underground railway system. It has 394 kilometers of route in total, which is nearly twice as large as the system in Paris. Kyoto, in contrast, has the smallest system. It only has 11 kilometers of route, which is more than 30 times less than that of London.

Interestingly, Tokyo, which only has 155 kilometers of route, serves the greatest number of passengers per year, at 1927 millions of passengers. The system in Paris has the second greatest number of passengers, at 1191 million passengers per year. The smallest underground railway system, Kyoto, serves the smallest number of passengers per year.

▶考官评分:7分

译文：

该图表展示的是关于六个城市地铁系统的详细说明。

在这六个城市当中，伦敦有最古老的地铁系统，它于1863年开通，现在已经有140年的历史了。其次是1900年开通地铁的巴黎。然后是东京，华盛顿和京都的铁路先后开通。最近才拥有地铁系统的是洛杉矶，它在2001年才开通地铁。

就地铁系统的规模来说，伦敦无疑有着最庞大的地铁系统，它的线路总长394公里，这将近是巴黎地铁总长的两倍。相比之下，京都的地铁系统是最小的，它的线路总长只有11公里，比伦敦的小了30倍。

有意思的是，东京地铁线路的总长只有155公里，每年能够运载乘客的数量却十分惊人，1927年有成百万的乘客。巴黎的地铁系统拥有第二大的客流量，每年有1191百万乘客。作为拥有最小地铁系统的京都，每年客流量最小。

10. 一个图表

The bar chart shows the petroleum production and consumption among 7 regions in 2002.
Write a report for a university lecturer describing the information shown below.

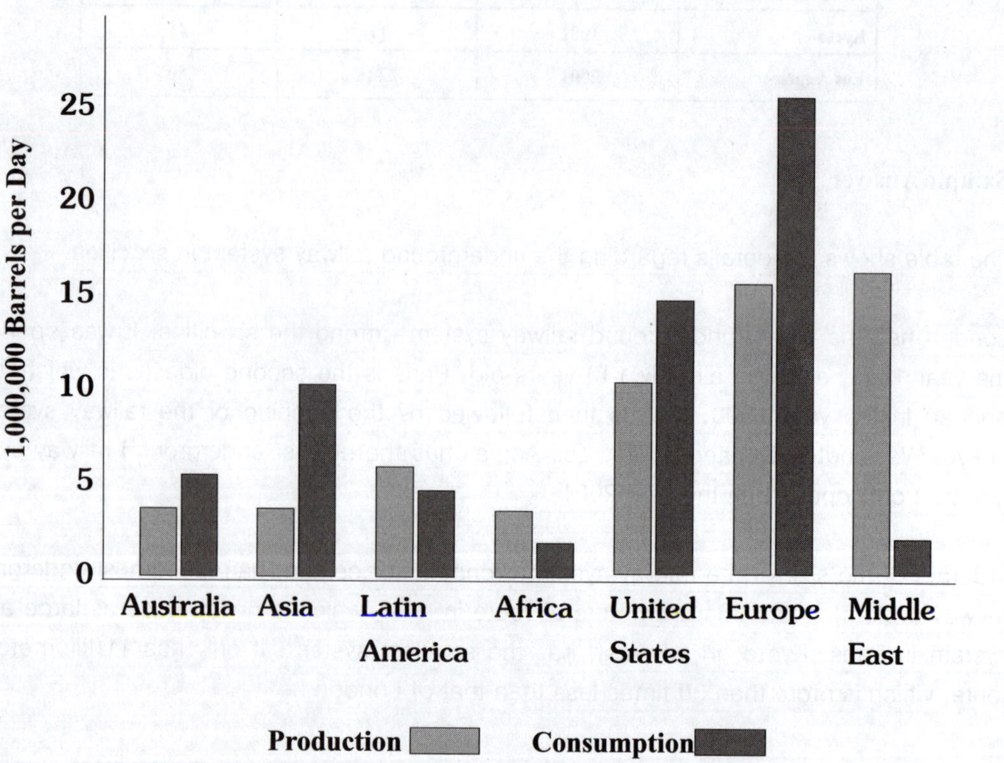

Sample Answer

The column graph compares the tremendous difference among 7 regions in petroleum production and consumption in 2002.

According to the graph, four regions—Australia, Asia, the US, and Europe—consumed more petroleum than they produced. The other regions—Latin America, Africa, and the Middle East—produced more petroleum than they consumed. Among them, the production of Latin America was only slightly over its need. The petroleum production of Africa doubled its consumption.

We can also see from the graph that the Middle East was the highest one in production (around 23 million barrels per day). The petroleum production of Europe and the US ranked the second and the third respectively, while Australia and Asia produced the least among the seven regions, with no more than 5 million barrels per day. However, the consumption of Europe and US ranked the first and the second respectively.

It seems that there was a big imbalance between petroleum production and consumption among the regions.

▶考官评分:7分

译文:

柱状图对比了在2002年七个地区石油产量和消耗量的极大差别。

通过图表可以看出，澳大利亚，亚洲，美国，以及欧洲这四个地区所消耗的石油总量比生产的数量大。其他地区——拉丁美洲，非洲，和中东——则生产了比其消耗量多的石油数量。在这三者之间，拉丁美洲的石油产量仅比所需要的数量略多。非洲的石油产量则是其消耗量的两倍。

我们还能看出中东的石油产量是最多的（每天两千三百万桶）。欧洲和美国的石油产量分别位于第二和第三位，澳大利亚和亚洲则在七个地区中产量最少，每天不超过五百万桶。然而，欧洲和美国的消耗量也分别的排在第一和第二位。

看起来在区域间的石油产量和消耗量存在着极大的不平衡。

11. 一个图表

The diagram below shows the distribution of men and women in key professions in Malaysia in 1970.
Describe the distribution of men and women in the professions in Malaysia, as indicated in the diagram.

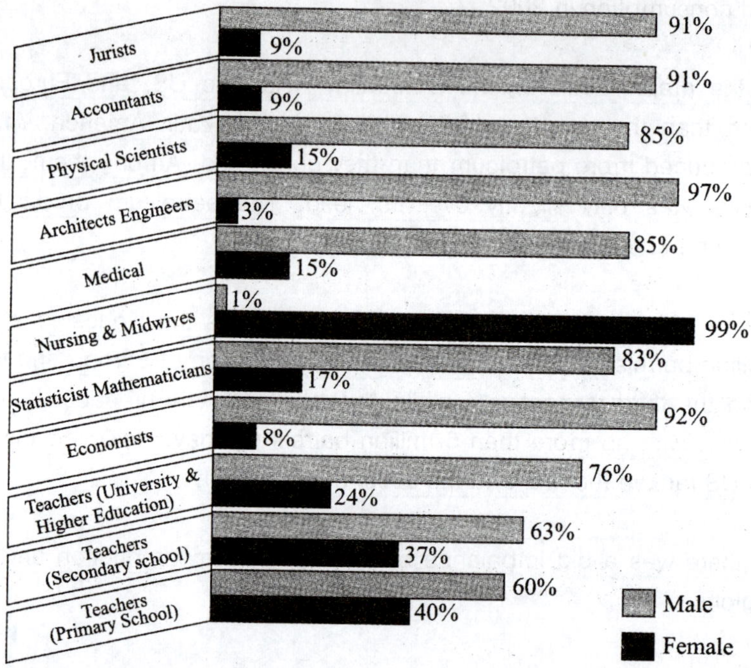

Sample Answer

The bar chart compares the male and female roles in key professions in Malaysia in 1970.

In 1970, the professions in Malaysia were almost totally dominated by men. Men occupied more than 90% of all positions in many key professions, including jurists, accountants, architects, engineers and economists. Architecture and engineering were particularly male-dominated, where men made up 97% but women only accounted for 3%.

Women were only slightly better in science and medicine, comprising around 15% of scientists, mathematicians, doctors and dentists. Women had considerably high percentage in the field of education. However, an interesting fact is that the proportion decreased according to the level, from around 40% of teachers in primary schools to under 25% of teachers in universities and higher education.

The only profession where women dominated was in nursing, the traditionally female area, with 99% of all nurses and midwives being women.

The diagram therefore shows that there existed serious sexual discrimination in employment in Malaysia in 1970.

▶考官评分:7分

译文：

该图显示了1970年在马来西亚男女角色在主要职业中的对比。

1970年，在马来西亚男性几乎控制了所有的职业。男性占据了很多主要职业的90%以上，其中包括法理学家，会计师，建筑师，工程师以及经济学家。在建筑学和工程学中这种现象表现得更为明显，在这两个领域中男性占97%，而女性只有3%。

女性在自然科学和医药领域的情况稍微好一点，在科学家，数学家，医生及牙医中有15%是女性。女性在教育领域有较高的比例。但是，有一个有趣的现象那就是随着级别的升高，比例降低，女性在初等学校中占40%，在大学或者高等教育领域占不到25%。

惟一女性占优势的职业是护理，它在传统意义上就是女性的领域，在护士和助产士中有99%都是女性。

因此这个图表显示了1970年马来西亚的职业统计中存在着严重的性别歧视。

12. 一个图表

The graph below shows the number of people at a London underground station from 6:00 to 22:00.
Write a report for a university lecturer describing the information shown below.

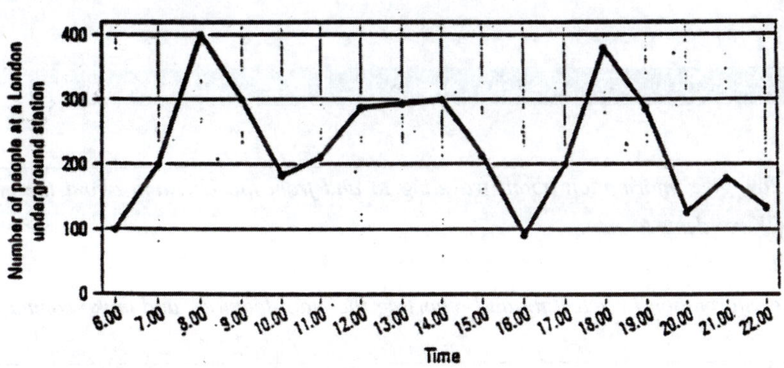

Sample Answer

The line graph describes the number of people using a London underground station over 16 hours (6 am to 10 pm).

We can see from the line graph that at 6 am the number of people at the station is only 100, which is one of its lowest points. After that, the number shoots up until 8 am, peaking at 400. However, there is a drastic drop in the number over the next two hours. The period between 10 am and 12 noon witnesses a moderate growth in the number of people in the station, with the number reaching 280 at mid-day. There is little change in the number from 12 noon to 2 pm and then the number plummets until 4 pm when it reaches its bottom at 100. The next two hours see a dramatic rise in the number again. After 6 pm, number suffers from a dramatic fall until 10 pm, with a slight rise from 8 pm to 9 pm.

It can be seen from the line graph that the number of people at the station reaches its highest point at the time when people go out for and return from work.

▶考官评分:8分

译文:

这个曲线图显示了在16个小时（上午6点到晚上10点）中，使用一个伦敦地铁站的人数。

我们从这个图中可以看到，在6点这个车站的人数是100，是最低点之一。之后，这个数字急剧上升，在8点达到最高点，是400。然后，这个数字在接下来的2个小时急剧下降。这个数字在10点到12点适度增加，中午12点达到280。从12点到下午2点，这个数字几乎没有变化。然后，这个数字从2点到4点急剧下降。在下午4点达到最低点100。接下来的2个小时，这个数字再次剧烈上升。6点以后直到10点，再次下降，但8点到9点轻微上升。

从曲线图中可以看出，站台上的人数在上下班时达到高峰。

杨凡老师点评:

这是一个图的第三类典型题目，占10%左右。它的特点是“只有不同的时间，没有不同的对象”。这样的题目，通常写2–3段：先写一个开头段，主体段落只写一段，描述这个对象在这段时间的变化。最后，可以写一个结尾段，指出图表所反映的规律。

13. 两个图表

The charts below give information about traveling to and from the UK, and about the most popular countries for UK residents to visit.

Summarise the information by selecting and reporting the main features, and make comparisons where relevant.

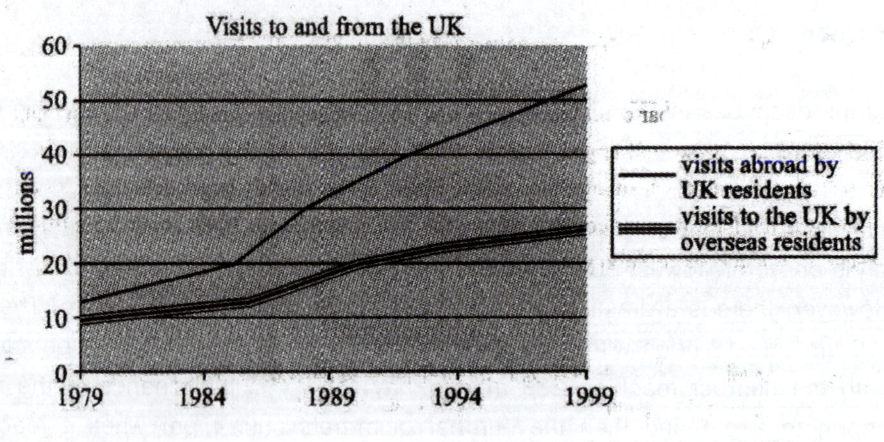

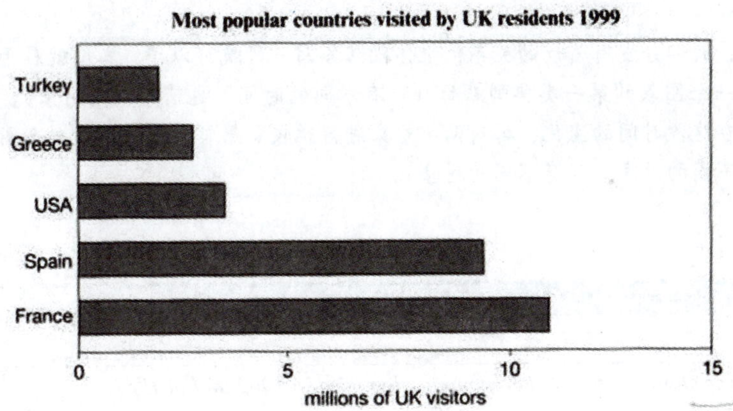

Sample Answer

The line graph shows the information about traveling to and from UK for 20 years to 1999. The bar chart compares the five most popular countries for UK residents in 1999.

We can see from the line graph that there was a slight increase in the number of visits abroad by UK residents from 12 million in 1979 to 20 million in 1985. However, after that, the number rose sharply until 1999, peaking at a little over 50 million. During the same time period, there was a slow growth in the number of visits to UK by overseas residents. From 1979 to 1999, the number of visits abroad was larger than that of visits to UK.

It can be seen from the bar chart that France was the most popular country for UK residents in 1999. Spain had the second largest number of UK visitors in the five countries. Although the number to USA was much smaller than that to Spain, it was slightly larger than that to Greece. Turkey was the least popular country among the five countries. In 1999, about 2.5 million of UK travelers had been to Turkey.

▶考官评分:8分

译文:

线状图显示了到1999年为止的20年间从英国出发旅游和来到英国旅游的信息。柱状图则对比了在1999年英国居民最喜爱的五个国家。

从线状图中我们可以看出英国居民出境旅游的人数从1979年的一千两百万人次轻微的增长到1985年的两千万人次。然而，在那之后，到1999年这个数字迅速的增长，最多时达到五千万以上。在同一时期，外国游客到英国旅游的人数只是缓慢的增长。从1979年到1999年，到国外旅游的人数要比到英国参观的人数多。

从柱状图中我们可以看出，在1999年对英国居民来说法国是最受欢迎的国家。在这五个英国旅游者最多的国家中西班牙位居第二。尽管前往美国的人数远远小于去西班牙的人数，但依旧比到希腊的人数略微多些。在这五个国家中土耳其是受欢迎程度最小的。在1999年，有大约两百五十万的英国游客来过土耳其。

杨凡老师点评：

两个图表，大部分没有密切的关系，主体段落各写一段就可以了。本图就属于这种情况。第一个图，属于一个图表的第一类典型题目（既有不同的时间，也有不同的对象）。所以，先分别描述两个对象在这段时间的变化，再对两个对象进行比较。第二个图，属于一个图表的第二类典型题目（没有不同的时间，只有不同的对象）。

14. 两个图表

The two pie charts show the types of communication used in 1962 and in 1982.
Write a report to describe the information shown in the graph.

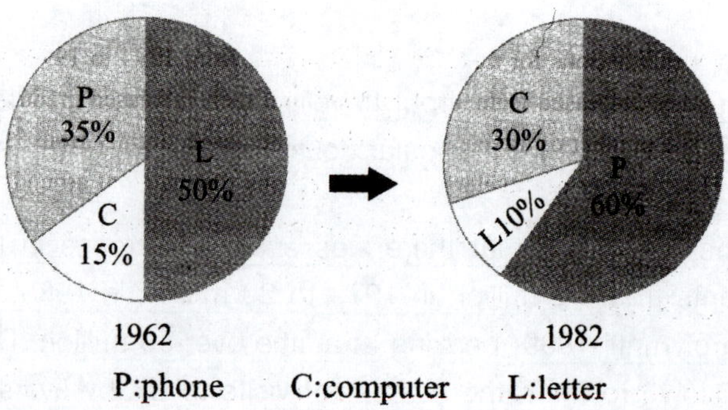

Sample Answer

The two pie charts compare different methods of communication used in 1962 and 1982.

We can see from the first pie chart that in 1962, letter writing was the most popular form of communication, taking up 50% of the total. At that time, the use of telephone just occupied 35% and computer was the least used form of the three methods (15%).

It can be seen from the second pie chart that in 1982, the telephone, at 60%, has become the most used form of communication. 30% of people used computers to communicate with others. However, writing letter, which was only 10%, was the least popular type of communication.

From 1962 to 1982, the use of the phone and computers both increased significantly. The use of phone increased from 35% to 60%. Similarly, the use of computers doubled to 30%. On the contrary, during this same period, the use of letter writing decreased dramatically.

▶考官评分:8分

译文：

这两个饼状图比较了1962年和1982年之间通讯方法的不同。

从第一个饼图，我们看到，在1962年，写信是最流行的通讯方式，占到了全部的50%。同时，使用电话的仅仅占35%。在三种方法中，使用电脑的最少(15%)。

从第二个图可以看到，在1982年，使用电话的占60%，成为了最常用的通讯方式。30%的人使用计算机与他人交流。然而，写信，只占10%，是最不受欢迎的交流方式。

从1962年到1982年，使用电话和计算机都有很明显的增长。电话从35%增加到60%。同样的，使用计算机的人数也翻倍到了30%。然而，这段时间，写信的使用人数急剧下降。

杨凡老师点评：

两个图表，少数情况下有密切的关系，主体段落写三段，先各用一段分别描述两个图表，再写一段，比较两个图表中的数据。本图就属于这种情况。这两个饼图，都属于一个图表的第二类典型题目（没有不同的时间，只有不同的对象）。

15. 两个图表

The line graph shows the percentage of people who have criminal records at different ages of both males and females, and the pie chart indicates the percentage of males and females in prison in the UK in 2000.

Write a report for a university lecturer describing the information shown below.

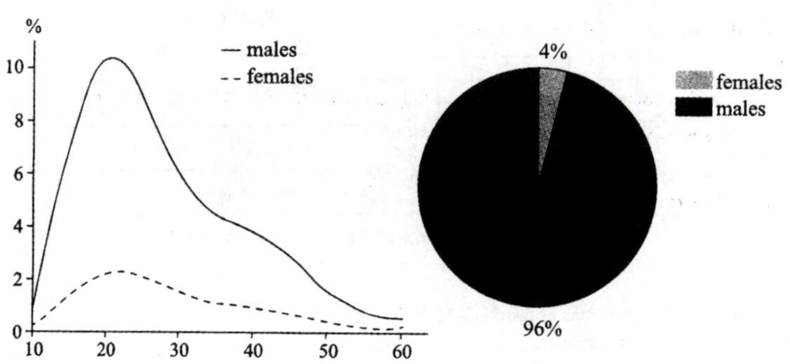

Sample Answer

The line graph compares the percentage of men and women who have criminal records at different ages. The pie chart shows the percentage of men and women in prison in the UK in 2000.

According to the line graph, the percentage of men who have criminal records increased sharply from 10 years old to 20 years old, peaking at around 10%. From 20 years old to 50 years old, the percentage decreased dramatically. The percentage of women also rose from 10 years old to 20 years old and declined from 20 years old to 50 years old but it was not so drastic. It reached its highest point at 2% when women are 20 years old. We can also see from the line graph that the percentage of men was much higher than that of women in every age.

From the pie chart, it can be seen that the percentage of men in prison, which was 96%, was substantially higher than that of women(4%).

▶考官评分:7分

译文:

线状图对比了不同年龄段男性与女性的犯罪比例。饼状图则显示了在2000年男性与女性的入狱比例。

通过线状图能看出从10岁到20岁男性的犯罪比例快速增长，最高时大约10%。从20岁到50岁之间，该比例急剧地下降。女性的犯罪比例从10岁到20岁间也有上升，从20岁到50岁也有下降，但都不是非常迅猛。女性在20岁时达到最高为2%。我们从线状图中还能看出每个年龄段男性的犯罪比例都远高于女性。

通过饼状图能看出男性的入狱比例大约是96%，该数字远远高于女性的4%。

16. 两个图表

The chart below shows the amount of money per week spent on fast foods in Britain. The graph shows the trends in consumption of fast foods.

Expenditure on fast foods by income groups

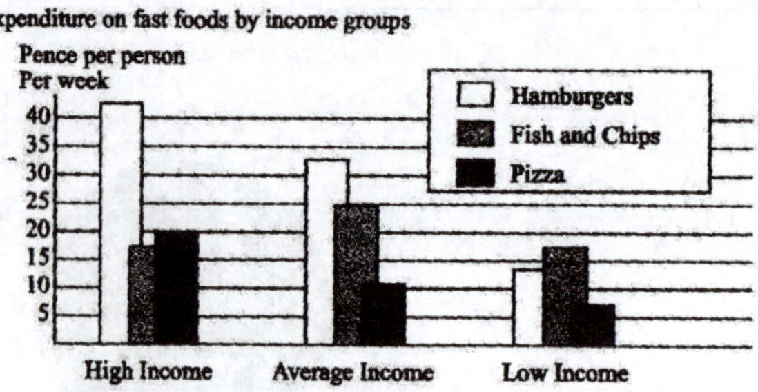

Consumption of fast foods 1970-1990

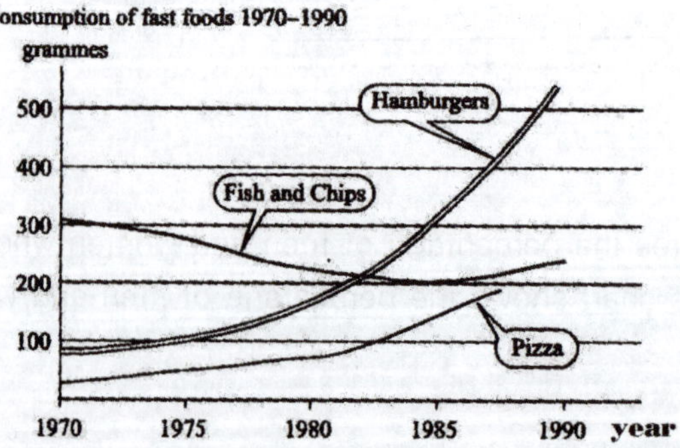

Sample Answer

The bar chart shows the amount of money expended on fast food according to three different income groups. Hamburger is the most popular fast food in the high and average income groups. People in high income spend over 40 pence per person per weak on the consumption of hamburger. Although fish and chips is the most popular food for those in low income, it is the least popular for those in the high income. Pizza, on the other hand, is not very popular among the low income group.

The line graph indicates the general pattern of fast food consumption between 1970 and 1990. Obviously, there was a sharp increase in the consumption of hamburger during this time period. In 1970, people in Britain ate less than 100 grams of hamburger per person per week. By 1990, this number increased to over 500 grams. Pizza also increased but it was not so dramatic. Fish and chips, however, dropped slightly. Before around 1983, Fish and chips was the most popular fast food. However, after that, hamburger increased sharply and it became much more popular than the other two fast foods.

▶考官评分:7分

译文:

该柱状图显示了三个不同收入群体在快餐上花费的钱数。汉堡在中高收入/中等收入群体中是最受欢迎的食物，高收入的人每人每周在汉堡上要花40多便士。虽然炸鱼和薯条是低收入群体最喜欢的食物，但它在高收入人群中却是最不受欢迎的。相反，比萨在中低收入人群中不太受欢迎。

曲线图显示了1970到1990间快餐消费的总体格局。显然，在这一时期内汉堡的消费量大幅度增加。1970年，在英国每人每周吃不到100克的汉堡。到1990年，这个数字已经增加到500克。比萨的消费量也在增加但没有这么显著。而炸鱼和薯条的消费量略有下降。约在1983年前，炸鱼和薯条是最受欢迎的快餐食品，然而在此之后，汉堡的消费量大幅增加并变得远比其他两种快餐食品更流行。

17. 两个图表

The first chart below shows the results of a survey which sampled a cross-section of 100,000 people asking if they traveled abroad and why they traveled for the period 1994-1998. The second chart shows their destinations over the same period.

Write a report for a university lecturer describing the information shown below.

VISITS ABROAD BY UK RESIDENTS BY PURPOSE OF VISIT (1994-1998)					
	1994	1995	1996	1997	1998
Holiday	15,246	14,898	17,896	19,703	20,700
Business	3,155	3,188	3,249	3,639	3,957
Visits to friends and relatives	2,689	2,628	2,774	3,051	1,181
Other reasons	982	896	1,030	1,054	990
TOTAL	22,072	21,610	24,949	27,447	28,828

DESTINATIONS OF VISITS ABROAD BY UK RESIDENTS BY MAIN REGION (1994-1998)				
	Western Europe	**North America**	**Other areas**	**Total**
1994	19,371	919	1,782	22,072
1995	18,944	914	1,752	21,610
1996	21,877	1,167	1,905	24,949
1997	23,661	1,559	2,227	27,447
1998	24,519	1,823	2,486	28,828

Sample Answer

The first table reveals reasons for travel by UK residents from 1994 to 1998. The number of travelers for holiday decreased from 1994 to 1995, but then increased gradually, peaking at 20,700 in 1998. The number of travelers for business increased slightly from 3,155 in 1994 to 3,957 in 1998. The number of travelers for other reasons fluctuated at around 1,000. Among the four reasons, holiday and business had the largest and second largest number. Comparatively, a smaller number of people had been to other countries to see friends and relatives. Other reasons had the smallest number.

The second table indicates which areas UK residents visited during this time period. The number of travelers to Western Europe increased from 19,371 in 1994 to 24,519 in 1998. The number of travelers to North America doubled from 919 in 1994 to 1,823 in 1998. The number of travelers to other areas increased from 1,782 in 1994 to 2,486 in 1998. Among the three destinations, Western Europe had the highest number and North America had the lowest number.

▶考官评分:7分

译文:

第一张表格显示在1994至1998年间英国居民旅游的目的。度假的旅行者从1994年至1995年呈递减的态势，但是随后逐渐增长，到1998年到达顶峰为20700人。商务出行者在1994至1998年间从3155轻微地增长至3957。其他原因的出行者大约在1000上下起伏不定。在这四个原因中间，度假和商务分别占到了第一位和第二位。相比较而言，去看望朋友或亲属的人相对较少。由于其他原因而出行的人占了最小的一部分。

第二张表显示出在这段时期英国居民出行的地区。到西欧的旅行者从1994年的19371人增长到1998年的24519人。去北美的人数则翻了一倍。从1994年的919人至1998年的1823人。去其他地区的人数也从1994年的1782人增长到了1998年的2486人。从这三个目的地来看，西欧仍是人们的首选，而去北美的人数则为最少。

18. 两个图表

The graphs below indicate the effect of treatment in two types of cancer in females.
Using the information in the graphs, describe and compare the situation with and without treatment for the two types of cancer.

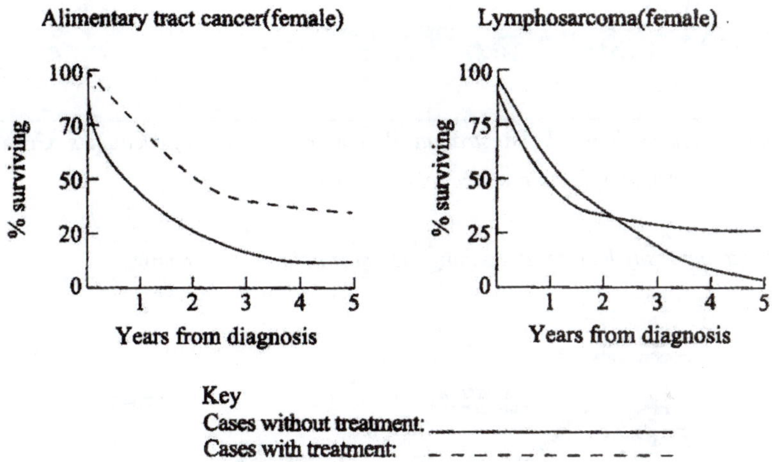

Sample Answer

The two graphs show the situation with and without treatment for two types of cancer in women: cancer of the alimentary tract and lymphosarcoma.

For cancer of the alimentary tract, treatment can be reasonably effective. Whereas only 30% of patients survive one year after diagnosis without treatment, when treatment is applied about 75% of patients survive one year. Without treatment, fewer than 25% of patients survive for five years after diagnosis, but with treatment the survival rate after five years increases to nearly 50%.

For lymphosarcoma, however, treatment can have a negative effect. The survival rate one year after diagnosis is around 30%, whether treatment is applied or not. However, survival rate with treatment is lower than that without treatment beyond one year. After five years, 25% of untreated patients are still alive, whereas none of the cases studied who have received treatment survive for five years after diagnosis.

▶考官评分:7分

译文:

这两个曲线图显示了接受治疗和没有接受治疗的两类癌症女性患者的状况：食道癌和淋巴癌。

对于食道癌，治疗可以取得相当的效果。虽然，在确诊后的一年里，没有接受治疗的患者中仅仅有30%的人幸存，与此同时，接受治疗的患者在一年后有75%的人幸存。在确诊5年后，没有接受治疗的患者中不到25%的人能够幸存，但是接受治疗的患者在5年后幸存的比率增长到接近50%。

然而，对于淋巴癌，治疗会起到副作用。不管是否接受治疗，确诊一年后的幸存比率大约在30%左右。然而，一年后接受治疗的人要比没有接受治疗的人的幸存比率低。5年后，没有接受治疗的患者有25%的人还活着，然而确诊5年后，在接受治疗的人中没有存活的案例。

19. 过程图

The diagram below shows how The Australian Bureau of Meteorology collects UP-to-the-minute information on the weather in order to produce reliable forecasts.

Write a report for a university lecturer describing the information shown below.

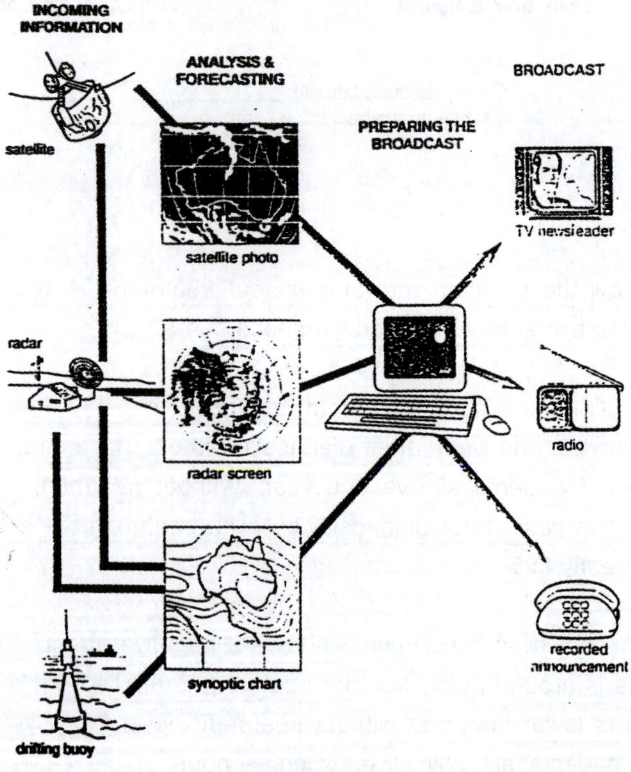

Sample Answer

The diagram illustrates in four stages how the Australian Bureau of Meteorology gets its weather information to make weather forecasts.

In the first stage, it can be seen from the diagram that there is the "incoming information". Raw data is collected from outer space, on land, or at sea, using satellite, radar, and drifting buoy respectively. Next, we can see from the diagram that this data is analyzed and forecasted by experts. At this stage, experts study satellite photos, radar screens, and synoptic charts to determine weather conditions. Stage three of the process is when the information is prepared for broadcast. At this point, it is done through computer which sends the weather data to the media. In the last stage, it is obvious from the diagram that the weather data is broadcast to the general public via TV, radio and telephone (recorded announcement).

To sum up, the process diagram shows how weather data is collected, studied, prepared, and finally broadcast.

▶考官评分:7分

译文:

这个图表显示出澳大利亚气象局为预报天气而获得天气信息的四个阶段。

通过图表可以看出，第一个阶段是信息搜集。从外层空间、陆地上、海洋中，使用卫星、雷达和各个漂流的浮筒得到原始数据。然后由专家分析这些数据并预测。在这个阶段，专家们研究卫星图片、雷达屏幕和气象图以确定气候条件。为预报准备信息是预报过程的第三个阶段。这是通过计算机发送有关天气数据到媒体的第四个阶段，在这个阶段，很明显，天气信息通过电视、广播和电话（录音公告）来向大众预报。

因此，这个过程图说明了气候信息是如何被搜集、研究、准备并最终预报的。

杨凡老师点评:

过程图，也叫流程图，出现的概率是20%。很多考生谈虎色变，生怕遇到这种图表。实际上，过程图并不那么可怕。它有完整的模板式句型。

20. 过程图

Using the information in the diagram, write a description of how a refrigerator works.
You may use your own knowledge and experience in addition to the diagram.

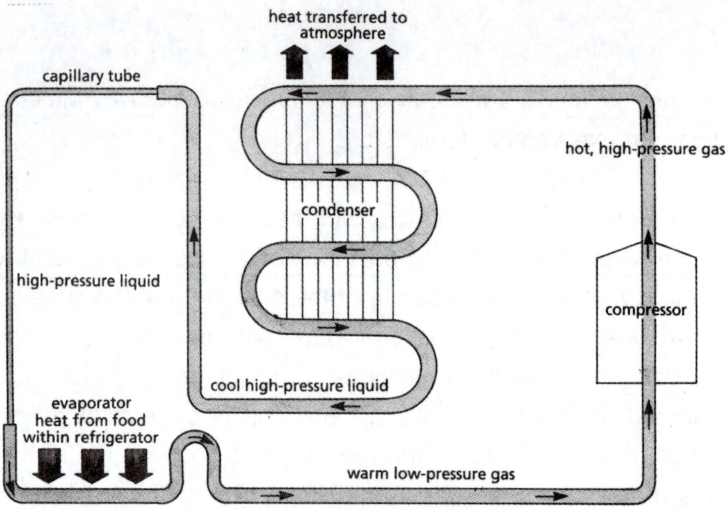

Sample Answer

The diagram shows in four stages how a refrigerator works.

According to the diagram, in the first stage, high-pressure liquid flows in the capillary tube. Food within the refrigerator sends out vapor. In this stage, the high-pressure liquid is heated by the vapor to warm low-pressure gas. Next, the warm low-pressure gas flows ahead, arriving at the compressor. At this stage, it is compressed to hot high-pressure gas. Stage three of the process is when the hot high-pressure gas passes the condenser, where it is cooled to high-pressure liquid. Where is the heat then? It is transferred to atmosphere. Finally, the cool high-pressure liquid continues to flow forward and enters the capillary tube. At this point, it is heated by the vapor from food within the refrigerator again and a new cycle begins.

Thus, the process diagram illustrates the principle of the refrigerator.

▶考官评分:7分

译文:

这张图表展示出电冰箱是如何工作的。

根据这个图表，在第一阶段，高压液体流进细管道。冰箱中的食物放出蒸气。在这一阶段，高压液体被蒸汽加热成低压气体。然后，低压温热气体向前运动至压缩机处。在这一阶段，它被压缩成高压热气体。这个过程的第三个阶段是这些高压热气体通过冷凝器，在那它们被冷却成高压液体。那么，热到什么地方去了呢？此时，它们已经被转移到了大气当中。最后，这些凉的高压液体继续流入细管道。此时，它再一次被冰箱中食物的蒸汽加热，一个新的循环开始了。

因此，这个图显示了冰箱的工作原理。

21. 过程图

As a class assignment you have been asked to write a description of how this plastic is produced and then broken down.

Using the information in the diagram, write a description of the cycle.
You may use your own knowledge and experience in addition to the diagram.

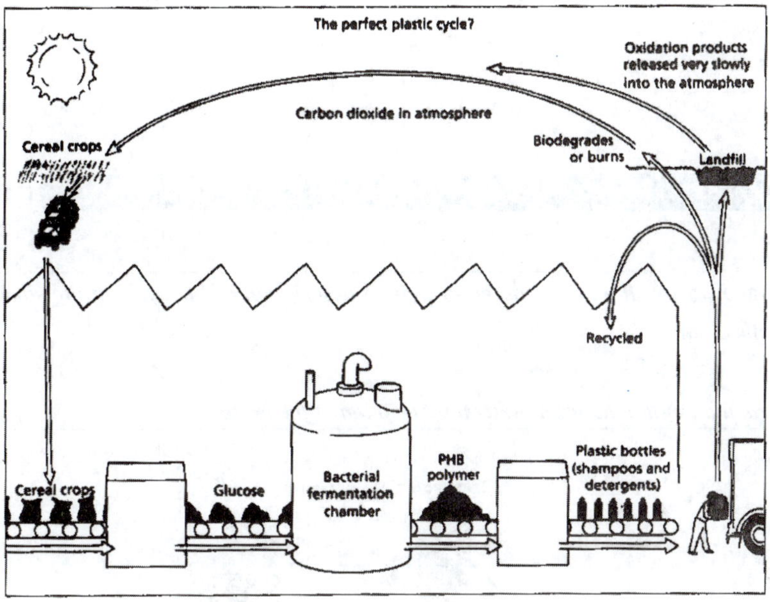

Sample Answer

The diagram shows in four stages how plastic is produced and then broken down.

According to the diagram, in the first stage, cereal crops are harvested and taken to a factory. Next, in the factory, glucose is extracted from cereal crops. Stage three of the process is when the glucose then passes into a bacterial fermentation chamber, where the process of fermentation produces a type of plastic called PHB polymer. This can be used to make plastic bottles to hold shampoos and detergents. When these plastic bottles are thrown away, they may be disposed in three ways. First, they may be recycled. Another way is that they may also be filled in land. In this way, the oxidation products from the landfill sites are released slowly into the atmosphere. Other discarded bottles are burnt or biodegraded and send out carbon dioxide into atmosphere. Finally, cereal crops require carbon dioxide in order to grow, and these crops are used in the manufacture of the new plastic.

Thus, the process diagram illustrates the cycle of the plastic.

▶考官评分:7分

译文:

这个图显示了在四个阶段里塑料是如何制成和分解的。

根据这个图，在第一阶段，谷物收获以后会被运到工厂去。然后，在工厂里，葡萄糖从谷物中萃取出来。这个过程的第三个阶段是葡萄糖通过细菌发酵室，在这里通过发酵过程产生一种塑料，叫做PHB聚合体。这种塑料可以被制作成用来装洗发水或清洁剂的瓶子。当这种塑料瓶子被丢弃以后，它们可能以三种方式被处理。首先，他们可能被回收。另一种方式是它们也有可能被掩埋到地下。这种情况下，掩埋地点的氧化物缓慢地释放到大气中。其他被丢弃的瓶子会被燃烧或被生物降解，并且会向大气中释放二氧化碳。最后，谷物为了生长需要二氧化碳，它们又会被用来制作成新的塑料。

因此，这个图显示了塑料的循环过程。

22. 过程图

As a class assignment you have been asked to write a description of life cycle of the silkworm and the production of silk cloth.

Using the information in the diagram, write a description of the cycle.

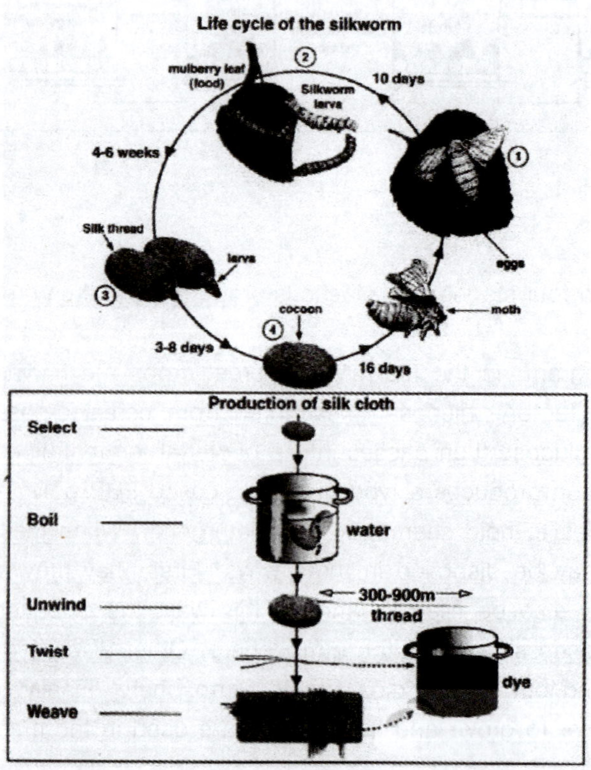

Sample Answer

The first diagram shows that there are four main stages in the life of the silkworm. First of all, eggs are produced by the moth and it takes ten days for each egg to become a silkworm larva that feeds on mulberry leaves. This stage lasts for up to six weeks until the larva produces a cocoon of silk thread around itself. After a period of about three weeks, the adult moths eventually emerge from these cocoons and the life cycle begins again.

The cocoons are the raw material used for the production of silk cloth. Once selected, they are boiled in water and the threads can be separated in the unwinding stage. Each thread is between 300 and 900 metres long, which means they can be twisted together, dyed and then used to produce cloth in the weaving stage.

Overall, the diagrams show that the cocoon stage of the silkworm can be used to produce silk cloth through a very simple process.

▶考官评分:8分

译文:

第一个图表展示了蚕的生命当中最主要的四个阶段。首先，蛾子产下卵，每个卵都要经过十天的时间孵化成以桑树树叶为食物的蚕的幼虫。这个阶段会持续多达六个星期，直到幼虫用吐出的蚕丝包裹着自己形成一个茧。大约三个星期后，成年蛾子终于从蚕茧中脱离出来，同时，一个新的生命周期又开始了。

蚕茧是用于生产制造丝质衣物的原始材料。一经选定，这些蚕茧就会被放到水中煮沸，蚕丝就会在这个退卷阶段分开。每根蚕丝大概有300到900米长，这也就意味着它们能够拧到一起，经过染色和编织然后用于制造衣物。

总的来说，这个图表所展示的就是从蚕茧阶段到能够用于制造丝质衣物的一个非常简单的过程。

23. 过程图

The chart below shows the shaping and growth of the forests in Yellowstone National Park after a fire disaster.

Write a report for a university lecturer describing the information shown below.

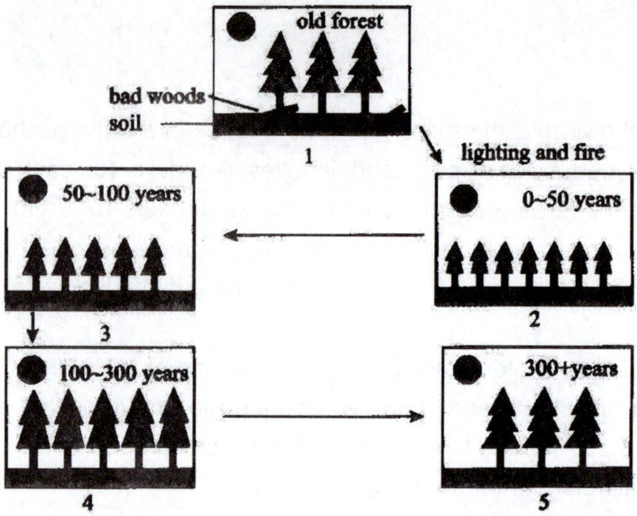

Sample Answer

The diagram illustrates in four stages the recovery of the forests in Yellowstone National Park after a fire disaster.

According to the diagram, in the first picture, while the old forests still exist, they drop bad wood to the soil under them, which makes the soil more fertile. Then lightning and fire strike, destroying the forests completely. And the growth of new forests starts right at this point. The second picture demonstrates that in the first 50 years after the devastating fire, saplings emerge where the old forests used to stand. The second five decades see the saplings grow in build while descend in overall number. In the next two centuries, the young trees continue to thrive in Yellowstone, because of the fertile soil and the ample sunlight. Then, three hundred years after the fire, the number of trees decline to roughly the same as the old forests.

These five pictures show us that it takes as long as three centuries for a destroyed forest to fully recover.

▶考官评分:7分

译文:

这个图表显示了火灾过后黄石国家公园恢复森林的四个阶段。

通过图表，在第一个图中，在曾经的森林尚在的时候，树木在它们下面的土地上落下朽木，使土壤更加肥沃。之后由于闪电和火灾，森林被完全破坏。新生森林的生长从这时候开始。第二图显示了在毁灭性火灾过后的50年中，树苗从那些曾经的森林上生长出来。随后的50年显示这些树苗在整体数目下降的同时个体在形态上继续生长。在接下来的两个世纪中，这些年轻的树木由于有着肥沃的土壤和充足的阳光，因而继续在黄石公园中茁壮生长。然后，在火灾发生的三百年之后，树木的数量下降到与原来森林树木数量大致相同的水平。

这五张图片为我们说明一个被破坏的森林只要经过三个世纪就可以完全恢复。

24. 地图

The diagrams below show the development of the village of Kelsbey between 1780 and 2000.

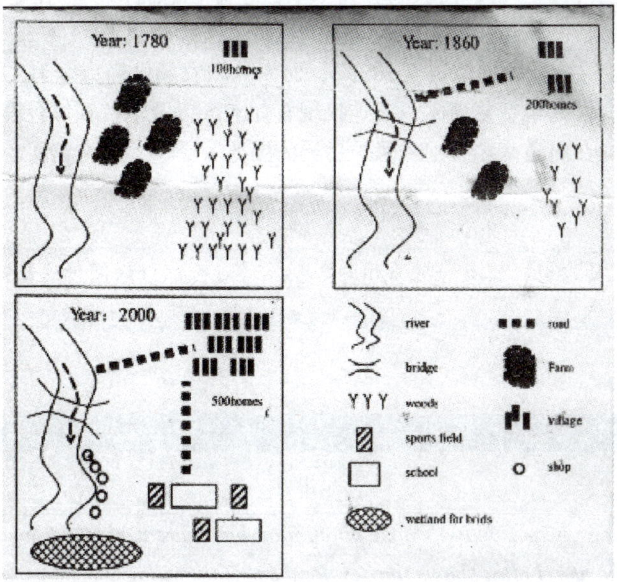

Sample Answer

The three diagrams illustrate what the village of Kelsbey looked like in 1780, 1860 and 2000.

In 1780, Kelsbey had only 100 homes in the northeast, but there were a lot of woods in the east of the village and four farms in the middle. In the western part of the village, there was a river running from north to south.

The year 1860 saw a doubling in the number of homes. However, the number of farms and woods decreased dramatically. At that time, a bridge could be seen over the river and a road was constructed, linking the river to the homes.

140 years later, the number of homes increased drastically to 500, but the farms and woods completely disappeared. Some schools and sports fields were established in the southeast of the village. A new southbound road was built, which connected the residential areas with the schools and sports facilities. Some shops opened along the eastern part of the river and to the south of the river, a wetland for birds came into being.

▶考官评分:8分

译文:

这三张图片显示了Kelsbey村1780年、1860年和2000年的情况。

1780年，在Kelsbey的东北部仅有100户人家，而村子的东部有大片的树林以及四个农场在村子的中部，村子西边一条河流贯穿南北。

1860年家庭的数量翻了一番，而农场和树木的数量却在急剧减少，在这个时候，可以看到一座桥梁横跨于河的上方，一条连接河流和住宅区的道路也被修建起来。

140年以后，房屋的数量大幅增长至500户，而树林和农场已经完全消失。村子的东南面修建了一些学校和体育场，同时也新修建了一条连接现有住宅区以及学校和体育设施的环南公路。在河的东岸开了很多店铺而在河道南端有一片保护鸟类的湿地。

杨凡老师点评:

地图题没有固定的模板，但有一些常用的句型。读者可以仔细阅读这篇范文，从中学习如何描述方位和有什么物体。

25. 地图

Chorleywood is a village near London whose population has increased steadily since the middle of the nineteenth century. The map below shows the development of the village.

Write a report for a university lecturer describing the development of the village.

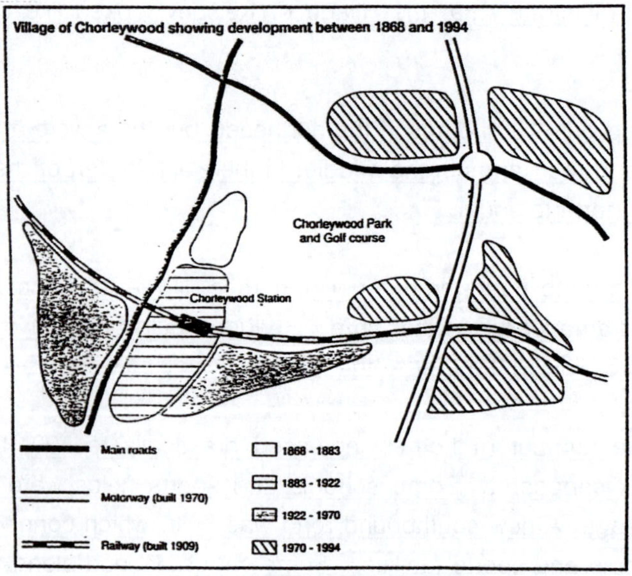

Sample Answer

This map illustrates in four stages the development of Chorleywood, a small London village, from 1868 to 1994.

According to the map, the first period was from 1868 to 1883. At this time, Chorleywood only had one small area and two crossing main roads. The next period was from 1883 to 1922. During this time, there emerged another habitation to the south of the original small area, which was almost twice bigger than the former one. In 1909, a railway, parallel with the eastbound main road, came into being. It went through the new habitation and formed an intersection with another main road as well. Next, from 1922 to 1970, along the western part of the newly-built railway, two large areas took shape. Finally, 1970 saw another great change in Chorleywood. A southbound motorway was built linking the railway and the eastbound main road. Since then, another five living areas were founded, scattering along the motorway.

Therefore, the map shows that thanks to the construction of the railway and the motorway, the land of Chorleywood expanded significantly from 1868 to 1994.

▶考官评分:7分

译文:

这张图表描述的是伦敦小镇Chorleywood从1868年到1994年的四个发展阶段。

通过这张图可知，第一个阶段是从1868年到1883年。在这段时间，该地只有一小块区域和两条交叉的主路。下一个时期是1883年到1922年。在这段时期，在原来地区的南部形成了另一个几乎相当于过去两倍的新居民区。1909年，开始修建一条与东西向主路平行的铁路。它穿过新居民区并且和另一条主路也有个交点。然后，从1922年到1970年，沿着新建铁路的西部形成两大地区。最后，1970年Chorleywood地区发生了新的变化。一条通向南北方向的高速路被建成，它和铁路以及东西向的主路相连。从那时候开始，新建了五个居住区，分散在高速公路周边。

因此，这个图表明，Chorleywood地区从1868年到1994年显著的发展归功于铁路和高速公路的建设。

26. 地图

The map below is of the town of Garlsdon. A new supermarket(S) is planned for the town. The map shows two possible sites for the supermarkets. Summarize the information by selecting and reporting the main features and make comparisons where relevant.

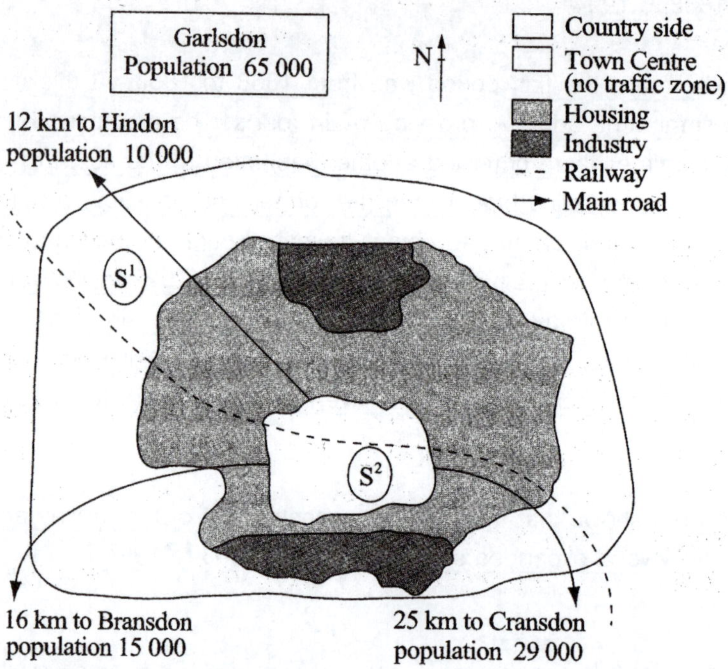

Sample Answer

The map displays two possible locations for the construction of a new supermarket in the town of Garlsdon.

As is indicated in the map, the first potential site for the new supermarket is located in the countryside. This site is 12 km to Hindon, an area with a population of 10,000, and lies between the railway and main road linking the city center. Therefore, it is quite convenient for people to do shopping at S1 by taking trains or driving cars. Moreover, S1 is in the outskits of Garlsdon, people doing shopping there will have no trouble with parking.

Conversely, the second suggested site is just in the center of Garlsdon and this will pose great challenges to parking. However, it has its advantages: as it is surrounded by residential areas and there are mature railway and mainroad system connecting Hindon, Bransdon and Cransdon, it is none the less an ideal choice. Bransdon is 16km from the city center, with a population of 15,000 while Cransdon is 25km from the city center and has 29.000 residents. In addition, lying in between Bransdon and Cransdon is an industrial zone. All these imply that the potential customer group is huge.

In conclusion, the two suggested sites both have their own advantages and disadvantages. It is better to take all these factors into consideration when making the final decision.

▶考官评分:7分

译文:

该地图展示了在加尔斯顿建一个新超市备选的两个场地。

从图上可以看出，新超市第一个备选地点位于郊外。这个地点距离拥有1万人口的辛顿12公里，而且处在连接市中心的铁路线和主干线的中间。因此，在S1购物的人们乘火车和开车去都很方便。此外，由于S1处在加尔斯顿的郊区，停车不会遇到困难。

相反，第二个建议的地点就在加尔斯顿的中央区域，这必然会对购物者停车造成很大的困难。然而，也有其有利的一面：由于周围都是居民区，又有发达的铁路和公路主干道与辛顿、布兰斯顿和克兰顿相连，所以也不失为一个上好的选择。布兰斯顿离市中心16公里，人口15000；克兰斯顿离市中心25公里，人口29000，两者之间是工业区，所以，蕴含的潜在客户群很大。

总之，这两个选址各有其优势和劣势。当最终拍板时，最好将这些因素都考虑在内。

第三章

书信题库全部题目和范文

1. 抱怨产品质量

Topic:

You have bought a mp3 at a shop. On reaching home, you discover a fault with it.

Write a letter to the shop authority explaining the situation, and ask that the problem be put right.

Sample Answer

Dear Sir/Madam,

I wish to make a complaint about a mp3 which I bought three days ago in your shop.

As is my habit, I made a point of trying it out on the spot. It worked perfectly well, and so I went ahead and purchased it. However, when I got home and tried it again, it seemed that the volume knob had ceased to work. Removing the back of the case, I found that the internal components of the mp3 were all rusted: Not only that but some of the wires were broken.

I am sure that you will agree that this is a most unsatisfactory situation. Therefore I request you to arrange to replace this mp3 with another one, which must be in perfect working order. Failing that, I will have to visit on a refund in full of the price which I paid for it.

Yours sincerely,

Fan Yang

▶考官评分:8分

译文:

尊敬的先生:

我想向您投诉三天前我在贵商店购买的一部mp3随身听。

根据我的习惯，我提出当场试一下。因为效果不错，所以我就买了下来。然而，当我回到家再次试用时，似乎调节音量的旋钮有点问题，打开后盖，我发现它的内部零件全部生锈了，不仅如此，一些电线也断了。

我相信您也会认为这是一种最令人不满的情况。所以，我请求您安排为我换一部mp3，而且必须是一部品质优良的mp3。如果您无法做到这一点，我将不得不要求全额退款。

此致

杨凡

2. 抱怨服务质量

Topic:

> *You booked a two-week holiday to Sydney with Holiday Travel. You are not happy with the holiday—no one met you at the airport, the hotel was unsatisfactory, and so on.*
>
> *Write to Holiday Travel to complain about the holiday giving details about the problems. Request some compensation or refund.*

Sample Answer

Dear Mr. Smith,

I am writing to complain about my recent holiday in Sydney which was organized by your company.

My wife and I selected the two-week tour starting on 29 December. On arrival at the airport, there was no one to meet us. We waited for half an hour and then had no choice but to take a taxi. This cost $ 30. The receipt is enclosed.

The hotel was not what I would consider three-star. The room was dirty; the beds were small and uncomfortable, and the hotel refused to provide us with dinner. We had to spend a further $500 on extra meals. Again, I enclose our restaurant receipts.

I find it dishonest and unacceptable that your company sold us a tour which in no way resembled the description, and my wife and I expect to be compensated for all our extra expenses. The receipts which are enclosed total $530. We expect to receive your cheque very soon.

Yours sincerely,
Fan Yang

▶考官评分:8分

译文:

亲爱的史密斯先生：

我写此信向您投诉不久前我参加的由贵公司组织的悉尼假日旅行。

我和我的妻子选择了12月29日开始的两周游。下了飞机以后，没有人来迎接我们。我们等了半个小时，最后别无选择只得搭乘出租车。这花掉了我们30美元。发票已随信附上。

那家酒店根本就不是我所想象的三星级酒店。房间不干净，床既窄小又不舒服，不提供晚餐。

我们不得不在吃饭方面又额外支出500美元。饭店的发票也随信附上。

贵公司承包的旅游与宣传完全是两码事，我觉得这是一种欺骗行为，对此我感到难以接受，我和妻子希望全额赔偿我们的额外开支。随附发票总额为530美元。我们希望能很快收到支票。

此致

杨凡

3. 抱怨服务质量

Topic:

Write a letter of complaint to a holiday company after spending a fortnight in one of their hotels which was unfinished, despite promises to the contract in their brochure.

Sample Answer

Dear Sir/Madam,

I am writing to complain about a holiday that I spent in your hotel in July of this year. My friend spent two weeks of hell in a half-finished hotel that was advertised as"a new jewel in the crown of this most gorgeous island". Our opinion was rather different after our two-week nightmare in this rain-soaked building site.

I have several reasons for complaining, but the main one is that there were no facilities whatsoever. The promised gyms and golf course were still an architect's pipe dream and the shopping mall was a simple outdoor market that packed up whenever it started to rain.

A further reason is that the flight to Paloma was delayed so that we missed nearly a day of our holiday by spending a day in Manchester Airport's departure lounge: this ended up being the high-point of our holiday since we were dry, warm and well-fed.

This brings me to my next area of complaint: Food. There was none. Your brochure stated food was"plentiful and traditional"and that it was available day and night. It was, in fact, available for fourteen days and nights because we marked a quiche and it was still there after fourteen days.

Therefore, after having endured two weeks of this ordeal, I feel that I and my friends are deserving of at least a refund or we will be forced to take this matter further and may release our photographs to the press.

Yours sincerely,

Fan Yang

▶考官评分:8分

译文：

尊敬的先生/女士：

我写此信的目的是想向您投诉我在今年7月于贵旅行社度假时的一些情况。我的朋友们在一间没有装修好的旅馆里过了两个星期地狱一般的日子，而这个旅馆就是贵公司广告上所说的“最美岛屿上的一颗明珠”。我们在这个漏雨的旅馆里度过了两个星期噩梦般的日子之后，对你们的广告不敢苟同。

有几方面原因让我对此投诉，但是主要的一点是这里没什么设施。所承诺的体育馆和高尔夫球场被一些建筑管线所取代，而所谓的商业街也只是一些室外市场，一下雨就收摊。

我投诉的另外一个理由是飞往帕洛山的飞机晚点了。因为飞机晚点，我们的假期不得不延期将近一整天，那一天我们是在曼彻斯特机场的候车室度过的。而在机场度过的这个晚上是我们整个假期中最好的一段时间。因为只有在这个晚上，我们没有被淋湿，没有受冻也没有挨饿。

这让我又想起另外一件投诉的事情——食物。我们什么也没有吃到。您的说明中声称食物“丰富、地道”，而且是昼夜供应。但是，事实上，这里的食物一般都陈列了14天以上。因为我们注意到了一个乳蛋饼，而这个饼在14天之后还摆在那里。

所以，在经历两个星期的这种“考验”之后，我和我的朋友应该得到相当可观的经济赔偿。否则，我们将深究此事，并向新闻公布我们的照片。

此致

杨凡

4. 抱怨服务质量

Topic:

You have booked a two-week holiday to Sydney with Fly-by-Night Travel. You are not happy with the holiday: the flight was delayed; the hotel was noisy, and the service was poor.

Write to Fly-by-Night Travel to complain about the holiday, giving details about the problems. Request some compensation or refund.

Sample Answer

Dear Sir/Madam,

We have just returned from our holiday, a two-week package tour to Sydney organized by your company. Unfortunately it was a miserable experience. We are writing to ask you for an explanation.

The first problem we encountered was a five-hour delay in your charter flight, so the activities arranged for that evening therefore had to be cancelled. To make matters worse, we did not manage to fall asleep the entire night after we checked in. There was constant noises, such as screaming and laughter, coming from the next room. The final thing we have to complain about is your tour guide service. The guide deliberately shortened our time for sightseeing and took us to one shopping centre after another.

We feel compelled to draw your attention to the trouble we had and the sense of our loss caused by your unsatisfactory service. Your company promised that any such loss or customer dissatisfaction would be compensated. For these reasons, we request to be refunded totally. We hope you will give these matters serious consideration and expect to hear from you soon.

Yours sincerely,

Fan Yang

▶考官评分:8分

译文:

尊敬的先生/女士:

我们刚刚参加完贵公司组织的悉尼之旅，这次旅行是一个组团旅行，为期两周左右。遗憾的是，这次旅行对于我来说是一次痛苦的经历。我写此信是希望贵公司能够对此做出解释。

我们所碰到的第一个问题就是贵公司的包机晚点5个小时，那天晚上既定的活动不得不因此取消。更糟糕的是在登机之后，我们整夜都无法入睡。隔壁的噪音不断，尖叫声和笑闹声不绝于耳。我们要投诉的最后一件事情就是贵公司的导游服务。导游故意缩短了我们的观光时间，而带我们去逛一家又一家的购物中心。

我们不得不提醒您注意一下，贵公司的糟糕服务给我们所带来的麻烦和精神上的损失。贵公司曾经承诺：旅客的任何不满均能够得到赔偿。鉴于此，我们希望贵公司能够全额退款。我们希望贵公司能够认真考虑这件事情，并期望您能够早日回信。

此致

杨凡

5. 抱怨房屋问题

Topic:

You rent a house through an agency. The heating system has stopped working. You phoned the agency a week ago but it has still not been mended.

Write a letter to the agency. Explain the situation and tell them what you want them to do about it.

Sample Answer

Dear Sir/Madam,

I am at present living in a house which I rented through your agency. I am sorry to inform you that the heating system in the house stopped working some time ago.

I phoned your agency and explained the problem one week ago, but you still have not sent anybody to fix the heating system. This is very inconvenient – not to mention dangerous to the health – as the weather is starting to get colder. I am puzzled as to why you have not paid attention to this urgent matter. I must remind you that a fully operative heating system is one of the terms of the lease of the house.

Therefore, I would very much appreciate it if you would send a technician to repair the system as soon as possible. He may call at any time during the day, as either I or my wife will be at home all this week.

Yours sincerely,

Fan Yang

▶考官评分:8分

译文:

尊敬的先生/女士:

我目前居住的房子是经贵中心介绍租下的。我很遗憾地通知您此房的供暖系统前几天坏了。

我曾就此事于一周前打电话给贵中心，但您至今仍未派人前来修理供暖系统。这给我带来了极大的不便——更不用说对健康不利——因为天开始越来越冷了。我很纳闷为什么这样一件紧急的事情却丝毫没能引起您的注意。我必须提醒您提供良好的供暖系统是承租此房的条件之一。

因此，如您能尽快派一位技术人员修复这个系统，我将不胜感激。他在白天任何时间来都行，因为我或我太太本周会全天在家。

此致

杨凡

6. 抱怨房屋问题

Topic:

You are a student living in a university accommodation. The heating has not worked for some time. Write a letter to the management to complain.

Sample Answer

Dear Sir or Madam,

I live in Room 201 in the first dormitory building. I am writing to express my dissatisfaction with the heating system.

When I got your brochure, I was very glad and thought that I had found a nice accommodation. However, when I moved in, I found everything was so different from what the brochure told me. Beyond my tolerance is the heating system, because it has not worked till now. I have told the janitor about this, but have not got any feedback. It is getting colder and colder, so it has become very urgent. I hope you will send someone to repair it as soon as possible.

I would be very grateful if you kindly consider my request and maintain the heating system at once. I am looking forward to the day when it starts to work. Or, I would like to move into a different room.

Yours sincerely,
Fan Yang

▶考官评分:8分

译文:

尊敬的先生或女士:

我住在第一宿舍楼201室。我想写信说明一下我对供暖系统的不满。

当我收到你的宣传册时,我感到非常高兴,认为我找到了一个很好的住宿。但是,当我搬进来,我发现这和宣传册里面提到的完全不同。供暖系统到现在都不能正常使用,这已经超出了我的容忍限度。我曾经向管理员反映过这个情况,但没有得到任何反馈。天气渐渐转冷,所以解决这个问题迫在眉睫。我希望你们能尽快派人来修理。

如果您能认真考虑我的意见并立刻对我的供暖系统进行维修,我将不胜感激。我希望能等到它正常使用的一天。否则,我将考虑换一个房间。

此致

杨凡

7. 抱怨银行账户出错

Topic:

You have had a bank account for a few years. Recently you received a letter from the bank stating that your account is $240 overdrawn and that you will be charged $70 which will be taken directly from your account. You know that this information is incorrect.

Write a letter to the bank. Explain what has happened and say what you would like them to do about it.

Sample Answer

Dear Sir,

I am writing in reply to a letter I received from you a few days ago. In your letter you state that my account is $240 overdrawn and that you will charge me $70.

I would like to point out that my account is overdrawn because of a mistake made by your bank. If you look through your records you will see that I wrote several weeks ago explaining the situation. For the last twelve months, I have been paying $300 a month for a car I bought last summer. The monthly payments were taken directly from my bank account. However, two months ago I sold the car and I wrote to you instructing you to stop paying the monthly installments. I received a letter from you acknowledging my request, but, for some reason, nothing was done about it. Another $300 installment has been paid this month and this is the reason why my account is overdrawn.

I would like you to contact the garage where I bought the car explaining your error. I would also like you to ask them to return the money.

Yours faithfully,

Fan Yang

▶考官评分:8分

译文:

尊敬的先生:

我写此信以回复几天以前我收到的您的来信。信中您称我透支了240美元并要收取我70美元的罚金。

我想指出我的透支是贵银行工作失误的结果。如果您仔细查看一下记录，您会发现几个星期以前我曾写信解释过这个问题。在过去的12个月中，我一直每月为我去年夏天购买的汽车支付300美元。该款项每月直接从我的银行账户上扣除。但是，两个月以前我卖掉了那部汽车，并写信通知你们停止支付每个月的分期付款款项。我收到了您确认我的请求的复函，但不知出于什么原因，贵行却没有采取任何措施，而这个月贵行又支付了300美元，这就是造成我透支的原因。

我想请您与我购买汽车的车行取得联系并解释一下您的失误，我还希望您请求他们退回该退回来的钱。

此致

杨凡

8. 说明信

Topic:

You have had an accident and are in hospital.
Write a letter to your college administration explaining why you will be absent from class for the next month. Ask for advice about how to continue your studies during this period.

Sample Answer

Dear Prof. Smith,

I am writing to explain my absence from classes since April 21, 1999.

On April 20, 1999, I was involved in a serious motor vehicle accident. I was transported to the hospital in an ambulance, where I was treated for a broken ankle, fractured collarbone, and 3 bruised ribs. My doctor advised complete bed rest for 6 weeks, and as a result, I have been unable to attend classes since April 21, 1999.

I am concerned about keeping up with my studies, and have been doing the required readings, as assigned by my professors. My biggest concern is whether I will be eligible to write the final exams in June. Would you please advise me regarding my courses and exams, specifically if there will be any special consideration given to me in light of my current situation?

Thank you for your kind assistance. I look forward to hearing from you soon.

Sincerely,

Fan Yang

▶考官评分:8分

译文:

亲爱的史密斯教授:

我写此信向您解释我自1999年4月21日以来一直缺课的原因。

1999年4月20日，我被卷入了一场严重的车祸。我被救护车送入了医院，在那里医生就我扭伤的踝关节、断裂的锁骨和三根挫伤的肋骨进行了治疗。医生建议我卧床休息六周，于是，我自1999年4月21日以来便一直未能上课。

我很想赶上学习进度，并一直在完成教授所布置的阅读任务。我最为关心的是我是否仍有资格参加6月份的期末考试。您能就课程和考试事情给我提些建议吗?尤其是针对我目前的情况，您是否会给予一些特殊的考虑?

谢谢您的热心相助，盼望着您尽快回信。

此致

杨凡

9. 说明物品丢失

Topic:

You have lost your credit card.

Write to the manager of your bank. Explain where and how you lost the card and any other relevant details. Ask the manager to cancel the old card and to send you a replacement.

Sample Answer

Dear Sir/Madam,

I am writing to confirm the loss of my credit card.

The details of my card are as follows. It is a Visa card in the name of Fan Yang. The credit card number is 4531 7602 2597 8413. I have had the card since 1994. This card is valid from August 2005 to August 2006.

I lost the card yesterday at about 10: 30 in the evening. The only time I used the card yesterday was to buy three dictionaries at the Haidian Bookstore. By accident, I left the card at the shop. When I realized what I had done, I telephoned the shop, but the shop assistants there could not find the card.

Could you please cancel my card immediately and make the necessary arrangements to issue me with a replacement card?

Thank you for your assistance.

Yours faithfully,

Fan yang

▶考官评分:8分

译文：

尊敬的先生/女士：

我写此信的目的是确认我的信用卡已经丢失。

我的信用卡的详细情况如下：它是一张Visa卡，持卡人是杨凡，卡号是4531 7602 2597 8413。自1994年起我就一直持有此卡。这张卡的有效期是2005年8月到2006年8月。

我大约于昨晚10：30丢失此卡。我昨天惟一一次使用此卡是在海淀书店用它买了三本词典。我不小心把信用卡丢在了店里。等我发现卡丢了，我给那家书店打了电话，但是店中服务员已找不到卡了。

您能立即注销我的信用卡并采取必要措施给我补办一张替代卡吗？

谢谢您的帮助。

此致

杨凡

10. 说明信

Topic:

You have moved to another city and changed your language school.
Write a letter to one of your friends to tell him about the new school and your impressions of it.

Sample Answer

Dear David,

Hope you are well. I have moved to London and therefore transferred to another language school. I am still getting used to this place, and I am not sure yet whether I prefer it.

The school's facilities are generally better than those of the previous one. What I am most satisfied with is the room, which I am sharing with a Japanese guy. It has a private bathroom and full kitchen facilities, and there is also access to the Internet in the room. A five-minute walk away from my dorm is a well-equipped indoor swimming pool. You know how important that is for a regular swimmer like me.

What worries me now is my part-time work. It is not easy to find a temporary job here, as there is a high unemployment rate. You can see how anxious I am if I am not in temporary employment, because it is one of the main sources of paying my living costs.

Let's keep in touch.

Yo

译文：

亲爱的大卫：

你一切都好吧？我已经搬家到了伦敦，所以转学到了另外一家语言学校。我在这里还基本适应，但是我不敢肯定我是否会喜欢这里。

学校的设施总体上比从前的那所学校要好。我最满意的就是我的宿舍（我与一个日本人合住这间宿舍）。宿舍里有单独的盥洗室，全套的厨房设施，而且还能够在房间里上网。从我们宿舍步行5分钟就可以走到一个设备精良的室内游泳馆。要知道对于一个像我这样的经常游泳的人来说，这是多么重要。

让我感到比较烦心的是我的兼职工作。在这里找临时工作非常不容易，因为这里的失业率非常高。你能够想象如果没有机会打零工我该是多么着急，因为这是我的生活费的主要来源之一。

经常保持联系！

此致

凡

11. 说明信

You are travelling and have lost something that is expensive. The lost item is insured. Write to the insurance company to describe how it happened and ask for compensation.

Sample Answer

Dear Sir or Madam,

I am one of your customers, and I just lost an expensive video recorder on a trip.

I joined in a holiday tour last week. But on March 12th, when I finished one day's sightseeing and went back to the hotel, I found my video recorder which was in a drawer missing. I had to recharge the batteries of the recorder so I did not bring it with me on that day. I asked the floor waiter about the recorder but he said he did not even notice it. I also complained to the manager of the hotel. He said he was sorry for my loss but he could do nothing about it. So I had to call the police. When I returned from the trip, I remembered that some of my properties, including the recorder, were insured by your company. Therefore, I am writing to let you know that I would like to claim compensation from you.

I have enclosed a copy of the police statement. I look forward to your timely reply.

Yours sincerely,

Fan Yang

▶**考官评分：8分**

译文：

尊敬的先生或女士：

我是你们公司的一名顾客，我在旅行途中丢失了一台贵重的摄像机。

上周我报团去旅游度假了。但是在3月12日这天，当我完成一天的观光，回到宾馆后，我发现锁在抽屉里的摄像机不见了。那天摄像机的电池没电了，因此我不得不把它留在宾馆充电。我问过楼层的服务生，但他说从来没有看到过我的摄像机。我也把这件事向宾馆的经理反映过。他说，他对我的损失深表歉意，但他没有办法。因此，我最后不得不打电话报警。当我旅行归来后，我想起我的部分财产曾经在贵公司买过保险，其中就包括这台摄像机。因此，我希望能得到你们公司的赔偿。

我已附上警方声明的复印件。我期待着您的及时答复。

此致

杨凡

12. 说明道歉和邀请

Topic:

Having finished your end-of-term exams, you have gone straight home without saying good-bye to your roommate.

Write a letter explaining the situation to him, and invite him home during the vacation.

Sample Answer

Dear David,

I am writing to apologize for the abrupt way I departed right after the exams finished. It was terribly rude of me to have left without saying good-bye to you, especially as we have been such good roommates. Not only did we help each other to study over the past term, but we also shared many leisure interests.

The fact is that when I learned that I had passed the exams with high marks, I was so excited that I could not wait to get home and tell the good news to my parents. You see, they had been worried about the low grades I had been getting. I'm sure you will understand my feelings.

Anyway, I want to let you know that I very much value our good relationship. To make up for my thoughtless behavior toward you, I want to invite you to come and stay with my family during the vacation. My hometown is located in a very scenic part of the country, and there are lots to do and see. You are welcome to stay for as long as you wish, so please write and let me know your decision.

Yours sincerely,

Fan

▶考官评分:8分

译文:

亲爱的大卫:

我写此信是想对一考完试便突然离开一事向你道歉。我的不辞而别是非常不礼貌的行为，尤其是我们是关系这么好的室友。在过去的一学期里，我们不仅在学习中相互帮助，而且还志趣相投。

事实是当我得知我以很高的分数通过了考试后，我兴奋得只想马上把这个好消息告诉给我父母。你知道，他们曾一直为我成绩较差而担心。我相信你能理解我的心情。

无论如何，我想让你了解我很珍惜我俩间的友情。为了弥补我欠缺考虑的行为，我想邀请你来我家共度假期。我的家乡在一个景色秀丽的地方，我们可以做很多事情，到很多地方去玩。你在我家愿住多久就住多久，请写信告诉我你的决定。

此致

凡

13. 咨询信息

Topic:

A friend is already attending Oxford college in the UK. You will be going to the UK next year. Write and ask him / her about what you should do before you go. Ask him / her about any problems he / she has had.

Sample Answer

Dear Danny,

How are you getting on in Oxford? I hope everything is going well and you are enjoying your studies. I'm writing to ask you for some information as I'm planning to come and study in the UK next year. I have applied to Oxford College to take the course in Tourism Management.

Could you tell me what I have to do to obtain a study visa and how long the process will take? The college said I also have to take out insurance before I come to the UK. How do I do this? I'd be really grateful if you can give me this information. I would also be grateful if you can tell me what I should bring with me, for example, clothes, books or anything else I cannot get in the UK.

I am sure that adjusting to a new culture was probably difficult. Have you had any particular problems that I should watch out for? I would appreciate any advice you give me.

Many thanks for your help.

Yours,

Fan

▶考官评分:8分

译文:

亲爱的丹尼:

你在牛津过得好吗? 我希望你一切都好并且学习生活愉快。我写信想向你了解一些情况，因为我明年也打算去英国学习。我已经向牛津学院申请攻读旅游管理课程。

请你告诉我如何才能获得学生签证以及这一过程需要多长时间。牛津学院说我在来英国之前还必须办理保险手续。我该如何处理此事? 如果你能给我提供有关信息，我将不胜感激。我还想知道我应该随身携带的物品，比如衣服、书或任何其他英国当地买不到的东西。

我敢说适应一种新的文化可能很不容易。你有没有遇到过一些我应该特别注意的问题? 对于你提供的任何忠告，我将十分感激。

谢谢你的帮助!

此致

凡

14. 咨询学校

Topic:

You wish to study at a certain foreign university.

Write a letter inquiring about the situation there as regards accommodation, fees and qualifications.

Sample Answer

Dear Sir/Madam,

I am a Chinese citizen who wishes to study at your university. My plan is to start my course next term, and I would be grateful if you would be kind enough to provide me with certain essential information.

First, what qualifications do I need to follow a course of study at your university? I already have a master's degree from a university here in China, but I wonder if there are any further academic requirements. Second, how much is the tuition fee? Although I intend to be self-supporting, I would be interested to hear if there are any scholarships available for international students. Third, what is the situation as regards accommodation? I would prefer a single room, which is more conducive to studying, but if single rooms are expensive, I would be willing to share.

I look forward to your reply, and to attending your esteemed institution.

Yours sincerely,
Fan Yang

▶考官评分:8分

译文:

尊敬的先生/女士:

我是一名希望在贵校学习的中国公民，我计划下学期开始我的课程学习，如果您能热心为我提供一些基本情况，我将十分感激。

首先，在贵校学习一门课程，我需要具备什么条件？我已经在中国的一所大学获得了硕士学位，但我想知道是否还有其他学术要求。第二，学费是多少？尽管我打算自己负担学费，但我也很想知道对外国学生是否提供奖学金。第三，住宿方面的条件怎么样？我愿意住一个单人间，这样更有助于学习，但是如果单人间费用太高，我也愿意与人合住。

盼望您的回信，希望很快能赴久负盛名的贵校深造。

此致
杨凡

15. 咨询信息

Topic:

You wish to enroll in a course at an Australian college. You have already written a letter to the college asking for information but have received no reply.

Write a letter to the college explaining your concern because the course will start in less than two months. You need to know if you can still enroll, and you also require further information about the course, including the cost.

Sample Answer

Dear Sir/Madam,

I am anxious to obtain information about the college's Graphics Design course which begins in less than two months. Actually, I wrote four weeks ago, but I have not yet heard from you. Perhaps you did not receive my letter.

First of all, I need to know if it is too late to enroll in the course. Can you write and tell me if there are any places left? I certainly hope that my enrolment is still possible.

I need to have more information about the course before I decide to apply, but I realize that I do not have much time. Would you be kind enough to send your reply by express mail? Especially, I need to know the cost of the course, and whether the certificate you offer at the end of the course will be sufficient qualification for me to apply full-time to one of the Graphic Design colleges in your city.

I look forward to your reply.

Yours sincerely,
Fan Yang

▶考官评分:8分

译文:

尊敬的先生/女士:

我十分急切地希望能得到关于贵校的图形设计课程的相关信息，而该课程还有不到两个月的时间就要开课了。实际上，我四周之前就写信询问了，但是到现在还没收到回信，我想也许是，你们没有收到吧。

首先，我需要知道现在报名是不是太迟了。你能告诉我现在是否还有名额，我现在报名还有可能被批准吗?

在申请这个课程之前，我需要了解更多课程信息，但是，我意识到我没有太多时间了。你能用邮件快递的方式告诉我吗？特别是，我需要知道课程的费用，以及在课程结束时所颁发的证书是否可以作为证明让我申请一所这个城市中图形设计学院的全职学生课程。

我盼望得到你们的回复。

此致
杨凡

16. 咨询信息

Topic:

Assume that you wish to study in England.

Write a letter of inquiry based on your interests. Ask what kind of clubs there are at the university, and what is the procedure for joining them.

Sample Answer

Dear Sir/Madam,

I have applied to enter your esteemed university to follow a course of study. However, although I find the academic curriculum suitable, I feel that the opportunities for leisure activities are also an important part of student life. Therefore, I would be grateful if you could give me some information about this aspect of the campus.

In my spare time, I indulge in a wide range of sports; I am also interested in music, especially playing the guitar. Specifically, I wish to know if there are any sports clubs, including soccer and tennis teams run by students. Furthermore, I would be keen to join a student band or orchestra, if there is one.

Please write and let me know what university clubs I am eligible to join. By the way, what is the procedure for joining campus clubs, what qualifications do I need, and what are the fees for taking part in their activities?

I look forward to your reply.

Yours sincerely,
Fan Yang

▶考官评分:8分

译文:

尊敬的先生/女士:

我已经申请进入贵校参加一门课程的学习。然而，尽管我认为学习课程安排得非常合理，但是我觉得有机会进行休闲活动在学生生活中也很重要。因此，如果您能向我介绍一下学校这方面的情况，我将十分感激。

在我的闲暇时间，我喜欢参加广泛的体育活动；我还喜欢音乐，尤其是弹吉他。我特别想知道贵校是否有体育俱乐部，其中包括由学生组建的足球队和网球队。此外，如果有学生乐队或乐团，我特别想加入。

请写信告诉我哪些俱乐部我够资格参加。顺便问一下，加入校园俱乐部需要哪些手续，我需要具备哪些条件，以及参加他们的活动需付多少费用。

盼望您的答复。

此致

杨凡

17. 咨询信息

Topic:

As part of a student social survey project, you are organizing a group to visit a historical exhibition in a small town.
Write a letter to the exhibition organizer asking for information regarding such things as the contents of the exhibition, and the dates of its opening and closing, and if there are any discounts available.

Sample Answer

Dear Sir/Madam,

I am organizing a group of students to pay a visit to the historical exhibition in your town. This visit will be part of our school's activities to encourage the students to take part in social surveys. Therefore, I would be grateful if you would supply me with the following information:

First of all, what are the opening and closing dates between which the exhibition will be held, and what are the daily opening hours? Secondly, what is the size of the exhibition, what is its theme and what objects are on display? Thirdly, are there any other activities being held in connection with the exhibition?

I should let you know that I hope to bring over 100 students to the exhibition. So I would like to inquire if there is any discount available on entrance tickets for students. If so, how much is the discount and what is the minimum number of students necessary to qualify for it?

I look forward to your reply.

Yours sincerely,

Fan Yang

▶考官评分:8分

译文：

尊敬的先生/女士：

我正在组织一批学生参观贵市的历史展览。本次参观将是我校鼓励学生参与社会调查活动的一部分。因此，如果您能够提供下列信息，我将不胜感激。

首先，展览的开始和截止日期分别是哪一天？每天在什么时间开放？第二，展览的规模有多大？它的主题是什么？有什么样的展品？第三，有没有与本次展览有关的其他活动？

我应告诉您的是我希望带100多名学生参观此次展览，所以我很想询问一下学生购门票是否可以打折。如果可以，折扣是多少？至少有多少学生才有资格享受打折？

盼回复。

此致

杨凡

18. 咨询信息

Topic:

You read in a newspaper an advertisement offering scholarships for overseas students.

Write a letter asking for detailed information, and explain why you think you are qualified for one of the scholarships. Also, state your study plan.

Sample Answer

Dear Sir/Madam,

I am writing in response to your advertisement in the *China Daily* on 4 October regarding scholarships available for international students. As a Chinese student, I wish to recommend myself as a promising scholarship candidate.

Let me begin by outlining my background and claims to such a scholarship. First of all, I obtained my master's degree from Peking University. Then I started working at CCTV as an English news reporter and have been there for four years. Therefore I am confident I fully meet the requirements of your scholarship programme.

If I am granted financial support, I will study with a carefully mapped out plan. My research will focus on how to boost China' s media industry and how to get it ready for fierce global competition after China becomes a member of the World Trade Organization. As I intend to work once more as an English reporter after graduation, I will also devote my time to the study of English writing and phonology.

I am looking forward to your early reply with full application details and trust that you will give my claims serious consideration. Thank you for your attention.

Yours sincerely,

Fan Yang

▶考官评分:8分

译文:

尊敬的先生/女士:

我在10月4日的《中国日报》上看到贵方刊登的广告，广告上说贵方能够为外国学生提供奖学金。我写此信就是为了这件事。我是一名中国学生，我认为自己符合贵方的奖学金要求。

我首先向贵方介绍一下我的基本情况和我在申请奖学金方面所具备的条件。首先，我在北京大学获得硕士学位。然后，我在CCTV做了四年的英文记者。因此，我符合贵方的奖学金要求，对此我非常自信。

如果能够获得经济支持，我会精心安排我的学习计划。我将专心研究如何使中国的传媒业兴旺发达，以及入世后如何应对激烈的国际市场竞争。我在毕业之后还希望从事英文记者工作，因此我也会倾注于英文写作和语言学方面的研究。

期待您能早日回信，告知详细申请细则，相信贵方会慎重考虑我的申请书。再次向您表示感谢。

此致

杨凡

19. 道歉信

Topic:

One of your pen pals will shortly be visiting your city. For some reasons, you can not manage to meet him at the airport on time.

Write a letter to ask him to wait for you at the airport and tell him how to identify you.

Sample Answer

Dear David,

I am very much looking forward to your visit to my city. After all these years of writing to each other, we will finally have the chance to meet! However, I regret to inform you that I will not be able to meet you at the airport when you arrive.

I was glad to hear that you would come to see me and I thought I must go to the airport to meet you. But yesterday I was informed that I must attend an important business meeting on the day when you arrive. The meeting is supposed to be over at 11:00 am, which will be an hour later than your arrival time.

Please wait for me in the arrival lounge. I'll go there as quickly as possible after the meeting. As we have never met, I must tell you how to recognize me: I am of medium height and have a small mustache. In addition, I will be carrying a copy of the morning newspaper tucked under my left arm.

Looking forward to our first meeting.

Yours sincerely,

Fan

▶考官评分:8分

译文:

亲爱的大卫:

我热切地盼望着你来参观我所在的城市。互通信件这么多年，我们终于有机会相见了！但是，我遗憾地告诉你我将不能在你初抵机场的那一刻前去迎接你。

听说你要来看我，我真的很高兴，我想我一定要去机场接你。但是昨天我接到通知在你到的那天我要参加一个重要的会议。会议预计在十一点结束，比你到达时间晚一小时。

请在休息大厅等我。会议结束后，我将尽快去机场。由于我们从未见过面，我想有必要向你描述一下我自己，以便你能认出我：我中等身材，留小胡子，此外，我左臂下将夹着一份晨报。

盼望着我们的初次见面。

此致

凡

20. 道歉信

Topic:

You've just been offered a job, but you will not be able to start work on the appointed day.
Write a letter to your boss explaining the problem and asking for an alternative day to start work.

Sample Answer

Dear Mr. Smith,

Thank you for offering me a position in your company. I am looking forward to working as a new member of your staff. However, I have to write to apologize, because I am afraid it is impossible for me to begin work on the date you mentioned, Monday, April 23.

The reason is that I will be in my travel on the date. I booked the trip at a special discount three weeks ago when I thought I could still have time for relaxation before starting a new job. When I received your job, I was delighted and called the travel agency to see if it was possible to cancel or delay my trip. However, they said no, because the trip was not refundable for any cancellations. As a result, I feel I have to go on my trip. Otherwise I will lose thousands of dollars.

I will return on Friday April 27, so I think the earliest possible starting date will be the following Monday. By then I will be fully refreshed after an exciting journey. Therefore, I hope you can accept my request for rescheduling the starting date and I am sorry again for any inconvenience this may cause.

Yours sincerely,

Fan Yang

▶考官评分:8分

译文:

亲爱的史密斯先生:

感谢贵公司为我提供的这一职务。我正期待着成为贵公司的一员。但是实在抱歉,我恐怕不能够按照你们的要求在4月23日(星期一)的早上去贵公司报到。

因为那天我将在旅途中。我在三个星期之前就已经预定了外出旅游的行程。这次旅行的费用非常低廉而且我希望能够在开始新的工作之前有时间好好休息一下。当我接到您的通知时,我感到非常高兴,并且和旅行社联系,看看是否可以取消或延期我的旅行。但是,他们说不可以,因为即使我取消旅行也不能退费。所以,我不得不继续我的旅行计划。否则,我的损失会很大。

我将于4月27日(星期五)返回。所以,我觉得我最早可以在下星期一开始工作。到那个时候,我的旅行圆满结束了,而我也能够精神焕发地投入工作。所以,我期望公司能够接受我延期入职的请求,对于此举给贵公司带来的不便,我再次表示歉意。

此致

杨凡

21. 道歉信

Topic:

You are a tenant and have unintentionally damaged something that is the property of the landlord. Write to the landlord to describe how it happened and apologize.

Sample Answer

Dear Mr. Johnson,

I am writing to express my apology for having damaged the television in my room and I would like you to know that I am prepared to pay for the repair or for purchasing a similar one.

I was watching TV yesterday evening, with a cup of coffee in my hand. Then I heard the telephone ringing. I put the coffee on the top of the TV and went to the sitting room to answer the phone. It was a friend who asked me to go to a movie. We talked for some time and then I returned to my room. I had totally forgotten the coffee that I left on the top of TV. When I was putting on my coat, somehow I swept the cup over and the coffee spilt, some of which went inside of the TV and caused damage. The TV is not working and I think it needs repairs from professional people.

I would like to know what I should do.

Yours sincerely,
Fan Yang

▶考官评分:8分

译文:

亲爱的约翰逊先生:

对于房间的电视机被损坏一事，我感到十分抱歉，我写这封信是想让您知道，我愿意支付维修费用，或者买一个一模一样的赔给您。

昨晚我看电视的时候，手里正好端着一杯咖啡。这时我听到电话铃响了，我就顺手把咖啡放在电视机顶上，去客厅接电话。电话是一个朋友打来的，邀请我一起看电影。我们聊了一会之后，我就回到屋里。我彻底忘记了被我放在电视机顶上的咖啡。当我穿衣服的时候，碰到了咖啡杯，咖啡洒了出来，一部分流到了电视机里面引起了故障。电视机现在已经不能用了，我认为应该送到专业人员那里进行维修。

我想知道我接下来该怎么做。

此致
杨凡

22. 感谢朋友探病

Topic:

After being involved in an accident, you were looked after by another person.
Write a special letter to express your thanks.

Sample Answer

Dear David,

I am writing to express my heartfelt gratitude. I am referring to that unfortunate accident the other day, when I was knocked off my bike by a taxi. If it had not been for your timely assistance in giving me first aid and taking me to a nearby hospital, I fear that the consequences might have been much more serious.

The doctor says that my broken leg is healing well, and the bruises and cuts I suffered will soon be completely better. In addition, the taxi company has agreed to pay my hospital bills. Everyone agrees that it was your quick-witted response in that emergency that has led to this satisfactory outcome.

Although nowadays many people talk about the need to be unselfish and to help others, we see very few people practicing what they preach. But you showed by your selfless action that you are an exception. If there were more people like you, this world would be a much nicer place.

Yours sincerely,

Fan

▶考官评分:8分

译文:

亲爱的大卫:

我写此信是想向您表达我由衷的感谢。我指的是几天前发生的那场不幸的车祸，当时我骑着自行车被一辆出租车撞倒了。要不是您及时地对我采取了急救措施并将我送进附近的一家医院，我想结果恐怕会更加严重。

医生说我跌断的腿恢复情况良好，而且身上的挫伤和伤口将会很快完全愈合。此外，出租车公司已同意支付我的住院费用。大家都说多亏您在紧急情况下反应敏捷，才会有了现在这样令人满意的结果。

尽管现在不少人大谈特谈大公无私和助人为乐的必要性，但我们很少看见有人能说到做到。但是您通过自己无私的举动证明了您是一个例外。如果有更多的人像您一样，这个世界将变得更加美好。

此致

凡

23. 感谢朋友帮助

Topic:

You have just arrived in the city where you are going to spend two years for your master's degree. You have a lot preparation to do before the new term starts, but you do not know how to go round the city. A friend you have newly acquainted offered you guidance and helps you through difficulties.
Write a letter to express your thanks.

Sample Answer

Dear David,

I am writing this letter to thank you for the guidance you gave me.

I was a perfect stranger when arriving at this city. Once I lost myself for not knowing the way in a downtown street, although I stopped to ask some people for direction. The streets and shops puzzled me so much that I would rather stay indoors. At that time, you came to see me and brought me a map of the city. You also spent a lot of your valuable time showing me around the city. Now I begin to know how to take the proper buses. Yesterday I went downtown with some of my schoolmates to buy some stationery.

Although nowadays many people talk about the need to be unselfish and to help others, we see very few people practicing what they preach. But you showed by your selfless action that you are an exception. If there were more people like you, this world would be a much nice place.

Yours sincerely,
Fan

▶考官评分:8分

译文:

亲爱的大卫:

我写此信是想感谢你给予我的帮助。

初来这座城市时，我感到很陌生。记得有一次在街上，虽然向人问路，可我还是迷了路。街道和商店使我搞不清方向，所以我宁愿待在屋内。在那个时候，你来看我，带给我城市的地图。你抽出许多宝贵的时间带我四处逛。现在我知道怎么坐公共汽车了。昨天我和我的同学去市区买了一些文具。

尽管现在不少人大谈特谈大公无私和助人为乐的必要性，却很少看见有人能说到做到。但是你通过自己无私的举动证明了你是一个例外。如果有更多的人像你一样，这个世界将变得更加美好。

此致

凡

24. 建议

Topic:

You have a friend who is about to enter university, and he wants you to advise him which subject to specialize in history, in which he is very interested or computer science, which offers better job prospects. Write a letter to your friend offering your advice.

Sample Answer

Dear David,

When we last spoke over the phone, you asked me whether you should specialize in history or in computer science. In your case, I see choosing history as the right decision.

By majoring in history, you will be "killing two birds with one stone". First of all, I know you are especially interested in history, which will motivate you to study hard through college to achieve the best academic results. Besides, if you graduate with a good degree, you are definitely going to get better career opportunities in the field. You will be one of those fortunate people who can combine work and pleasure.

As everybody knows, the subject of computer science is very popular. Therefore, even if you complete a computer degree, you are still likely to face the problem of finding a job. What is more, I don't think you would enjoy working with computers.

As your good friend, I really wish to see you always enjoy what you do and get on the road to success. I am confident you will make it if you major in history. Hope to hear from you soon with some good news. Good luck!

Yours sincerely,

Fan

▶考官评分:8分

译文：

亲爱的大卫：

上次我们通电话，你问我你应该选择计算机专业还是历史专业。鉴于你的实际情况，我认为你比较适合学习历史。

选择历史专业对于你来说可谓一举两得。首先，我知道你特别喜欢历史，这一点会激励你努力学习并取得优异的成绩。其次，如果你能以优异的成绩毕业的话，当然会在你这个领域里获得很好的就业机会。你会非常幸运地将工作和爱好合二为一。

众所周知，计算机专业非常热门。因此，即使你计算机专业毕业，你仍然会面临就业的难题。而且，我认为你不会喜欢从事计算机方面的工作。

作为你的好朋友，我希望你工作愉快，并踏上成功之路。我相信如果选择历史专业，你一定会取得成功。希望能够很快听到你的好消息。祝你好运。

此致

凡

25. 求职

Topic:

You are a college student who applies for a part-time job in a shop during the summer vacation.

Write a letter to the shop owner explaining why you are a suitable person for the job.

Sample Answer

Dear Sir/Madam,

I would like to apply for the position of part-time shop assistant, as advertised on our college notice board. I am a marketing major at Beijing University, and hope to find suitable work through my summer vacation.

I am certain that you will find me to be a worthy employee for several reasons. As mentioned, my specialty is marketing. In the last semester, I completed several courses including Business Communication which included information on how to talk with customers and how to persuade them to purchase certain products. Other relevant courses included Consumer Psychology. I am therefore confident that I will be able to put some of my academic knowledge into practice and thus enhance your profits.

Besides this, my personality is also suitable for the job. I am outgoing, a team player, compassionate and helpful. You will find me to be creative and resourceful, adept at handling any complaints from customers.

I hope that you will give my application serious consideration. I am available at your convenience for an interview and look forward to your early reply.

Yours sincerely,

Fan Yang

▶考官评分:8分

译文:

尊敬的先生/女士:

在我们学校的留言板里我看到了贵公司招聘兼职的商店售货员的广告。我写此信是希望能够应聘这一职务。我是北京大学市场营销专业的学生，想在暑假找到一份适合的工作。

我相信您一定会发现我是一名非常出色的雇员，理由如下：如前所述，我的专业是市场营销。在上个学期我完成了几门课程，其中包括《商务交流》。在《商务交流》这门课中介绍了如何与客户谈话以及如何劝说他们购买某种产品。还有《消费心理学》。因此，我确信能够把我的理论只是运用到实践中，从而为您创造更多的利润。

此外，我的个性也非常适合这项工作。我是一个性格外向的人，具有团队精神，富有同情心并乐于助人。您会发现我非常有创造力，足智多谋，善于处理各类顾客投诉。

我希望你能够认真考虑我的申请。如果方便的话，我希望能够与您面谈。我盼望您能够早日回信。

此致

凡

附录

剑8写作真题解析

A类

Test 1

Task 1

Topic:

The pie chart below shows the main reasons why agricultural land becomes less productive. The table shows how these causes affected three regions of the world during the 1990s.
Summarise the information by selecting and reporting the main features, and make comparisons where relevent.

Causes of worldwide land degradation

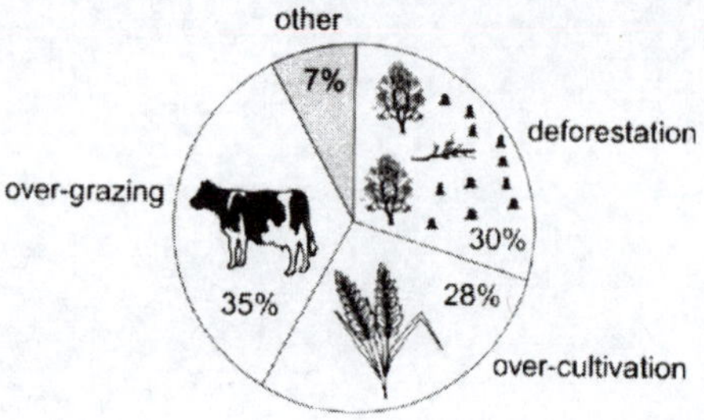

Causes of land degradation by region

Region	% land degraded by...			
	deforestation	over-cultivation	over-grazing	Total land degraded
North America	0.2	3.3	1.5	5%
Europe	9.8	7.7	5.5	23%
Oceania*	1.7	0	11.3	13%

* A large group of islands in the South Pacific including Australia and New Zealand

Sample Answer

The pie chart illustrates why agricultural land is becoming less productive. The table describes three regions affected by the reasons during the 1990s.

We can see from the pie chart that over-grazing has the highest percentage in the four reasons, which is 35%. Deforestation ranks the second position with 30%. The percentage of over-cultivation is much higher than that of other reasons. Interesting, the percentage of over-cultivation is four times as much as that of other reasons (28% and 7% respectively).

It can be seen from the table that in terms of total land degraded and deforestation, Europe had the highest percentage in the three regions. The percentage of Oceania was much higher than that of North America. As for over-cultivation, Europe occupied the first place with 7.7%, which was followed by North America (3.3%) and the percentage of Oceania was 0. However, in the area of over-grazing, Oceania had the highest percentage in the three regions, which was 11.3%, while North America had the lowest, which was only 1.5%.

▶考官评分:8

译文:

该饼状图说明了农田产量下降的原因。表格描述了90年代3个受这些原因影响的地区。

从饼状图中我们可以看到过度放牧是这四个原因中占比例最高的，其所占比例是35%。森林砍伐以30%的比例排在第二位。过度耕种的比例比其他原因所占的比例高许多。有趣的是，过度耕种的比例是其他原因的4倍（分别是28%和7%）。

从表格中可以看出关于总土地退化和森林砍伐，欧洲在这3个地区中的比例最高。大洋洲所占的比例比北美洲的高很多。关于过度耕种，欧洲以7.7%的比例占据第一位，紧接着的是北美洲（3.3%），大洋洲的比例是0。但是，在过渡放牧方面，大洋洲在3个地区中的比例最高，比例是11.3%，而北美洲最低，只有1.5%。

范文点评:

统计数据图表，两个图。第一个图是pie chart，第二个图是table。两个图都属于典型题目二（此题是统计数据图表，有两个图。只有不同的对象，没有不同的时间），两个图之间没有密切的关系。

写了三段：

第一段：改写题目中的文字说明。

第二段：描述第一个图表。

第三段：描述第二个图表。

Task 2

Topic:

Some people think that parents should teach children how to be good members of society. Others, however, believe that school is the place to learn this.
Discuss both these views and give your own opinion.

Sample Answer

Recently, there is a tendency for parents to attach greater importance to their children' s education. Some people take the view that parents should take the responsibility to conduct their children' s behaviour, and tell them what is right or wrong, while others advocate that it is the school' s responsibility.

People who hold the opinion that the school should shoulder the major responsibility to educate children have some sound reasons. In the first place, most of the children' s waking time is spent in schools, and their purpose to attend school is to receive education. Secondly, the parents of the children pay for the education of their children, so they have the rights to receive correspondent services. As an institution of education, the school has the sole responsibility to educate the younger generation. Finally, there are well-equipped facilities and well-trained teachers in schools. The school provides an environment, in which children can not only master knowledge and skills, but also learn how to adapt themselves to the society and how to become responsible citizens.

However, the other side of the coin voices its strong opposition, saying that the parents should assume the main duty of children' s education. First of all, the parents know their children more than the school, and they know what to teach and in what way it can be accepted. The parents function as the first teachers of their children so that they should be responsible for the education of the children. In the second place, it is beneficial to teach children in accordance with their specific features. However, in school, each child gets inadequate individual attention, and sometimes his particular needs are passed over.

Admittedly, there are merits to both arguments. From my own perspective, I would like to take a more balanced position. Schools and parents are both essential to children' s all-round development and they should take the responsibility together. They should make joint efforts to create a harmonious atmosphere conducive to children' s healthy growth.

▶考官评分:8

题目:

有些人认为父母应该教育孩子如何成为好的社会成员。然而另外一些人认为学校应该做这件事情。讨论双方观点并且给出你的观点。

译文:

最近，父母更重视他们孩子的教育。有些人认为父母应负责规范子女的言行，并教导他们如何分辨是非。有些人则认为这是学校的责任。

认为学校应该承担主要教育责任的人有一些理由。第一，孩子的绝大多数非睡眠时间是在学校度过的，他们去学校的目的是接受教育。第二，家长为他们孩子的教育付钱，所以孩子有权利接受相应的服务。作为一个教育机构，学校有责任教育年轻的一代。最后，学校有装备良好的设施和训然而，另一方强烈反对，认为父母应该承担主要责任。首先，家长比学校老师更了解他们的孩子，而且知道应该教孩子什么和以何种方式教孩子能更容易让孩子接受。父母是孩子的第一个老师，所以他们应该负责孩子的教育。第二，因材施教对孩子是有益的。然而，在学校，孩子无法得到特殊的关照，有时他们的特殊需求被忽视。

必须承认，双方都有道理。我愿意站在一个更平衡的立场。学校和父母对孩子的全面发展都很重要。他们应该一起承担责任。他们应该共同努力来创造一个有利于孩子健康成长的和谐环境。

范文点评：

题目类型：
辩论型题目。题目要求中有Discuss both these views。所以必须使用对称式结构。
话题类型：
教育类话题。从内容上看，比较好写。
使用对称式结构。写了四段：
第一段：写了两句话。第一句介绍背景。第二句介绍双方观点。
第二段：写学校应该负责教育孩子。
第三段：写父母应该负责教育孩子。
第四段：提出自己的观点，采取折中方案：学校和父母都应该负责教育孩子。

Test 2

Task 1

Topic:

The three pie charts below show that changes in annual spending by a particular UK school in 1981, 1991 and 2001.
Summarise the information by selecting and reporting the main features, and make comparisons where relevent.

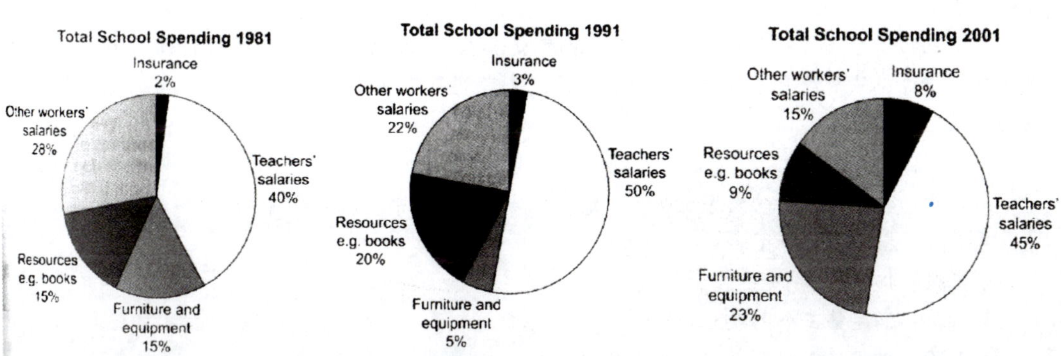

Sample Answer

The three pie charts illustrate the changes in the cost of a British school from 1981 to 2001.

We can see from the first pie chart that teachers' salaries had the highest percentage in the five aspects in 1981, which was 40%. Other workers' salaries occupied the second place with 28%. The percentage of resources was the same as that of furniture and equipment. Insurance had the lowest percentage.

It can be seen from the second pie chart that in 1991, teachers' salaries still ranked the first place and insurance had the lowest percentage (50% and 3% respectively). Although the percentage of resources was slightly lower than that of other workers' salaries, it was much higher than that of furniture and equipment.

In 2001, teachers' salaries had the highest percentage, which was followed by furniture and equipment. Insurance still had the lowest percentage, which was 8%.

According to the three pie charts, the percentage of teachers' salaries increased from 1981 to 1991, but then decreased from 1991 to 2001. However, there was a rise in the percentage of insurance over the 30 years.

▶考官评分:8

译文:

这三个饼状图说明了1981到2001年英国学校费用的变化。

我们可以从第一个饼状图看出，在1981年教师的薪金在这5个方面的比例最高，比例是40%。其他员工的薪水以28%的比例占据第二位。资源的比例同家具和设备的相同。保险费的比例最低。

从第二幅饼状图中可以看出，在1991年，教师薪金比例仍然排在第一位，并且保险费比例最低(分别是50%和3%)。虽然资源比例略低于其他员工薪金的比例，但其远高于家具和设备的比例。

2001年，教师薪金比例最高，后面是家具和设备比例。保险费比例仍然最低，比例是8%。

根据这3幅饼状图，从1981年到1991年教师薪金比例增长，而从1991年到2001年比例下降。然而，30年来保险费比例是增长的。

范文点评:

此题包括三个图，都是pie chart。每个图都是典型题目三，三个图之间有密切的关系。我们在课堂中讲过，从来没有考过一个pie chart的，一考就是两个甚至三个、四个。它们之间都有密切的关系。

写了五段:

第一段：改写题目中的文字说明。

第二段：描述第一个图表。

第三段：描述第二个图表。

第四段：描述第三个图表。

第五段：描述三个图表之间的关系。

Task 2

Topic:

Nowadays the way many people interact with each other has changed because of technology.
In what ways has technology affected the types of relationships people make?
Has this become a positive or negative development?

Sample Answer

Communication is very important both in the past and at present and tends to be more essential in modern society. The development of technology has changed the way we live and the way we relate to other people. For example, some inventions, such as the telephone and the Internet, make it unnecessary for people to meet face-to-face. The telephone has almost killed the ancient art of letter writing, which used to be the only method of long distance communication. Some people worry about its negative effects on people' s relationship. However, I believe that individuals can benefit from the development.

First of all, technology brings us great convenience and efficiency. For example, we can send E-mails to our friends in other countries in a few minutes while sending a traditional letter takes us at least a week and costs much. One of the advantages of telephone communication is that it can allow us to begin instantly to communicate no matter how far we are away from each other. As a result, fire alarm, robbery alarm and other emergency cases are often reported through telephone.

Some people are slightly frightened by the fact that the development of technology may lead to the alienation among families and friends. In fact, technology broadens our horizons and we can make friends with people from all parts of the world. It overcomes the geographical barriers and makes the world smaller. It is with the help of technology that we can communicate with more people and communicate more frequently. For example, traveling to see my parents living in another city would be prohibitively expensive and take a great deal of time, so I can only visit them twice a year. However, I can call them almost every week.

To sum up, technology has changed the way people communicate with each other and it is a positive development. Technology not only provides the most convenient and efficient means for personal communication but also shortens the distance between the people in the world.

▶考官评分:8

题目：

现在，科技使人们相互交流的方式已经改变了。科技怎样改变了人们相互交流的方式？这是一个正面的还是负面的发展？

译文：

不论是过去还是现在，信息交流都是十分重要的，在现代社会里更是重要。科技的发展改变了我们的生活方式以及和他人的相处之道。有些发明，例如电话和互联网，使得人们不需要面对面交谈。写信过去一向是长途通讯的惟一方式，可电话几乎扼杀了这个古代的写信艺术。有些人担心它对人们关系产生负面的影响。但是，我认为人们会从这种发展中获益。

第一，科技带给我们很大的便利和效率。比如，我们给国外的朋友发电子邮件只需要几分钟时间，传统的邮件至少要花费我们一周的时间并且费用也很高。用电话交流的优点之一是不论你在多么遥远的地方，它都让你和外界即刻地进行交流。因此，对火灾、抢劫及其他紧急情况一般都是用电话通知的。

有人有点儿担心科技的发展可能会导致家人和朋友之间关系疏远。实际上，科技开阔了我们的眼界，而且我们可以和世界各地的人交朋友。它克服了地理上的障碍，使世界变得更小。正是在科技的帮助下，我们能和更多的人交流，而且交流更频繁。比如，旅行去看我住在另一个城市的父母不仅很费钱，而且要花很多时间，所以，我一年只能去看他们两次。然而，我可以几乎每个星期都给他们打电话。

总之，科技改变了人们相互交流的方式，这是一个好的发展。科技不仅提供了人际交往中最方便、最便捷的通讯工具，而且缩短了世界各国人们之间的距离。

范文点评：

辩论型题目。题目有两个问号，一个是辩论型的，一个是解释型的，以辩论型的问号为主，相当于辩论型题目。解释型的问号如果在前面，用开头段的介绍背景来处理，写3句左右。

话题类型：

科技类话题。此话题要求谈科技对人们交流方式的影响，从内容上看，不是很好写。

使用一边倒结构。写了四段。

第一段：先介绍背景，科技是如何影响人们交流的方式的。最后说出自己的观点：人们会从中受益。

第二段：一个理由：科技带给我们很大的便利和效率。

第三段：反驳对方，科技的发展不会导致家人和朋友之间关系疏远。相反，在科技的帮助下，我们能和更多的人交流，而且交流得更频繁。

第四段：重申自己的观点：这是一个正面的发展。

Test 3

Task 1

Topic:

The diagrams below show the stages and equipment used in the cement-making process, and how cement is used to produce concrete for building purposes.
Summarise the information by selecting and reporting the main features, and make comparisons where relevent.

Cement Production

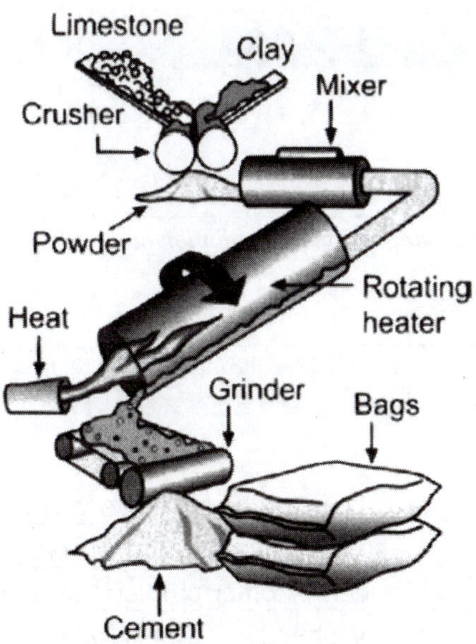

Concrete Production

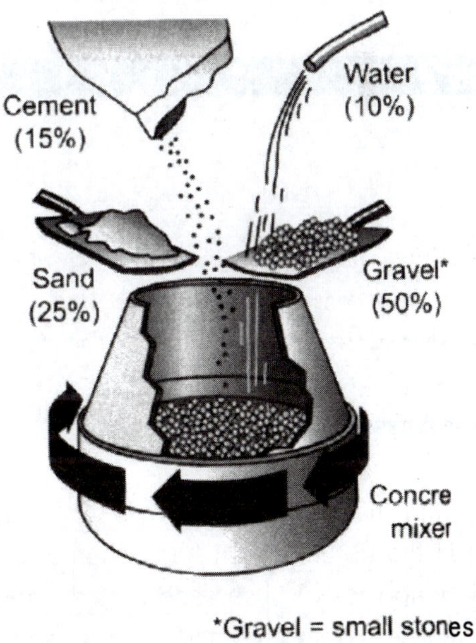

Sample Answer

The first diagram describes in 4 stages how cement is produced. The second diagram illustrates how concrete for building purposes is produced.

We can see from the first diagram that in the first stage, limestone and clay are poured into a crusher, where they are crushed into powder. Next, after fully mixed in a mixer, the powder arrives at a rotating heater. At this stage, it is continuously roasted by an external heat source at the bottom of the heater. The last stage of the process is when the heated mixture falls onto the surface of a grinder, where it is finally changed to cement and will be packaged into big bags as a product.

It can be seen from the second diagram that 4 ingredients are completely blended in a concrete mixer which is rotating all the time. And the ingredients are composed of cement, sand, gravel (small stones) and water with proportions of 15%, 25%, 50% and 10% respectively. Concrete is made in this way.

▶考官评分:8

译文:

第一张图描述了水泥生产的四个阶段，第二张图描述了建筑用的混凝土是怎样生产的。

我们能在第一张图中看到，第一步,石灰石和黏土被倒入粉碎机中，在这里它们被挤压成粉末。接下来，经过搅拌器的充分搅拌后，这些粉末到达一个旋转加热器，在这个阶段，它会被位于加热器底部的外界热源不断的烘烤，生产过程的最后一步是当加热后的混合物落在研磨机表面时，它将最终变成水泥并装入大袋子中成为产品。

在第二张图中我们可以看到，有四种原料在一个不断旋转的混凝土搅拌机中充分混合，这些原料由水泥，沙子，碎石子和水组成，用料比例分别是15%，25%，50% 和10%。混凝土就是这样制成的。

Task 2

Topic:

Increasing the price of petrol is the best way to solve growing traffic and pollution problems.
To what extent do you agree or disagree?
What other measures do you think might be effective?

Sample Answer

Along with the rapid development of urban traffic, certain problems have arisen, one of which is the traffic jam. It has become common to see passengers and drivers having to wait in long lines of buses and cars during the rush hours. Another problem is the pollution from vehicles. I am convinced that a rise in the price of petrol is the best way to deal with these two problems.

Because it is undeniable that private car use is one of the main causes of the increase in traffic and pollution, higher fuel costs will definitely compel drivers to give up driving their own cars and turn to public transportation. Researches reveal that in most cases, a car carries only one or two people, while it occupies almost half the space a bus does. The policy would also help to reduce some unnecessary traveling.

Through the practice of increasing the price of petrol, the government could collect a great sum of money. With the money, the government is able to invest more in the construction of new roads, which can lead to the reduction of traffic jams. The money could also be used to develop cleaner fuels. For example, persuading manufacturers and travelers to adopt electric cars would be an effective strategy for improving air quality, especially in cities.

To sum up, I believe increasing the price of petrol is the best way to solve growing traffic and pollution problems. Other measures include building more roads, giving priority to the development of public transportation, and working out cleaner fuels. However, these methods are not as effective as the rise of petrol price and some of them may need the fund collected from the policy.

▶考官评分:8

题目:

解决交通和污染问题的最好方法是提高汽油的价格。你在何种程度上同意或不同意？你认为还有什么有效的措施？

译文:

随着城市交通的迅速发展，出现了一些问题，其中之一是交通堵塞。我们通常看到在高峰时期公交车和汽车中的乘客和司机不得不排着长队等待。另一个问题是车辆造成的污染。我深信，提高汽油价格是处理这两大难题的最好方式。

因为不可否认的是，私家车的使用是导致交通和污染问题增加的主要原因之一，能源价格上涨肯定会迫使司机放弃驾驶自己的车而转向大众运输工具。研究表明，在大多数情况下，一辆车只载一或两个人，但它几乎占据了公共汽车行驶空间的一半。该政策也将有助于减少一些不必要的出行。

通过提高汽油价格的做法，政府可以征收一大笔钱。有了这笔资金，政府可以投资于建设新的道路，从而缓解交通拥堵。这些钱也可以用来开发更清洁的燃料。例如，说服制造商和旅游者采用电动汽车，这将成为改善空气质量的有效策略，尤其是在城市。

综上所述，我认为提高汽油价格是解决日趋严重的交通和污染问题的最好方式。其他措施包括兴建更多道路，优先发展公共交通，研发清洁燃料。但是这些方法都不如提高汽油价格有效。其中一些措施可能需要通过政策集资。

Test 4

Task 1

Topic:

The graph below shows the quantities of goods transported in the UK between 1974 and 2002 by four different modes of transport.

Summarise the information by selecting and reporting the main features, and make comparisons where relevent.

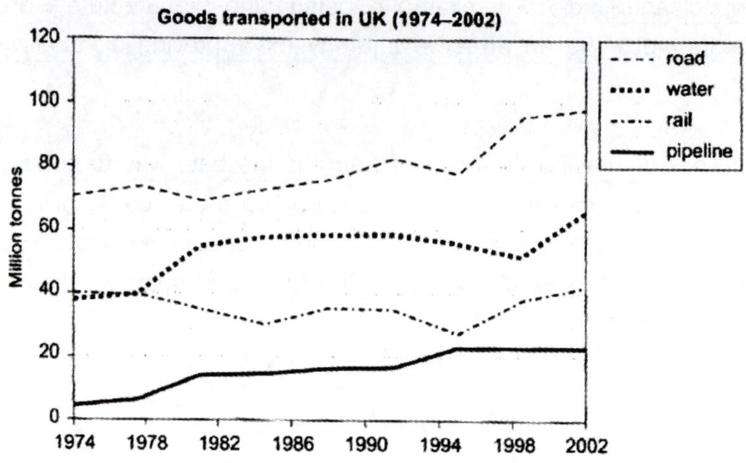

Sample Answer

The line graph illustrates the quantities of goods transported by four different modes of transport in the UK from 1974 to 2002.

The number of road increased slightly from 1974 to 1993, with a slight decrease from 1978 to 1982. After that the number decreased slowly until 1996. The next 3 years witnessed a sharp increase in the number and then there was a moderate rise in the number from 1999 to 2002. However, there was a sharp increase in the number of water from 1974 to 1982. After that, the number remained stable until 1998. The next four years saw a dramatic rise in the number.

There was a slight drop in the number of rail from 1974 to 1986. After that, the number fluctuated until 1994 and the period from 1994 to 2002 experienced a drastic growth in the number. In contrast, the number of pipeline increased gradually from 1974 to 1994 and then there was no change in the number over the next 8 years.

From 1974 to 2002, road had the highest number in the four modes of transport. Water occupied the second place. The number of rail was higher than that of pipeline.

▶考官评分:8

译文:

这张曲线图阐明了1974年到2002年英国的大部分商品由四种不同的交通工具运输。

公路的数量从1974年到1993年上升缓慢，其中在1978年到1982年略微有所下降，在这之后直到1996年数量都在缓慢下降。接下来的3年目睹了一个缓慢的增长过程，从1999年到2002年其数量平稳增加。然而，1974年到1982年水路数量显著增加，之后该数量一直保持到1998年，接下来的四年其数量又急剧增加。

铁路运输的数量自1974年到1986年略有下降，之后其数量一直波动，直到1994年。而1994年到2002年这段时间其数量急剧上升。相比之下，地下管道的数量从1974年到1982年稳步增加，之后的8年就再没什么变化了。

从1974年到2002年，在这四种运输体系中，公路数量最多，水路占据第二位，铁路的数量比地下管道的数量多。

Task 2

Topic:

In some countries the average weight of people is increasing and their levels of health and fitness are decreasing.
What do you think are the causes of these problems and what measures could be taken to solve them?

Sample Answer

As some people in poor countries are vastly underweight as a result of poverty, others elsewhere in the world are suffering from another problem—obesity, as a consequence of improved living conditions. A recent study has shown the latter problem is becoming an epidemic, as the number of obese people keeps rising alarmingly. I believe there are several factors responsible for this increase.

The first reason is the poor diet. Nowadays people face fierce competition and suffer from great pressure and they have to devote more time and energy to their careers. Consequently fast food has been gaining its popularity at an amazing rate. Although fast food is time-saving, it lacks nutritive value. Medical researches reveal that eating too much fast food will result in excessive intake of calories, salt and sugar, which leads to overweight.

It is not only a question of what people eat, but also a matter of lifestyles. TV and the Internet have produced sedentary lifestyle. People who watch TV passively or use computers for hours every day simply do not get enough physical exercises. Besides, a growing number of people have come to rely on private cars, rather than walking or using bicycles. Lack of activity gradually contributes to overweight.

In view of the seriousness of the problem, effective measures must be taken before things get worse. In the first place, a proper diet consisting of more vegetables and fruit and fewer fatty foods may assist. In the second place, it is of great importance that people participate in different sports including running, walking, and cycling.

▶考官评分:8

题目：

在一些国家，人们的平均体重在增加，健康水平正在下降。你认为这些问题的原因是什么，可以采取什么措施来解决这些问题？

译文：

一些贫穷国家的人由于贫穷造成体重过轻，而世界其他地方的人正在面临着另一个问题——肥胖，这是由于生活条件的改善而造成的后果。最近的一项研究表明，后者正在成为一种流行病，因为肥胖人数不断上升使人担忧。我认为有一些因素引起了肥胖人数增加。

第一个原因是不良的饮食习惯。现在人们面临着激烈的竞争和承受着巨大的压力，他们不得不花费更多的时间和精力在自己的工作中。因此快餐一直在以惊人的速度越来越受欢迎。虽然快餐省时，但它缺乏营养价值。医学研究表明，食用过多快餐会导致摄入更多的热量、盐和糖，从而导致肥胖。

这不仅是人们吃什么的问题，更是生活方式的问题。电视和互联网已经造成久坐的生活方式。人们每天看电视或使用电脑几个小时几乎没有得到足够的体育锻炼。此外，越来越多的人依赖于私家车，而不是步行或使用自行车。缺乏运动逐渐导致超重。

鉴于问题的严重性，在事态进一步恶化之前必须采取有效措施。首先，适当的饮食——更多的蔬菜和水果，少量高脂肪食品合理组合。其次，人们参加各种各样的运动是非常重要的。包括跑步、散步和骑自行车。

G类

Test A

Task 1

Topic:

You have recently moved to a different house.
Write a letter to an English-speaking friend. In your letter
- *explain why you have moved*
- *describe the new house.*
- *invite your friend to come and visit.*

Sample Answer

Dear Dave,

I am writing to let you know that at last we have moved to a bigger house! We just couldn't go on living in the two-bedroom bungalow now that the twins are growing up and the new baby has arrived. So we started looking and finally here we are in our new home.

I'm sure you'll like it. We have three bedrooms now, and a very modern bathroom and kitchen. The kids are happy because there is much more space with the big living room and the garden outside. But Michel is the happiest of all because he doesn't need to do much decorating.

Why don't you come round this weekend and see what you think of our new place? We would all love to see you and if the weather is good we can have a barbecue in the garden.

Our new address and phone number are below, so give us a call and let us know when to expect you.

Lots of love,
Francoise

▶考官评分:8

译文：

亲爱的大卫：

我写信给你是想告诉你我们最终搬入了一个大房子！随着我们的双胞胎的成长和一个方才出世的孩子的到来，我们此刻确实无法继续居住在那个有着两个卧室的平房了。

我确信你会喜欢我们的新房子。现在我们的房子有三个卧室，和一个极其时尚的盥洗室和厨房。孩子们都很高兴，因为大的起居室和户外花园给他们提供了更大的空间。而迈克是其中最高兴的，因为他不需要去做过多的装饰。

你何不在这周顺便过来看看你所认为的我们的新住处呢？我们都很高兴能见到你，而且如果天气好的话，我们还可以在花园中享受一顿烤肉野餐。

我们的新住址和电话号码写在下面，打给我们以便我们知道你到来的时间。

想念你的

弗朗索瓦丝

Task 2

Topic:

Today more people are travelling than ever before.

Why is this the case?

What are the benefits of travelling for the traveller?

Sample Answer

With the improvement of living standard, more and more people are able to make a holiday trip to places of interest. What was once reserved for only the rich, is now within everybody' s grasp.

The reasons for this increase are many and varied. On a simplistic level, there are larger numbers of means of transportation-there are more cars, buses and trains in operation. The cost of travelling, even though it is at present increasing due to an economic slow-down globally, is still relatively affordable to many people. This affordability is further enhanced by the use of credit cards and loans in order to fund travel, especially for holiday purposes. An increase of travel companies in competition with each other has also helped bring package prices down. At the same time, an increase in the number of operating flights globally has also increased, giving rise to falling air-fare prices. In addition, people now have more leisure time and disposable incomes.

Travelling brings tremendous benefits to travelers. In the first place, traveling gives them direct experiences. It is necessary for a person to expand his horizon. It will make his life more pleasant and make him have a deep understanding of the people and the world. In the second place, travelling is much more exciting and active. Travelling helps travelers to see new customs, eat new foods, and do new things. It also helps them to make new friends. Wherever they go, they are bound to meet with people from different backgrounds.

In conclusion, there are many reasons why more people are travelling both internationally and locally and travelling is beneficial to travelers in many aspects.

▶考官评分:8

题目:

译文:

随着生活水平的提高，越来越的人能去风景名胜区享受假期。曾几何时那些只有富人可以享受的旅行，现在人人都可以享有。

这个现象的成因多种多样。简单来说，有很多交通方式可供选择，我们那里有更多的小汽车、公共汽车和火车在运作。旅游之费用，尽管它因目前的经济增长速度有所放缓，但全球范围内，仍有许多相对负担得起的人。通过使用信用卡和贷款来增强负担能力，从而获得旅行基金，特别是度假的目的。现在旅行社之间的不断竞争使包团游价格下降。与此同时，由于飞机票价格下降，所以在全球范围内操作飞机的价格有所上升。除此之外，人们现在有更多的闲暇时间，更多可支配收入。

旅行会给旅行者带来巨大的利益。首先，旅行给了他们直接的经验。它是必要的，因为一个人需要去开阔自己的眼界。它将使人们的生活更加舒心，让他对人们和世界有了深刻的了解。第二，旅行是比较令人兴奋和活跃的事情。旅游使游客了解新的风俗、品尝独特的食物、尝试新鲜的事物。它也帮助他们结交新朋友。无论他们去哪里，他们注定要感受来自不同文化背景的人。

总之，有很多原因促使越来越多的人正在当地或世界各地旅行，并且旅行在很多方面都对旅行者有益。

Test B

Task 1

Topic:

You recently bought a piece of equipment for your kitchen but it did not work. You phoned the shop but no action was taken.
Write a letter to the shop manager. In your letter
- *describe the problem with the equipment*
- *explain what happened when you phoned the shop*
- *say what you would like the manager to do.*

Sample Answer

Dear Sir/Madam,

I am writing to make a complaint about the microwave oven which I bought five days ago in your shop.

As is my habit, I made a point of trying it out on the spot. It worked perfectly well, and so I decided to purchase it. However, when I got home and tried it again, it seemed that the knob did not work. In the instruction booklet you have not mentioned this defect and neither have you told the user how to solve the problem. I phoned your shop and explained the problem three days ago, but you still have not sent anybody to address it.

I am sure that you will agree that this is a most unsatisfactory situation. Therefore I request you to arrange to replace this microwave oven with another one, which must be in perfect working order. Failing that, I will have to visit on a refund in full of the price which I paid for it.

Yours sincerely,

Fan Yang

▶考官评分:8

译文:

尊敬的先生/女士，

我写信给你们是要投诉我五天前在你们商店所购买的微波炉。

作为我的习惯，我特意现场试用。它当时运转得相当好，所以我决定购买。然而，当我回到家并且再次试用它的时候，它那球形的把手便不再奏效了。它的说明手册里面并没有提及这个缺陷，也没有告诉使用者怎么样去解决这个问题。我三天前打通了你们商店的电话说明了问题所在，但是你们仍旧没有派人来处理这个问题。

我相信您也会认同这不是个令人满意的局面。因此我要求你们安排替换一个可以完好运转的微波炉给我。不然的话，我将不得不迁怒于你们将我已支付的款项全额退还于我。

谨上，

杨凡

Task 2

Topic:

Some people think that it is better to educate boys and girls in separate schools. Others, however, believe that boys and girls benefit more from attending mixed schools.
Discuss both these views and give your own opinion.

Sample Answer

Some countries have single-sex education models, while in others both single sex and mixed schools co-exist and it is up to the parents or the children to decide which model is preferable.

Some educationalists think it is more effective to educate boys and girls in single-sex schools because they believe this environment reduces distractions and encourages pupils to concentrate on their studies. This is probably true to some extent. It also allows more equality among pupils and gives more opportunity to all those at the school to choose subjects more freely without gender prejudice. For example, a much higher proportion of girls study science to a high level when they attend girls' schools than their counterparts in mixed schools do. Similarly, boys in single-sex schools are more likely to take cookery classes and to study languages, which are often thought of as traditional subjects for girls.

On the other hand, some experts would argue that mixed schools prepare their pupils better for their future lives. Girls and boys learn to live and work together from an early age and are consequently not emotionally underdeveloped in their relations with the opposite sex. In this way, boys do not grow up imaging that women are mysterious creatures and girls do not grow up scared of men. They are also able to learn from each other, and to experience different types of skill and talent that might be evident in a single gender environment.

Personally, I think that although there are advantages to both systems, I prefer to go to a mixed school. We should first think about the aim of education at school. Cramming children's heads full of knowledge is by no means the main purpose. The more important goal is to prepare them to take their place in adult society. As this society is made up of males and females, a segregated school consisting only of members of the same sex cannot serve this purpose well.

▶考官评分:8

题目:

一些人认为在男女分校中教育男生和女生会更好。然而，另外一些人认为男生女生会从混合学校中受益更多。讨论双方观点并给出你的观点。

译文:

一些国家已经采取单一性别的教育模式，而在另一些国家单一性别教育模式的学校和混合教学的学校是共存的，并且应由父母或孩子们来决定哪个模式更佳。

一些教育家认为单一性别的学校对教育男孩和女孩是更有效的，因为他们相信这种环境减少干扰，并鼓励学生专注于他们的学习。这可能在一定程度上是对的。它也允许在小学生中有更多的平等机会，让所有在学校的孩子更自由地选择科目并不再遭受性别偏见。例如，与混合学校相比女子学校中有更大比例的女生去学习科学课程并能取得较高的水平。同样地，上男子学校的孩子更有可能接触常被认为是女孩传统领域的烹饪课程和语言学习。

另一方面，一些专家会指出混合学校为他们的将来生活做准备。从幼年开始，女孩和男孩就学会在一起生活和工作并且在感情上不会疏远异性。因此，男孩在长大成人后，不会认为女人都是神秘的生物，女孩也不会害怕男人。但他们也可以互相学习，并且体验不同类型的技能和天赋，相对于单一性别环境这可能是显而易见的。

就我个人而言，尽管两种模式都有好处，我还是喜欢去一个混合的学校。我们应该首先考虑在学校教育的目的。让孩子们的头脑中充满知识绝不是主要目的。更重要的目标是想让他们准备好去扮演他们在成人社会中的角色。因为这个社会是由男性和女性构成的，只由同一性别成员组成的单一性别学校不能完成这个目标。